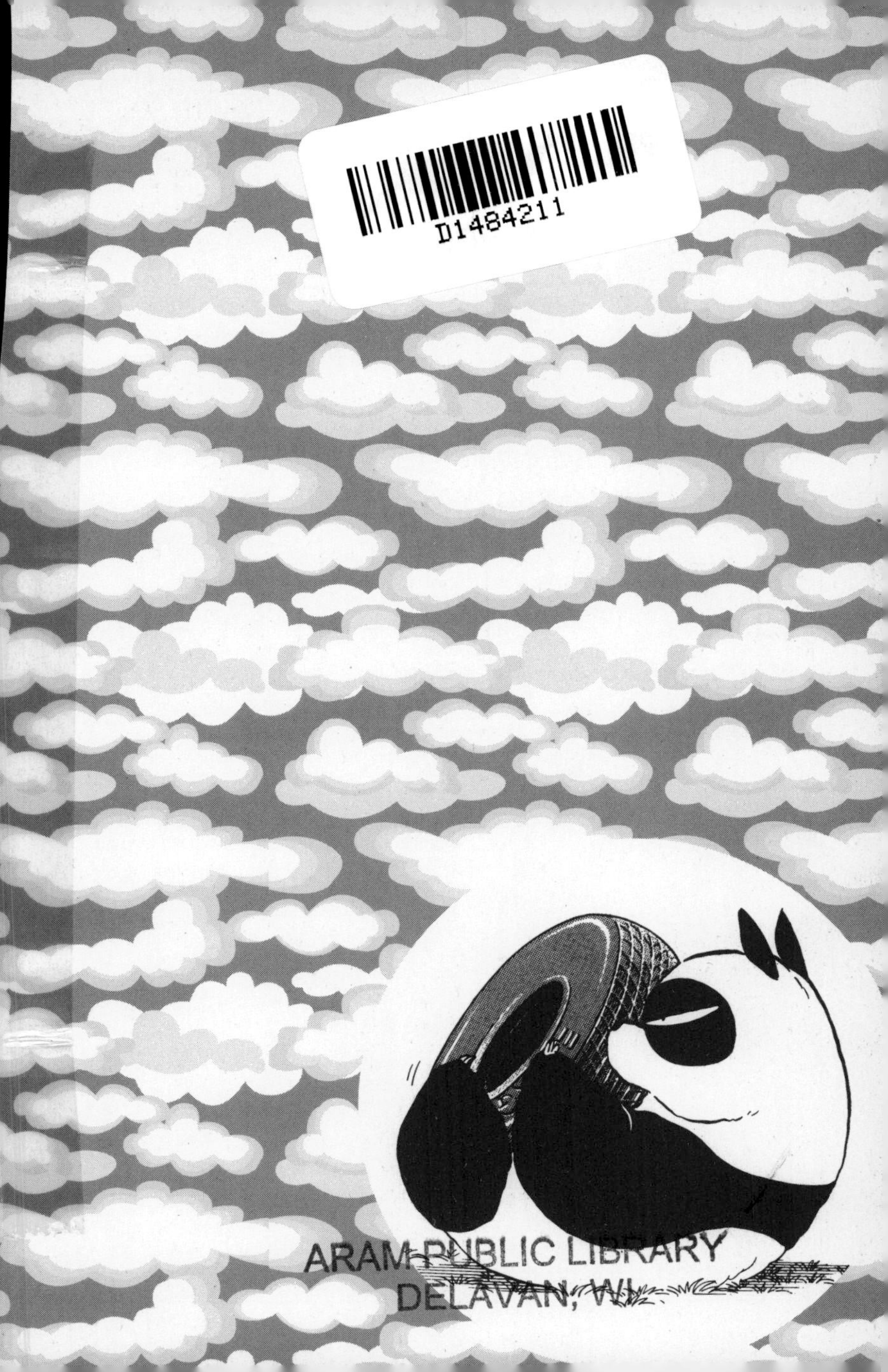

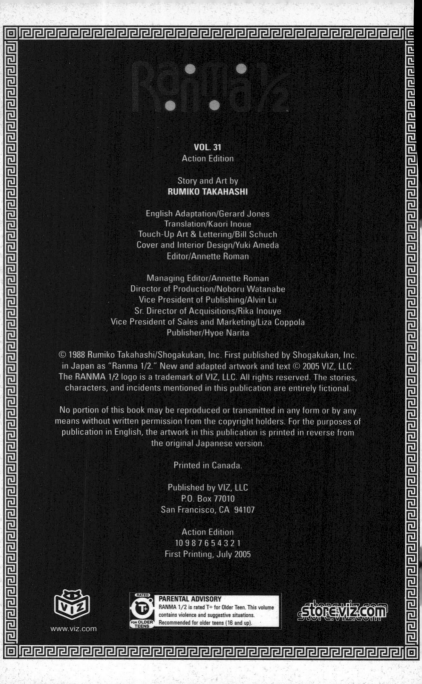

Ranma ½

VOL. 31
Action Edition

Story and Art by
RUMIKO TAKAHASHI

English Adaptation/Gerard Jones
Translation/Kaori Inoue
Touch-Up Art & Lettering/Bill Schuch
Cover and Interior Design/Yuki Ameda
Editor/Annette Roman

Managing Editor/Annette Roman
Director of Production/Noboru Watanabe
Vice President of Publishing/Alvin Lu
Sr. Director of Acquisitions/Rika Inouye
Vice President of Sales and Marketing/Liza Coppola
Publisher/Hyoe Narita

Printed in Canada.

Published by VIZ, LLC
P.O. Box 77010
San Francisco, CA 94107

Action Edition
10 9 8 7 6 5 4 3 2 1
First Printing, July 2005

www.viz.com

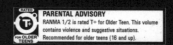

PARENTAL ADVISORY
RANMA 1/2 is rated T+ for Older Teen. This volume contains violence and suggestive situations. Recommended for older teens (16 and up).

RATED **T+** FOR OLDER TEENS

store.viz.com

Ranma 1/2

VOL. 31 — Action Edition

STORY & ART BY

RUMIKO TAKAHASHI

STORY THUS FAR

The Tendos are an average, run-of-the-mill Japanese family—on the surface, that is. Soun Tendo is the owner and proprietor of the Tendo Dojo, where "Anything Goes Martial Arts" is practiced. Like the name says, anything goes, and usually does.

When Soun's old friend Genma Saotome comes to visit, Soun's three lovely young daughters—Akane, Nabiki and Kasumi—are told that it's time for one of them to become the fiancée of Genma's teenage son, as per an agreement made between the two fathers years ago. Youngest daughter Akane—who says she hates boys—is quickly nominated for bridal duty by her sisters.

Unfortunately, Ranma and his father have suffered a strange accident. While training in China, both plunged into one of many "cursed" springs at the legendary martial arts training ground of Jusenkyo. These springs transform the unlucky dunkee into whoever—or whatever—drowned there hundreds of years ago.

From then on, a splash of cold water turns Ranma's father into a giant panda, and Ranma becomes a beautiful, busty young woman. Hot water reverses the effect...but only until next time. As it turns out, Ranma and Genma aren't the only ones who have taken the Jusenkyo plunge—and it isn't long before they meet several other members of the Jusenkyo "cursed."

Although their parents are still determined to see Ranma and Akane marry and assume ownership of the training hall, Ranma seems to have a strange talent for accumulating surplus fiancées...and Akane has a few stubbornly determined suitors of her own. Will the two ever work out their differences and get rid of all these "extra" people, or will they just call the whole thing off? What's a half-boy, half-girl (not to mention all-girl, *angry* girl) to do...?

CAST OF CHARACTERS

THE SAOTOMES

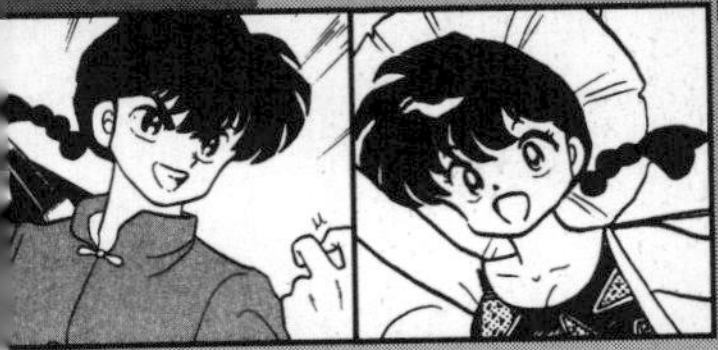

RANMA SAOTOME
Martial artist with far too many fiancées, and an ego that won't let him take defeat. Changes into a girl when splashed with cold water.

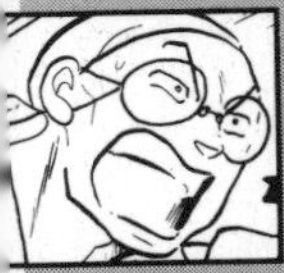

GENMA SAOTOME
Genma's father. Changes into a roly-poly, sign-talkin' panda when wet.

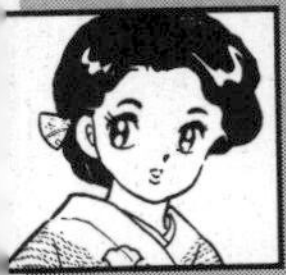

NODOKA SAOTOME
Genma's oh-so-traditional wife and Ranma's oh-so-deadly mom, Nodoka has taken an oath to do *both* her dearly beloveds in should her boy grow up to be less than manly. Um....

THE MASTER

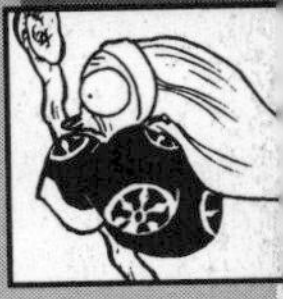

COLOGNE
Chinese Amazon martial artist, owner of the Cat Café, and great-grandmother to Shampoo. Almost always knows where the bodies are buried (so to speak).

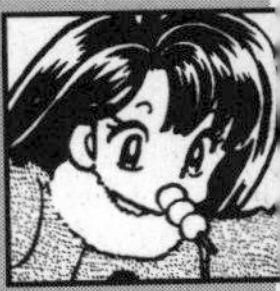

HINAKO NINOMIYA
Teacher at Ranma and Akane's school. Can use various techniques to instantly "grow up" from child to adult...provided there's *ki* or "battle-energy" around for her to absorb.

THE TENDOS

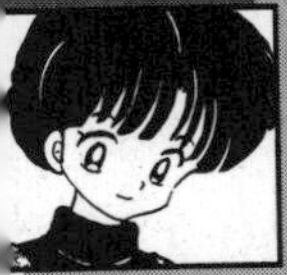

AKANE TENDO
Martial artist, tomboy, and Ranma's reluctant fiancée. Still totally in the dark about the "Ryoga/P-chan" thing.

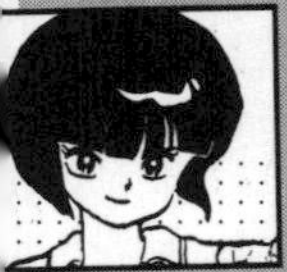

NABIKI TENDO
Middle Tendo daughter. Loves nothing as much as she loves money.

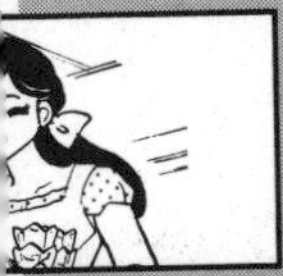

KASUMI TENDO
Eldest Tendo daughter and sweet-natured stay-at-home type.

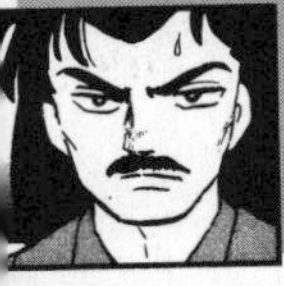

SOUN TENDO
Tendo family patriarch and former Happosai disciple. Easily excitable.

THE SUITORS

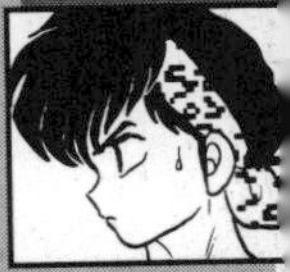

RYOGA
Martial artist with no sense of direction, a huge crush on Akane, and the rotten (or is it?) luck to change when wet into "P-chan," Akane's pet miniature black pig.

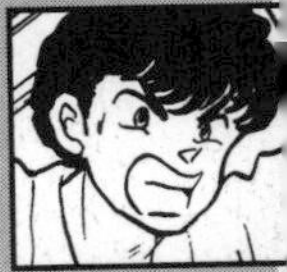

TATEWAKI KUNO
Seventeen-year-old kendo enthusiast in love with both Akane and the mysterious "pig-tailed girl" (girl-type Ranma).

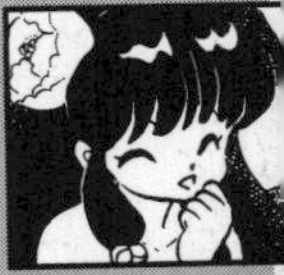

SHAMPOO
Has come all the way from China to either kill Ranma or marry him. Still hasn't quite decided what to do.

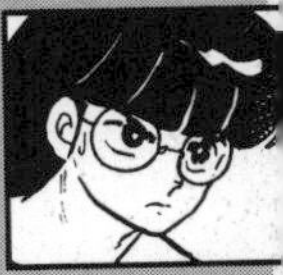

MOUSSE
Myopic master of hidden weapons. Continually thwarted (however inadvertently) in his pursuit of Shampoo by Ranma.

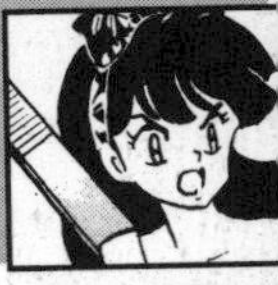

UKYO KUONJI
Spatula-wielding, childhood-betrothed, would-be sweetheart of Ranma.

CONTENTS

PART 1
LOVE MEDICINE

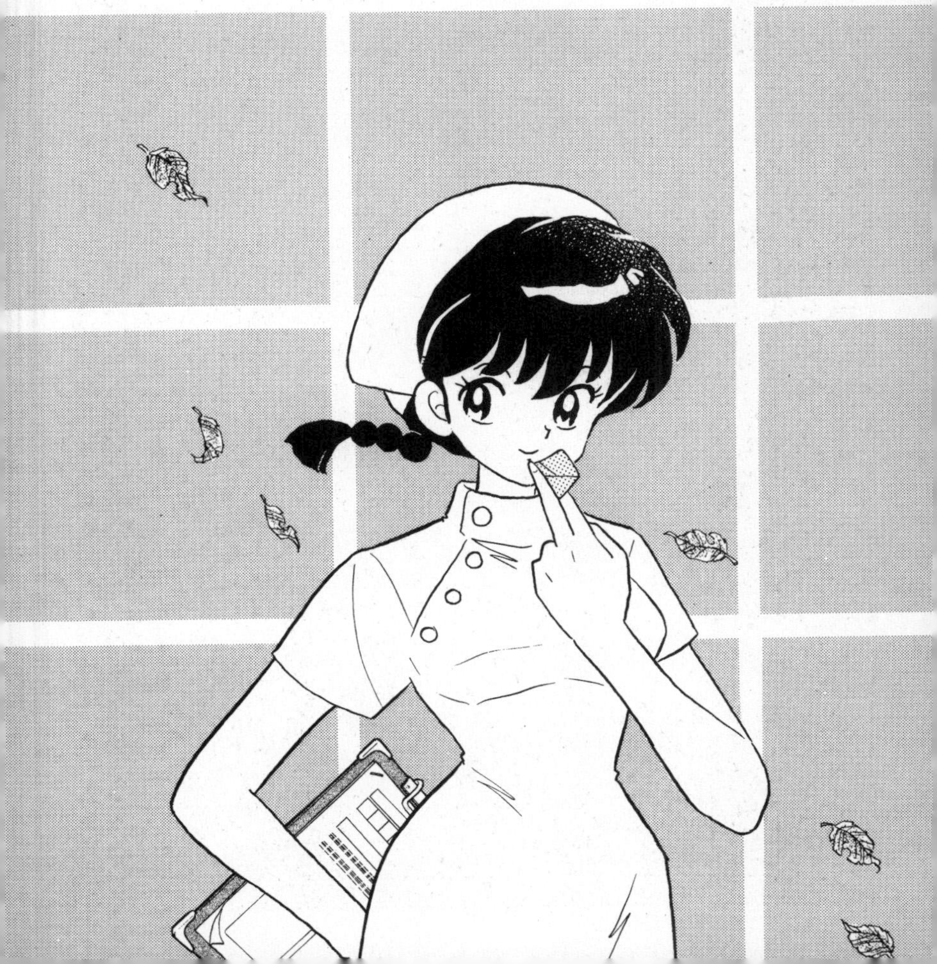

THE FRUITS
OF THE
PERSIMMON
TREE ARE
FULL AND
RIPE.

IT'S
FALL.

IT IS MY
TIME...

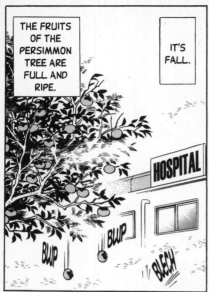

HOSPITAL

BLUP

BLUP

BLECH

I WILL BE
SUMMONED
TO HEAVEN,

NEVER TO
GREET THE
COMING
WINTER.

WHEN THE LAST
FRUIT OF THE
PERSIMMON
TREE FALLS...

MY LIFE
ALSO
WILL...

HYOI

...

PLUK

PLUK

PLUK

SCRAPE

YAH!

VOOSH

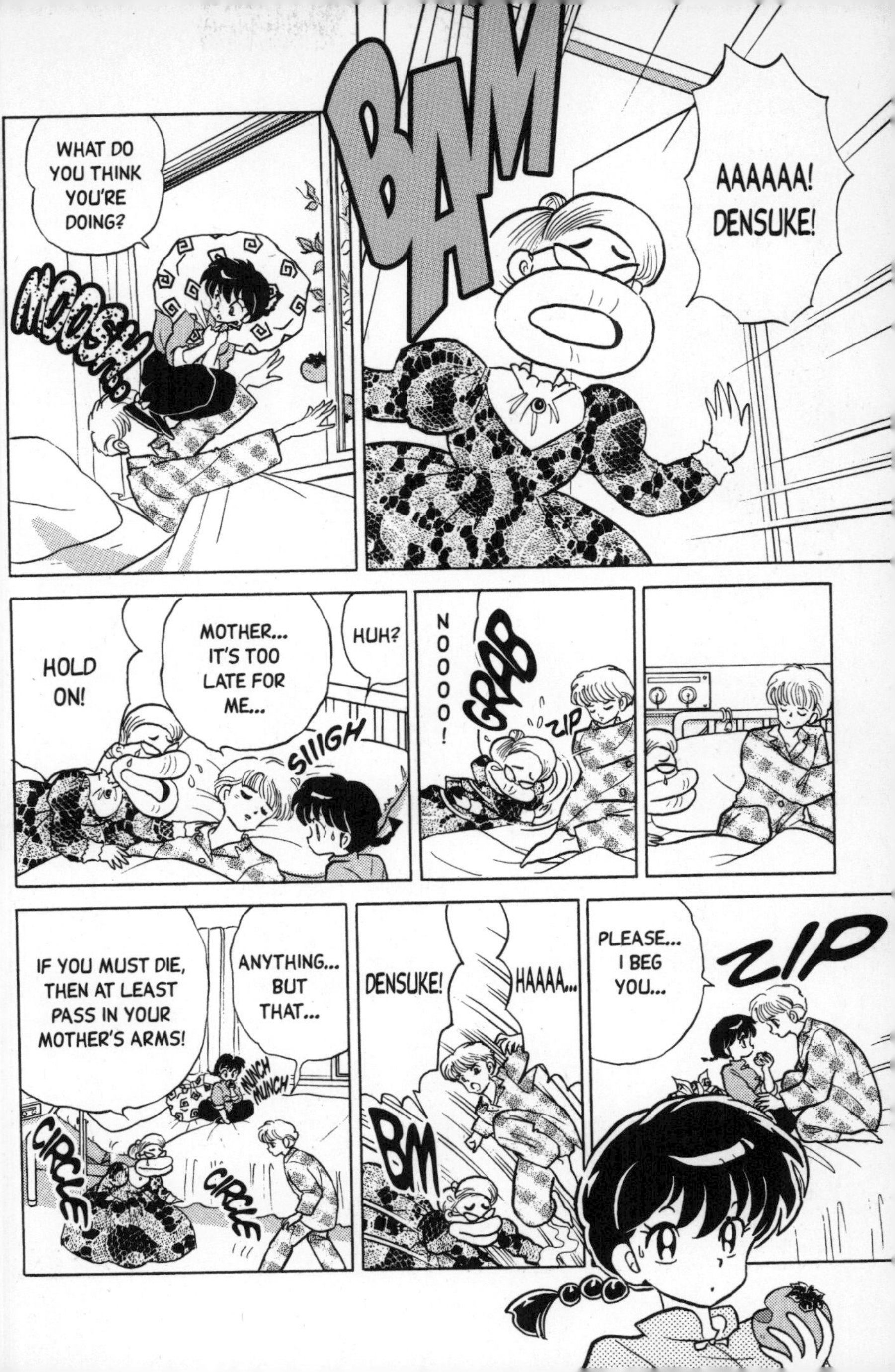
WHAT DO YOU THINK YOU'RE DOING?
WHOOSH
BAM
AAAAAA! DENSUKE!
HOLD ON!
MOTHER... IT'S TOO LATE FOR ME...
HUH?
SIIIGH
NOOOOO!
GRAB
ZIP
IF YOU MUST DIE, THEN AT LEAST PASS IN YOUR MOTHER'S ARMS!
ANYTHING... BUT THAT...
MUNCH MUNCH
CIRCLE
CIRCLE
DENSUKE!
HAAAA...
BM
PLEASE... I BEG YOU...
ZIP

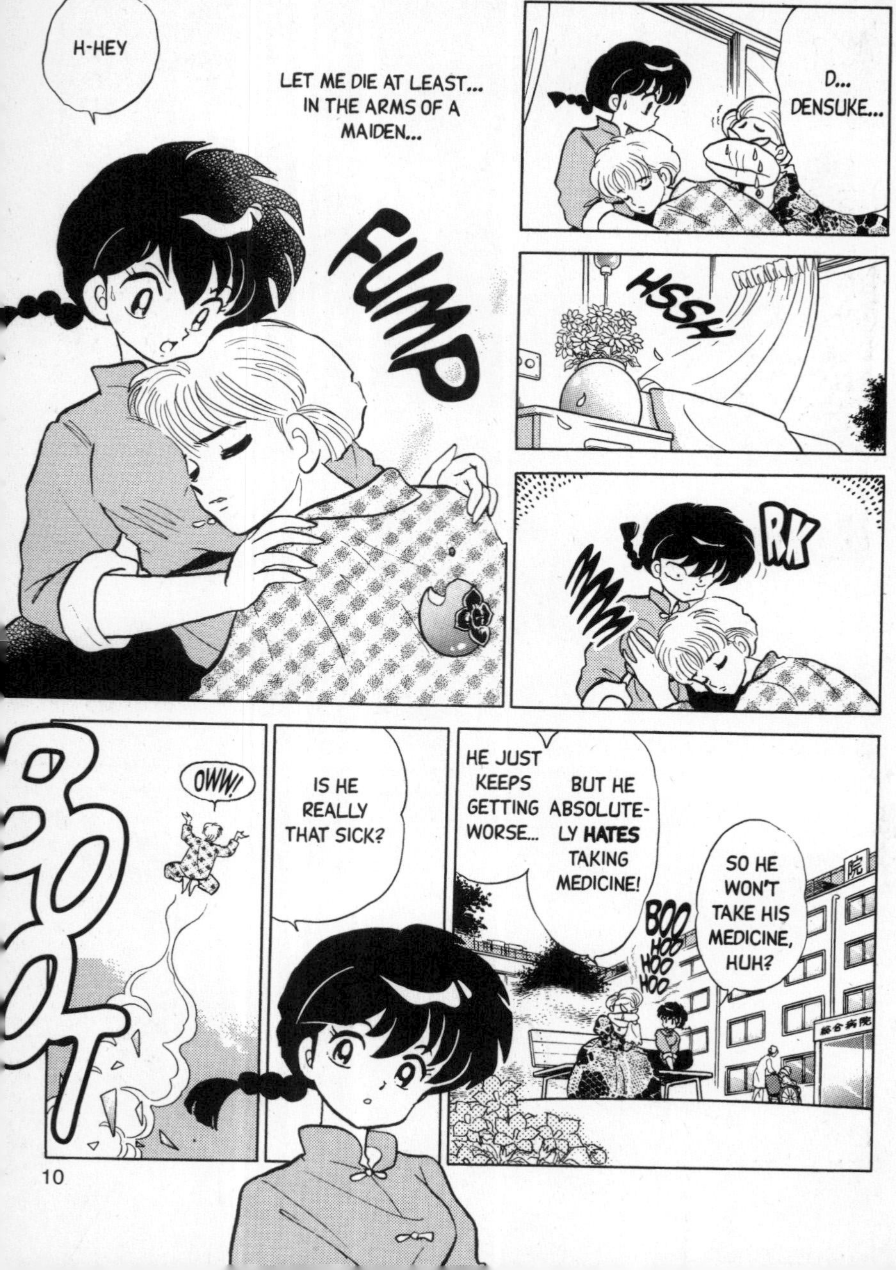
H-HEY
LET ME DIE AT LEAST... IN THE ARMS OF A MAIDEN...
FUMP
D... DENSUKE...
HSSH
RK
OWW!
IS HE REALLY THAT SICK?
HE JUST KEEPS GETTING WORSE...
BUT HE ABSOLUTE-LY **HATES** TAKING MEDICINE!
BOO HOO HOO HOO
SO HE WON'T TAKE HIS MEDICINE, HUH?
総合病院

ACCORDING TO THE DOCTOR...

WE DON'T HAVE A MOMENT TO LOSE! HE MUST TAKE IT OR ELSE HE WILL DIE!

WE DON'T KNOW WHAT TO DO EITHER!

POP!

I SEE...

...

MA'AM THIS MIGHT NOT BE ANY OF MY BUSINESS...

BUT YOU DON'T LOOK **ANYTHING** ALIKE.

NONE OF YOUR BUSINESS IS RIGHT.

"SIGH"

I'M SO SORRY, EVERYONE...

BUT I CANNOT OVERCOME MY AVERSION TO MEDICINE.

OF COURSE, I AM A YOUTH IN THE FIRST FLUSH OF LIFE...

...AND IF I WERE FED THIS MEDICINE SLOWLY AND TENDERLY...

...BY A YOUNG, FEMALE NURSE WITH A BEAUTIFUL BODY... HEH HEH...

OH, DEN-CHAN DON'T YOU KNOW HOW YOU SOUND?

BOO HOO HOO

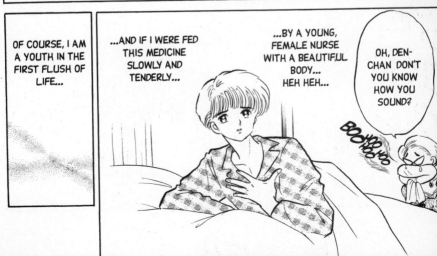

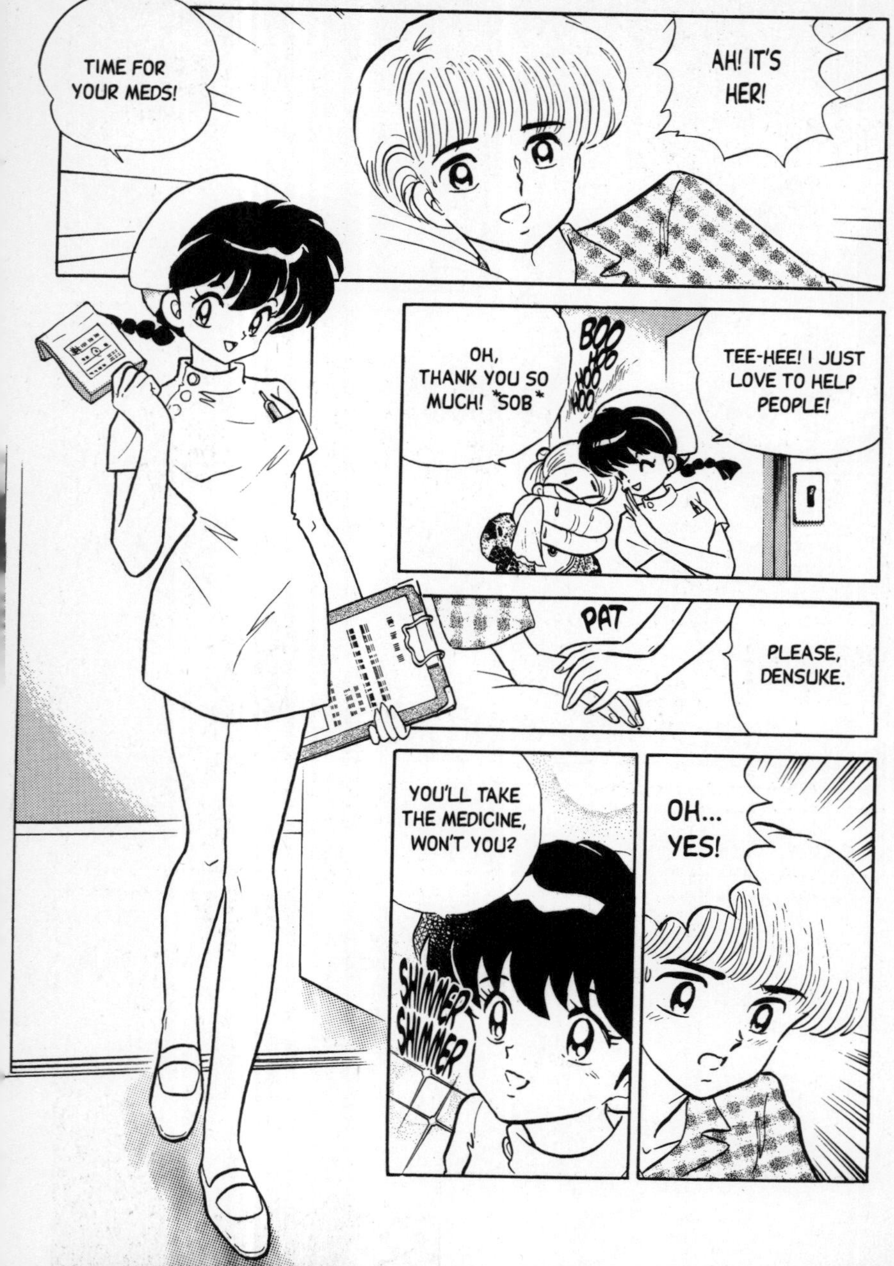
TIME FOR YOUR MEDS!
AH! IT'S HER!
OH, THANK YOU SO MUCH! *SOB*
BOO HOO HOO HOO
TEE-HEE! I JUST LOVE TO HELP PEOPLE!
PAT
PLEASE, DENSUKE.
YOU'LL TAKE THE MEDICINE, WON'T YOU?
SHIMMER SHIMMER
OH... YES!

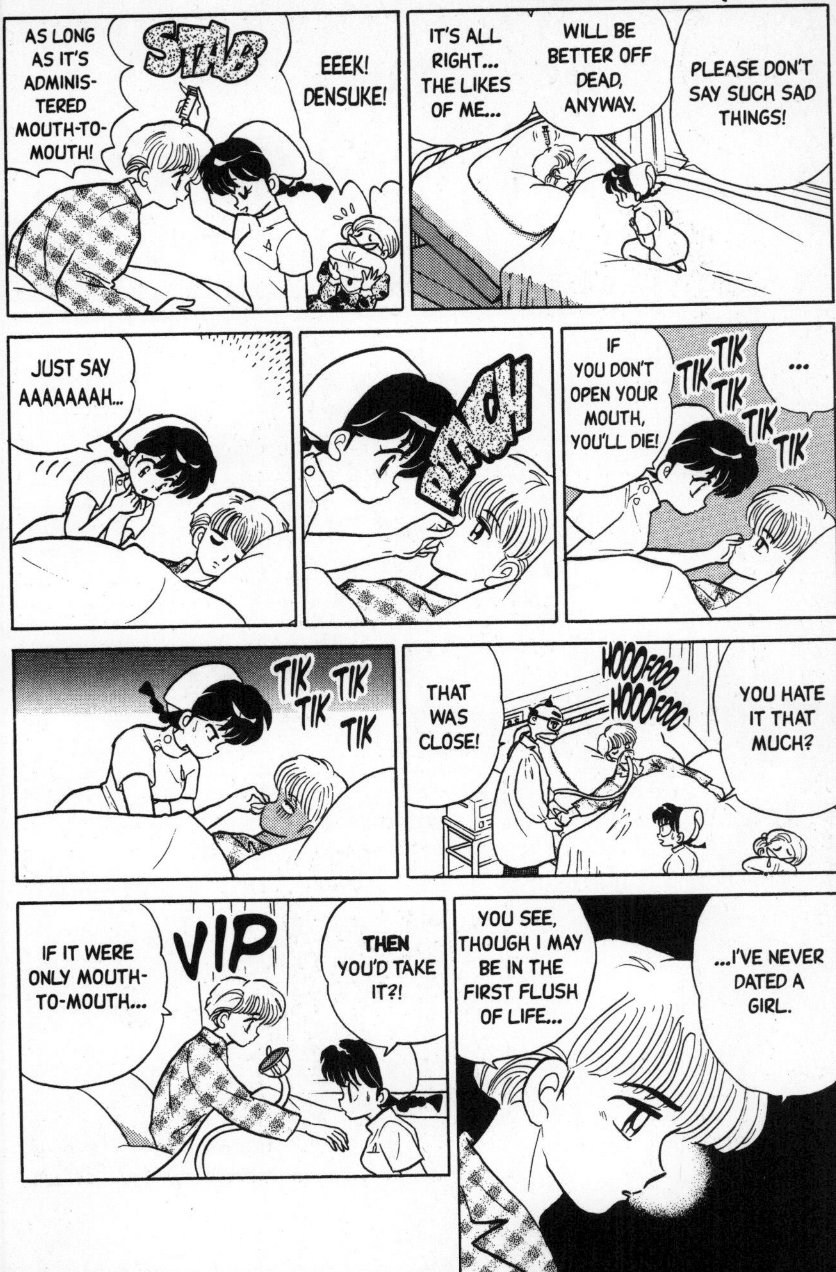
AS LONG AS IT'S ADMINIS-TERED MOUTH-TO-MOUTH!
STAB
EEEK! DENSUKE!
IT'S ALL RIGHT... THE LIKES OF ME...
WILL BE BETTER OFF DEAD, ANYWAY.
PLEASE DON'T SAY SUCH SAD THINGS!
JUST SAY AAAAAAAH...
PINCH
IF YOU DON'T OPEN YOUR MOUTH, YOU'LL DIE!
TIK TIK TIK TIK TIK TIK
...
TIK TIK TIK TIK
THAT WAS CLOSE!
HOOOFOOO HOOOFOOO
YOU HATE IT THAT MUCH?
IF IT WERE ONLY MOUTH-TO-MOUTH...
VIP
THEN YOU'D TAKE IT?!
YOU SEE, THOUGH I MAY BE IN THE FIRST FLUSH OF LIFE...
...I'VE NEVER DATED A GIRL.

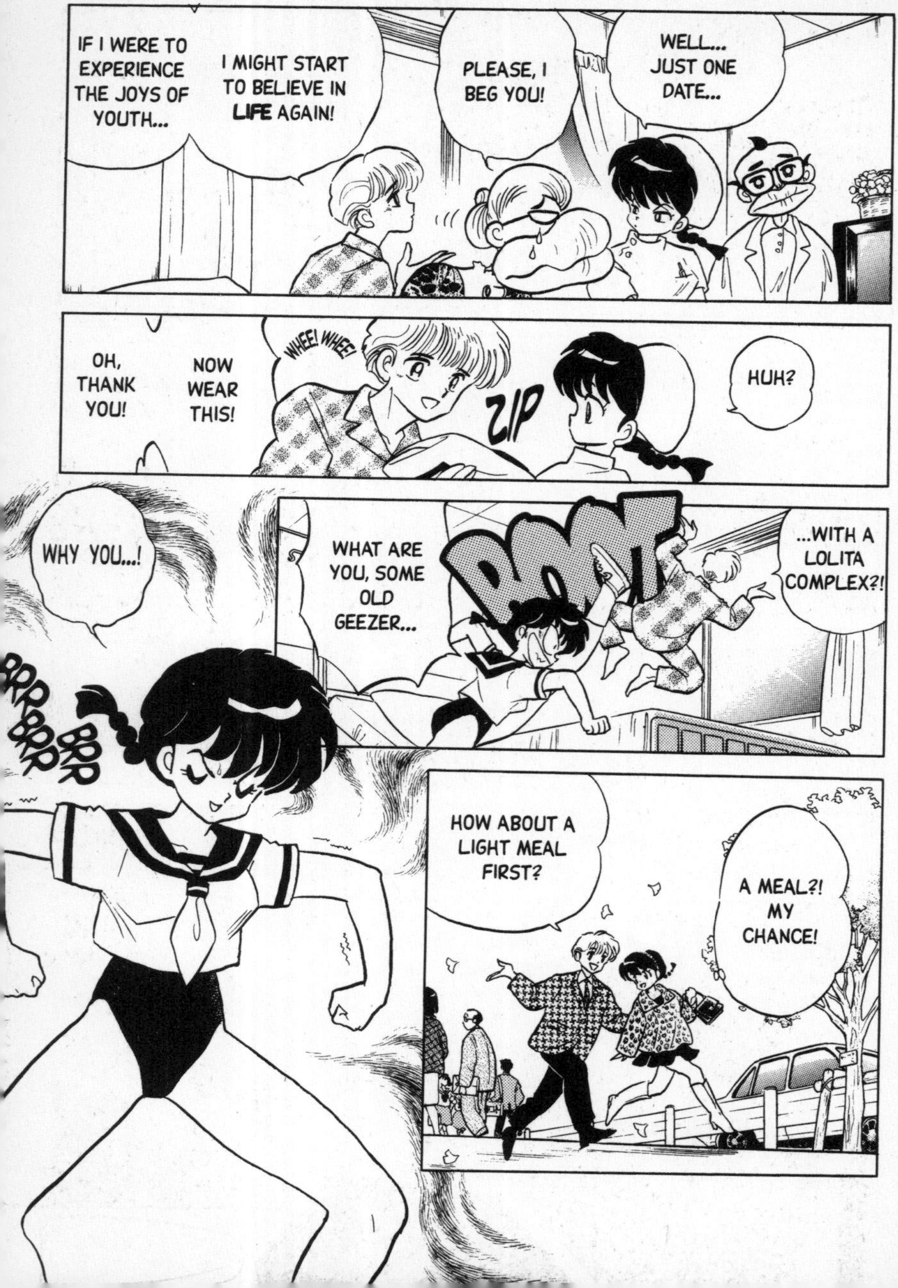
IF I WERE TO EXPERIENCE THE JOYS OF YOUTH...
I MIGHT START TO BELIEVE IN LIFE AGAIN!
PLEASE, I BEG YOU!
WELL... JUST ONE DATE...
OH, THANK YOU!
NOW WEAR THIS!
WHEE! WHEE!
ZIP
HUH?
WHY YOU...!
BRRR BRRR
WHAT ARE YOU, SOME OLD GEEZER...
...WITH A LOLITA COMPLEX?!
HOW ABOUT A LIGHT MEAL FIRST?
A MEAL?! MY CHANCE!

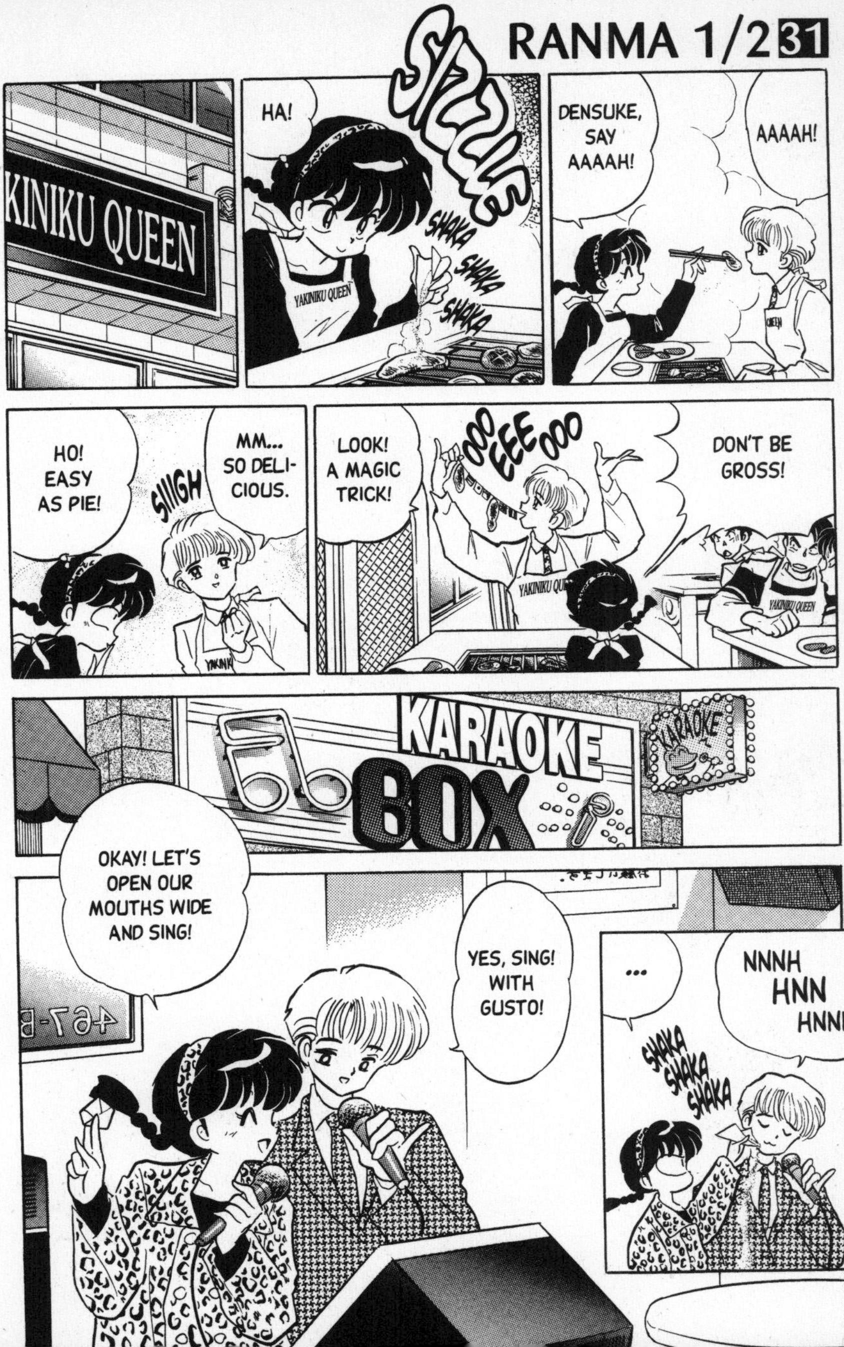
KINIKU QUEEN
HA!
SIZZLE
YAKINIKU QUEEN
SHAKA
SHAKA
SHAKA
DENSUKE, SAY AAAAH!
AAAAH!
QUEEN
HO! EASY AS PIE!
SIIIGH
MM... SO DELI- CIOUS.
YAKINIK
LOOK! A MAGIC TRICK!
OOO EEE OOO
YAKINIKU QUE
DON'T BE GROSS!
YAKINIKU QUEEN
KARAOKE BOX
KARAOKE
OKAY! LET'S OPEN OUR MOUTHS WIDE AND SING!
YES, SING! WITH GUSTO!
...
NNNH HNN HNNN
SHAKA SHAKA SHAKA

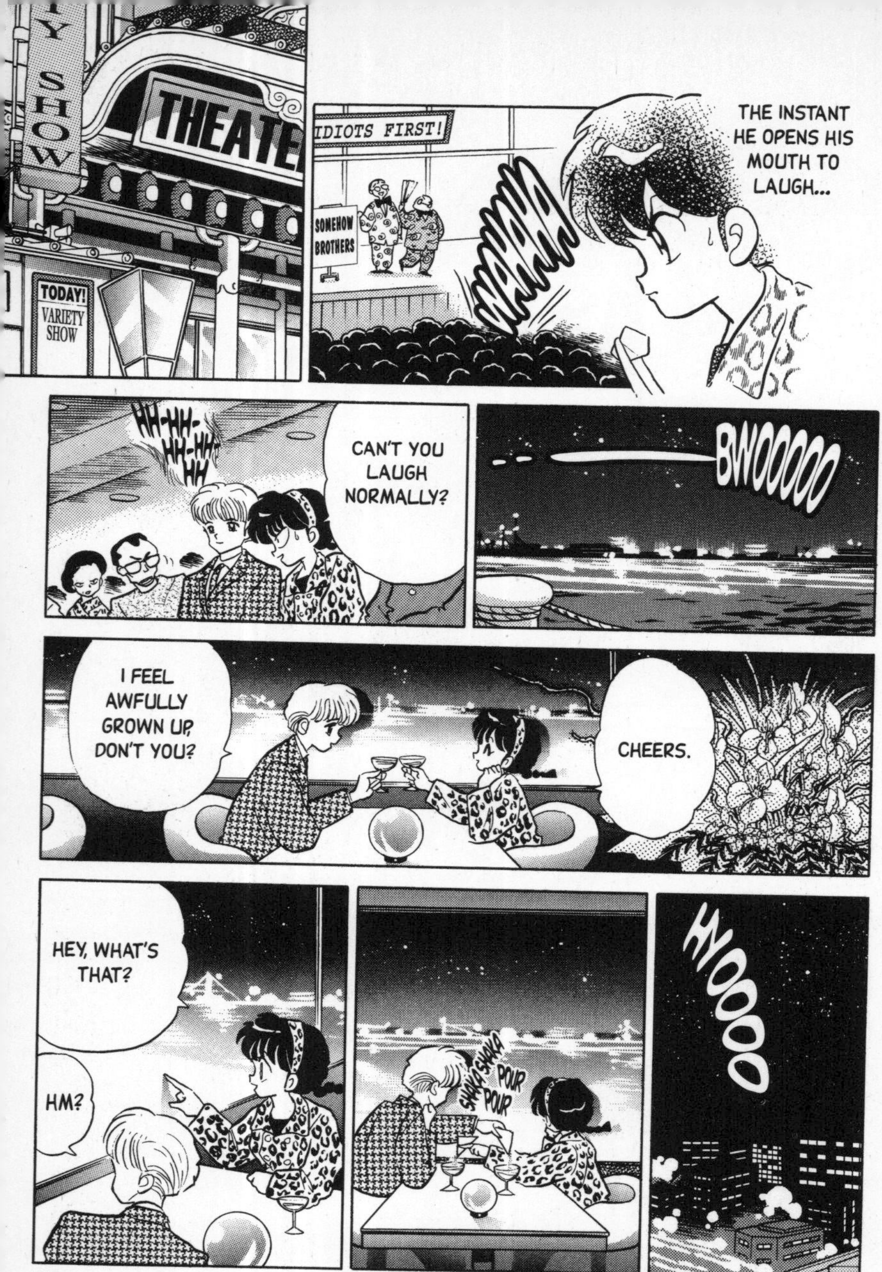
Y SHOW
THEATE
TODAY! VARIETY SHOW
IDIOTS FIRST!
SOMEHOW BROTHERS
THE INSTANT HE OPENS HIS MOUTH TO LAUGH...
HH-HH-HH-HH-HH
CAN'T YOU LAUGH NORMALLY?
BWOOOOO
I FEEL AWFULLY GROWN UP, DON'T YOU?
CHEERS.
HEY, WHAT'S THAT?
HM?
SHAKA SHAKA
POUR POUR
HYOOOO

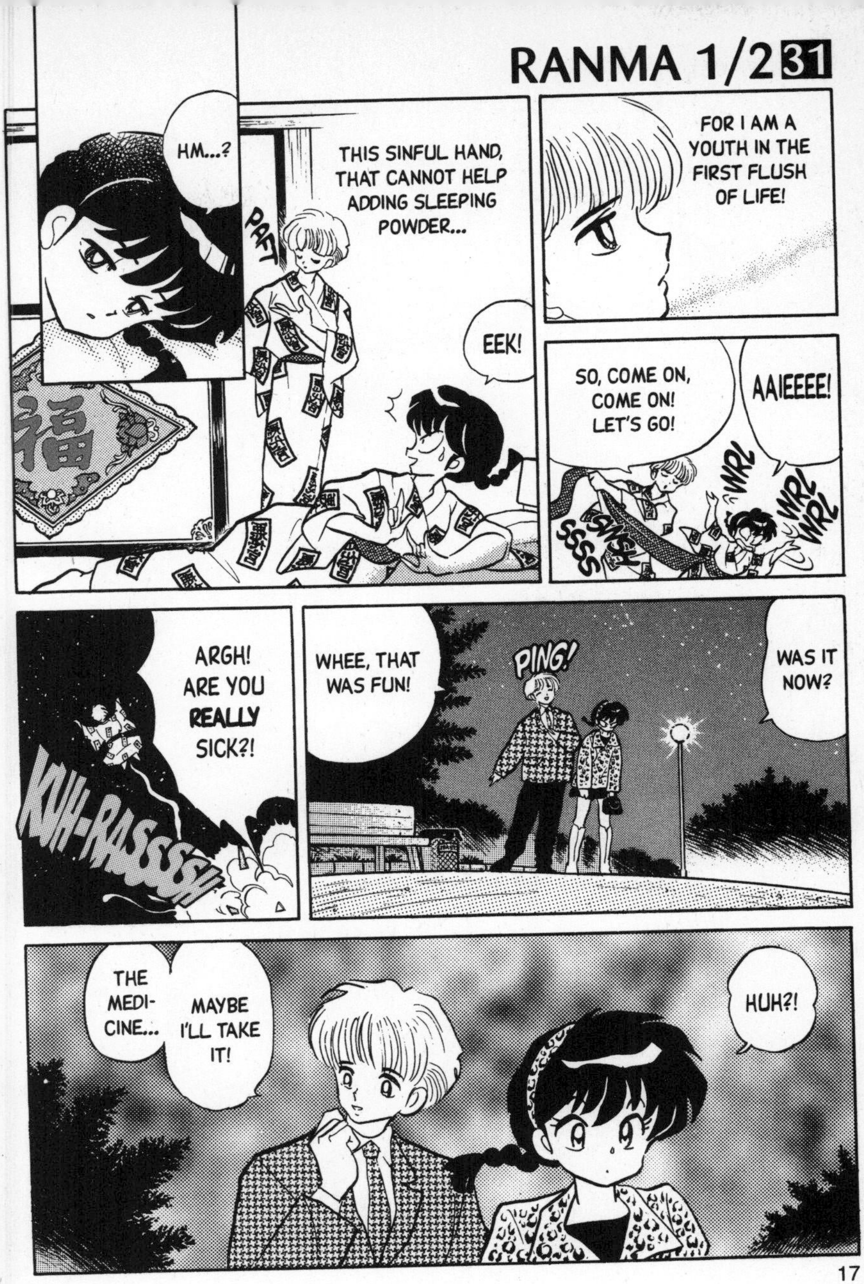
HM...?
THIS SINFUL HAND, THAT CANNOT HELP ADDING SLEEPING POWDER...
PAFT
EEK!
FOR I AM A YOUTH IN THE FIRST FLUSH OF LIFE!
SO, COME ON, COME ON! LET'S GO!
AAIEEEE!
SWISH
SSSS
WRL
WRL WRL
ARGH! ARE YOU REALLY SICK?!
KUH-RASSSH
WHEE, THAT WAS FUN!
PING!
WAS IT NOW?
THE MEDI- CINE...
MAYBE I'LL TAKE IT!
HUH?!

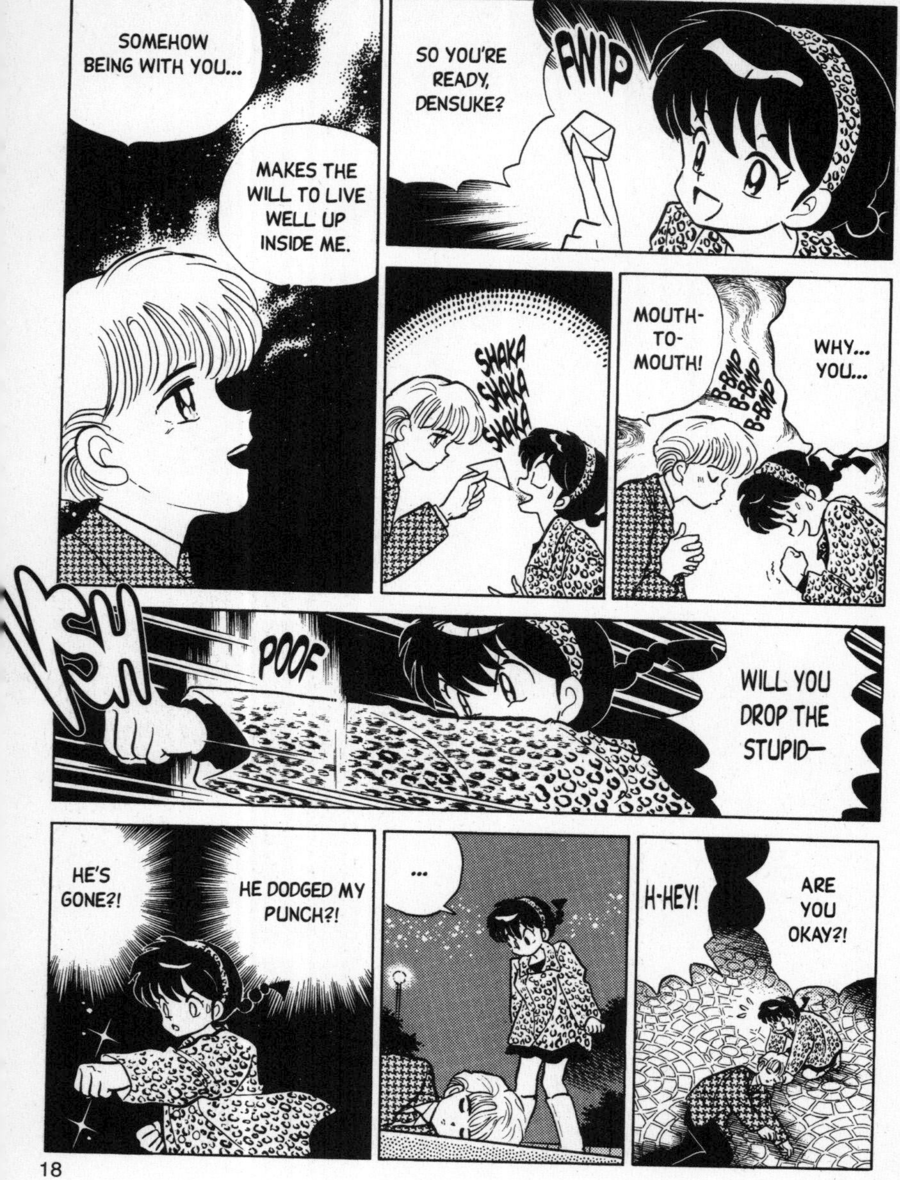
SOMEHOW BEING WITH YOU...
MAKES THE WILL TO LIVE WELL UP INSIDE ME.
SO YOU'RE READY, DENSUKE?
FWIP
SHAKA SHAKA SHAKA
MOUTH-TO-MOUTH!
B-BMP B-BMP B-BMP
WHY... YOU...
VSH
POOF
WILL YOU DROP THE STUPID—
HE'S GONE?!
HE DODGED MY PUNCH?!
...
H-HEY!
ARE YOU OKAY?!

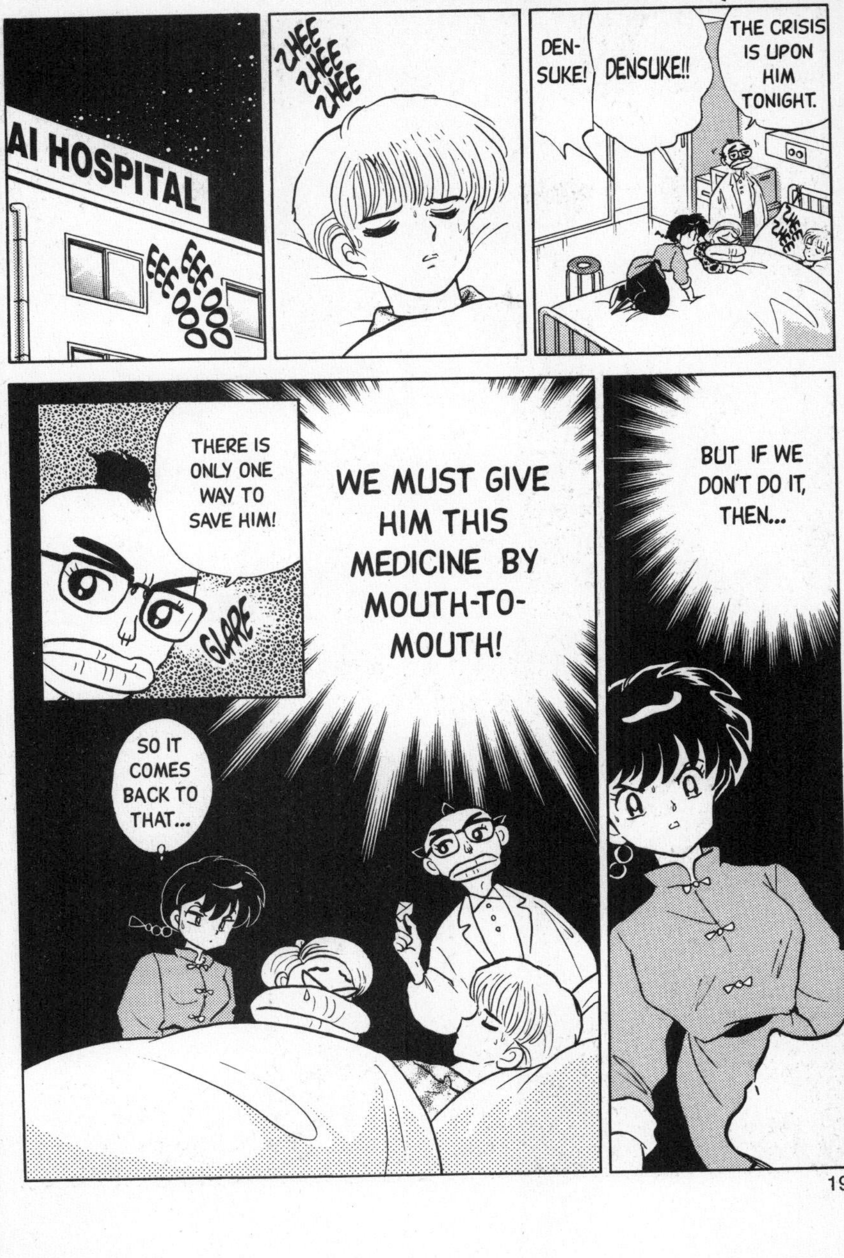
AI HOSPITAL
EEEOOO EEEOOO
ZHEE ZHEE ZHEE
DEN-SUKE!
DENSUKE!!
THE CRISIS IS UPON HIM TONIGHT.
ZHEE ZHEE
THERE IS ONLY ONE WAY TO SAVE HIM!
GLARE
WE MUST GIVE HIM THIS MEDICINE BY MOUTH-TO-MOUTH!
SO IT COMES BACK TO THAT...
BUT IF WE DON'T DO IT, THEN...

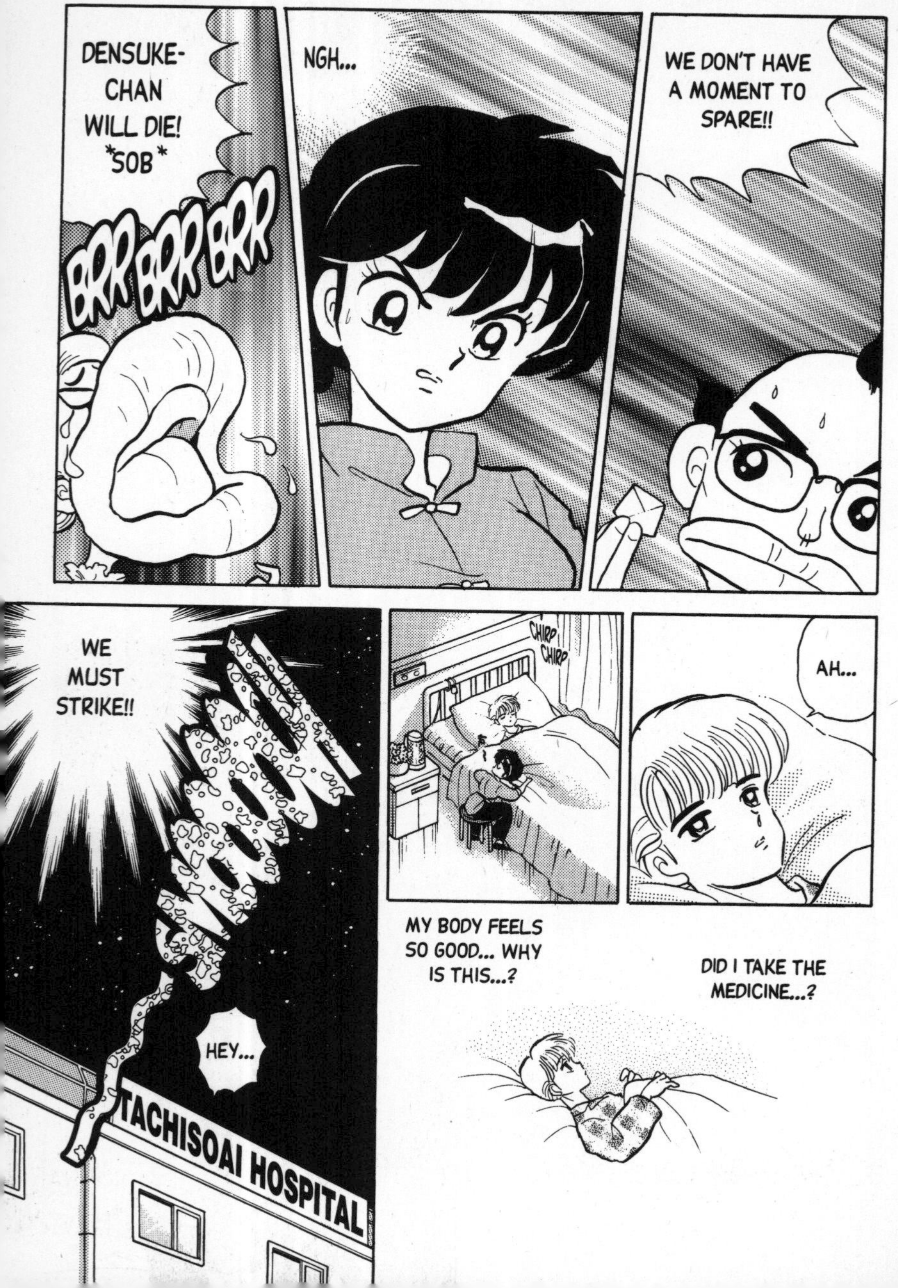
DENSUKE-CHAN WILL DIE! *SOB*
BRR BRR BRR
NGH...
WE DON'T HAVE A MOMENT TO SPARE!!
WE MUST STRIKE!!
HEY...
TACHISOAI HOSPITAL
CHIRP CHIRP
AH...
MY BODY FEELS SO GOOD... WHY IS THIS...?
DID I TAKE THE MEDICINE...?

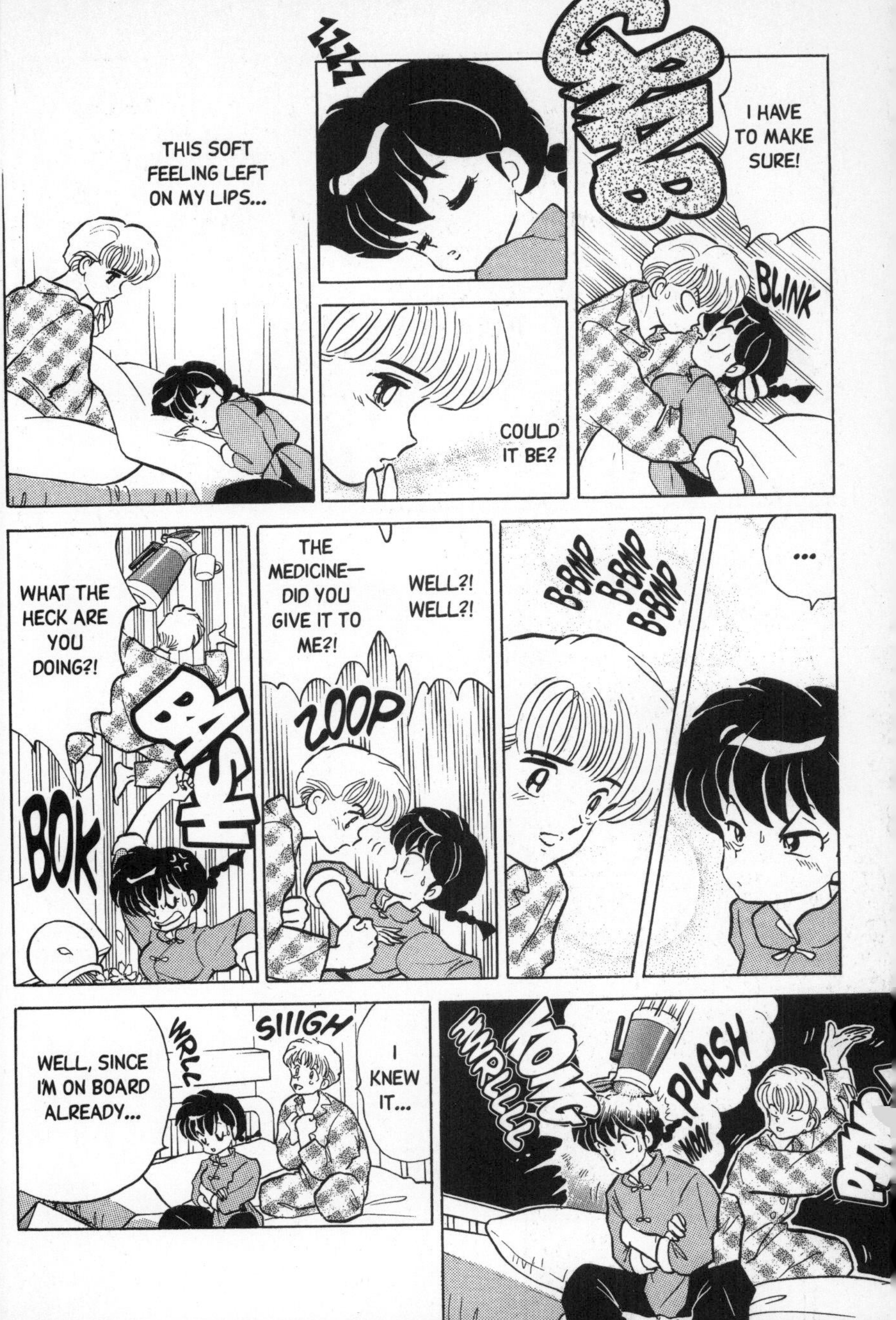
THIS SOFT FEELING LEFT ON MY LIPS...
ZZZ
COULD IT BE?
GRAB
I HAVE TO MAKE SURE!
BLINK
WHAT THE HECK ARE YOU DOING?!
BASH
BOK
THE MEDICINE— DID YOU GIVE IT TO ME?!
WELL?! WELL?!
ZOOP
B-BMP B-BMP B-BMP
...
WELL, SINCE I'M ON BOARD ALREADY...
WRLL
SIIIGH
I KNEW IT...
KONG
HWRLLL
PLASH

...
I PREFER TO LEAVE WITHOUT REVEALING MY TRUE IDENTITY.
WELL, JUST BE THANKFUL THAT YOUR LIFE WAS SAVED...
PAT
WEIRDO.
LOOK WHO'S TALKING!
KRASSSSH
SOME THINGS IN LIFE ARE BETTER LEFT UNKNOWN...
SO YOU REALLY GAVE HIM MOUTH-TO-MOUTH?
HEH
IT'S FOR HIS OWN GOOD TO LET HIM THINK SO.
SO DENSUKE REGAINS HIS WILL TO LIVE...
I WAS KISSED BY A GIRL!
SOB SOB
JUST KNOWING THAT HAS HEALED MY POOR, SICK SOUL!
HE WAS SAVED... THANKS TO YOU, DOCTOR!
BOW BOW
HAHAHA! IT WAS NOTHING!
AND HE'LL MOST LIKELY KEEP HIS WILL TO LIVE, AS LONG AS HE NEVER LEARNS THE CRUEL TRUTH...

PART 2
KASUMI GETS MAD

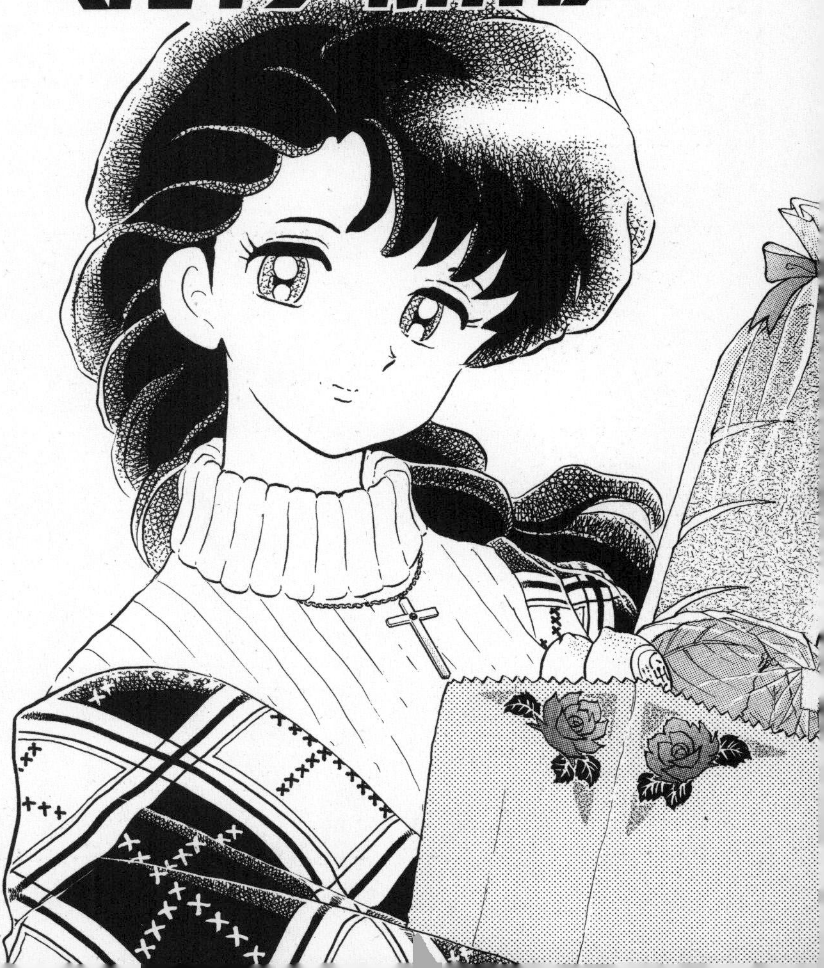

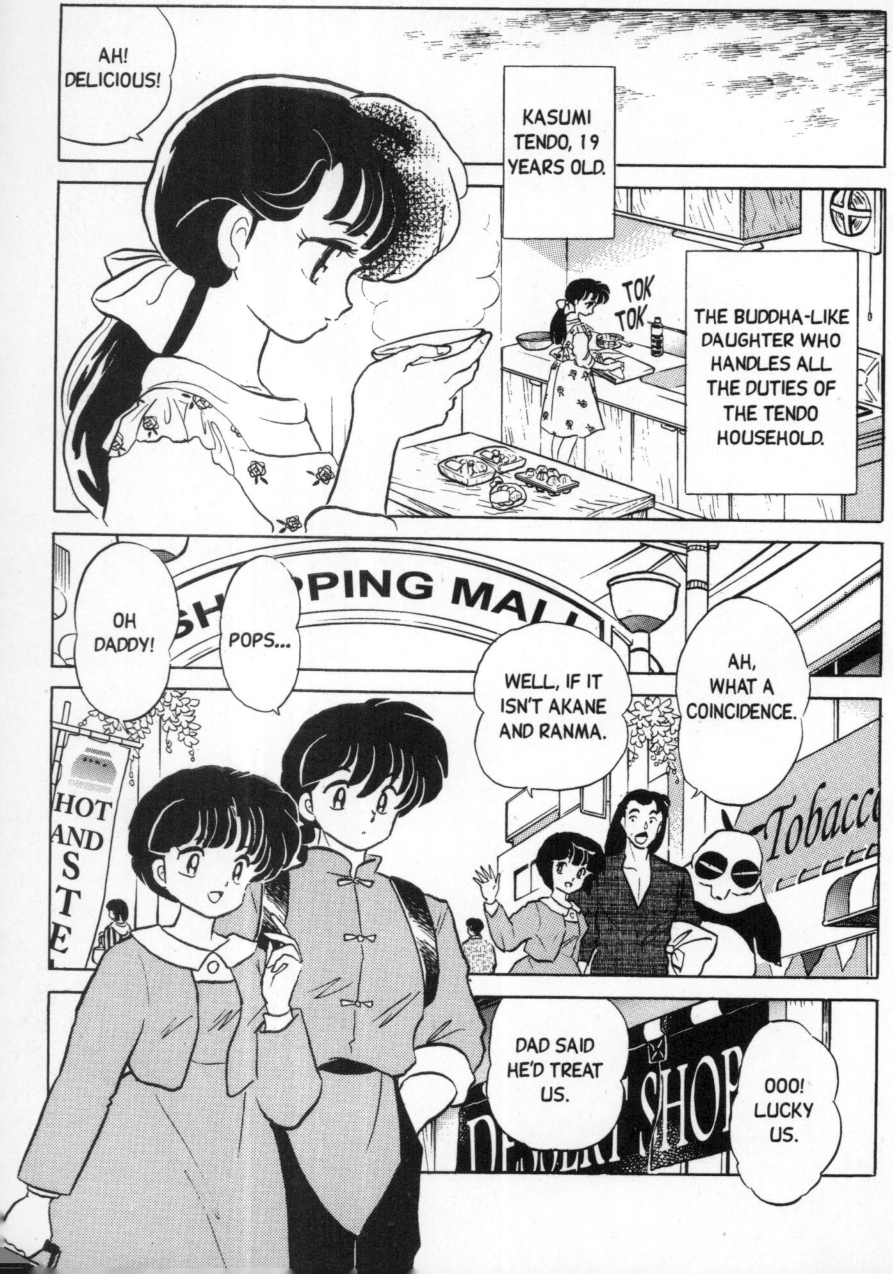
AH! DELICIOUS!
KASUMI TENDO, 19 YEARS OLD.
TOK TOK
THE BUDDHA-LIKE DAUGHTER WHO HANDLES ALL THE DUTIES OF THE TENDO HOUSEHOLD.
OH DADDY!
POPS...
PPING MALL
WELL, IF IT ISN'T AKANE AND RANMA.
AH, WHAT A COINCIDENCE.
HOT AND STE
Tobacco
DAD SAID HE'D TREAT US.
OOO! LUCKY US.
SHOP

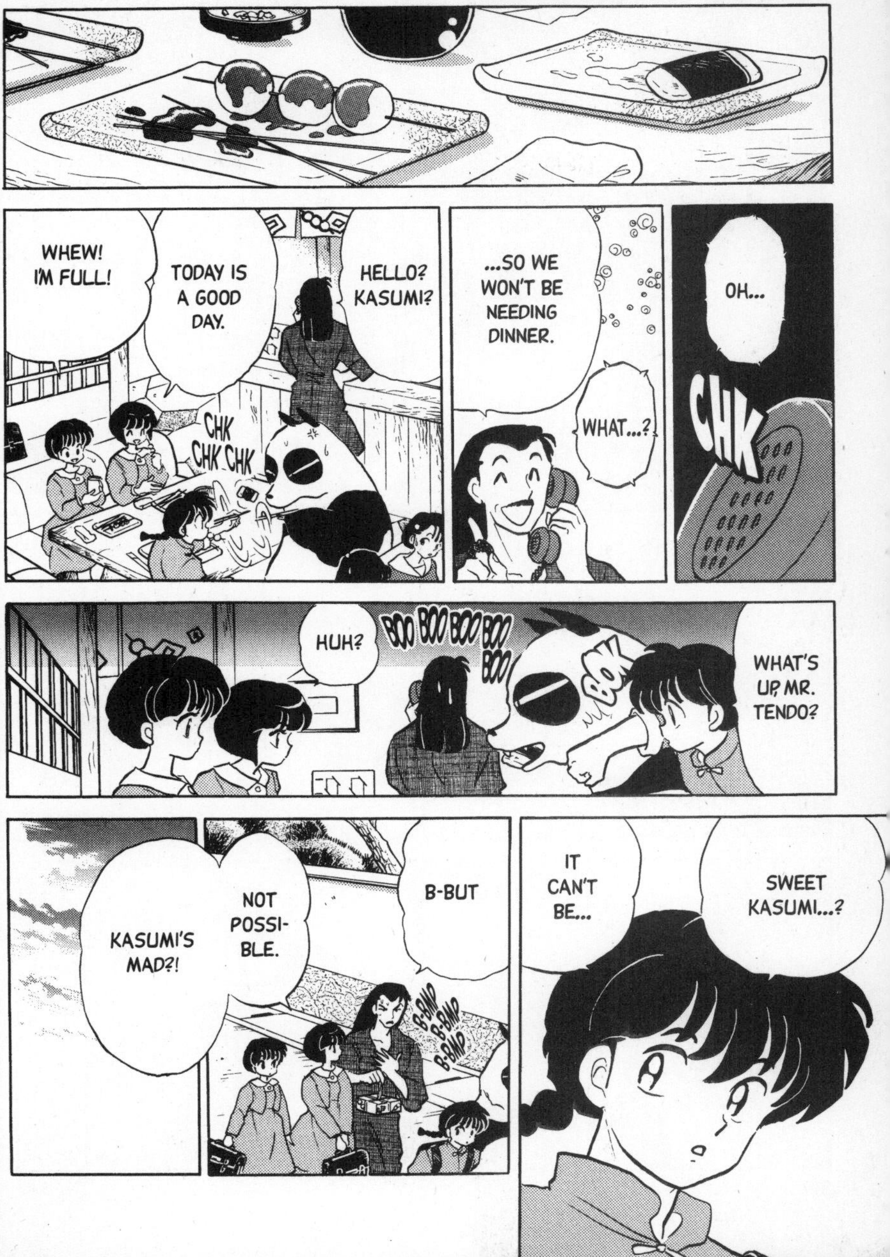
WHEW! I'M FULL!
TODAY IS A GOOD DAY.
HELLO? KASUMI?
CHK CHK CHK
...SO WE WON'T BE NEEDING DINNER.
WHAT...?
OH...
CHK
HUH?
BOO BOO BOO BOO BOO
BOK
WHAT'S UP, MR. TENDO?
KASUMI'S MAD?!
NOT POSSI-BLE.
B-BUT
B-BMP B-BMP B-BMP
IT CAN'T BE...
SWEET KASUMI...?

HUH...?

NO LIGHTS ON...

HYOOOO

HAS SHE G- GONE **OUT**...?!

B-BMP B-BMP

HIOOO KATATA

KASUMI...

!

LOOKS LIKE SOMEBODY THREW IT...

IT... IT CAN'T BE...

KASUMI...?

HYOI

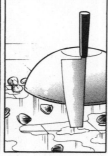

HYOOOO

26

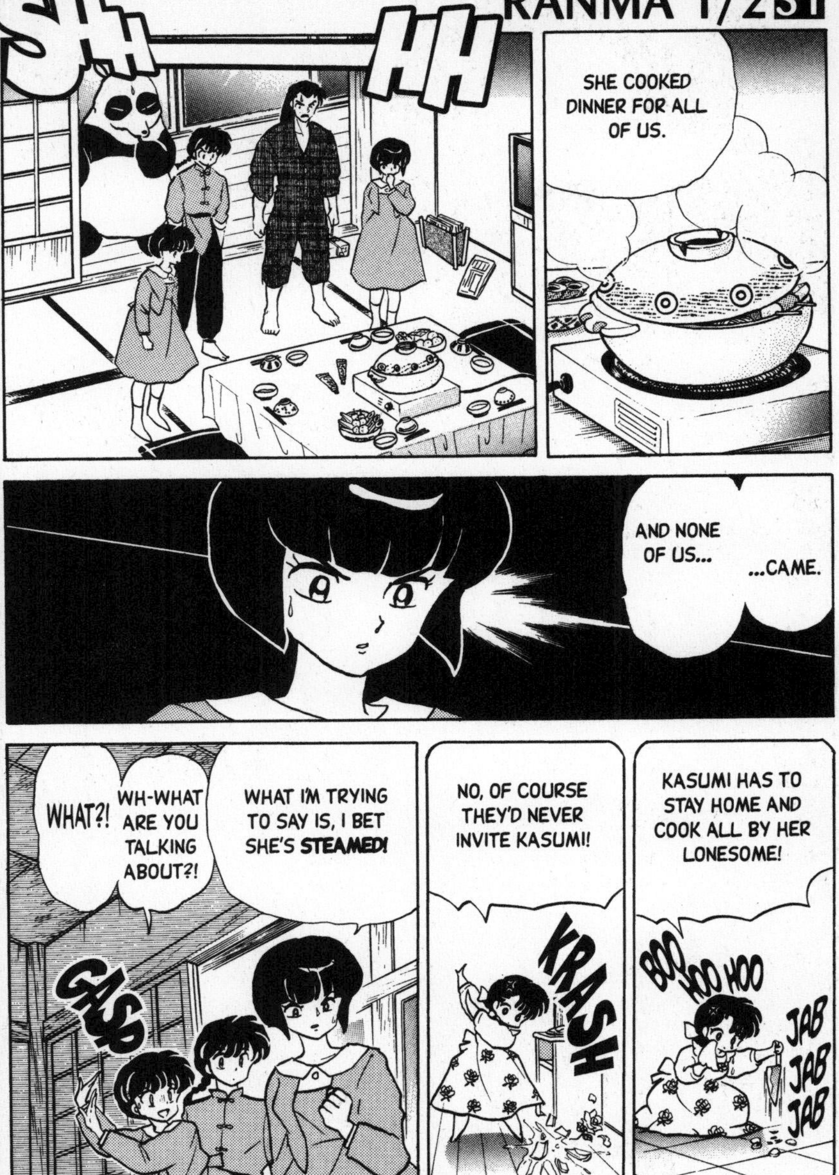
SHHHHH
SHE COOKED DINNER FOR ALL OF US.
AND NONE OF US...
...CAME.
WHAT?!
WH-WHAT ARE YOU TALKING ABOUT?!
WHAT I'M TRYING TO SAY IS, I BET SHE'S **STEAMED!**
GASP
NO, OF COURSE THEY'D NEVER INVITE KASUMI!
KRASH
KASUMI HAS TO STAY HOME AND COOK ALL BY HER LONESOME!
BOO HOO HOO
JAB JAB JAB

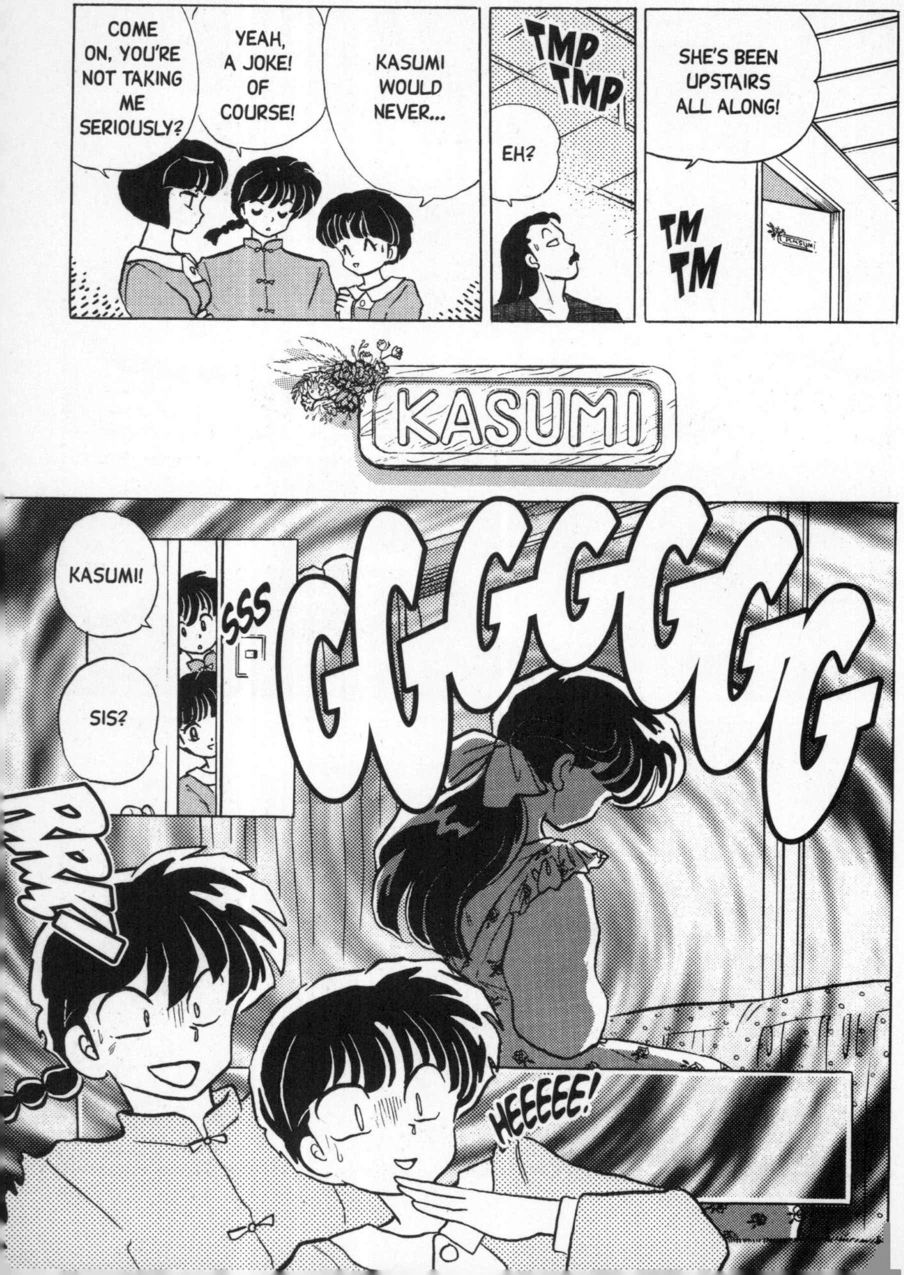
COME ON, YOU'RE NOT TAKING ME SERIOUSLY?
YEAH, A JOKE! OF COURSE!
KASUMI WOULD NEVER...
TMP TMP
EH?
SHE'S BEEN UPSTAIRS ALL ALONG!
TM TM
KASUMI
KASUMI!
SIS?
SSS
GGGGGG
RRK!
HEEEEEE!

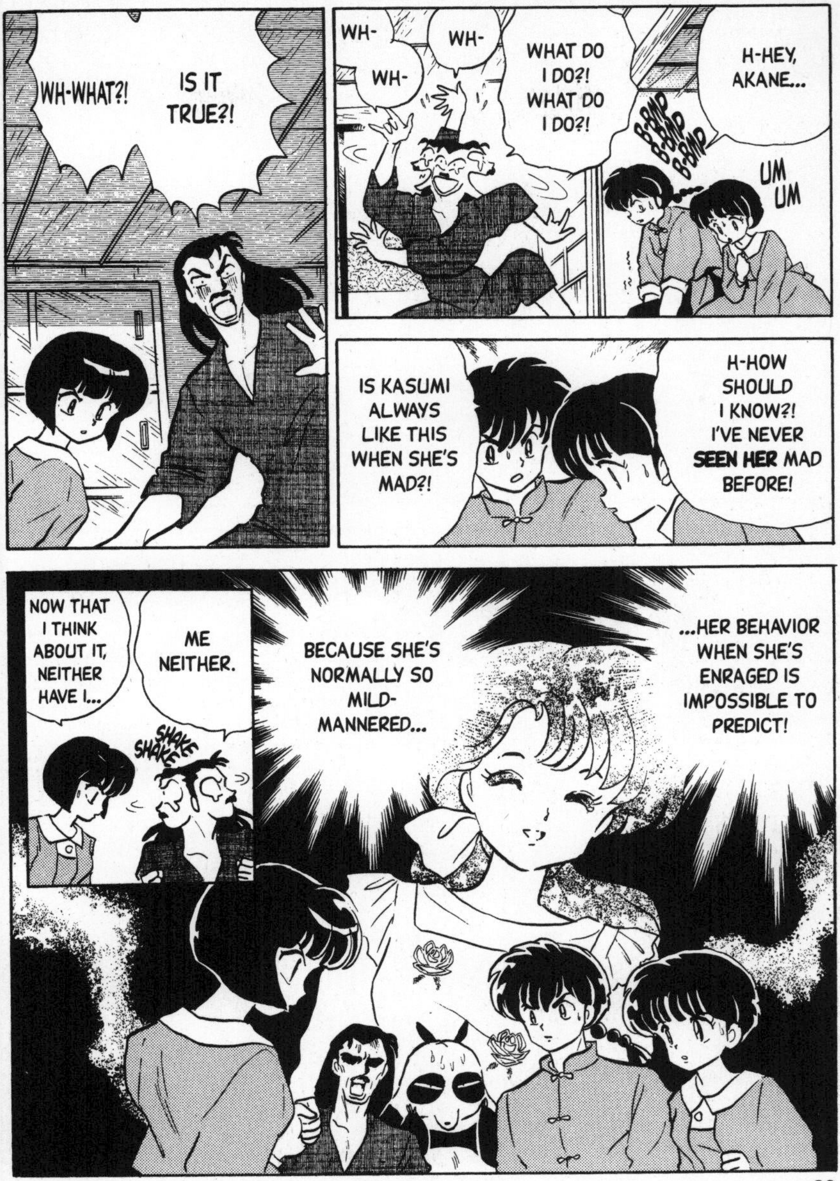
WH-WHAT?!
IS IT TRUE?!
WH-
WH-
WH-
WHAT DO I DO?! WHAT DO I DO?!
H-HEY, AKANE...
B-BMP B-BMP B-BMP
UM UM
IS KASUMI ALWAYS LIKE THIS WHEN SHE'S MAD?!
H-HOW SHOULD I KNOW?! I'VE NEVER **SEEN HER** MAD BEFORE!
NOW THAT I THINK ABOUT IT, NEITHER HAVE I...
ME NEITHER.
SHAKE SHAKE
BECAUSE SHE'S NORMALLY SO MILD-MANNERED...
...HER BEHAVIOR WHEN SHE'S ENRAGED IS IMPOSSIBLE TO PREDICT!

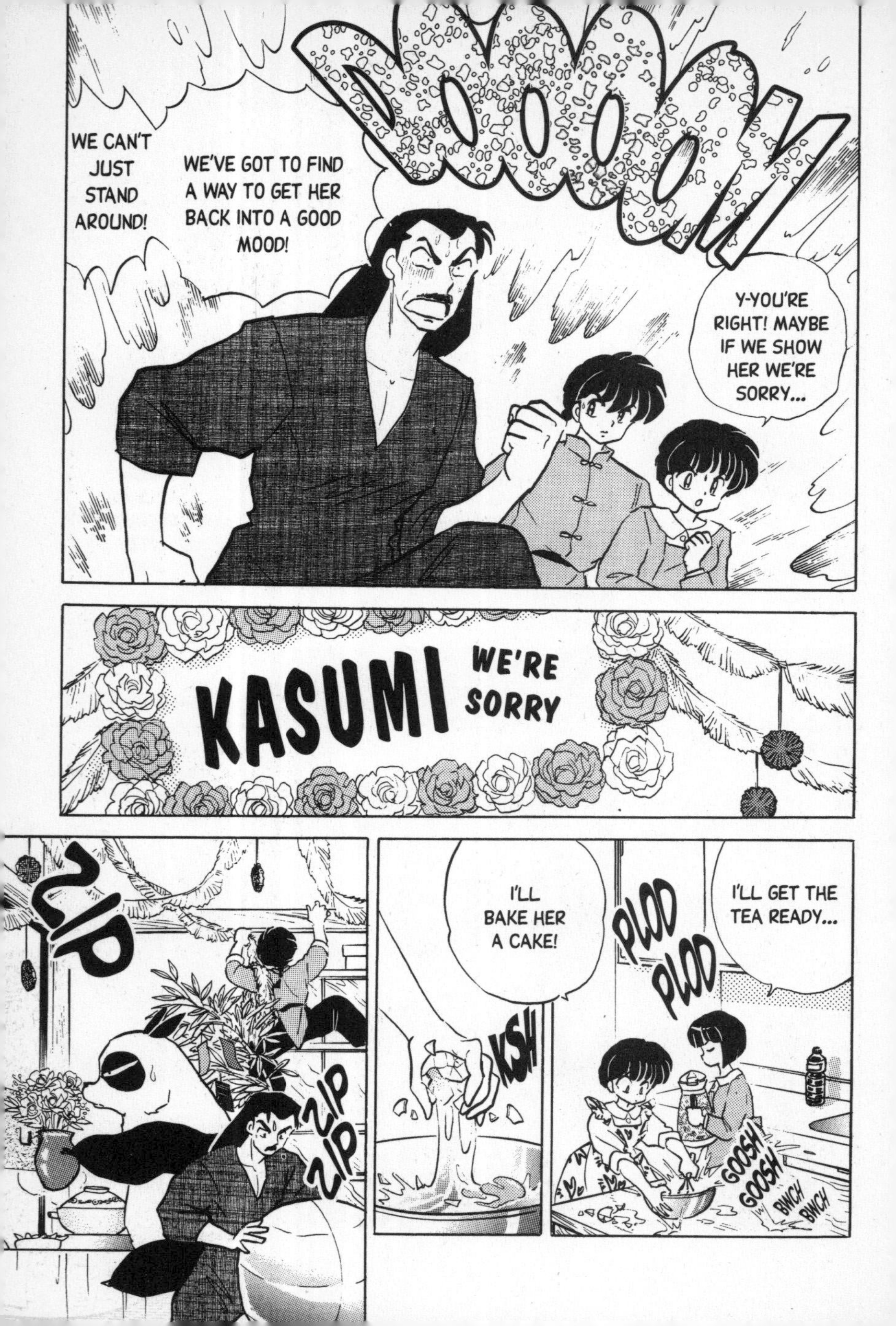
WE CAN'T JUST STAND AROUND!
WE'VE GOT TO FIND A WAY TO GET HER BACK INTO A GOOD MOOD!
DOOOOOM
Y-YOU'RE RIGHT! MAYBE IF WE SHOW HER WE'RE SORRY...
KASUMI WE'RE SORRY
ZIP
ZIP ZIP
I'LL BAKE HER A CAKE!
PLOD PLOD
KSH
I'LL GET THE TEA READY...
GOOSH GOOSH
BWCH BWCH

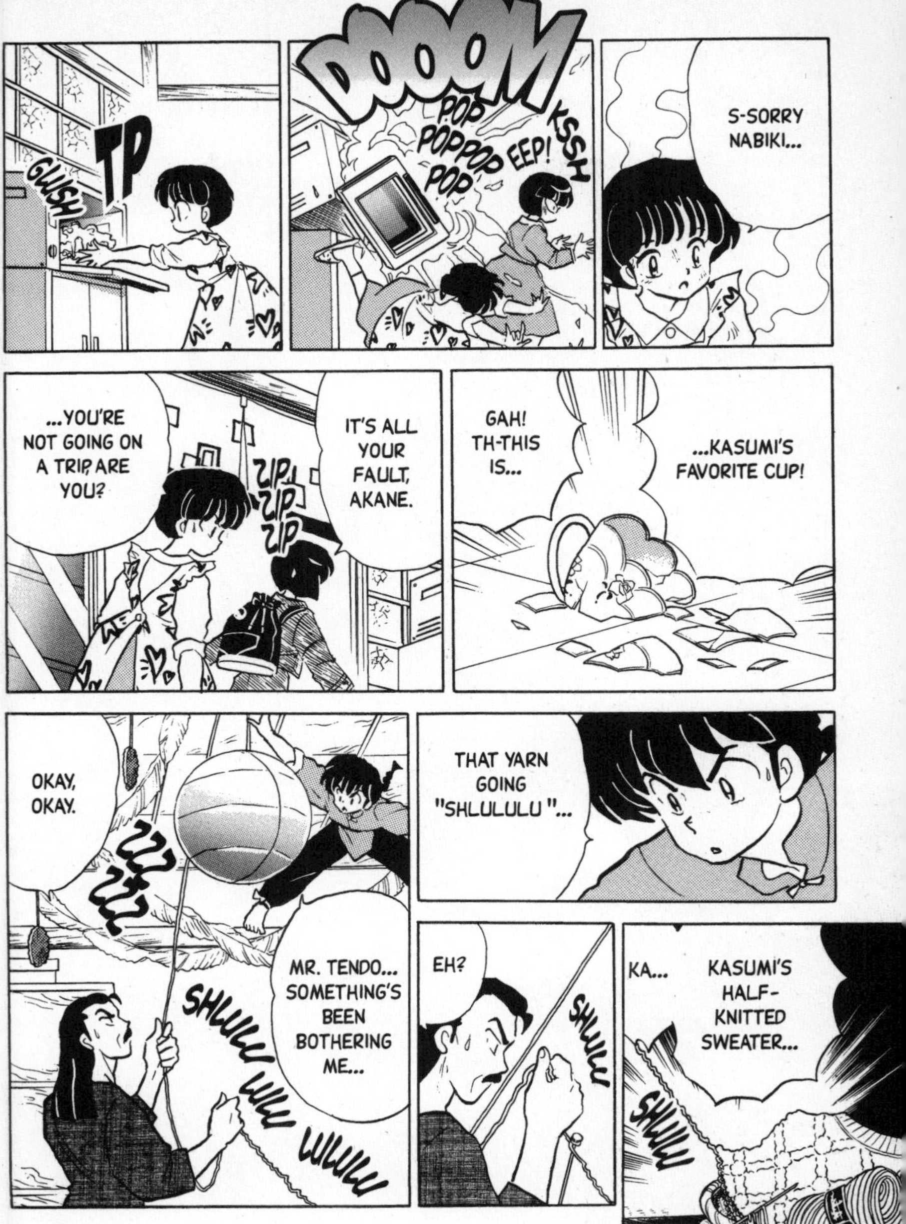
GUSH
TP
DOOOM
POP
POPPOP
POP
POP
EEP!
KSSH
S-SORRY NABIKI...
...YOU'RE NOT GOING ON A TRIP, ARE YOU?
ZIP ZIP ZIP ZIP
IT'S ALL YOUR FAULT, AKANE.
GAH! TH-THIS IS...
...KASUMI'S FAVORITE CUP!
OKAY, OKAY.
ZZZ ZZZ
MR. TENDO... SOMETHING'S BEEN BOTHERING ME...
SHLULU LULU LULULU
THAT YARN GOING "SHLULULU "...
EH?
SHLULU
KA...
KASUMI'S HALF-KNITTED SWEATER...
SHLULU

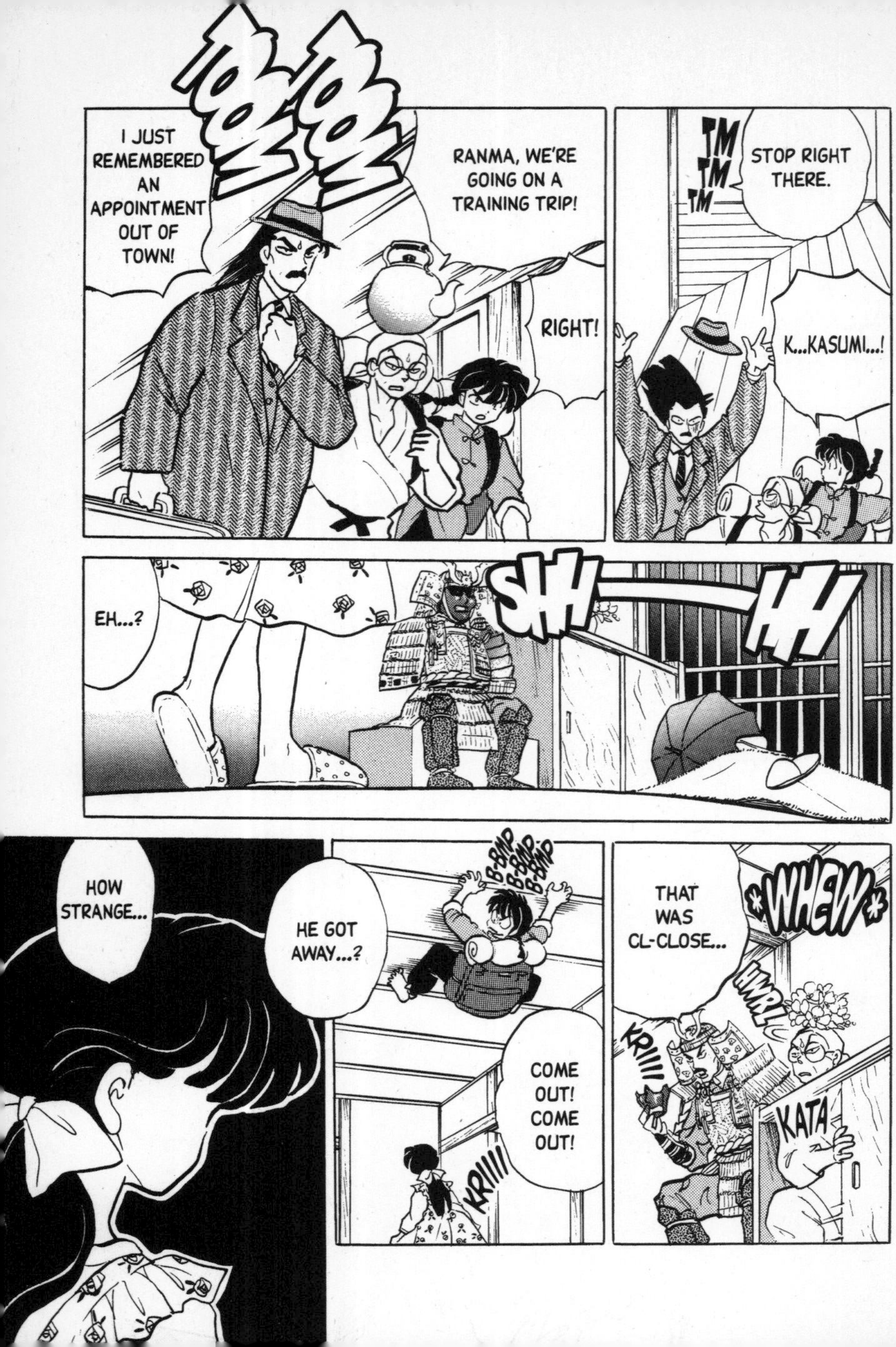
TOOM
TOOM
I JUST REMEMBERED AN APPOINTMENT OUT OF TOWN!
RANMA, WE'RE GOING ON A TRAINING TRIP!
RIGHT!
TM TM TM
STOP RIGHT THERE.
K...KASUMI...!
EH...?
SHH—HH
HOW STRANGE...
HE GOT AWAY...?
B-BMP B-BMP B-BMP
COME OUT! COME OUT!
KRIIII
WHEW
THAT WAS CL-CLOSE...
HWRL
KRIIII
KATA

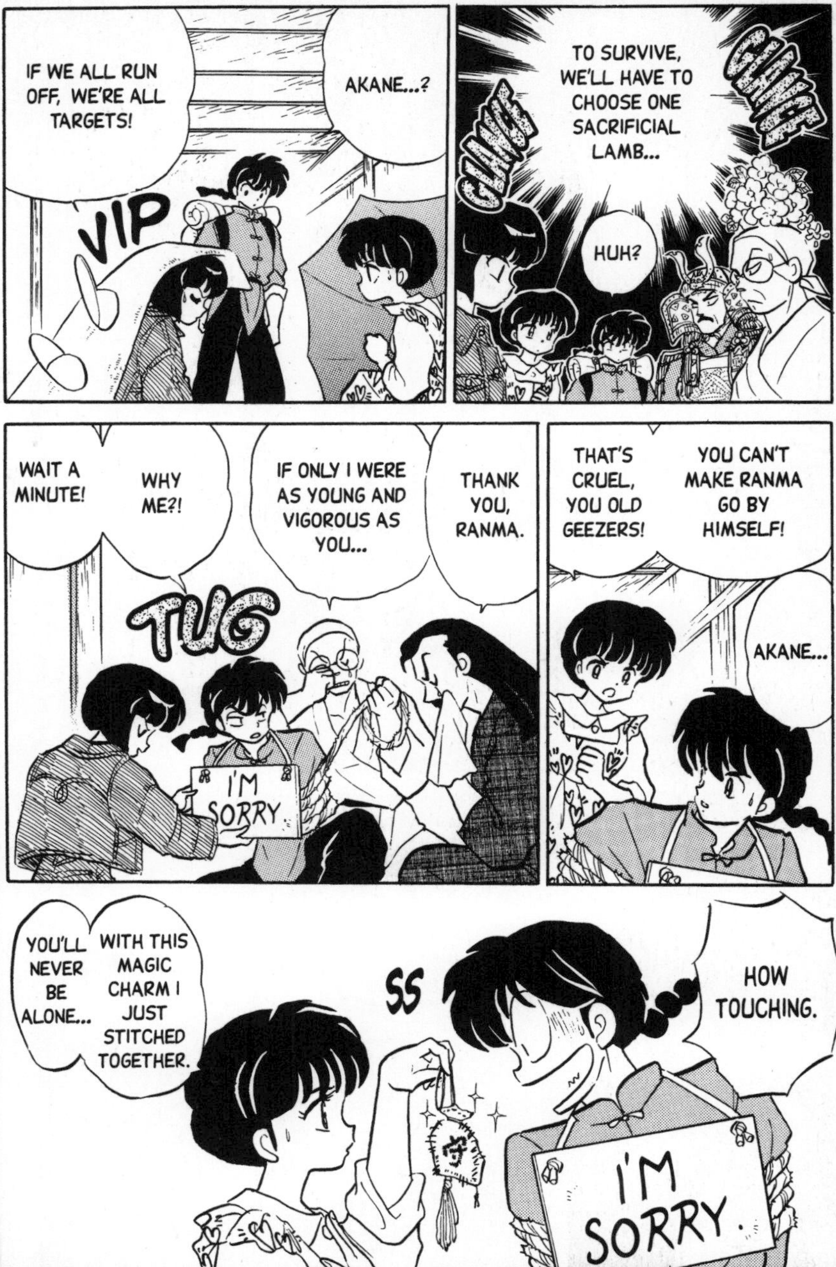
IF WE ALL RUN OFF, WE'RE ALL TARGETS!
AKANE...?
VIP
TO SURVIVE, WE'LL HAVE TO CHOOSE ONE SACRIFICIAL LAMB...
HUH?
WAIT A MINUTE!
WHY ME?!
IF ONLY I WERE AS YOUNG AND VIGOROUS AS YOU...
THANK YOU, RANMA.
TUG
I'M SORRY
THAT'S CRUEL, YOU OLD GEEZERS!
YOU CAN'T MAKE RANMA GO BY HIMSELF!
AKANE...
YOU'LL NEVER BE ALONE...
WITH THIS MAGIC CHARM I JUST STITCHED TOGETHER.
SS
HOW TOUCHING.
I'M SORRY.

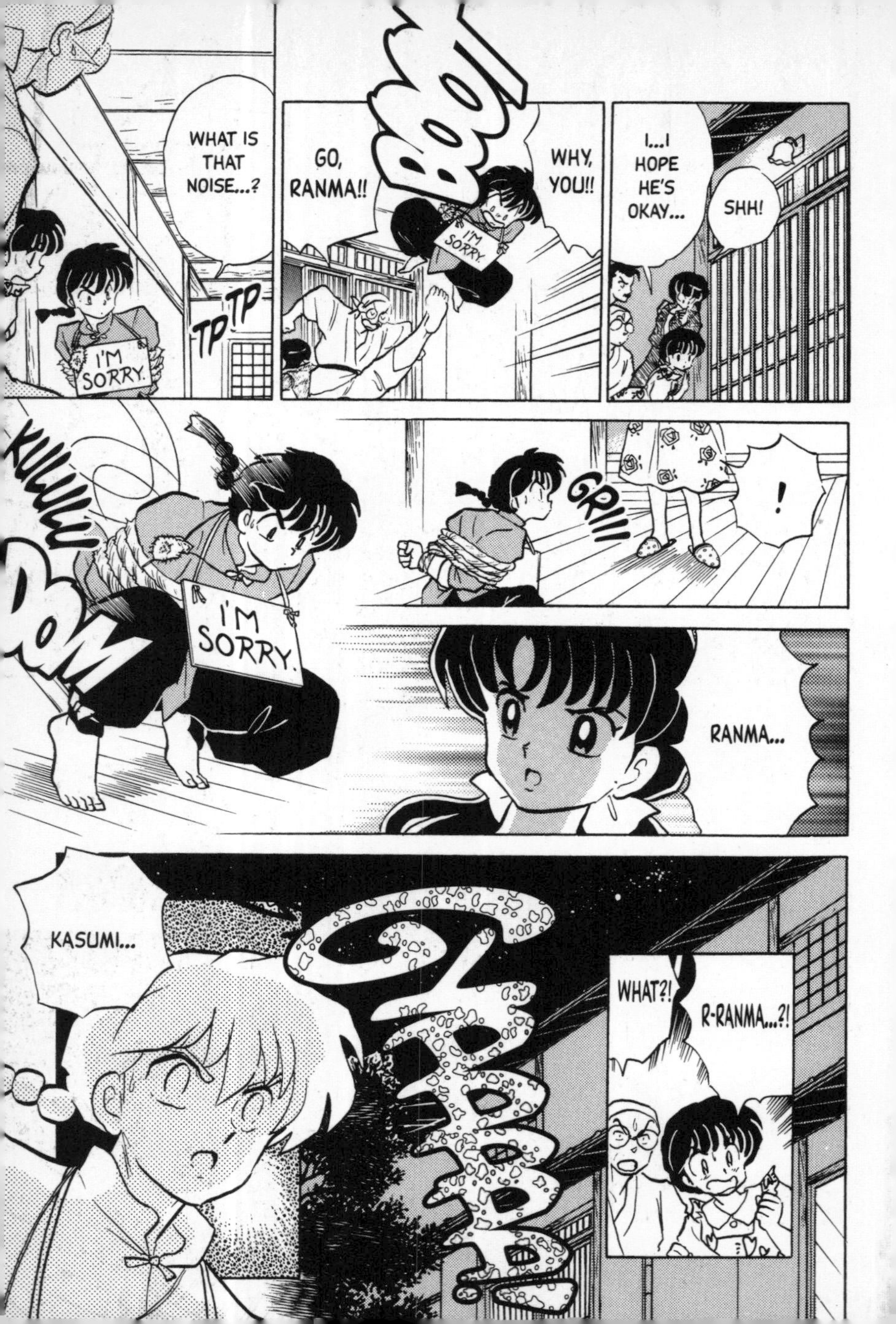
WHAT IS THAT NOISE...?
TP TP
I'M SORRY.
GO, RANMA!!
WHY, YOU!!
I'M SORRY.
I...I HOPE HE'S OKAY...
SHH!
I'M SORRY.
GRIIII
!
RANMA...
KASUMI...
WHAT?!
R-RANMA...?!

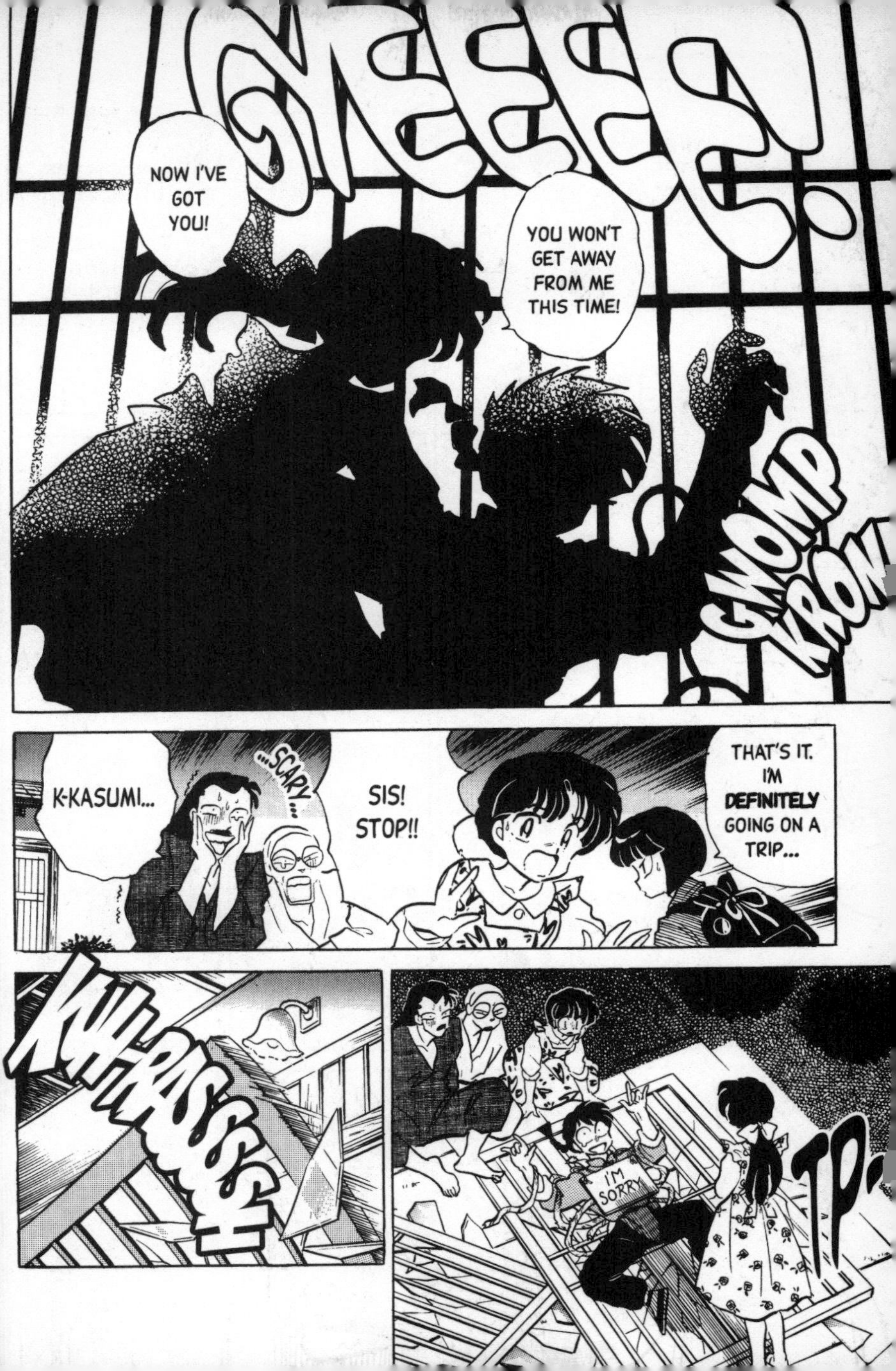
NOW I'VE GOT YOU!
YOU WON'T GET AWAY FROM ME THIS TIME!
GWOMP
K-KASUMI...
...SCARY...
SIS! STOP!!
THAT'S IT. I'M **DEFINITELY** GOING ON A TRIP...
I'M SORRY
TP-

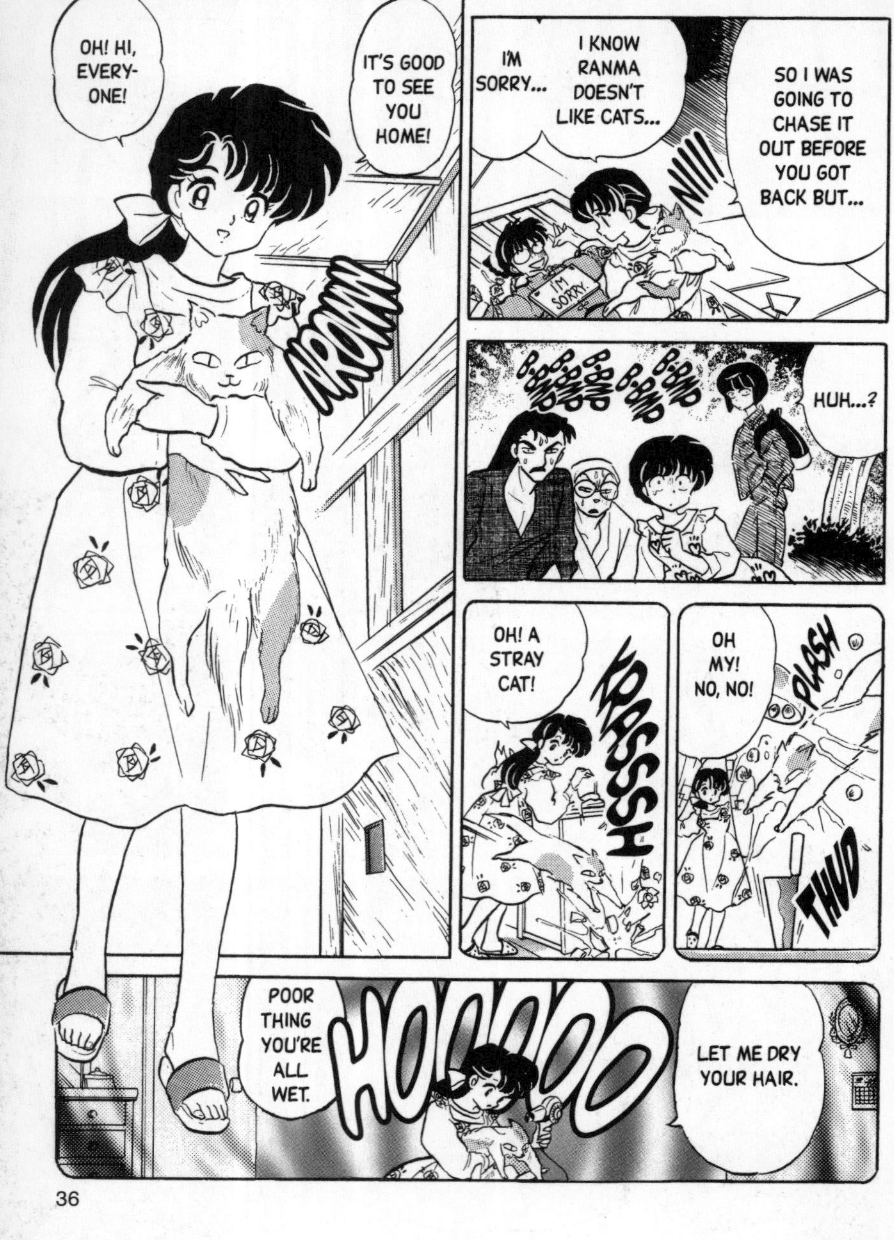
OH! HI, EVERY-ONE!
IT'S GOOD TO SEE YOU HOME!
I'M SORRY...
I KNOW RANMA DOESN'T LIKE CATS...
NI!!
SO I WAS GOING TO CHASE IT OUT BEFORE YOU GOT BACK BUT...
I'M SORRY.
B-BMP B-BMP B-BMP B-BMP B-BMP
HUH...?
OH! A STRAY CAT!
KRASSSH
OH MY! NO, NO!
PLASH
THUD
POOR THING YOU'RE ALL WET.
HOOOOOO
LET ME DRY YOUR HAIR.

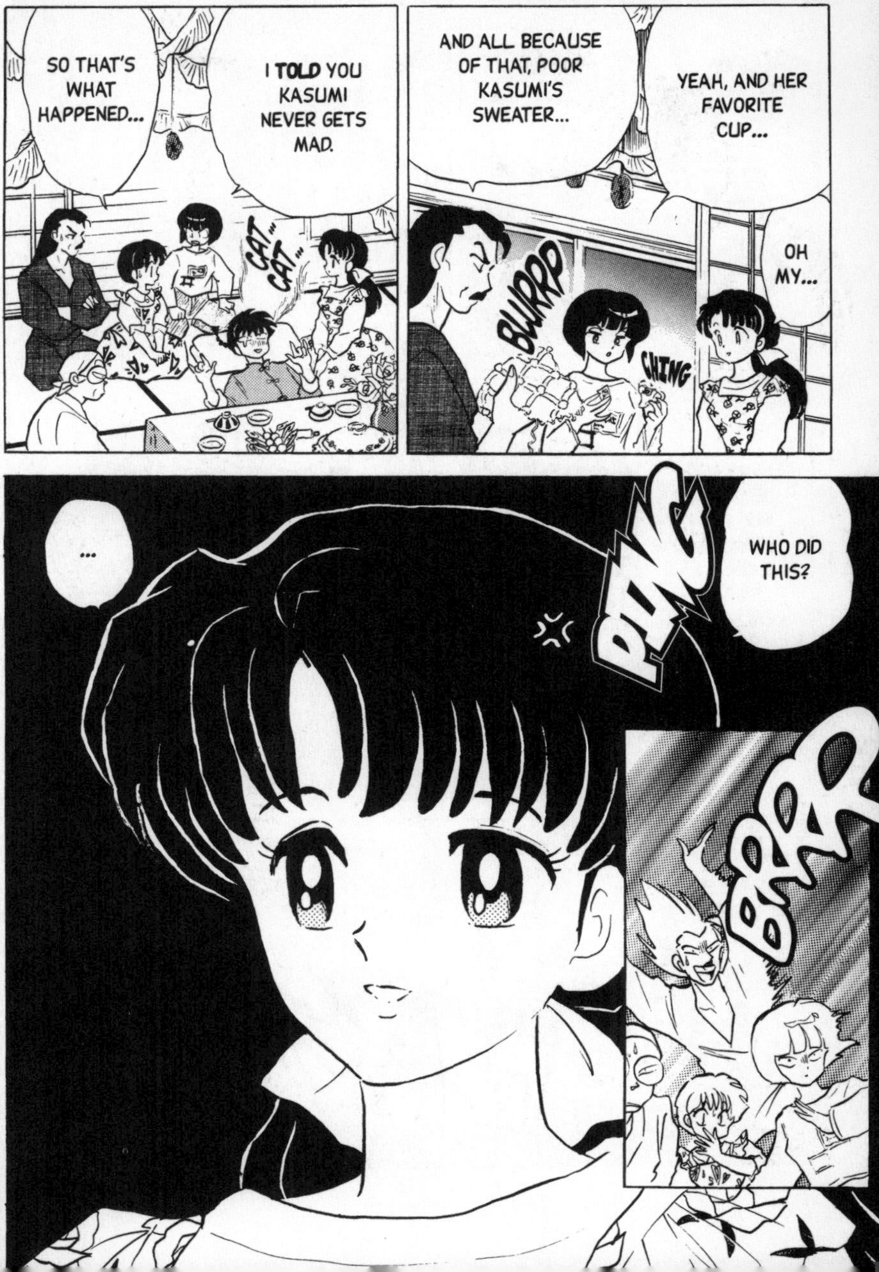
SO THAT'S WHAT HAPPENED...
I **TOLD** YOU KASUMI NEVER GETS MAD.
CAT... CAT...
AND ALL BECAUSE OF THAT, POOR KASUMI'S SWEATER...
YEAH, AND HER FAVORITE CUP...
BWRRP
CHING
OH MY...
...
PLING
WHO DID THIS?
BRRR

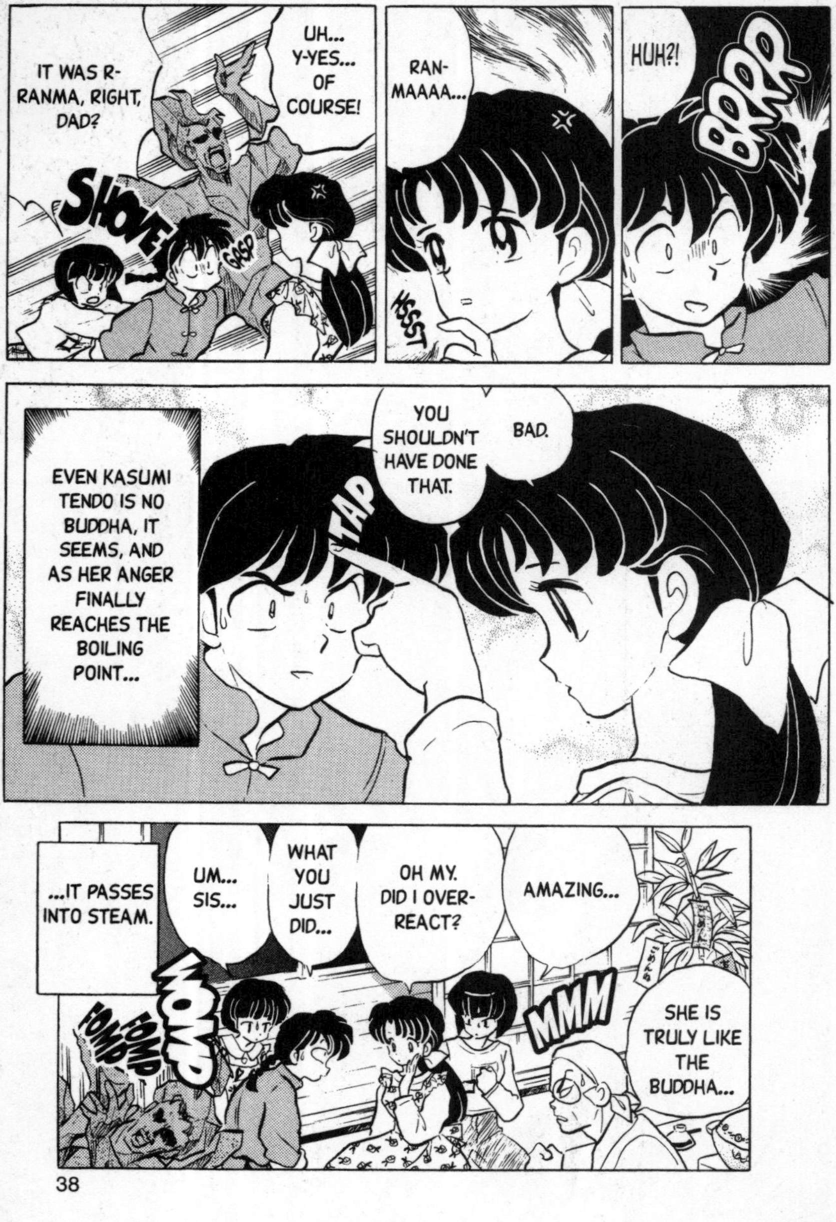
IT WAS R-RANMA, RIGHT, DAD?
UH... Y-YES... OF COURSE!
SHOVE
GASP
RAN-MAAAA...
HSSST
HUH?!
BRRP
EVEN KASUMI TENDO IS NO BUDDHA, IT SEEMS, AND AS HER ANGER FINALLY REACHES THE BOILING POINT...
TAP
YOU SHOULDN'T HAVE DONE THAT.
BAD.
...IT PASSES INTO STEAM.
UM... SIS...
WHAT YOU JUST DID...
OH MY. DID I OVER-REACT?
AMAZING...
WOMP
FOMP FOMP
MMM
SHE IS TRULY LIKE THE BUDDHA...

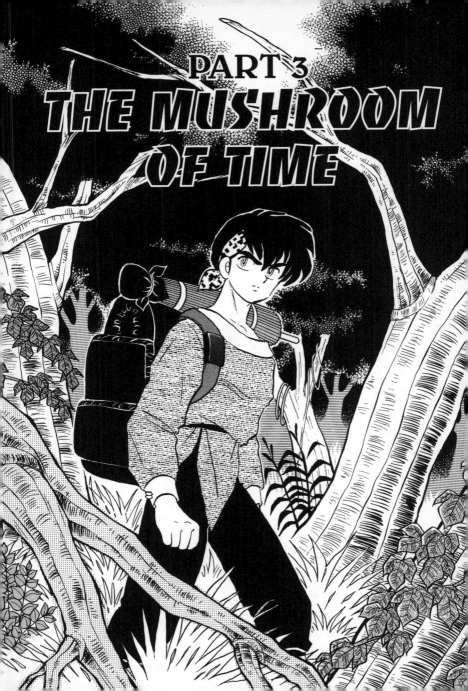

PART 3
THE MUSHROOM OF TIME

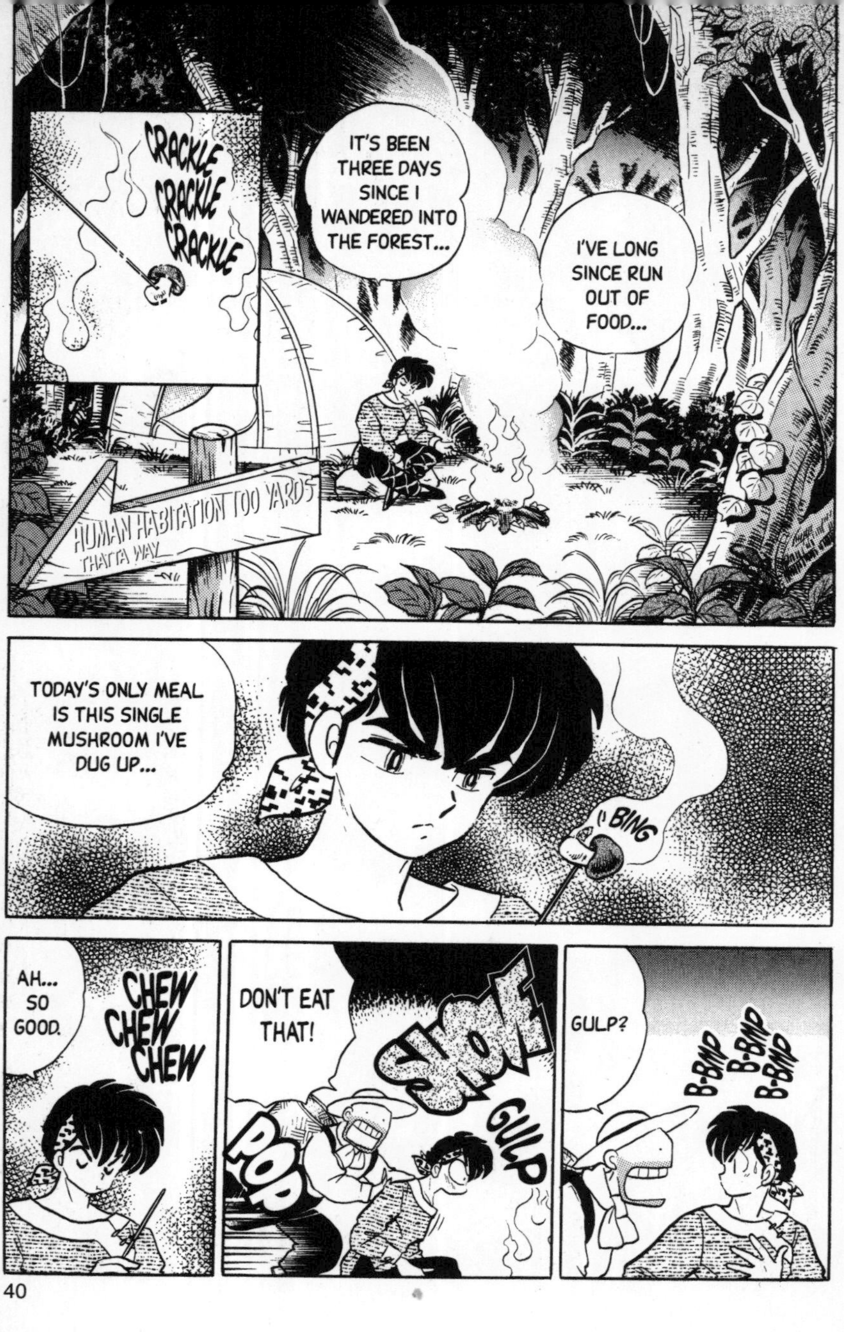
CRACKLE CRACKLE CRACKLE
IT'S BEEN THREE DAYS SINCE I WANDERED INTO THE FOREST...
I'VE LONG SINCE RUN OUT OF FOOD...
HUMAN HABITATION 100 YARDS
THATTA WAY
TODAY'S ONLY MEAL IS THIS SINGLE MUSHROOM I'VE DUG UP...
BING
AH... SO GOOD.
CHEW CHEW CHEW
DON'T EAT THAT!
SHOVE
POP
GULP
GULP?
B-BMP B-BMP B-BMP

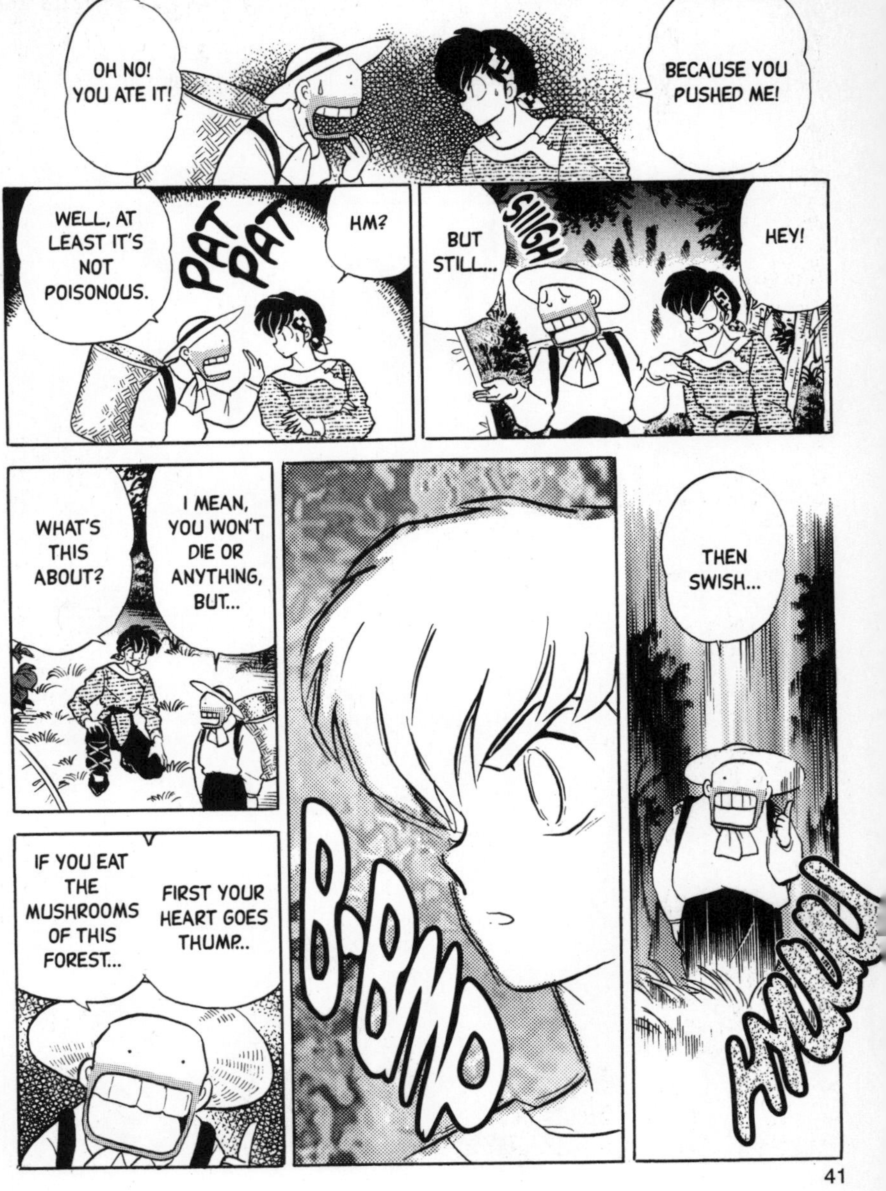
OH NO! YOU ATE IT!
BECAUSE YOU PUSHED ME!
WELL, AT LEAST IT'S NOT POISONOUS.
PAT PAT
HM?
BUT STILL...
SIIIGH
HEY!
WHAT'S THIS ABOUT?
I MEAN, YOU WON'T DIE OR ANYTHING, BUT...
IF YOU EAT THE MUSHROOMS OF THIS FOREST...
FIRST YOUR HEART GOES THUMP...
B-BMP
THEN SWISH...
HMM!!

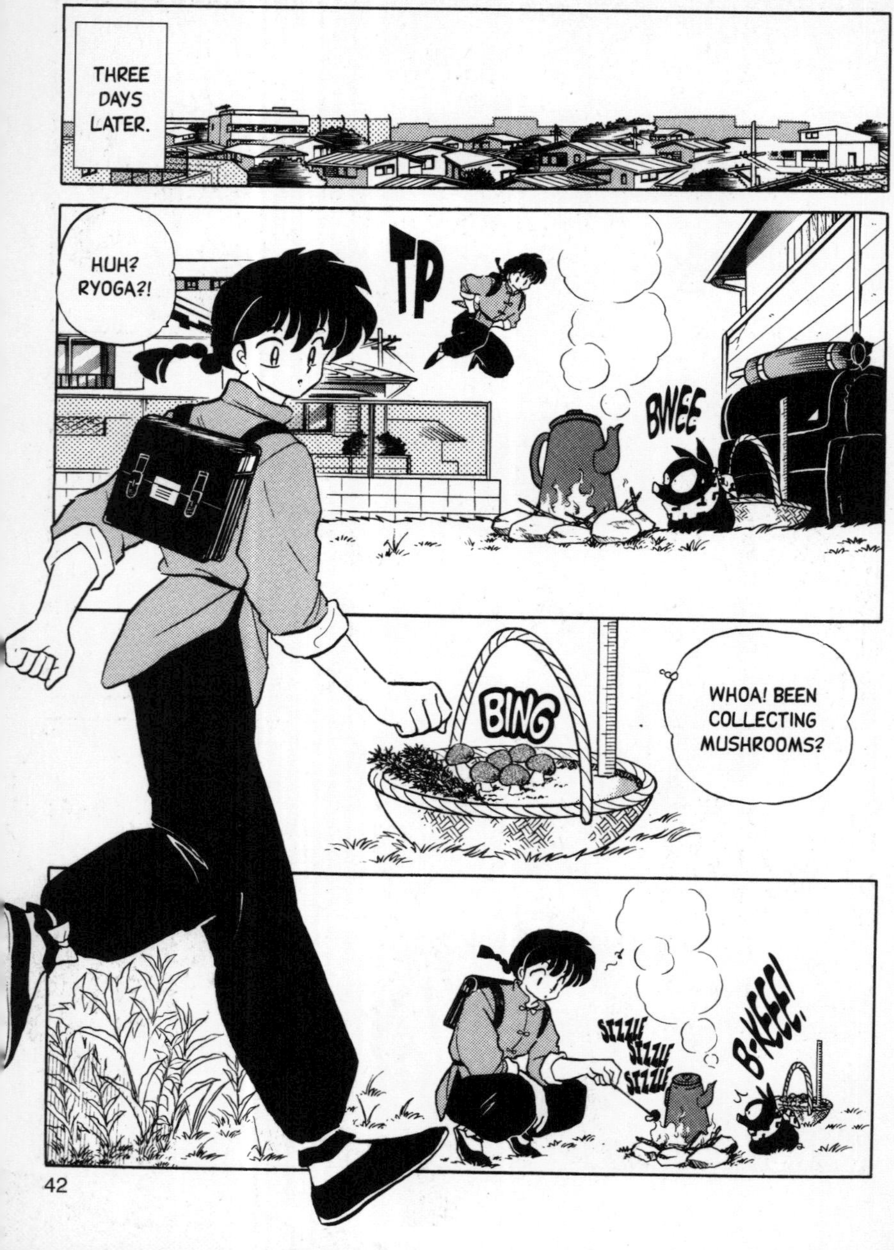
THREE DAYS LATER.
HUH? RYOGA?!
TP
BWEE
BING
WHOA! BEEN COLLECTING MUSHROOMS?
SIZZLE SIZZLE SIZZLE
B-KEEE!

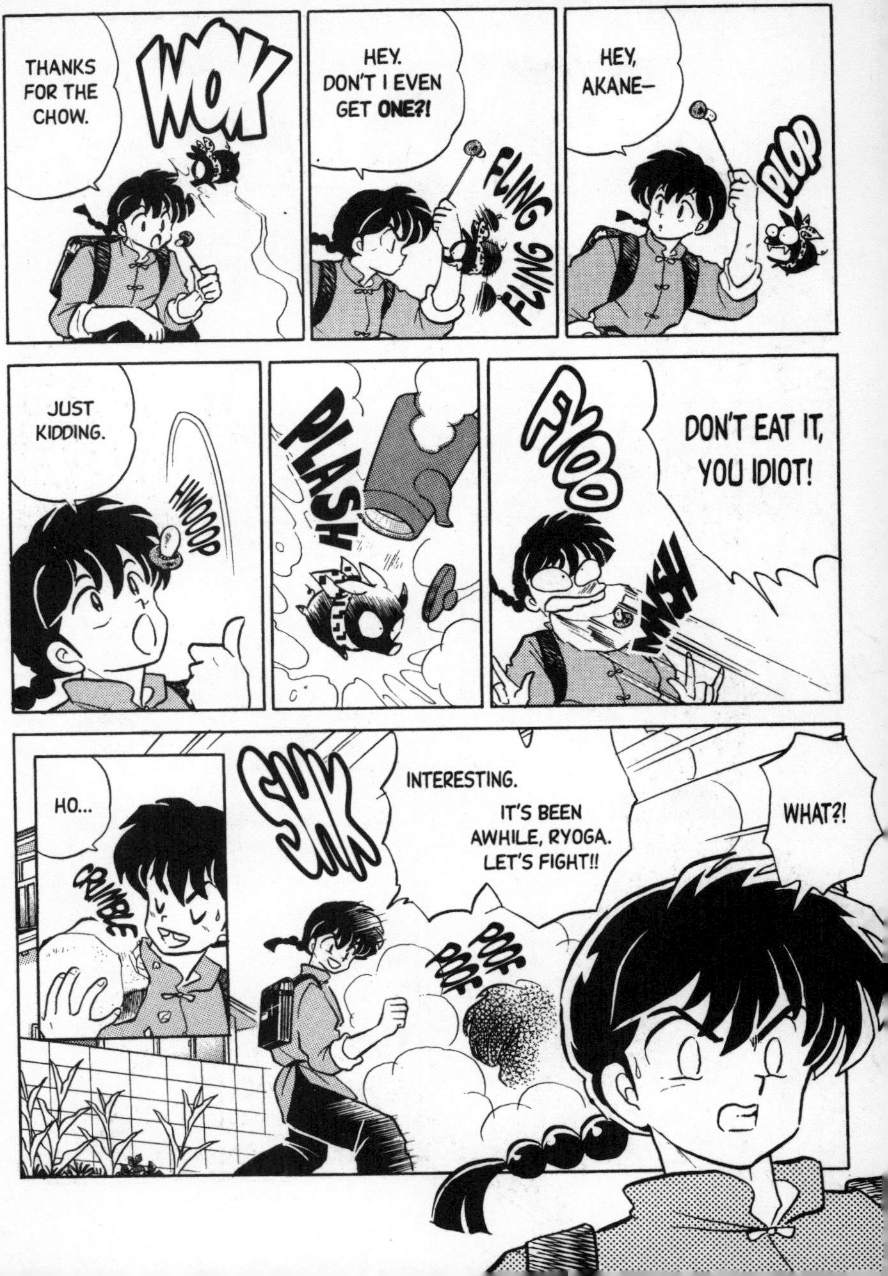
THANKS FOR THE CHOW.
WOK
HEY. DON'T I EVEN GET ONE?!
FLING FLING
HEY, AKANE—
PLOP
JUST KIDDING.
HWOOOP
PLASH
FYOOO
DON'T EAT IT, YOU IDIOT!
HO...
CRUMBLE
SHK
INTERESTING.
IT'S BEEN AWHILE, RYOGA. LET'S FIGHT!!
POOF POOF
WHAT?!

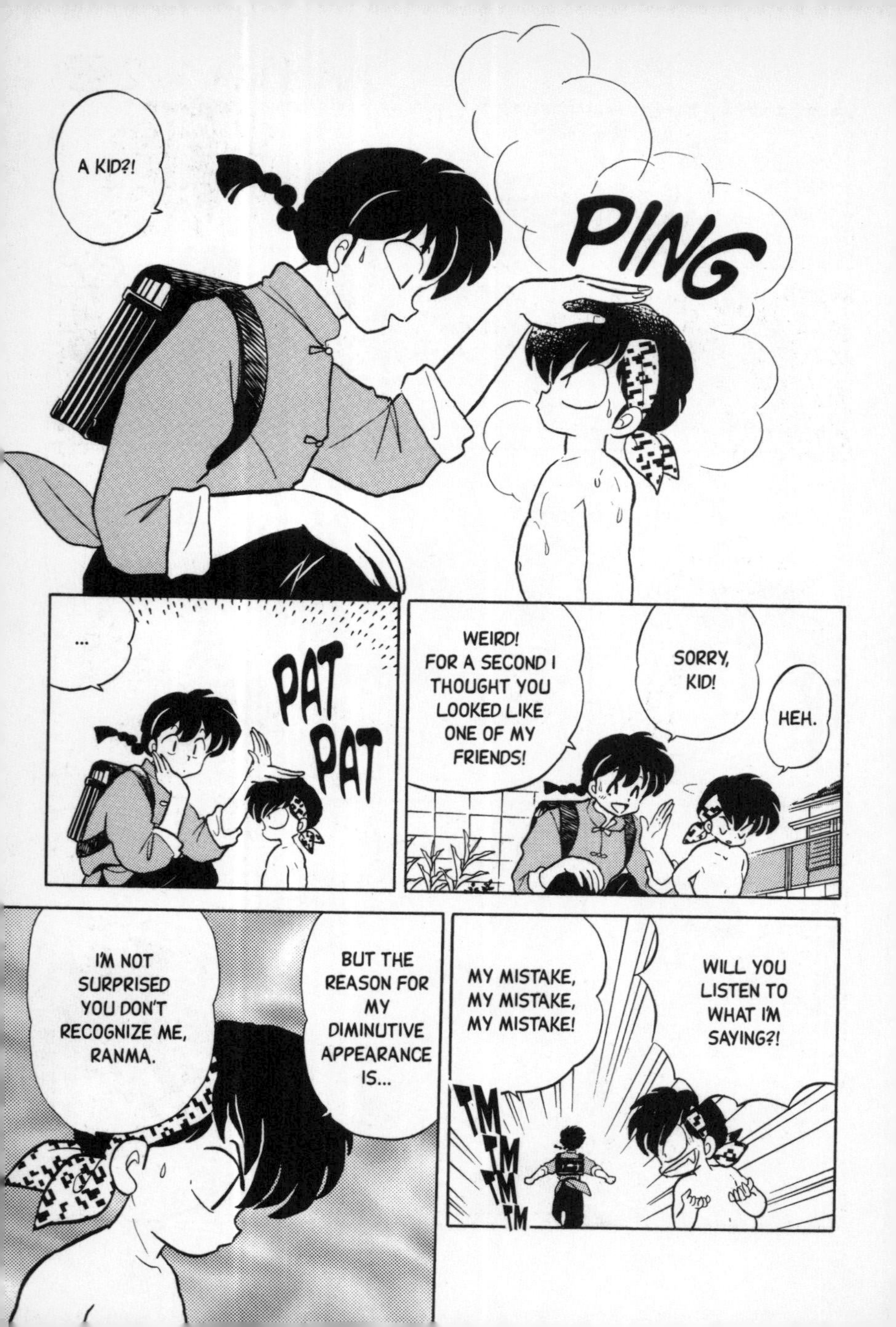
A KID?!
PING
...
PAT PAT
WEIRD! FOR A SECOND I THOUGHT YOU LOOKED LIKE ONE OF MY FRIENDS!
SORRY, KID!
HEH.
I'M NOT SURPRISED YOU DON'T RECOGNIZE ME, RANMA.
BUT THE REASON FOR MY DIMINUTIVE APPEARANCE IS...
MY MISTAKE, MY MISTAKE, MY MISTAKE!
WILL YOU LISTEN TO WHAT I'M SAYING?!
TM TM TM TM TM TM

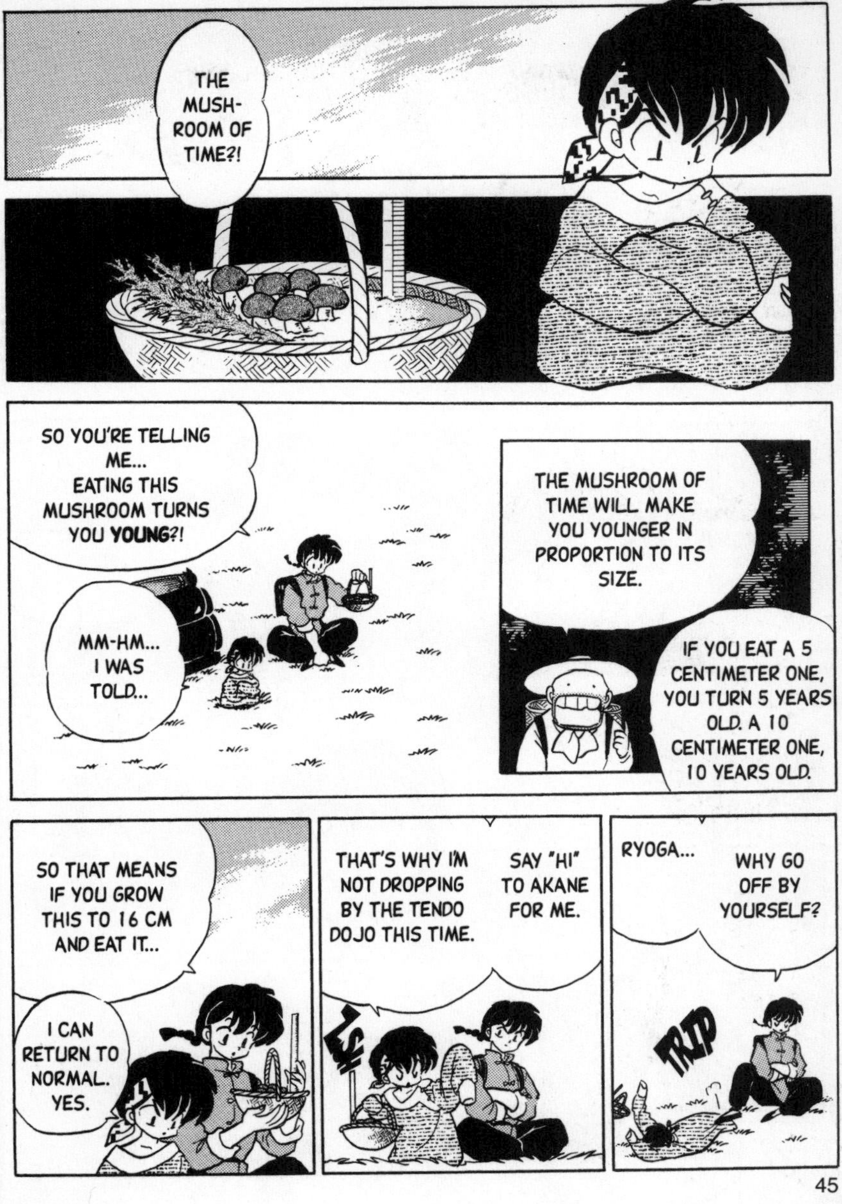
THE MUSH-ROOM OF TIME?!
SO YOU'RE TELLING ME... EATING THIS MUSHROOM TURNS YOU **YOUNG**?!
MM-HM... I WAS TOLD...
THE MUSHROOM OF TIME WILL MAKE YOU YOUNGER IN PROPORTION TO ITS SIZE.
IF YOU EAT A 5 CENTIMETER ONE, YOU TURN 5 YEARS OLD. A 10 CENTIMETER ONE, 10 YEARS OLD.
SO THAT MEANS IF YOU GROW THIS TO 16 CM AND EAT IT...
I CAN RETURN TO NORMAL. YES.
THAT'S WHY I'M NOT DROPPING BY THE TENDO DOJO THIS TIME.
SAY "HI" TO AKANE FOR ME.
RYOGA...
WHY GO OFF BY YOURSELF?
TRIP

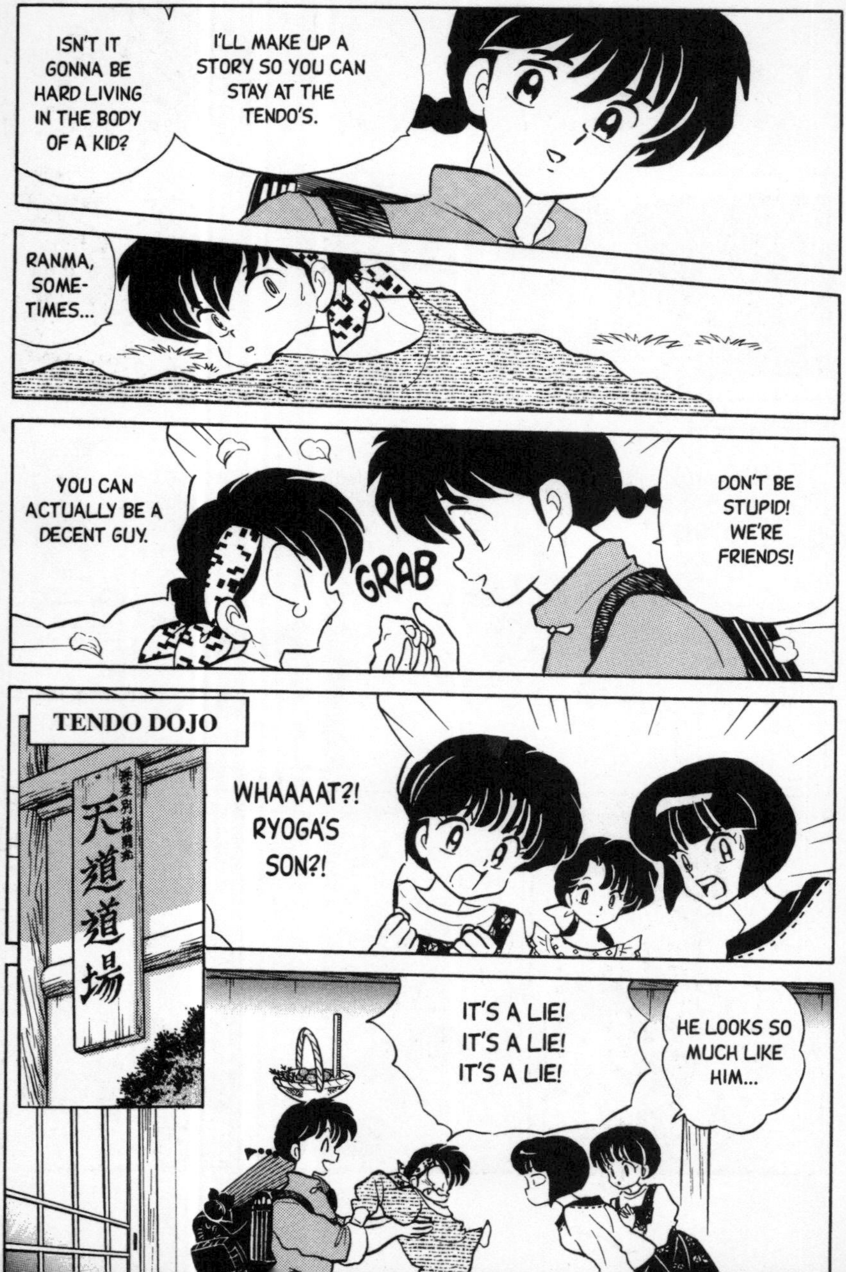
ISN'T IT GONNA BE HARD LIVING IN THE BODY OF A KID?
I'LL MAKE UP A STORY SO YOU CAN STAY AT THE TENDO'S.
RANMA, SOME- TIMES...
YOU CAN ACTUALLY BE A DECENT GUY.
GRAB
DON'T BE STUPID! WE'RE FRIENDS!
TENDO DOJO
天道道場
WHAAAAT?! RYOGA'S SON?!
IT'S A LIE! IT'S A LIE! IT'S A LIE!
HE LOOKS SO MUCH LIKE HIM...

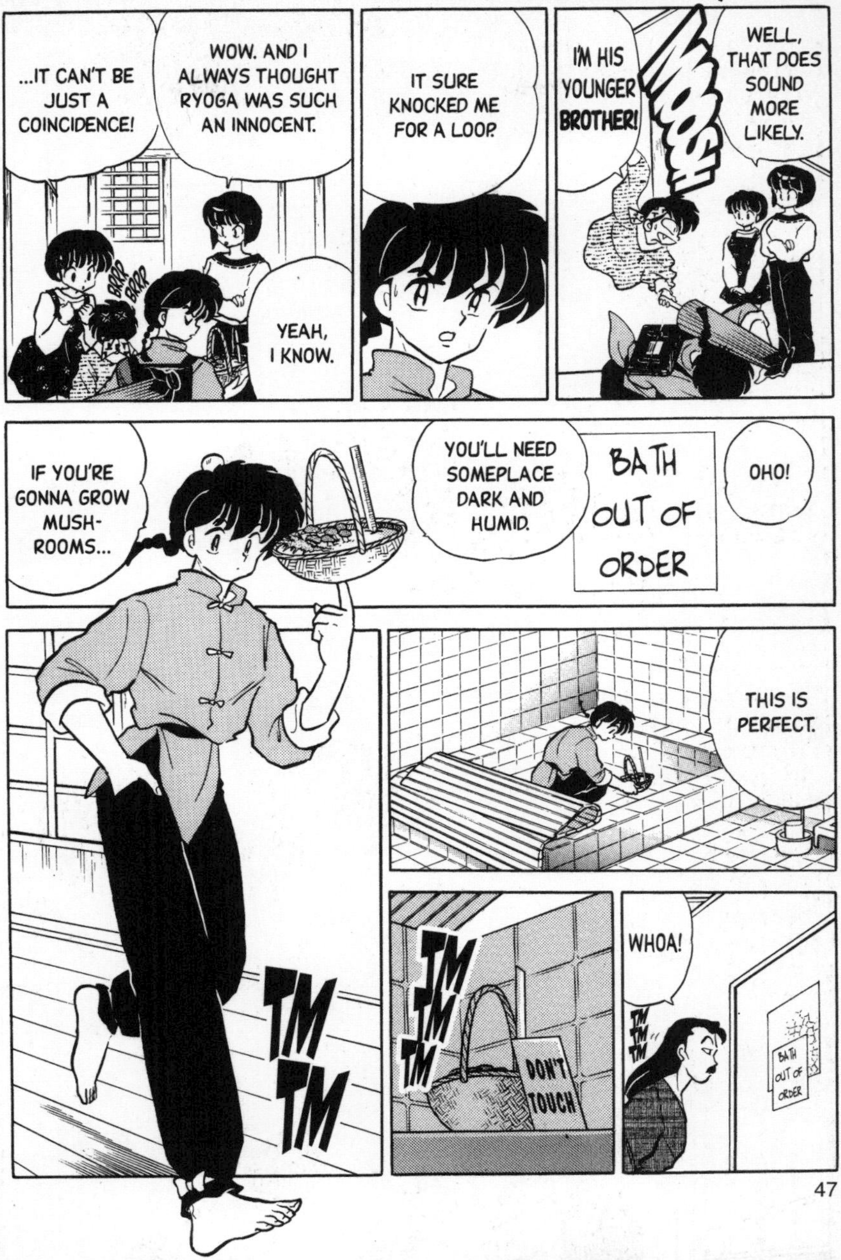
...IT CAN'T BE JUST A COINCIDENCE!
WOW. AND I ALWAYS THOUGHT RYOGA WAS SUCH AN INNOCENT.
BRRR BRRR
YEAH, I KNOW.
IT SURE KNOCKED ME FOR A LOOP.
I'M HIS YOUNGER **BROTHER!**
WOOSH
WELL, THAT DOES SOUND MORE LIKELY.
IF YOU'RE GONNA GROW MUSH-ROOMS...
YOU'LL NEED SOMEPLACE DARK AND HUMID.
BATH OUT OF ORDER
OHO!
TM TM
THIS IS PERFECT.
TM TM TM
DON'T TOUCH
WHOA!
TM TM TM
BATH OUT OF ORDER

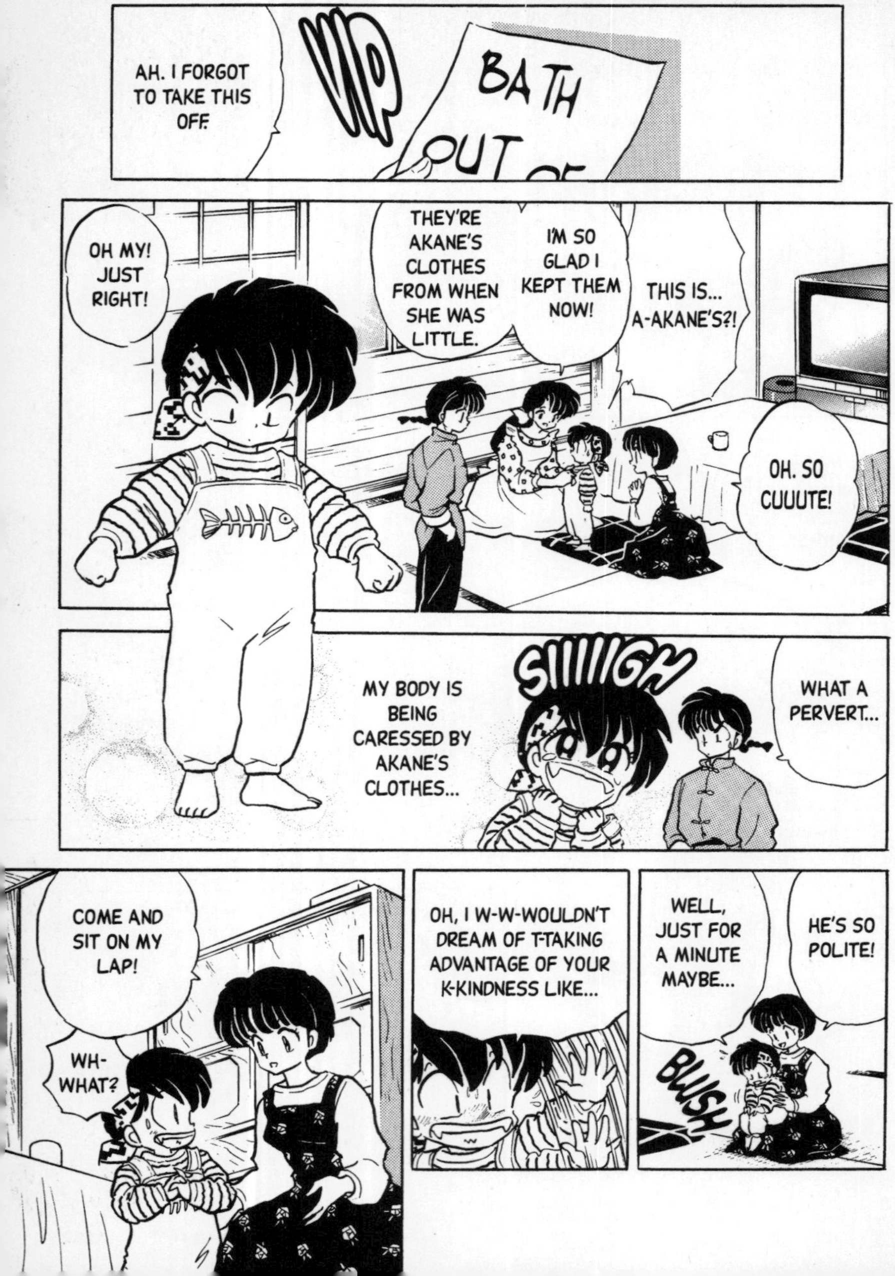
AH. I FORGOT TO TAKE THIS OFF.
BATH
OUT
OH MY! JUST RIGHT!
THEY'RE AKANE'S CLOTHES FROM WHEN SHE WAS LITTLE.
I'M SO GLAD I KEPT THEM NOW!
THIS IS... A-AKANE'S?!
OH. SO CUUUTE!
MY BODY IS BEING CARESSED BY AKANE'S CLOTHES...
SIIIIGH
WHAT A PERVERT...
COME AND SIT ON MY LAP!
WH-WHAT?
OH, I W-W-WOULDN'T DREAM OF T-TAKING ADVANTAGE OF YOUR K-KINDNESS LIKE...
WELL, JUST FOR A MINUTE MAYBE...
HE'S SO POLITE!
BWISH!

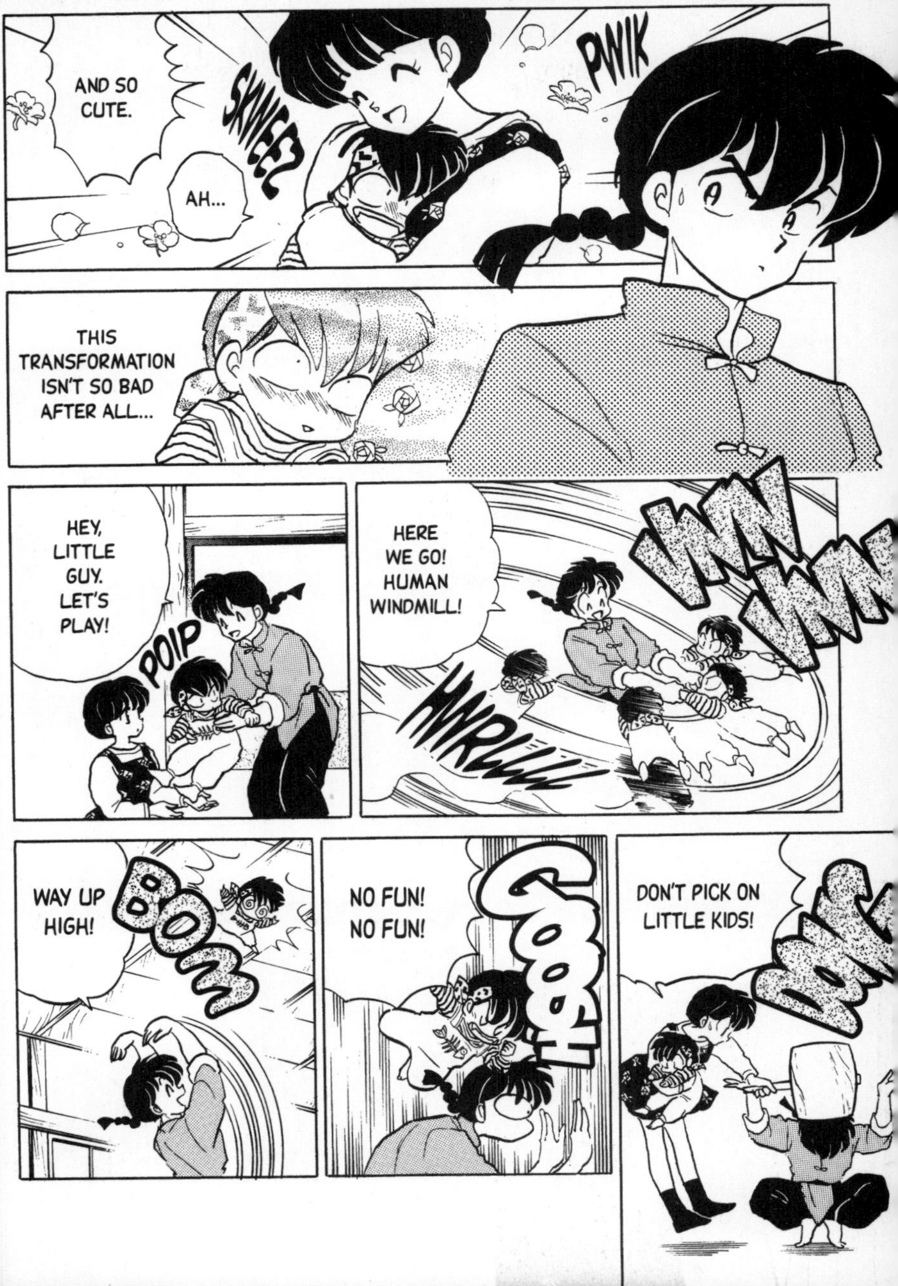
AND SO CUTE.
SKWEEZ
AH...
PWIK
THIS TRANSFORMATION ISN'T SO BAD AFTER ALL...
HEY, LITTLE GUY. LET'S PLAY!
POIP
HERE WE GO! HUMAN WINDMILL!
HWRLLLL
WAY UP HIGH!
BOM
NO FUN! NO FUN!
GOOOH
DON'T PICK ON LITTLE KIDS!

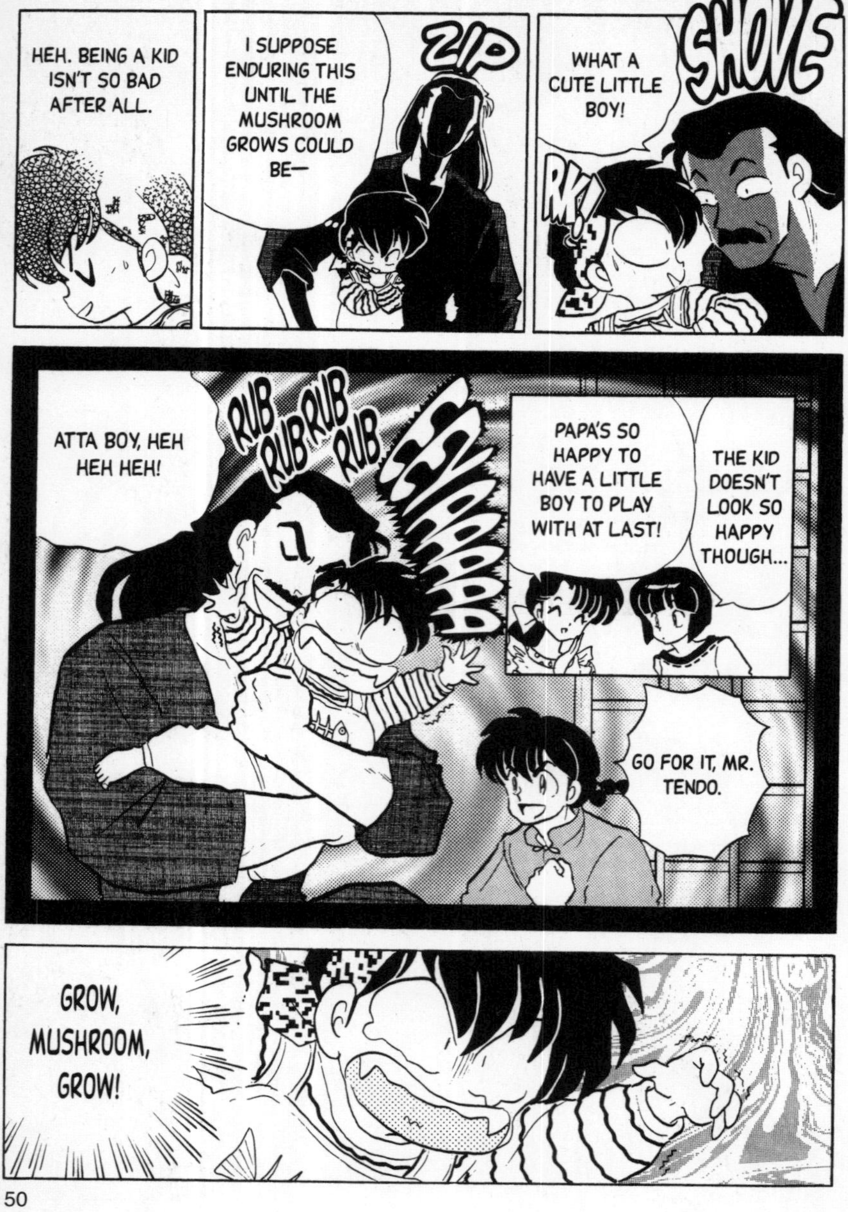
HEH. BEING A KID ISN'T SO BAD AFTER ALL.
I SUPPOSE ENDURING THIS UNTIL THE MUSHROOM GROWS COULD BE—
ZIP
WHAT A CUTE LITTLE BOY!
SHOVE
RK!
ATTA BOY, HEH HEH HEH!
RUB RUB RUB RUB
PAPA'S SO HAPPY TO HAVE A LITTLE BOY TO PLAY WITH AT LAST!
THE KID DOESN'T LOOK SO HAPPY THOUGH...
GO FOR IT, MR. TENDO.
GROW, MUSHROOM, GROW!

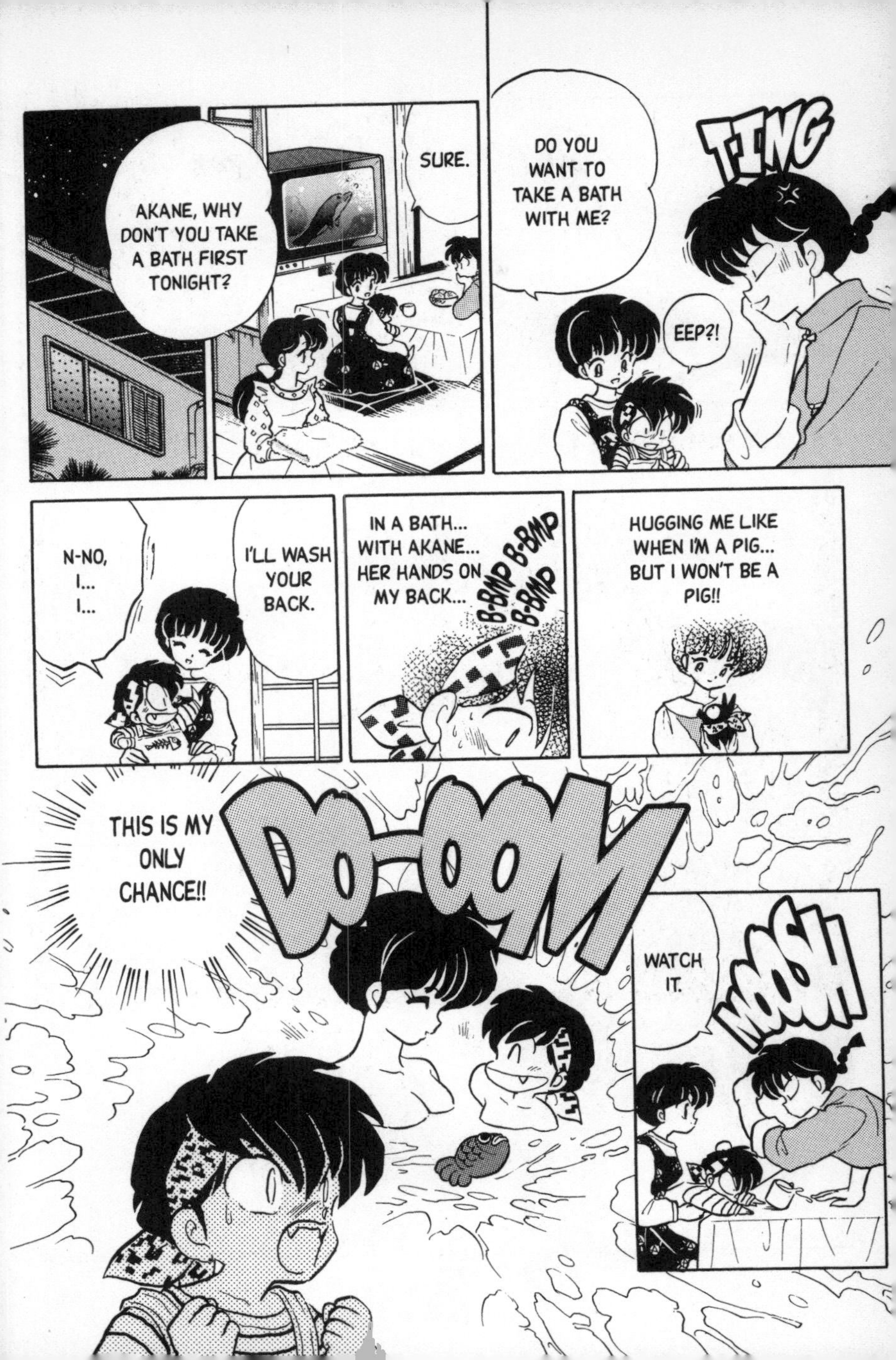
AKANE, WHY DON'T YOU TAKE A BATH FIRST TONIGHT?
SURE.
DO YOU WANT TO TAKE A BATH WITH ME?
TING
EEP?!
N-NO, I... I...
I'LL WASH YOUR BACK.
IN A BATH... WITH AKANE... HER HANDS ON MY BACK...
B-BMP B-BMP
B-BMP B-BMP
HUGGING ME LIKE WHEN I'M A PIG... BUT I WON'T BE A PIG!!
THIS IS MY ONLY CHANCE!!
DO-OOM
WATCH IT.
WOOSH

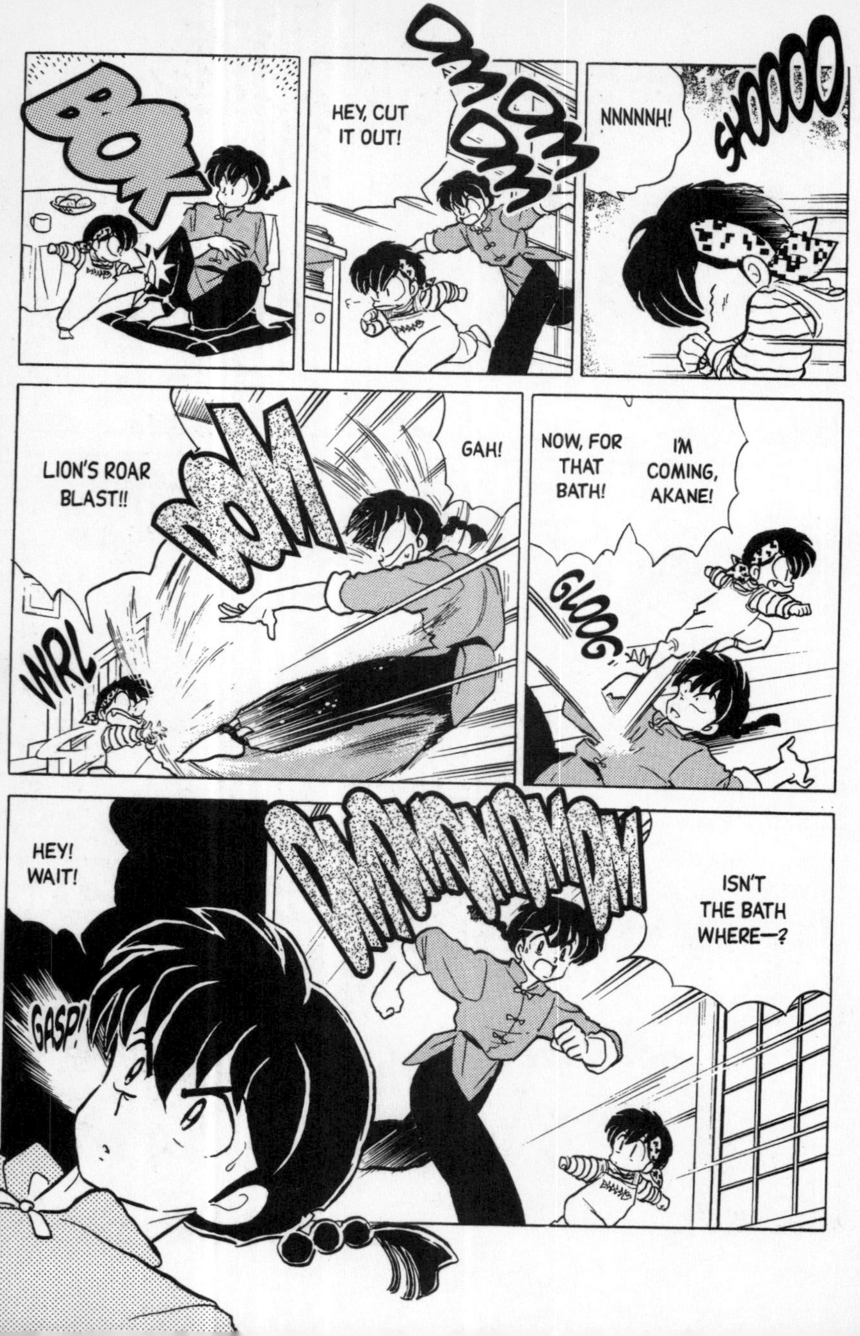
SHOOOO
NNNNNH!
HEY, CUT IT OUT!
BOK
I'M COMING, AKANE!
NOW, FOR THAT BATH!
GLOOG
GAH!
BOM
LION'S ROAR BLAST!!
WRL
ISN'T THE BATH WHERE—?
HEY! WAIT!
GASP!

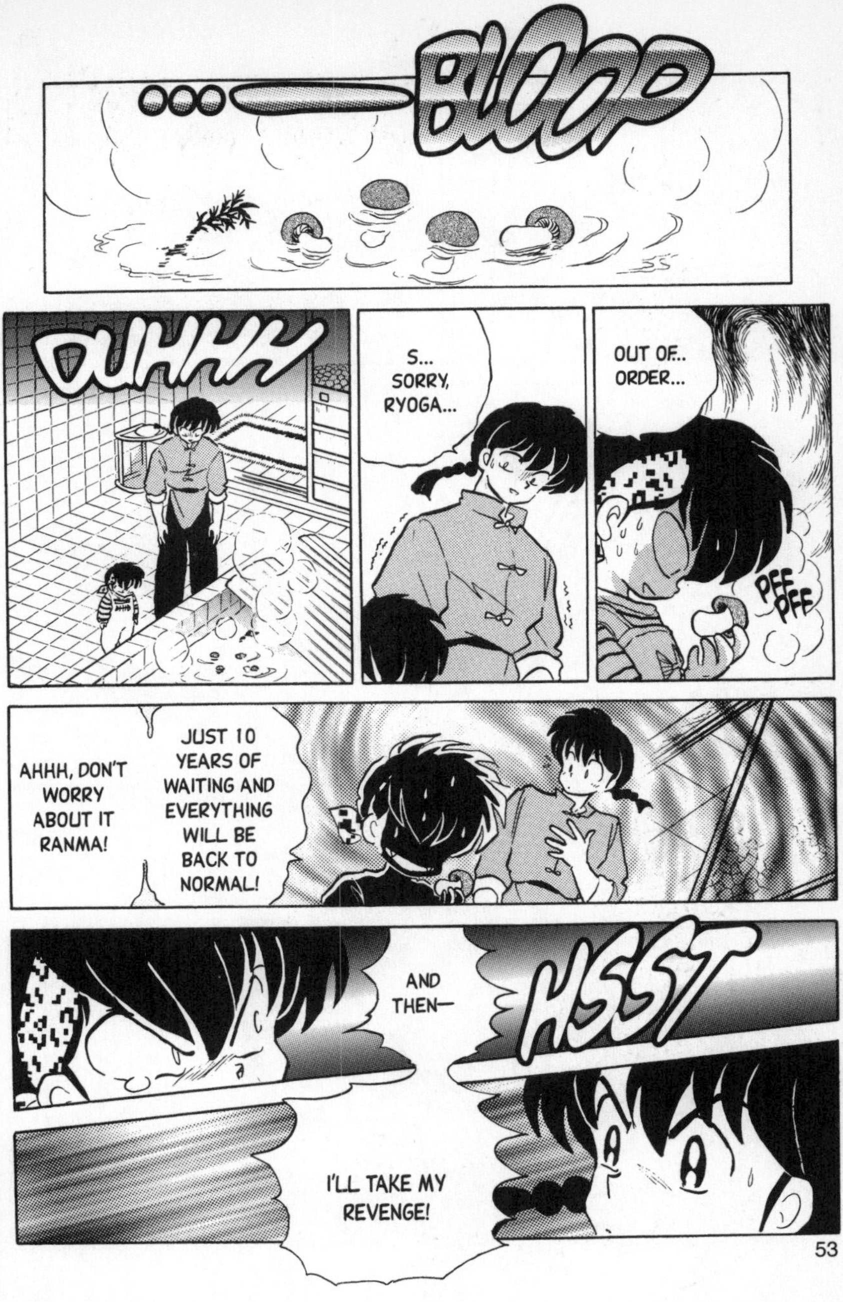
...—BLOOP
DUHHH
S... SORRY, RYOGA...
OUT OF.. ORDER...
PFF PFF
AHHH, DON'T WORRY ABOUT IT RANMA!
JUST 10 YEARS OF WAITING AND EVERYTHING WILL BE BACK TO NORMAL!
AND THEN—
HSST
I'LL TAKE MY REVENGE!

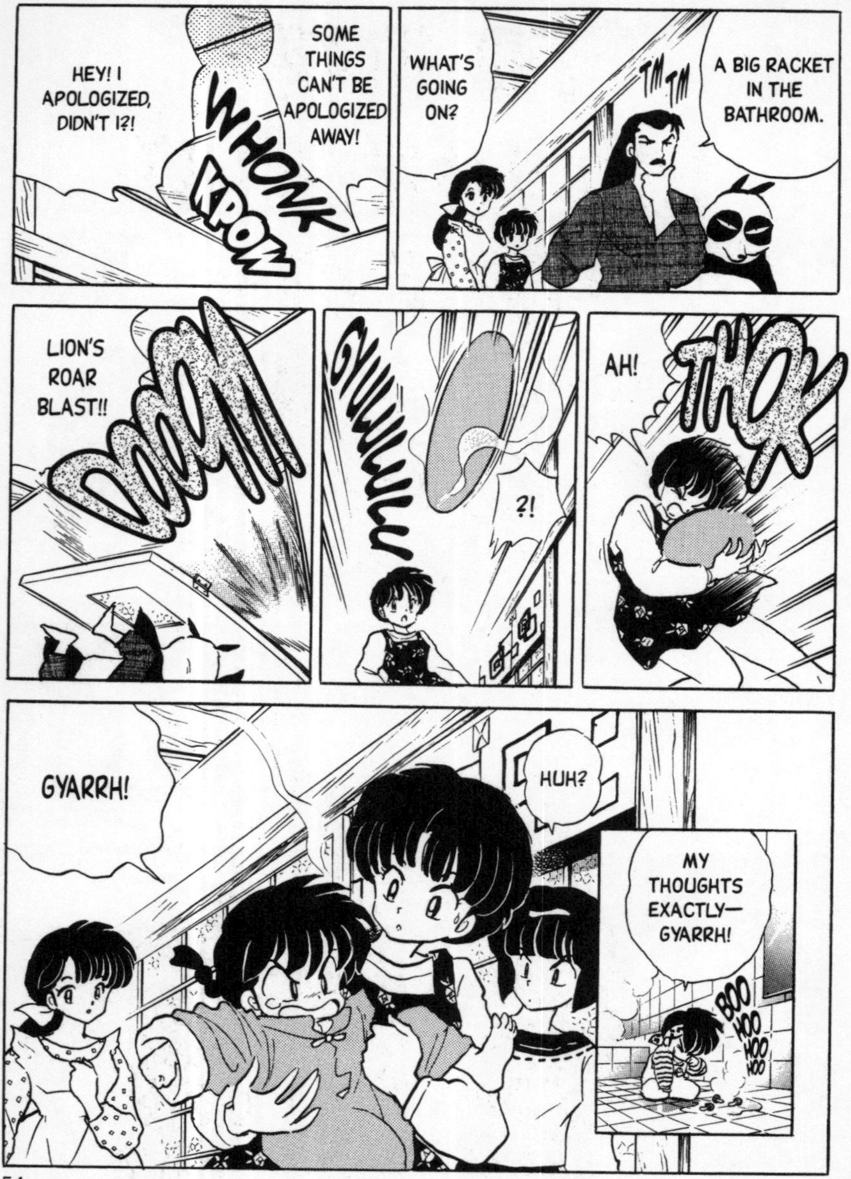
HEY! I APOLOGIZED, DIDN'T I?!
SOME THINGS CAN'T BE APOLOGIZED AWAY!
WHONK
KPOW
WHAT'S GOING ON?
TM TM
A BIG RACKET IN THE BATHROOM.
LION'S ROAR BLAST!!
GYUUUUUU
?!
AH!
THOK
GYARRH!
HUH?
MY THOUGHTS EXACTLY— GYARRH!
BOO HOO HOO HOO

PART 4

TO THE MUSHROOM FOREST!

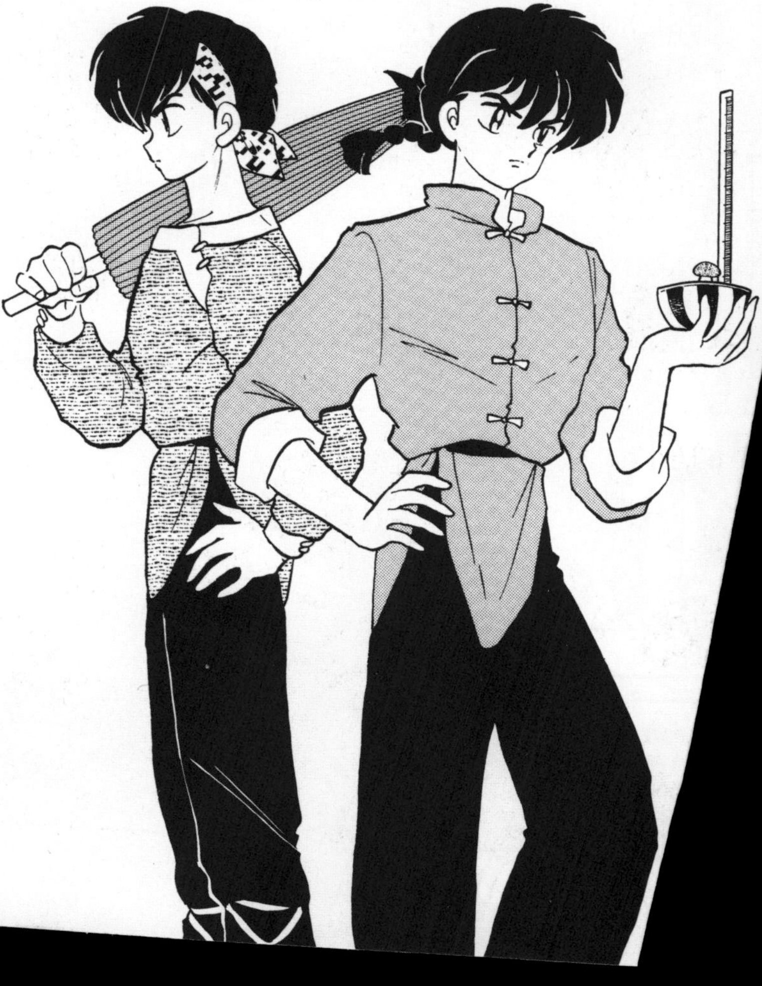

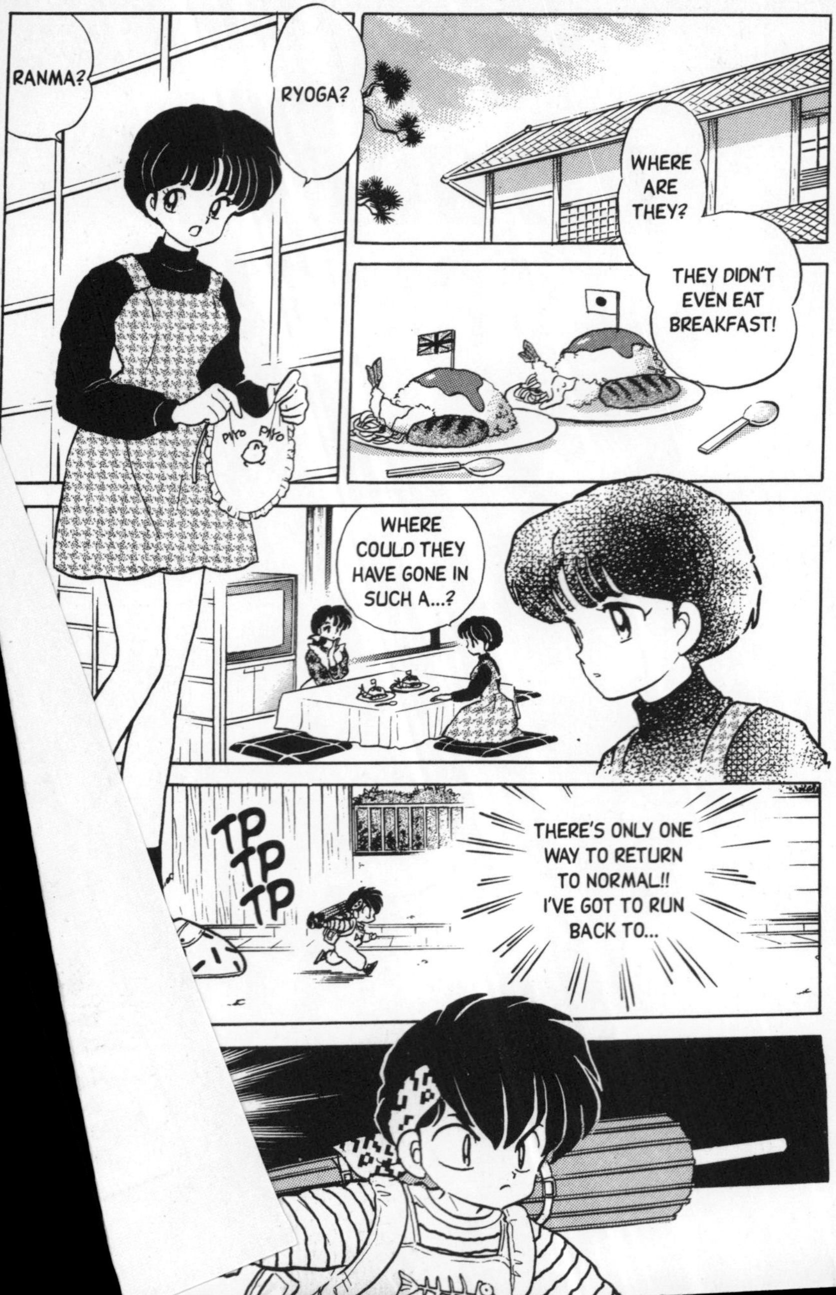
RANMA?
RYOGA?
WHERE ARE THEY?
THEY DIDN'T EVEN EAT BREAKFAST!
PIYO PIYO
WHERE COULD THEY HAVE GONE IN SUCH A...?
THERE'S ONLY ONE WAY TO RETURN TO NORMAL!! I'VE GOT TO RUN BACK TO...
TP TP TP

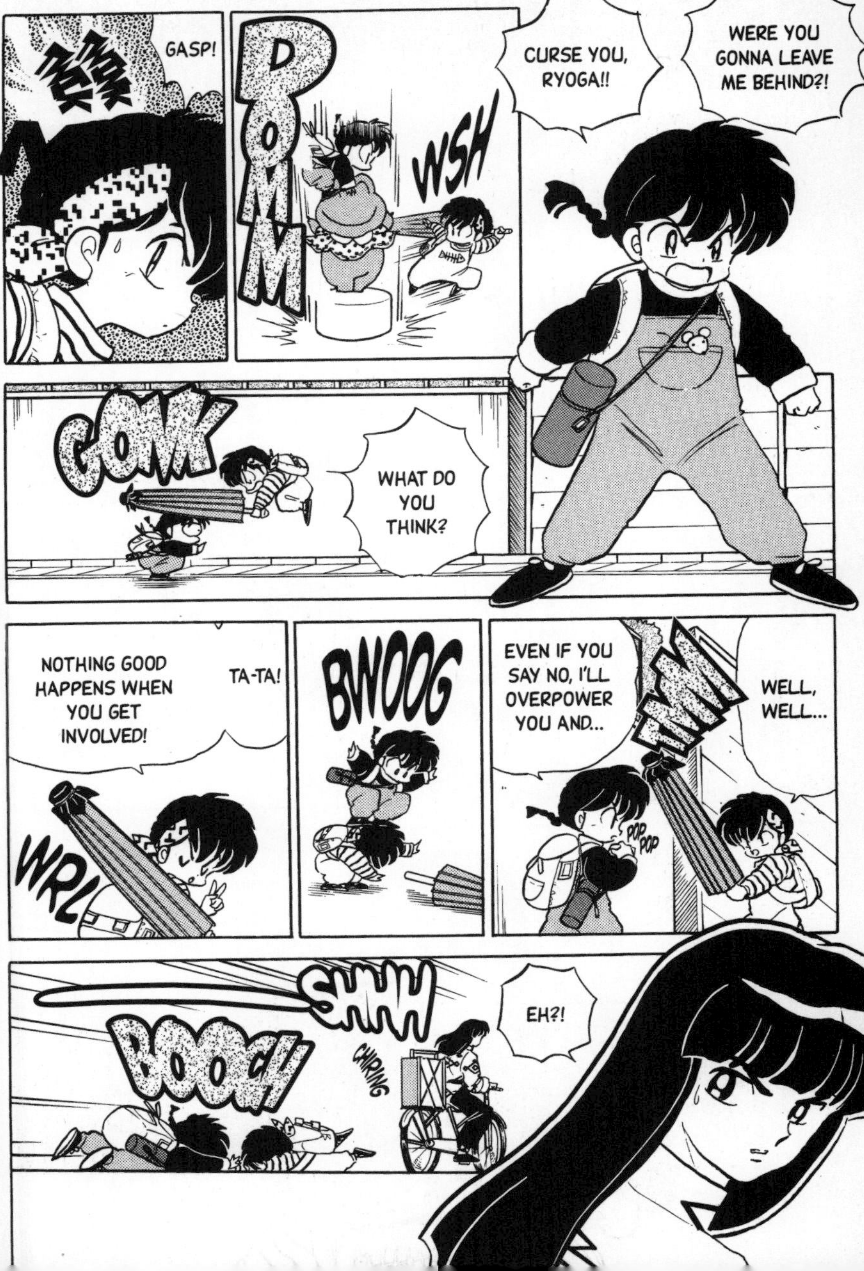
GASP!
POMM
WSH
CURSE YOU, RYOGA!!
WERE YOU GONNA LEAVE ME BEHIND?!
GONK
WHAT DO YOU THINK?
NOTHING GOOD HAPPENS WHEN YOU GET INVOLVED!
TA-TA!
WRL
BWOOG
EVEN IF YOU SAY NO, I'LL OVERPOWER YOU AND...
POP POP
WELL, WELL...
BOOCH
CHIRING
EH?!

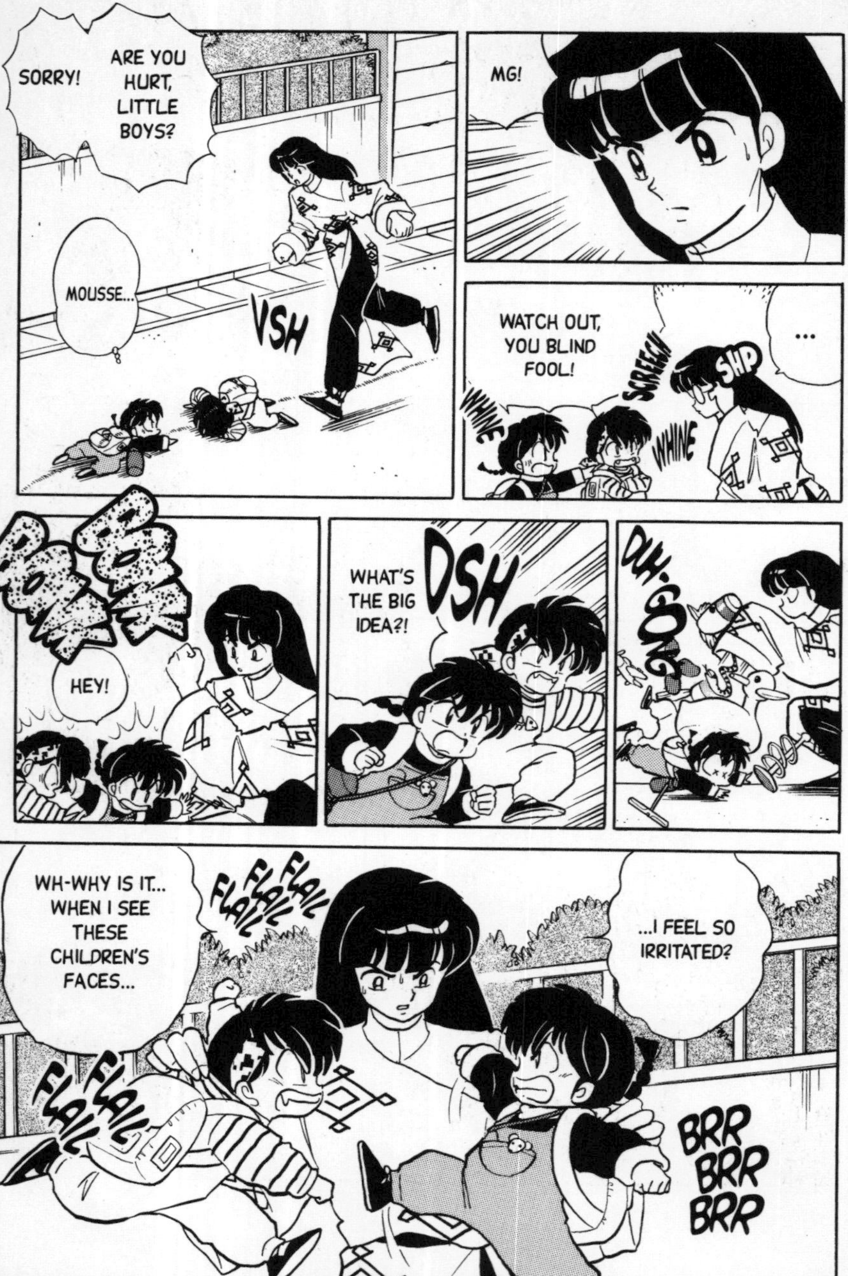

SORRY!
ARE YOU HURT, LITTLE BOYS?
MOUSSE...
VSH
MG!
WATCH OUT, YOU BLIND FOOL!
SCREECH
WHINE
WHINE
SHP
...
BONK BONK
HEY!
WHAT'S THE BIG IDEA?!
DSH
DUH-GONG
WH-WHY IS IT... WHEN I SEE THESE CHILDREN'S FACES...
FLAIL FLAIL FLAIL
...I FEEL SO IRRITATED?
FLAIL FLAIL
BRR BRR BRR

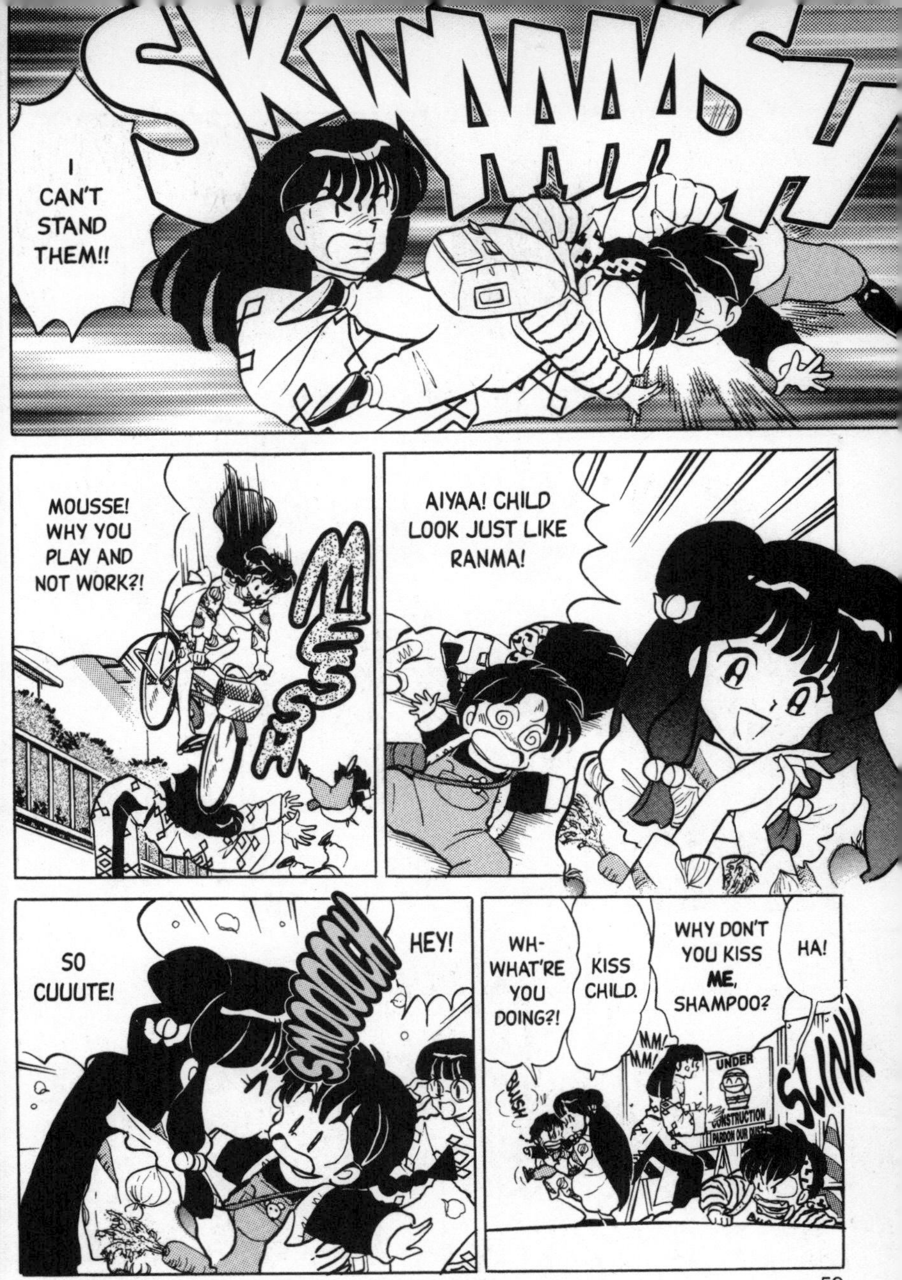
SKWAAASH
I CAN'T STAND THEM!!
MOUSSE! WHY YOU PLAY AND NOT WORK?!
AIYAA! CHILD LOOK JUST LIKE RANMA!
SO CUUUTE!
SMOOOOCH
HEY!
WH-WHAT'RE YOU DOING?!
KISS CHILD.
WHY DON'T YOU KISS ME, SHAMPOO?
HA!
MM! MM!
BLUSH
UNDER CONSTRUCTION
PARDON OUR DUST
SLINK

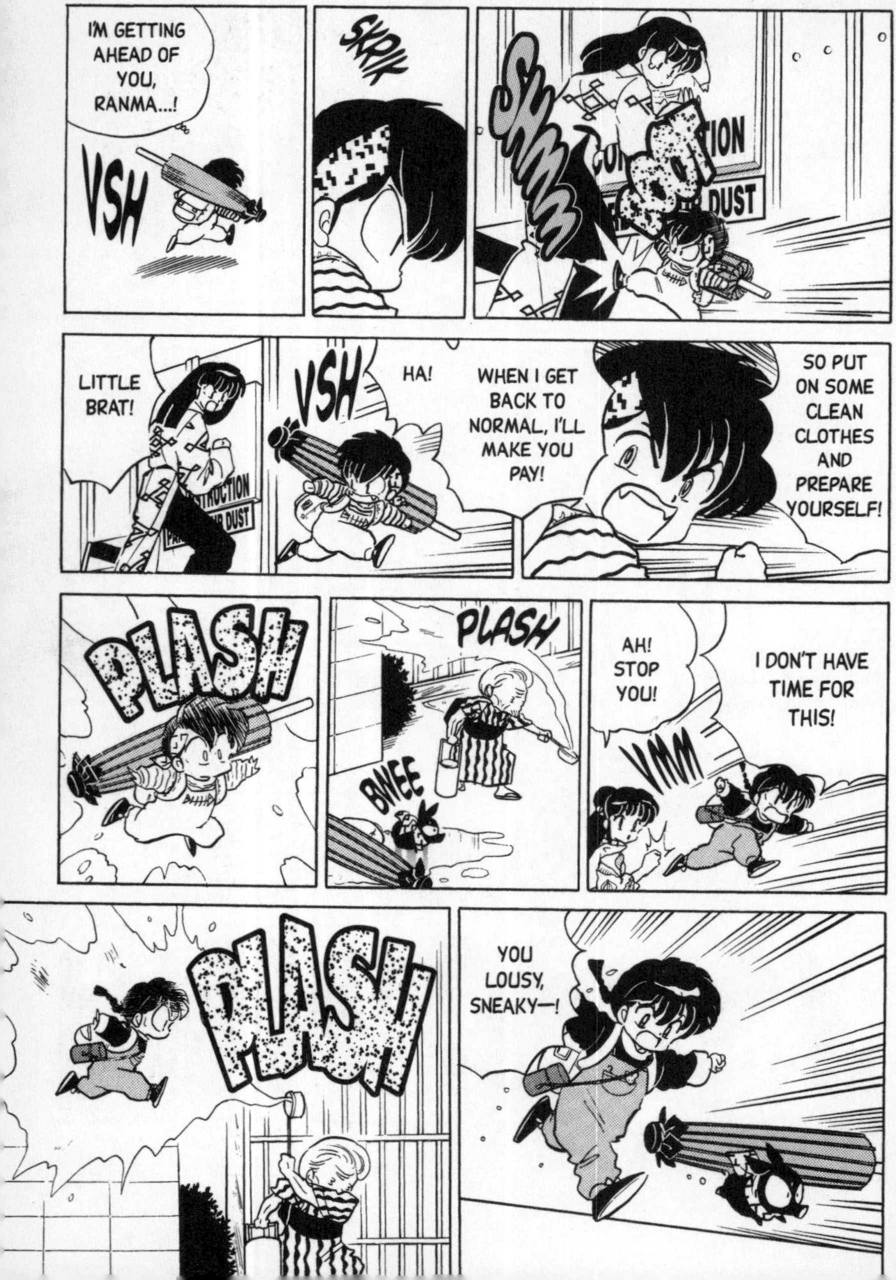
I'M GETTING AHEAD OF YOU, RANMA...!
VSH
SKRIK
SHWMM
LITTLE BRAT!
VSH
HA!
WHEN I GET BACK TO NORMAL, I'LL MAKE YOU PAY!
SO PUT ON SOME CLEAN CLOTHES AND PREPARE YOURSELF!
PLASH
PLASH
BWEE
AH! STOP YOU!
I DON'T HAVE TIME FOR THIS!
VMM
PLASH
YOU LOUSY, SNEAKY—!

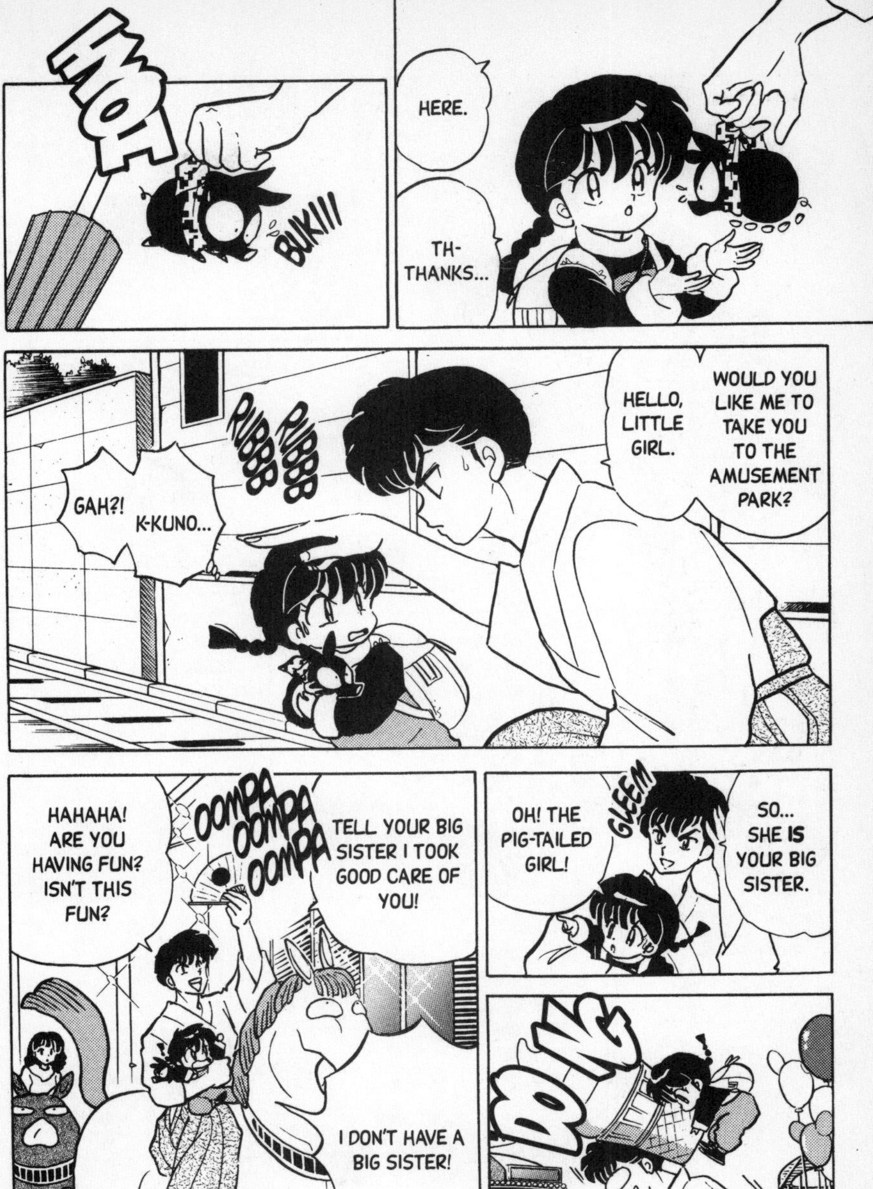
KNOT
BUKIII
HERE.
TH-
THANKS...
GAH?! K-KUNO...
RUBBB RUBBB
HELLO, LITTLE GIRL.
WOULD YOU LIKE ME TO TAKE YOU TO THE AMUSEMENT PARK?
HAHAHA! ARE YOU HAVING FUN? ISN'T THIS FUN?
OOMPA OOMPA OOMPA
TELL YOUR BIG SISTER I TOOK GOOD CARE OF YOU!
I DON'T HAVE A BIG SISTER!
OH! THE PIG-TAILED GIRL!
GLEEM
SO... SHE IS YOUR BIG SISTER.
DOING

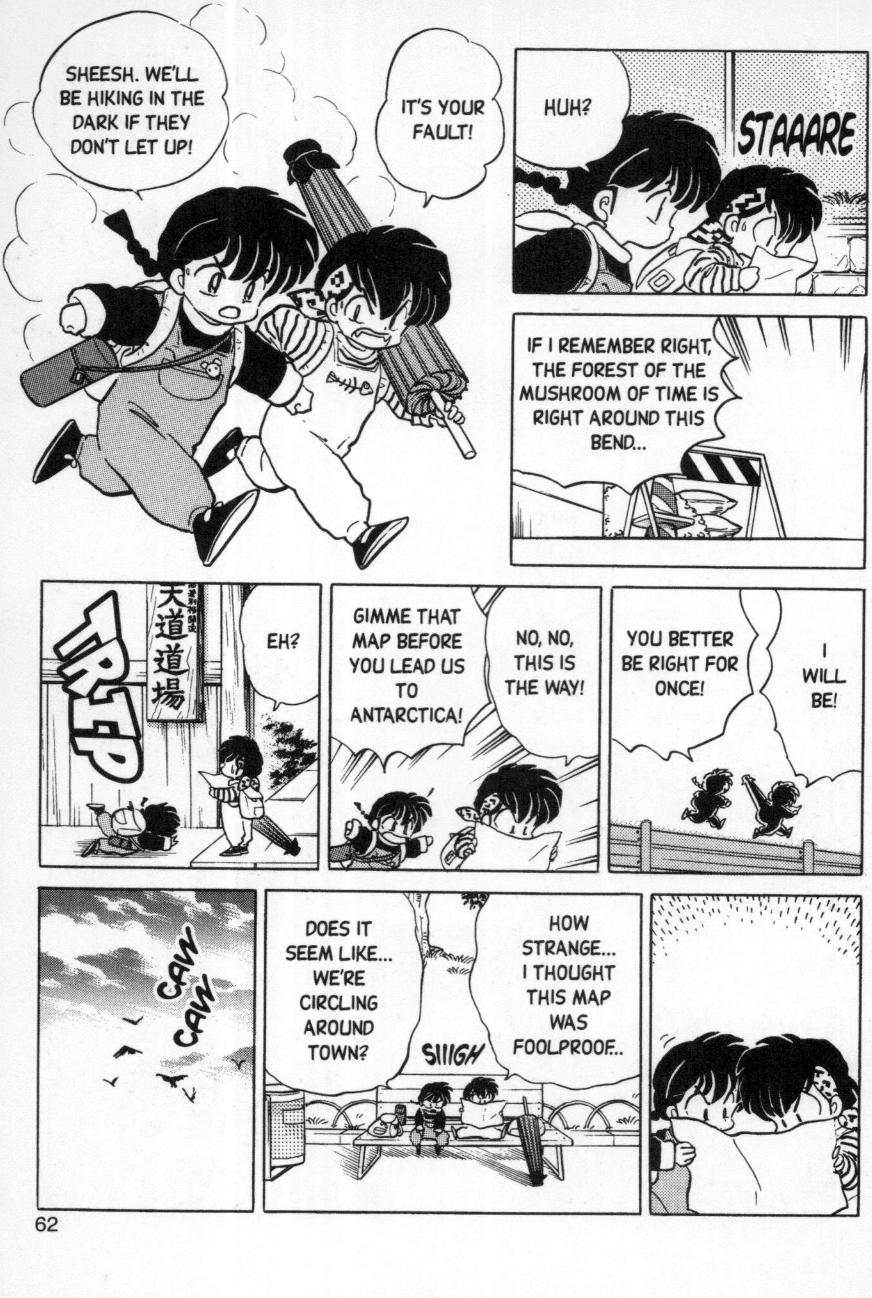
SHEESH. WE'LL BE HIKING IN THE DARK IF THEY DON'T LET UP!
IT'S YOUR FAULT!
HUH?
STAAARE
IF I REMEMBER RIGHT, THE FOREST OF THE MUSHROOM OF TIME IS RIGHT AROUND THIS BEND...
TRIP
天道道場
EH?
GIMME THAT MAP BEFORE YOU LEAD US TO ANTARCTICA!
NO, NO, THIS IS THE WAY!
YOU BETTER BE RIGHT FOR ONCE!
I WILL BE!
CAW
CAW
DOES IT SEEM LIKE... WE'RE CIRCLING AROUND TOWN?
HOW STRANGE... I THOUGHT THIS MAP WAS FOOLPROOF...
SIIIGH

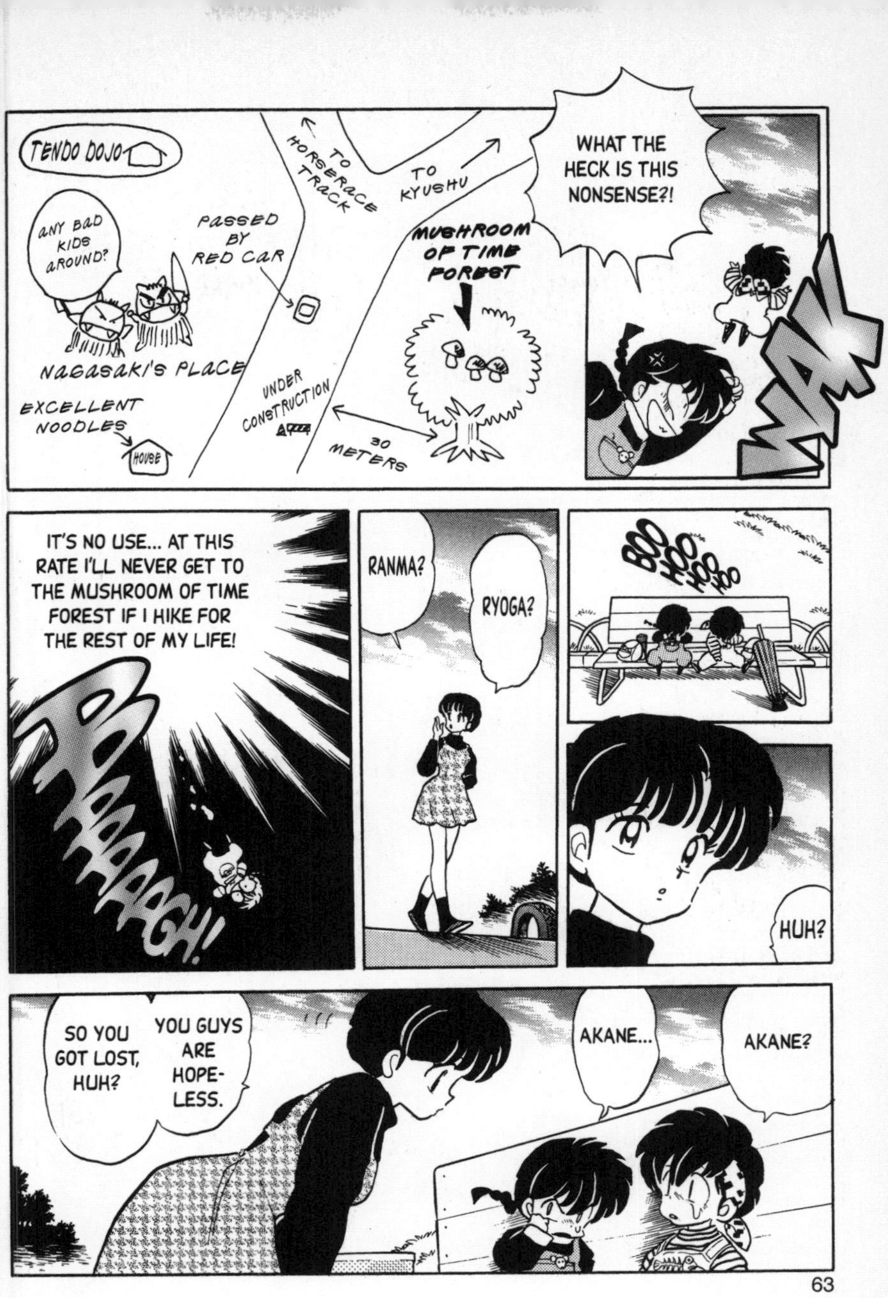
TENDO DOJO
TO HORSERACE TRACK
TO KYUSHU
ANY BAD KIDS AROUND?
PASSED BY RED CAR
MUSHROOM OF TIME FOREST
NAGASAKI'S PLACE
UNDER CONSTRUCTION
EXCELLENT NOODLES
HOUSE
30 METERS
WHAT THE HECK IS THIS NONSENSE?!
WAK
IT'S NO USE... AT THIS RATE I'LL NEVER GET TO THE MUSHROOM OF TIME FOREST IF I HIKE FOR THE REST OF MY LIFE!
BAAAAAAAGH!
RANMA?
RYOGA?
BOO HOO HOO HOO
HUH?
SO YOU GOT LOST, HUH?
YOU GUYS ARE HOPE-LESS.
AKANE...
AKANE?

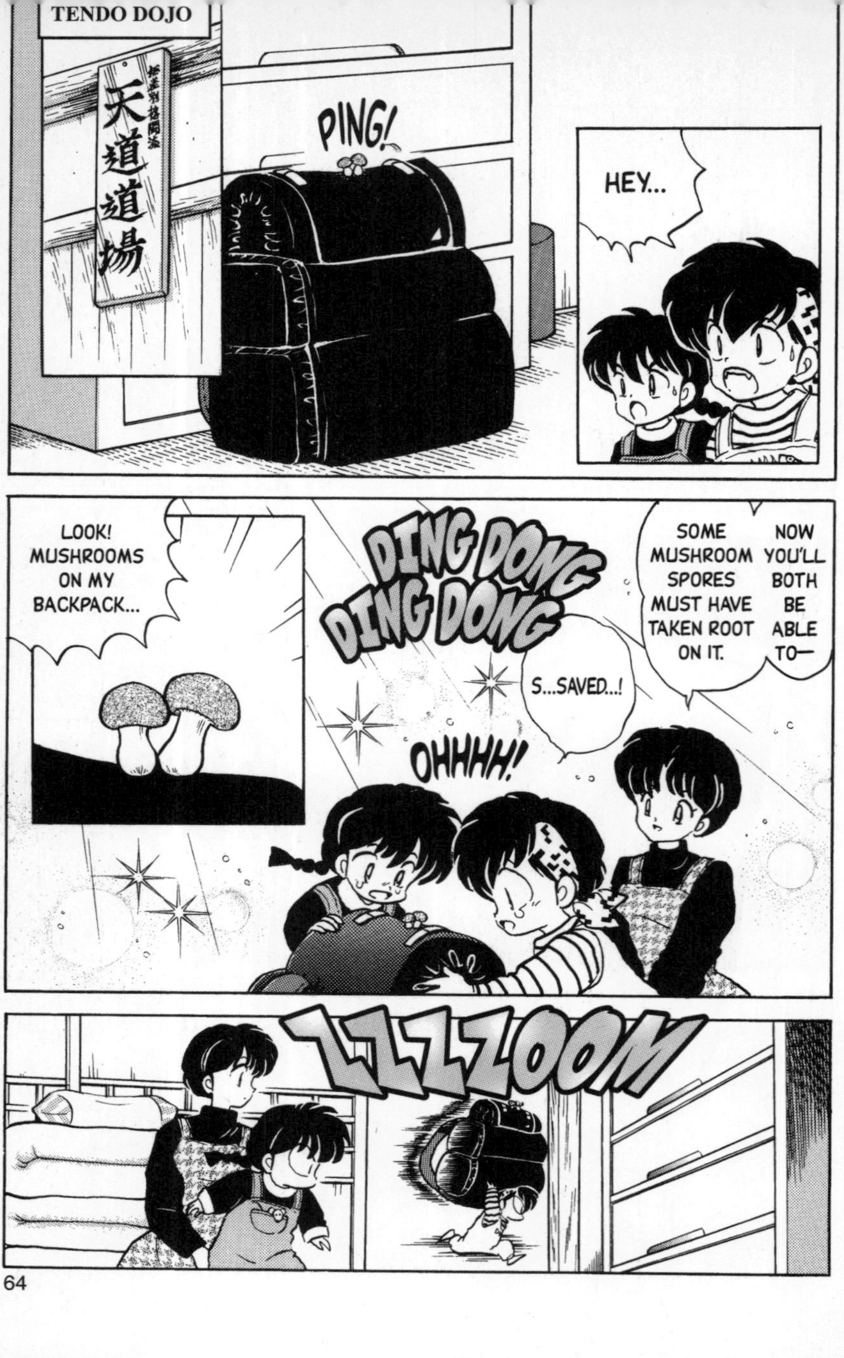
TENDO DOJO
天道道場
PING!
HEY...
LOOK! MUSHROOMS ON MY BACKPACK...
DING DONG DING DONG
SOME MUSHROOM SPORES MUST HAVE TAKEN ROOT ON IT.
NOW YOU'LL BOTH BE ABLE TO—
S...SAVED...!
OHHHH!
ZZZZOOM

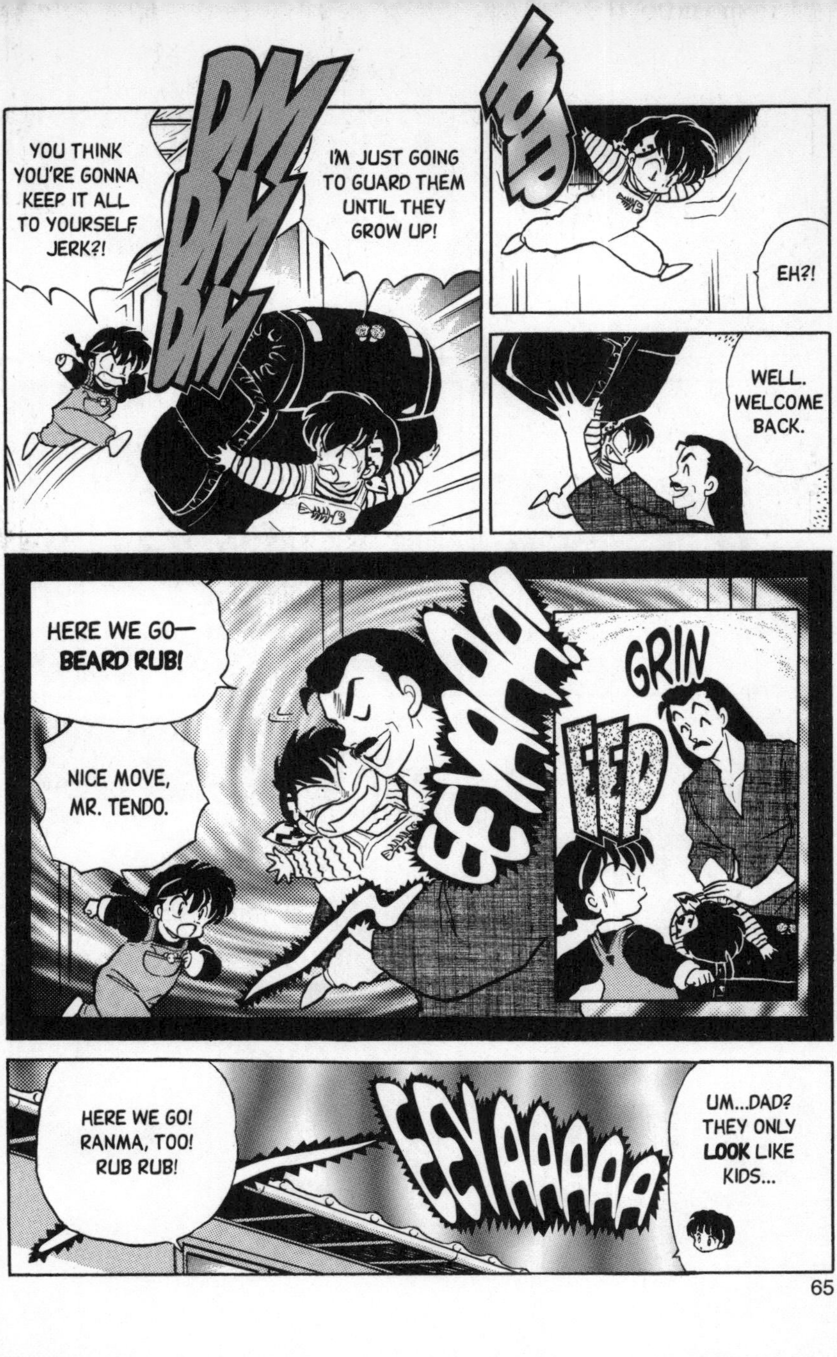
YOU THINK YOU'RE GONNA KEEP IT ALL TO YOURSELF, JERK?!
I'M JUST GOING TO GUARD THEM UNTIL THEY GROW UP!
EH?!
WELL. WELCOME BACK.
HERE WE GO— **BEARD RUB!**
NICE MOVE, MR. TENDO.
GRIN
EEP
HERE WE GO! RANMA, TOO! RUB RUB!
EEYAAAAAA
UM...DAD? THEY ONLY **LOOK** LIKE KIDS...

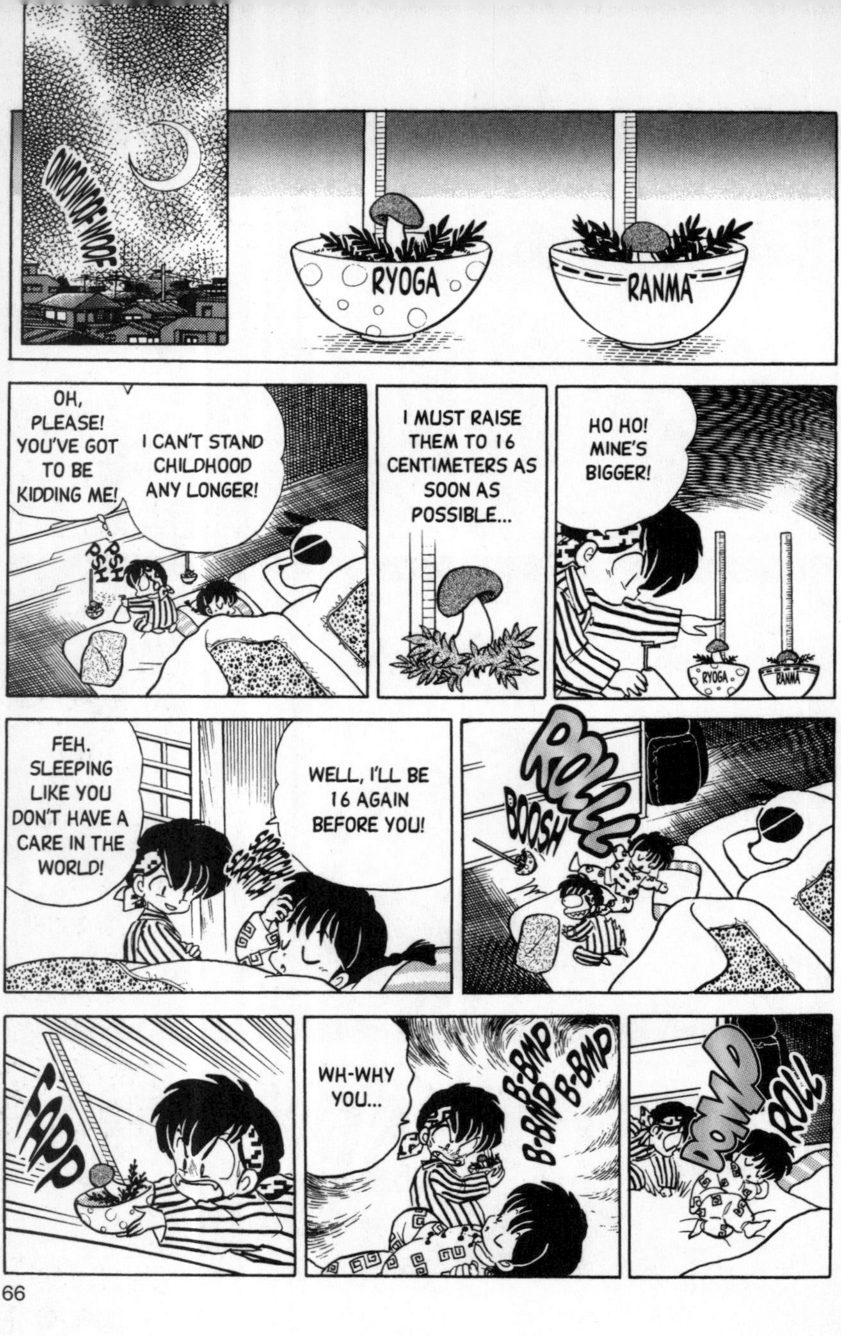
OWOOWOOF WOOF
RYOGA
RANMA
OH, PLEASE! YOU'VE GOT TO BE KIDDING ME!
I CAN'T STAND CHILDHOOD ANY LONGER!
PSH PSH
I MUST RAISE THEM TO 16 CENTIMETERS AS SOON AS POSSIBLE...
HO HO! MINE'S BIGGER!
RYOGA
RANMA
FEH. SLEEPING LIKE YOU DON'T HAVE A CARE IN THE WORLD!
WELL, I'LL BE 16 AGAIN BEFORE YOU!
SCRATCH SCRATCH
ROLL
BOOSH
FAPP
WH-WHY YOU...
B-BMP B-BMP B-BMP
BOMP
ROLL

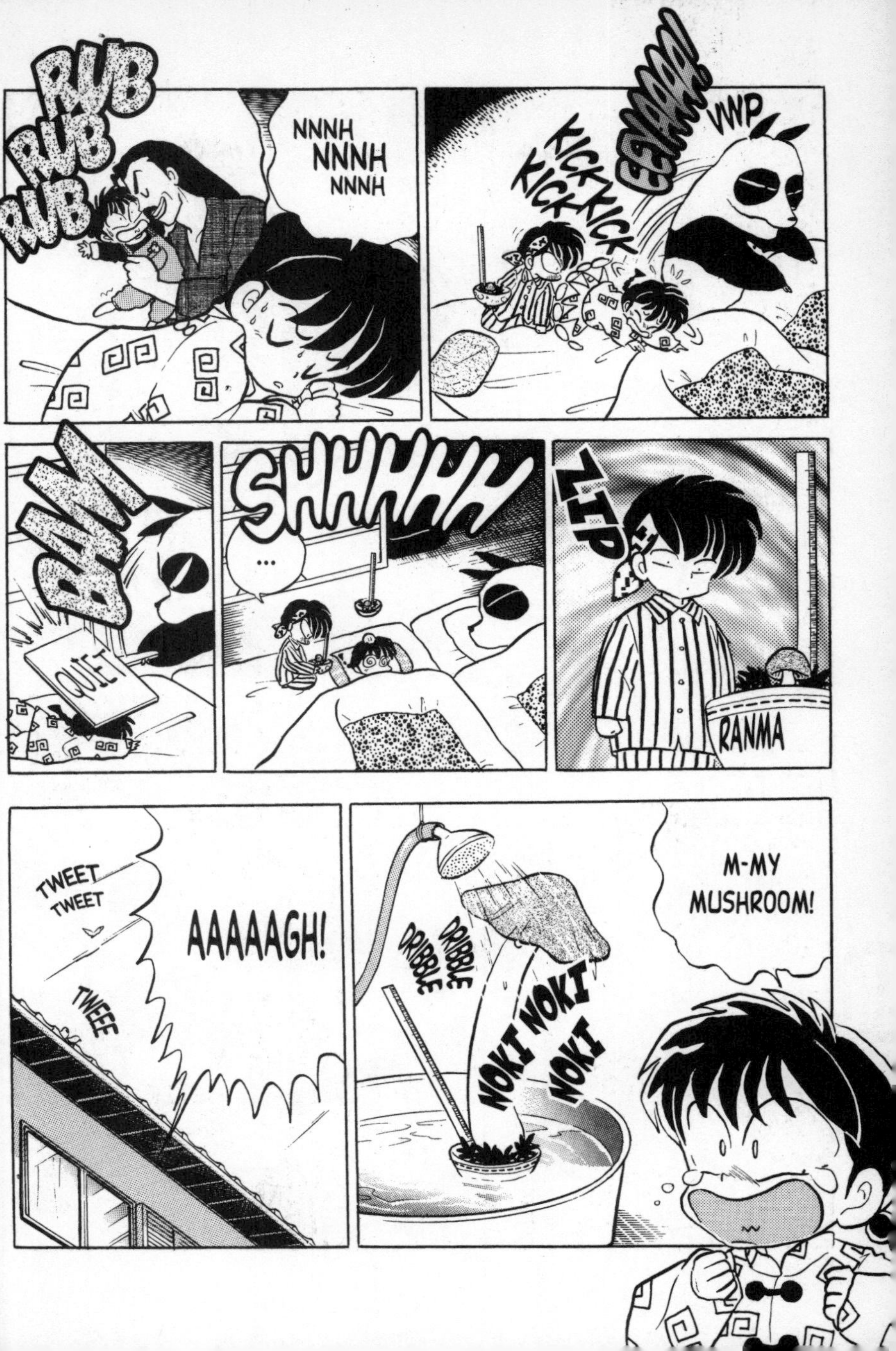
RUB RUB RUB
NNNH NNNH NNNH
KICK KICK KICK KICK
VWP
BAM
QUIET
SHHHHH
...
ZIP
RANMA
TWEET TWEET
TWEEE
AAAAAGH!
DRIBBLE DRIBBLE
NOKI NOKI NOKI
M-MY MUSHROOM!

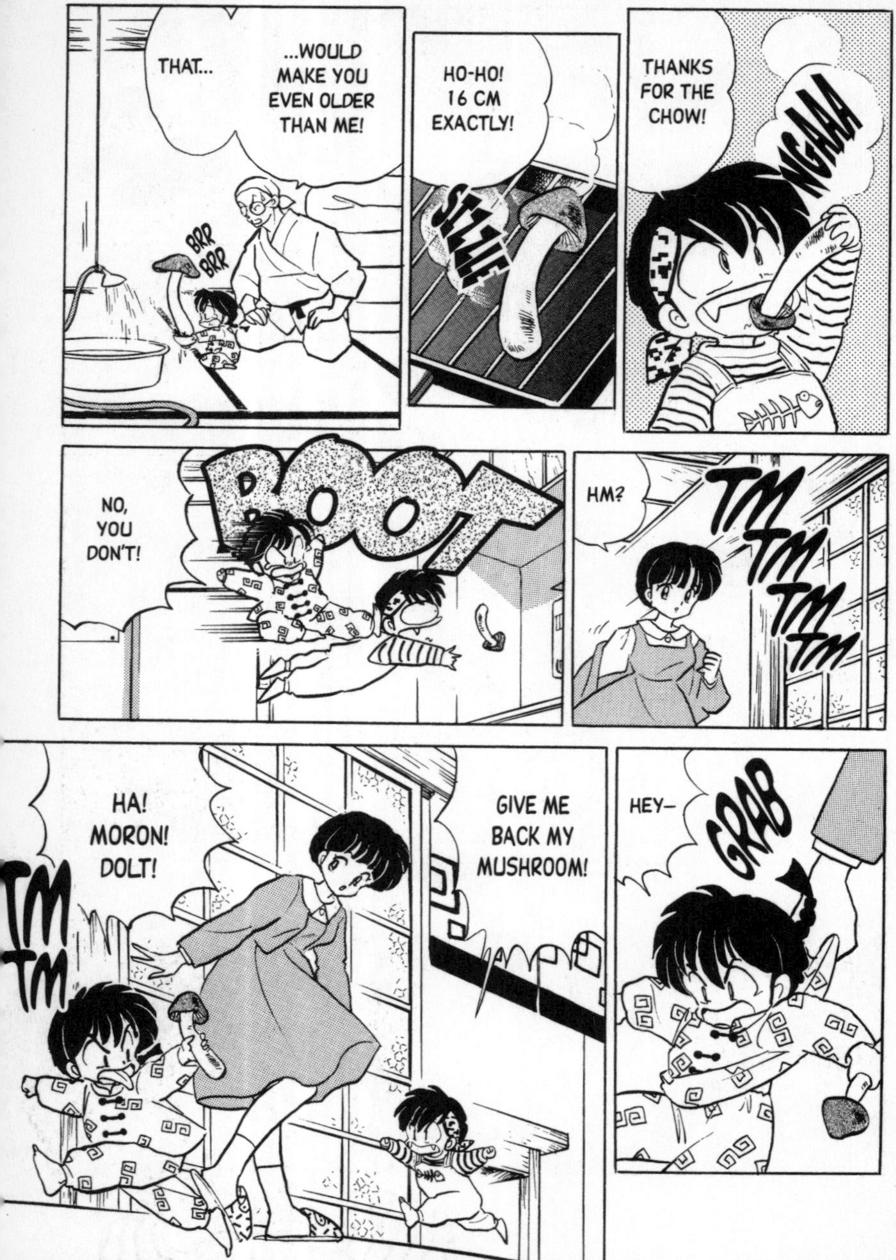
THAT...
...WOULD MAKE YOU EVEN OLDER THAN ME!
BRR BRR
HO-HO! 16 CM EXACTLY!
SIZZLE
THANKS FOR THE CHOW!
NGAAA
NO, YOU DON'T!
BOOT
HM?
TM TM TM TM
HA! MORON! DOLT!
TM TM
GIVE ME BACK MY MUSHROOM!
HEY—
GRAB

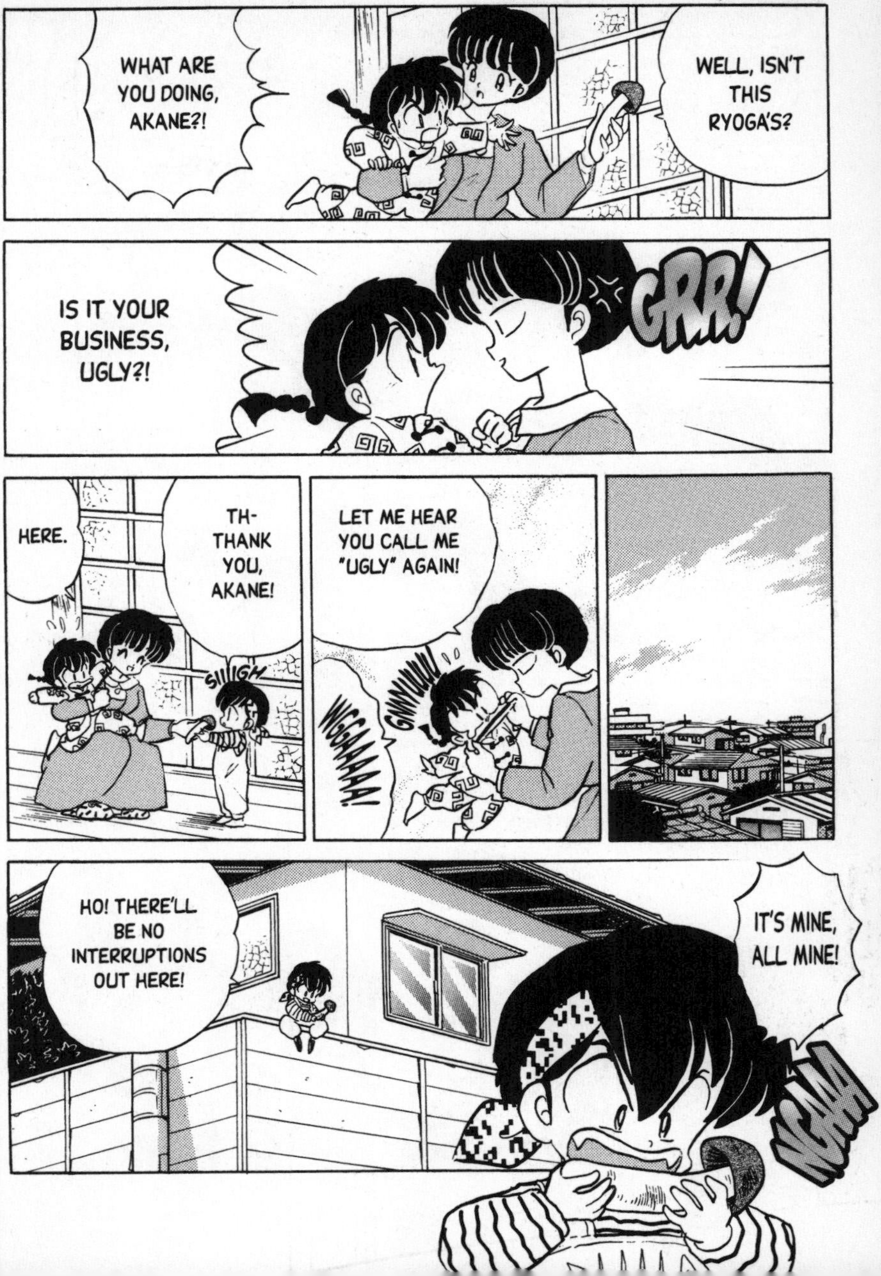
WHAT ARE YOU DOING, AKANE?!
WELL, ISN'T THIS RYOGA'S?
IS IT YOUR BUSINESS, UGLY?!
GRR!
HERE.
TH- THANK YOU, AKANE!
SHIIGH
LET ME HEAR YOU CALL ME "UGLY" AGAIN!
WIGGAAAAA!
GNNYUUUU
HO! THERE'LL BE NO INTERRUPTIONS OUT HERE!
IT'S MINE, ALL MINE!

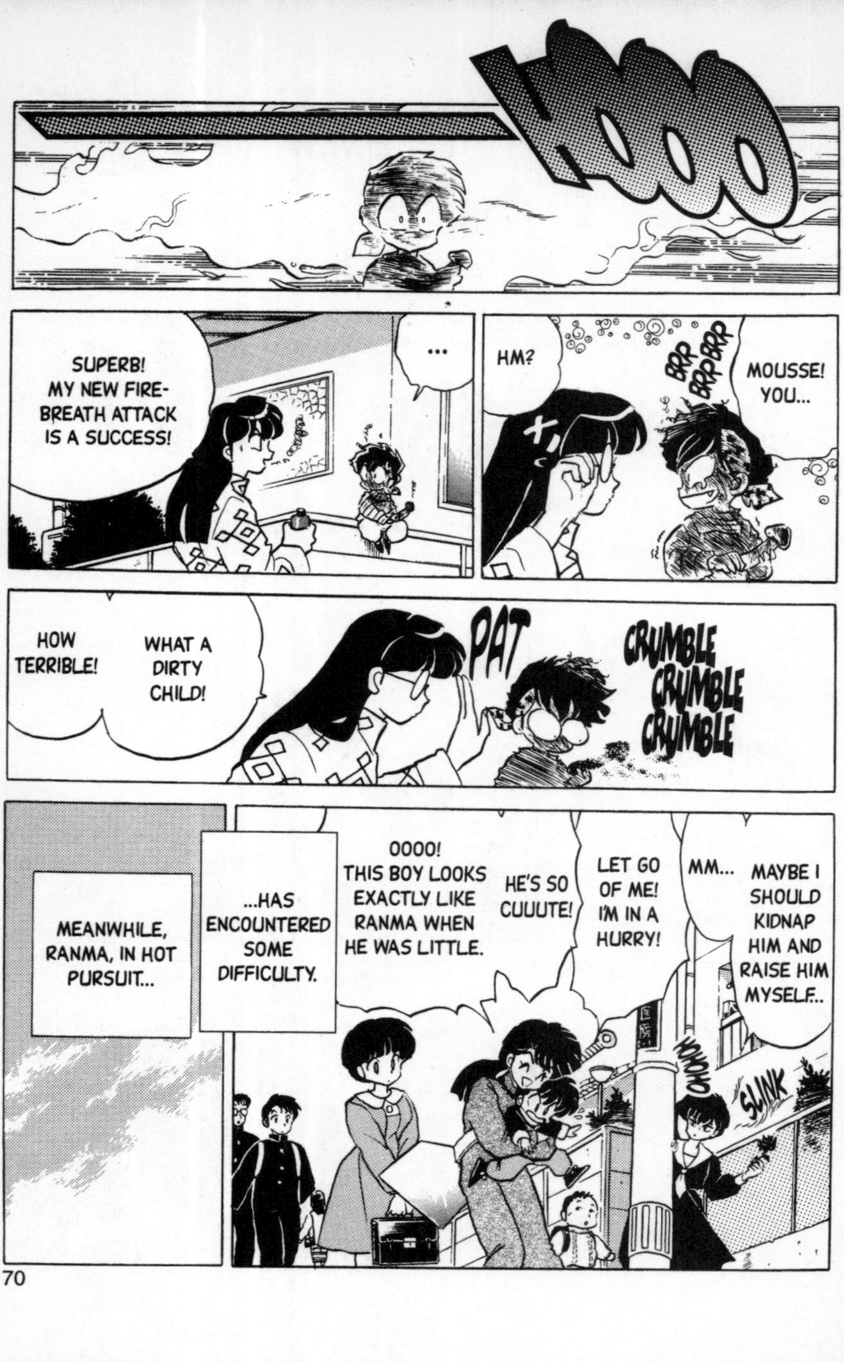
HOOOO
SUPERB! MY NEW FIRE-BREATH ATTACK IS A SUCCESS!
...
HM?
BRR BRRBRR
MOUSSE! YOU...
HOW TERRIBLE!
WHAT A DIRTY CHILD!
PAT
CRUMBLE CRUMBLE CRUMBLE
MEANWHILE, RANMA, IN HOT PURSUIT...
...HAS ENCOUNTERED SOME DIFFICULTY.
OOOO! THIS BOY LOOKS EXACTLY LIKE RANMA WHEN HE WAS LITTLE.
HE'S SO CUUUTE!
LET GO OF ME! I'M IN A HURRY!
MM...
MAYBE I SHOULD KIDNAP HIM AND RAISE HIM MYSELF...
OHOHOHO
SLINK

PART 5

16 CM SHORT

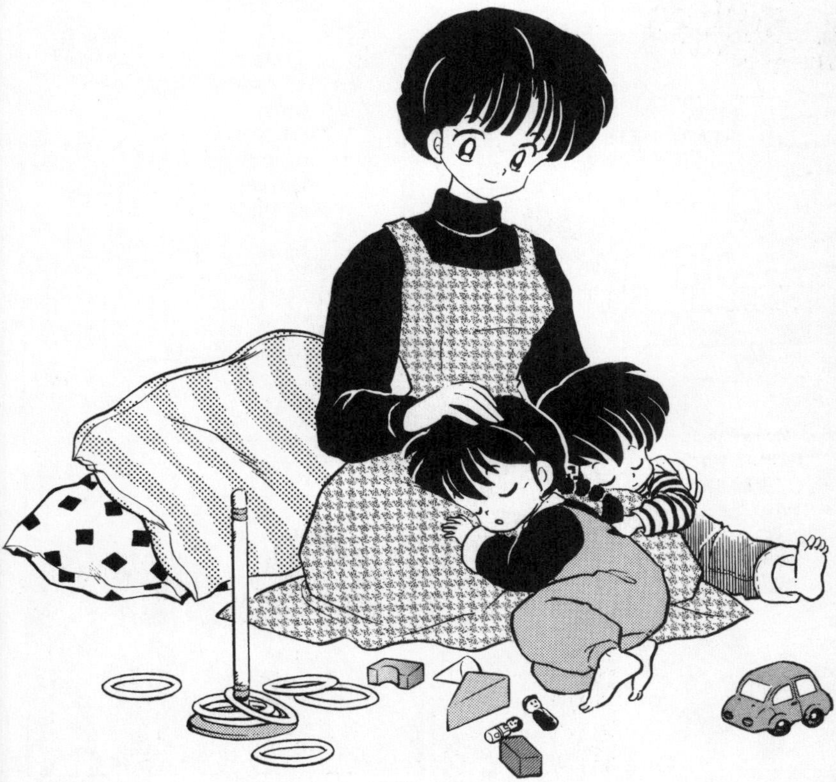

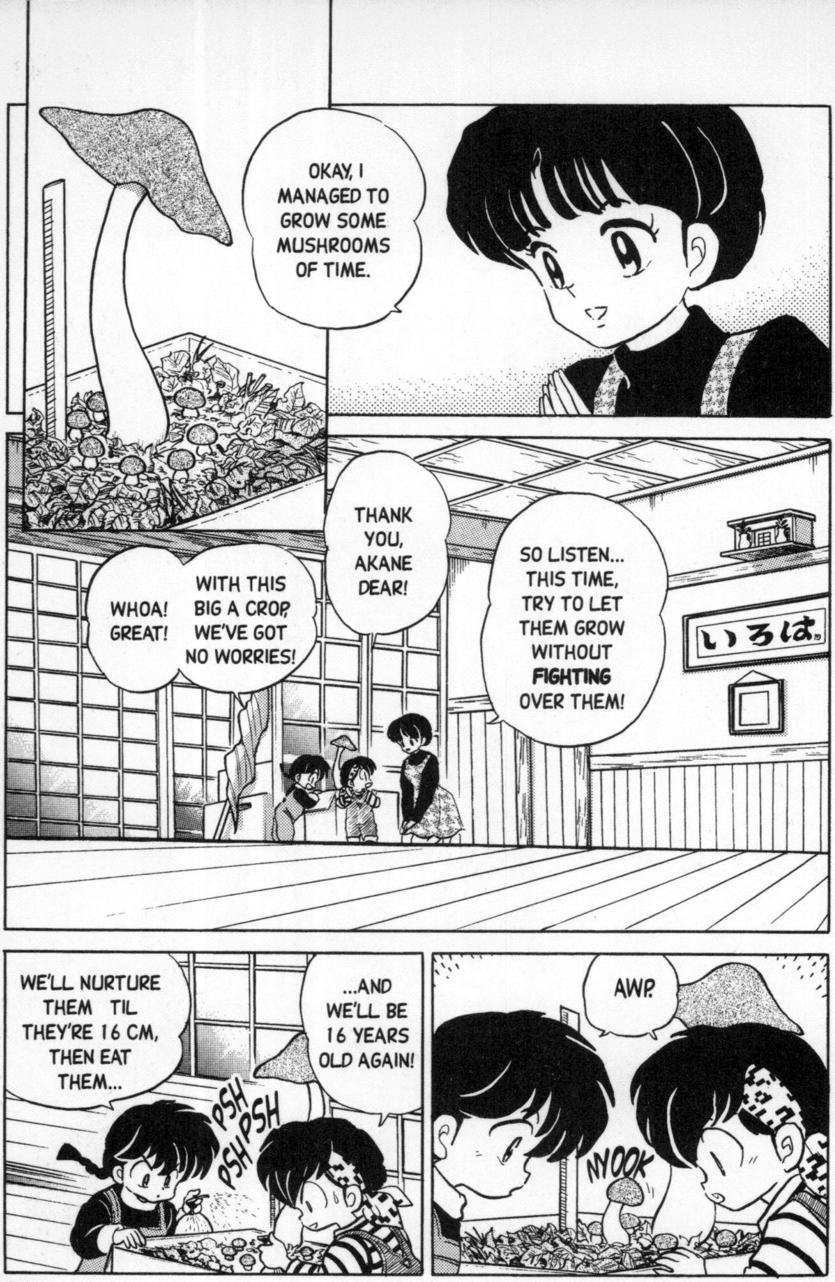
OKAY, I MANAGED TO GROW SOME MUSHROOMS OF TIME.
WHOA! GREAT!
WITH THIS BIG A CROP, WE'VE GOT NO WORRIES!
THANK YOU, AKANE DEAR!
SO LISTEN... THIS TIME, TRY TO LET THEM GROW WITHOUT **FIGHTING** OVER THEM!
いろは
WE'LL NURTURE THEM TIL THEY'RE 16 CM, THEN EAT THEM...
...AND WE'LL BE 16 YEARS OLD AGAIN!
PSH PSH PSH
AWP?
NYOOK

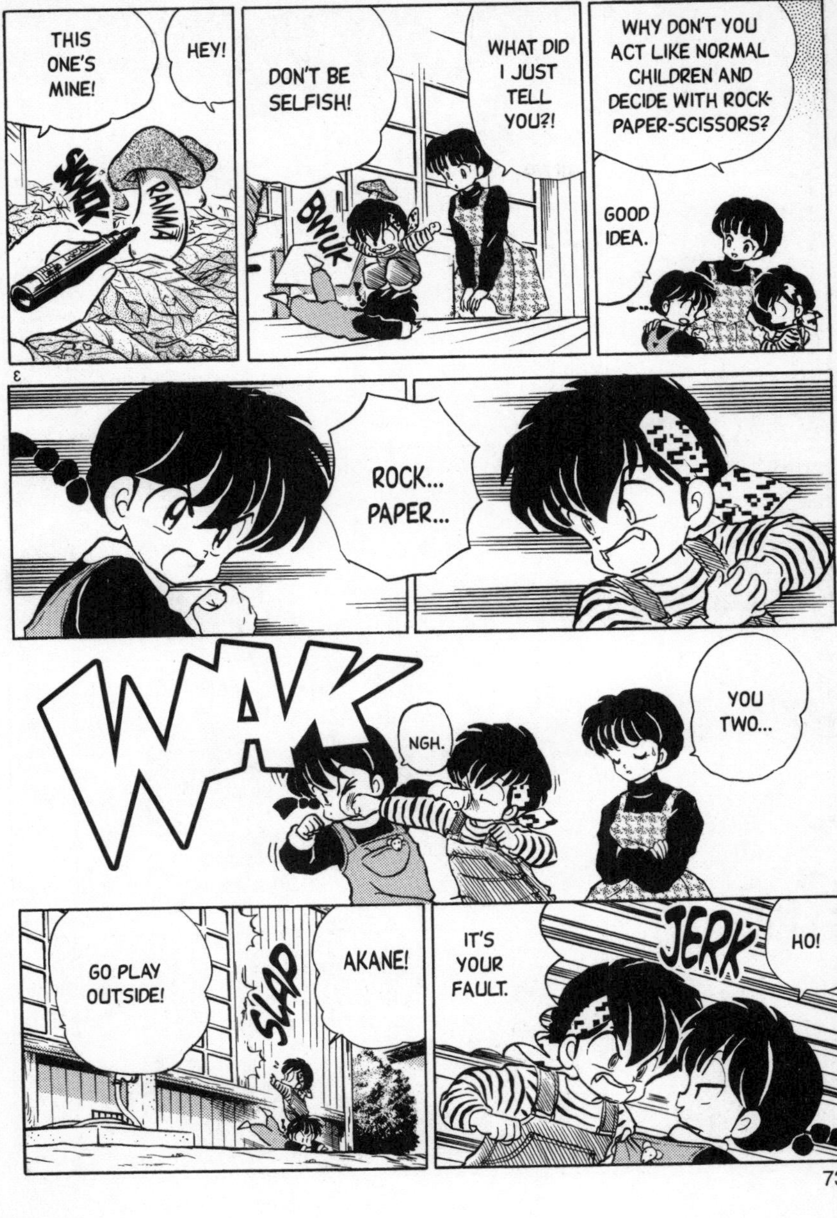
THIS ONE'S MINE!
HEY!
SNOK
RANMA
DON'T BE SELFISH!
WHAT DID I JUST TELL YOU?!
BWUK
WHY DON'T YOU ACT LIKE NORMAL CHILDREN AND DECIDE WITH ROCK-PAPER-SCISSORS?
GOOD IDEA.
ROCK... PAPER...
WAK
NGH.
YOU TWO...
GO PLAY OUTSIDE!
SLAP
AKANE!
IT'S YOUR FAULT.
JERK
HO!

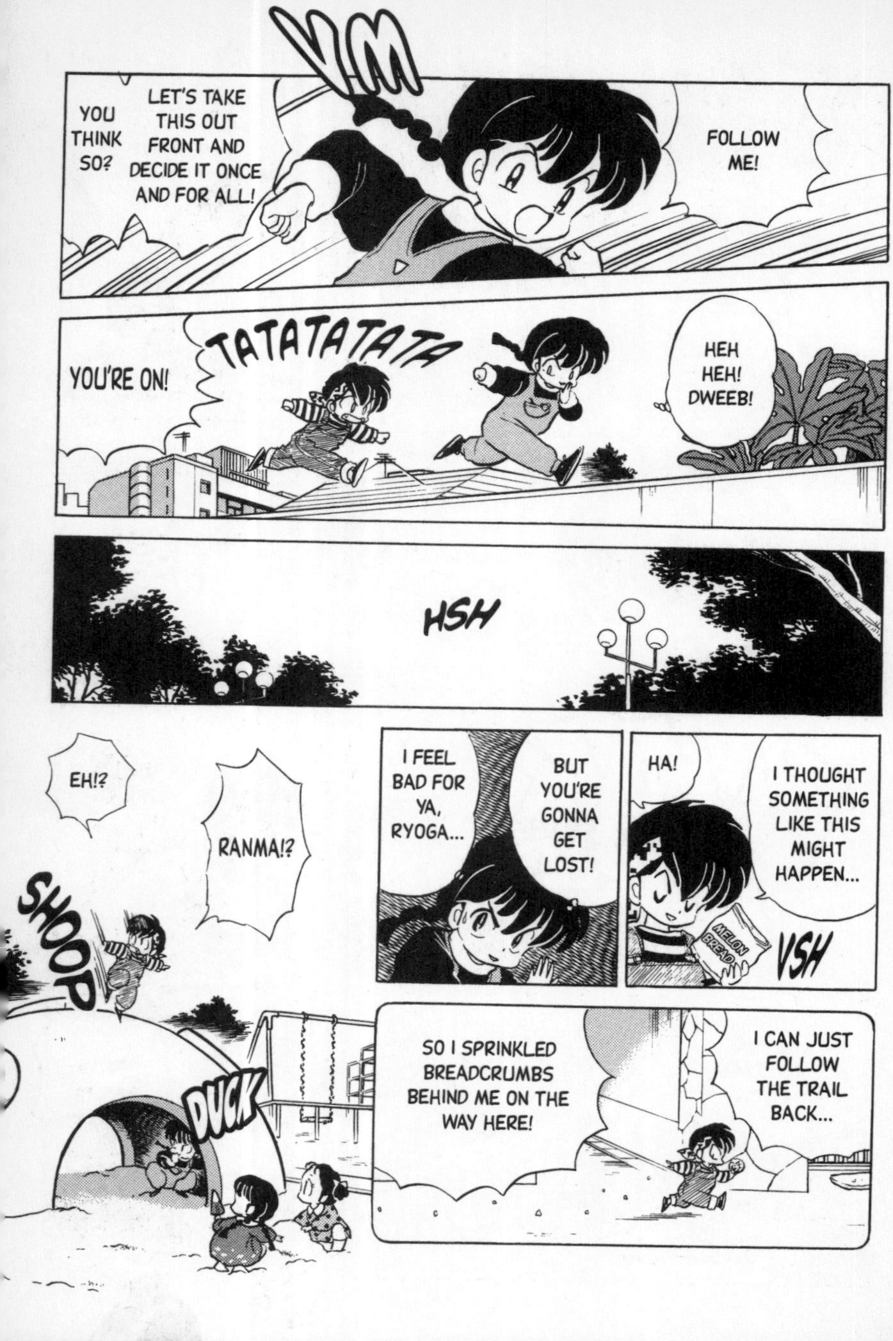
VM
YOU THINK SO?
LET'S TAKE THIS OUT FRONT AND DECIDE IT ONCE AND FOR ALL!
FOLLOW ME!
YOU'RE ON!
TATATATATA
HEH HEH! DWEEB!
HSH
EH!?
RANMA!?
SHOOP
DUCK
I FEEL BAD FOR YA, RYOGA...
BUT YOU'RE GONNA GET LOST!
HA!
I THOUGHT SOMETHING LIKE THIS MIGHT HAPPEN...
MELON BREAD
VSH
SO I SPRINKLED BREADCRUMBS BEHIND ME ON THE WAY HERE!
I CAN JUST FOLLOW THE TRAIL BACK...

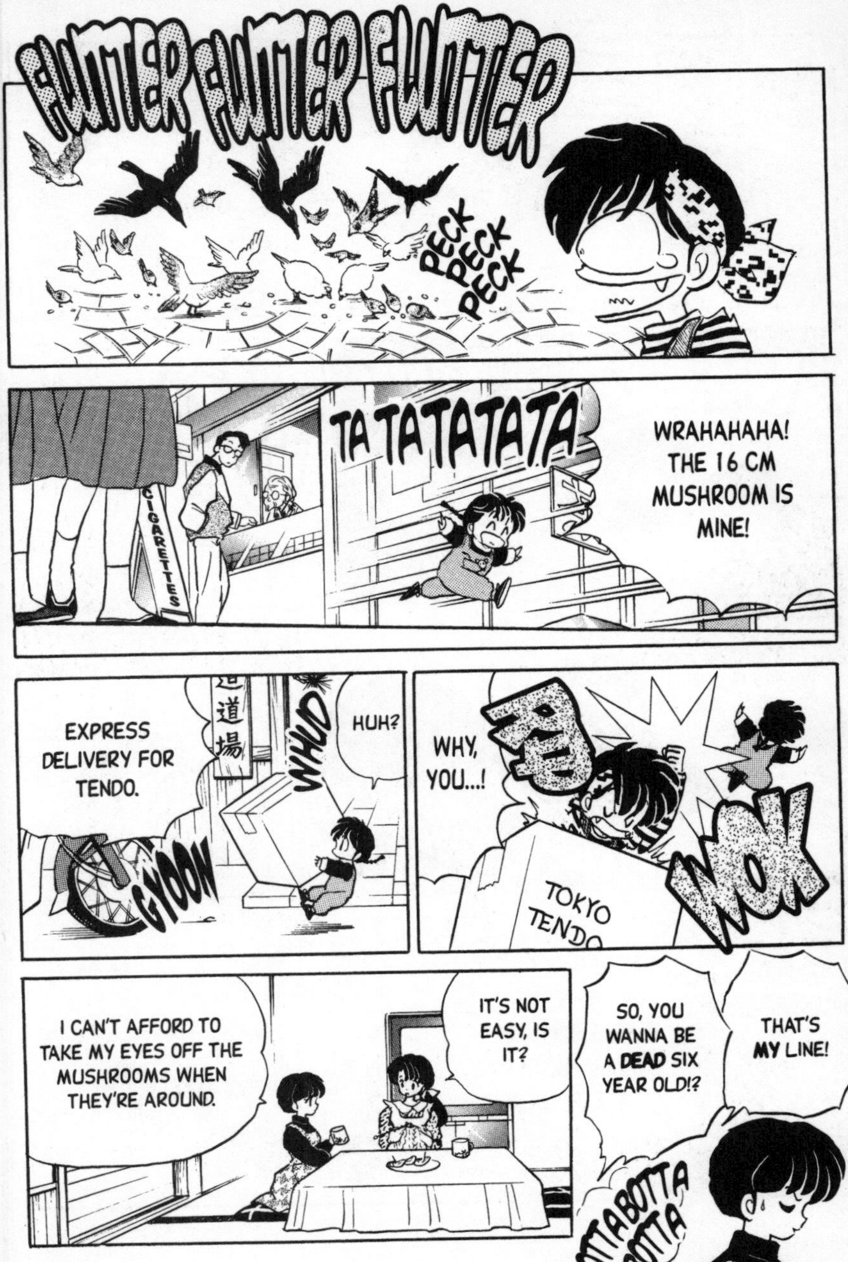
FLUTTER FLUTTER FLUTTER
PECK PECK PECK
CIGARETTES
TA TATATATA
WRAHAHAHA! THE 16 CM MUSHROOM IS MINE!
EXPRESS DELIVERY FOR TENDO.
道場
WHUD
HUH?
GYOON
WHY, YOU...!
WOK
TOKYO TENDO
I CAN'T AFFORD TO TAKE MY EYES OFF THE MUSHROOMS WHEN THEY'RE AROUND.
IT'S NOT EASY, IS IT?
SO, YOU WANNA BE A **DEAD** SIX YEAR OLD!?
THAT'S **MY** LINE!
BOTTA BOTTA BOTTA

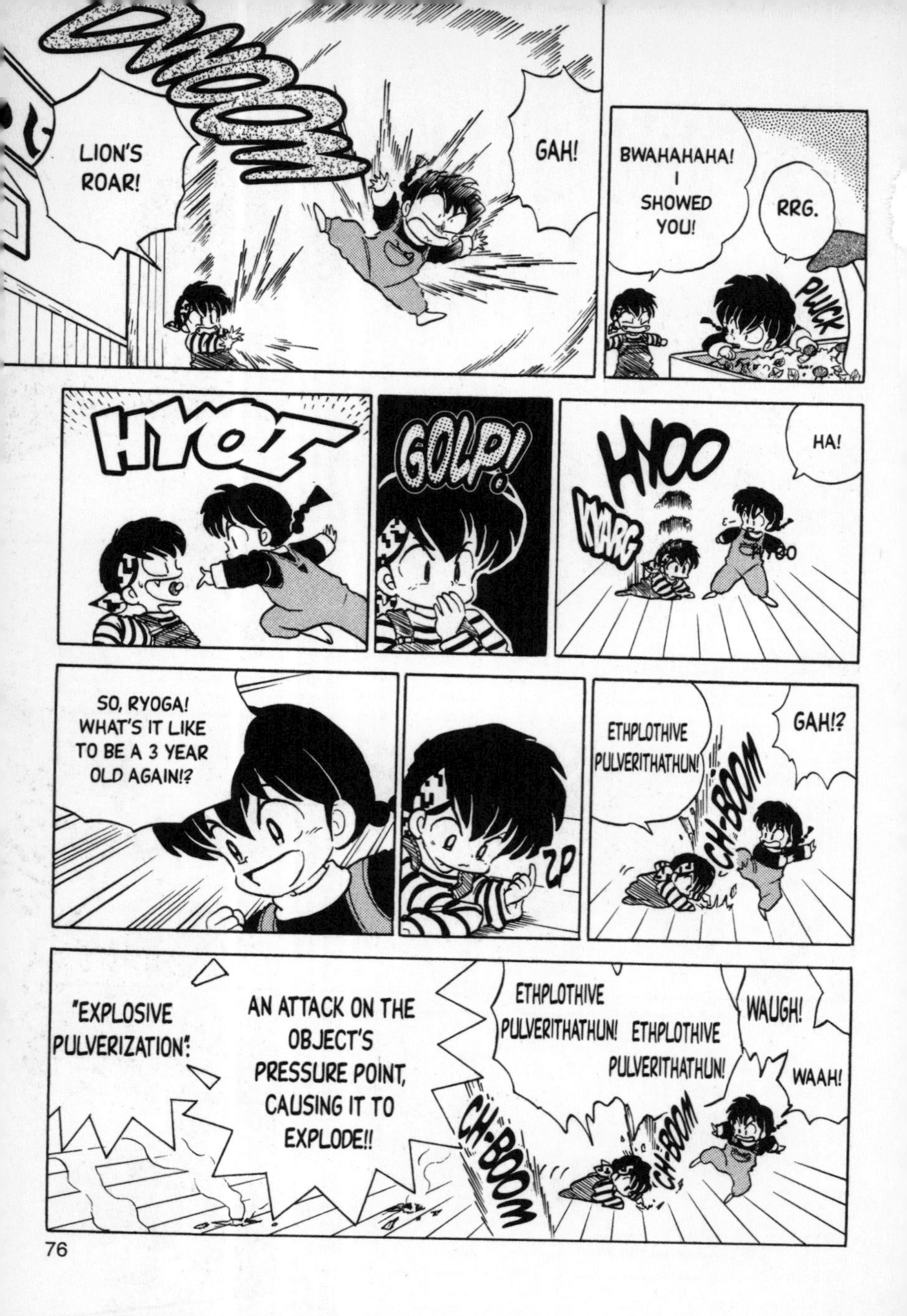
BWOOOM
LION'S ROAR!
GAH!
BWAHAHAHA! I SHOWED YOU!
RRG.
PWICK
HYOI
GOLP!
HYOO
KYARG
HA!
HYOO
SO, RYOGA! WHAT'S IT LIKE TO BE A 3 YEAR OLD AGAIN!?
ZP
ETHPLOTHIVE PULVERITHATHUN!
GAH!?
CH-BOOM
"EXPLOSIVE PULVERIZATION":
AN ATTACK ON THE OBJECT'S PRESSURE POINT, CAUSING IT TO EXPLODE!!
ETHPLOTHIVE PULVERITHATHUN!
ETHPLOTHIVE PULVERITHATHUN!
WAUGH!
WAAH!
CH-BOOM
CH-BOOM

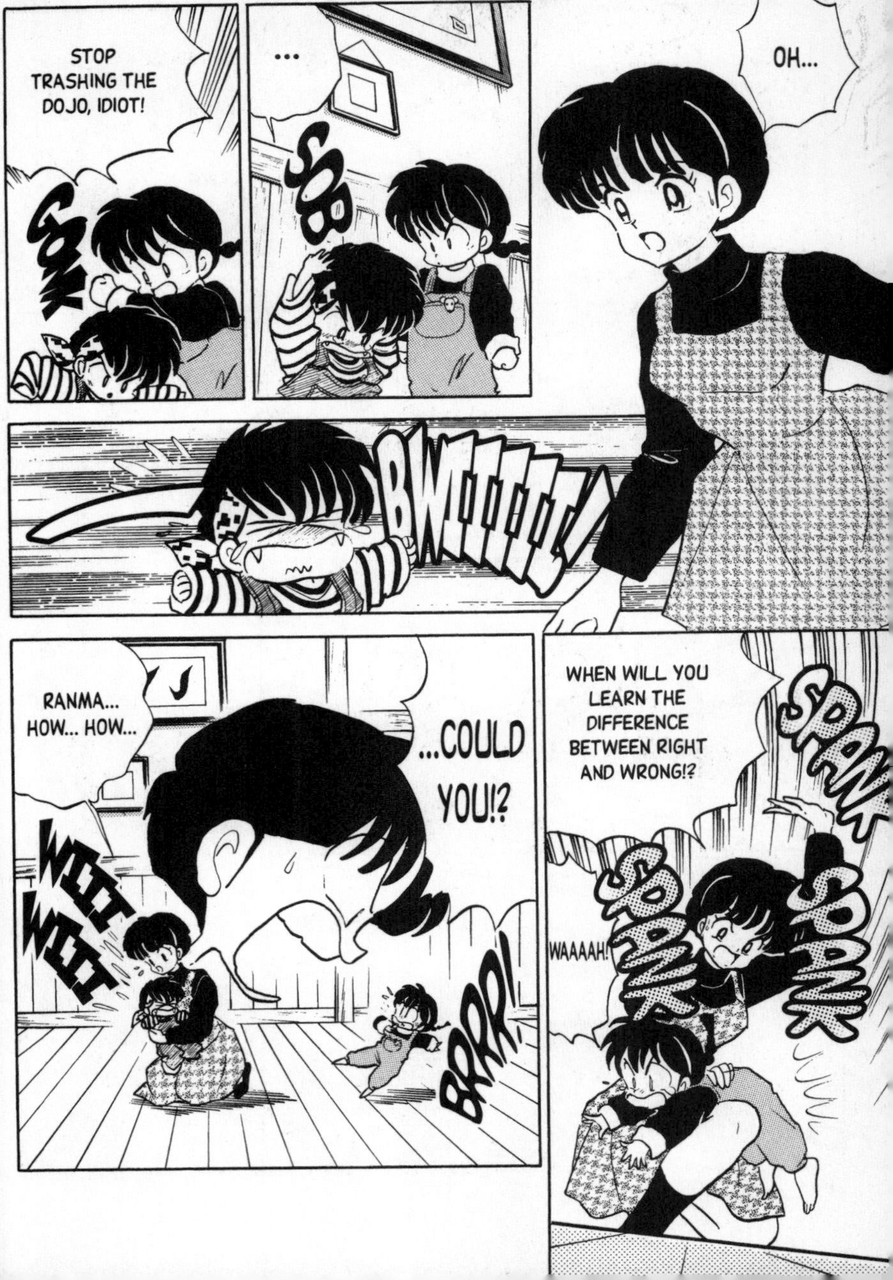
STOP TRASHING THE DOJO, IDIOT!
GONK
...
SOB
BWEEEE!
OH...
RANMA... HOW... HOW...
...COULD YOU!?
WEEE WEEE
BRRR!
WHEN WILL YOU LEARN THE DIFFERENCE BETWEEN RIGHT AND WRONG!?
SPANK
SPANK
SPANK
SPANK
WAAAAH!

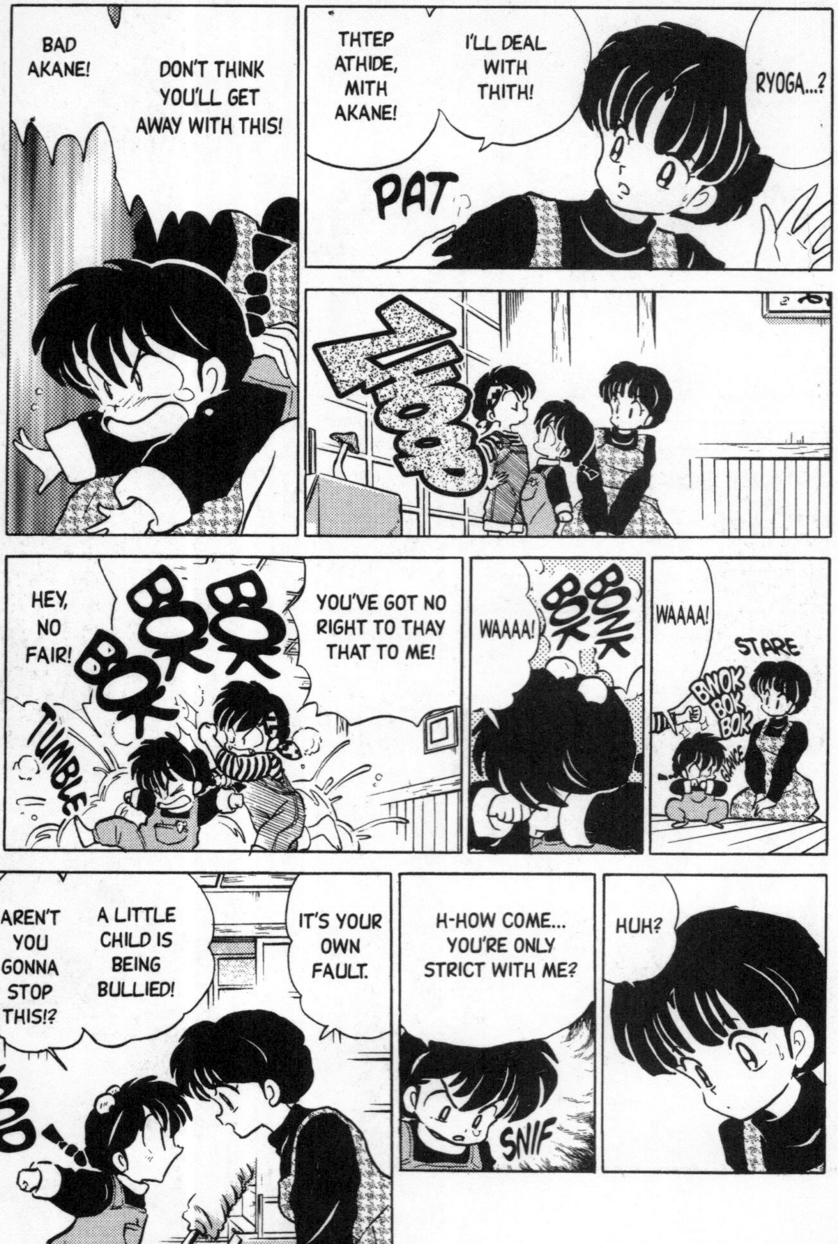
BAD AKANE!
DON'T THINK YOU'LL GET AWAY WITH THIS!
THTEP ATHIDE, MITH AKANE!
I'LL DEAL WITH THITH!
PAT
RYOGA...?
HEY, NO FAIR!
BOK BOK BOK
TUMBLE
YOU'VE GOT NO RIGHT TO THAY THAT TO ME!
WAAAA!
BONK BOK
WAAAA!
STARE
BWOK BOK BOK
GLANCE
AREN'T YOU GONNA STOP THIS!?
A LITTLE CHILD IS BEING BULLIED!
IT'S YOUR OWN FAULT.
SHOOP
H-HOW COME... YOU'RE ONLY STRICT WITH ME?
SNIF
HUH?

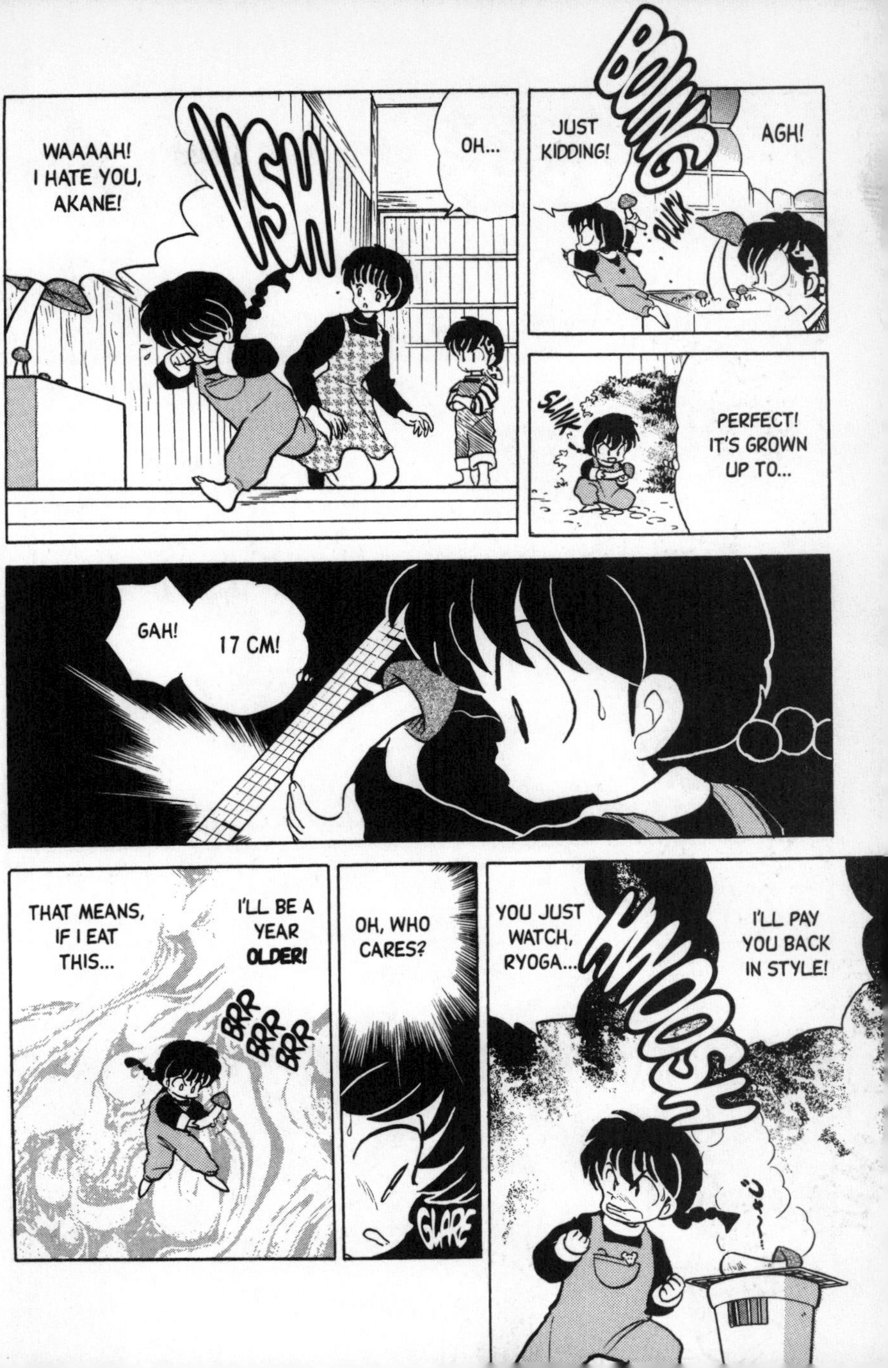
WAAAAH! I HATE YOU, AKANE!
VSH
OH...
BOING
JUST KIDDING!
AGH!
PLUCK
SLINK
PERFECT! IT'S GROWN UP TO...
GAH!
17 CM!
THAT MEANS, IF I EAT THIS...
I'LL BE A YEAR **OLDER!**
BRR BRR BRR
OH, WHO CARES?
GLARE
YOU JUST WATCH, RYOGA...
WHOOSH
I'LL PAY YOU BACK IN STYLE!

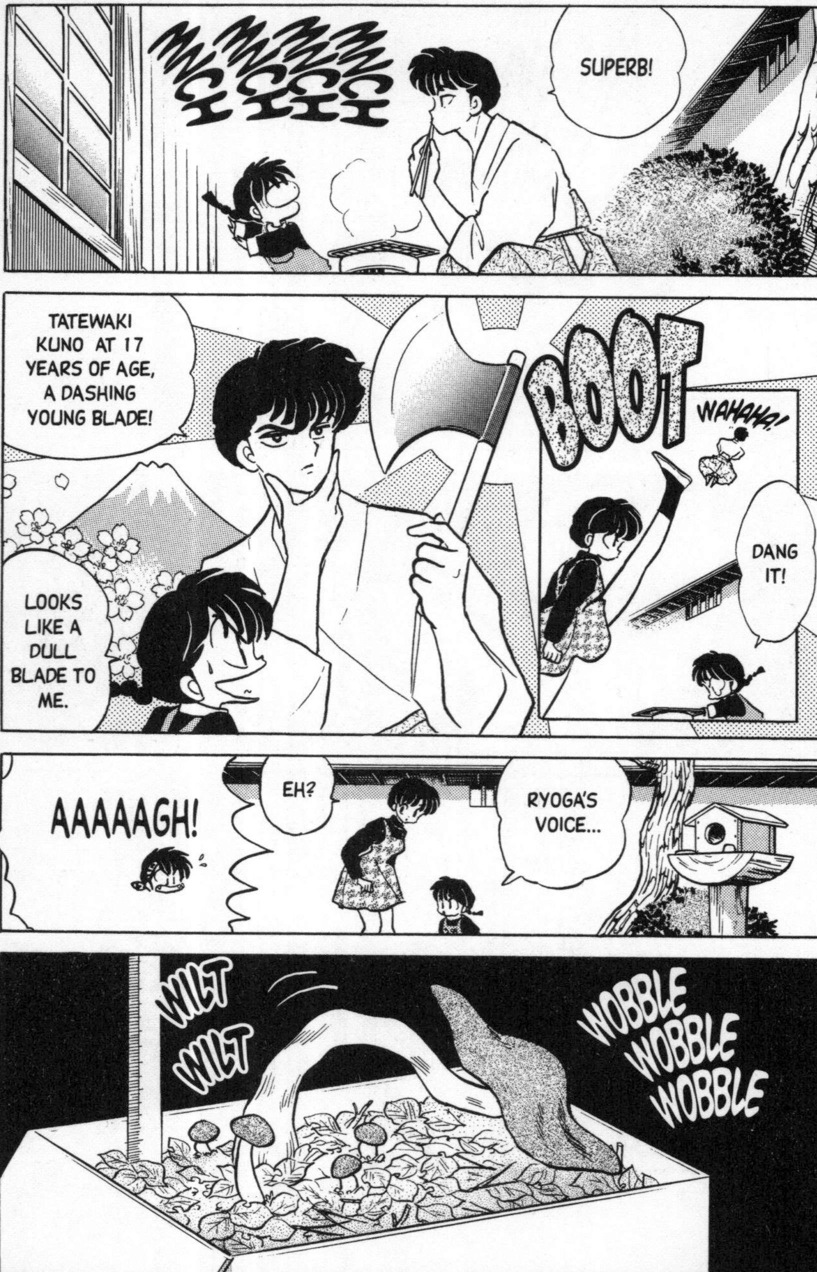
SUPERB!
TATEWAKI KUNO AT 17 YEARS OF AGE, A DASHING YOUNG BLADE!
LOOKS LIKE A DULL BLADE TO ME.
BOOT
WAHAHA!
DANG IT!
AAAAAGH!
EH?
RYOGA'S VOICE...
WILT WILT
WOBBLE WOBBLE WOBBLE

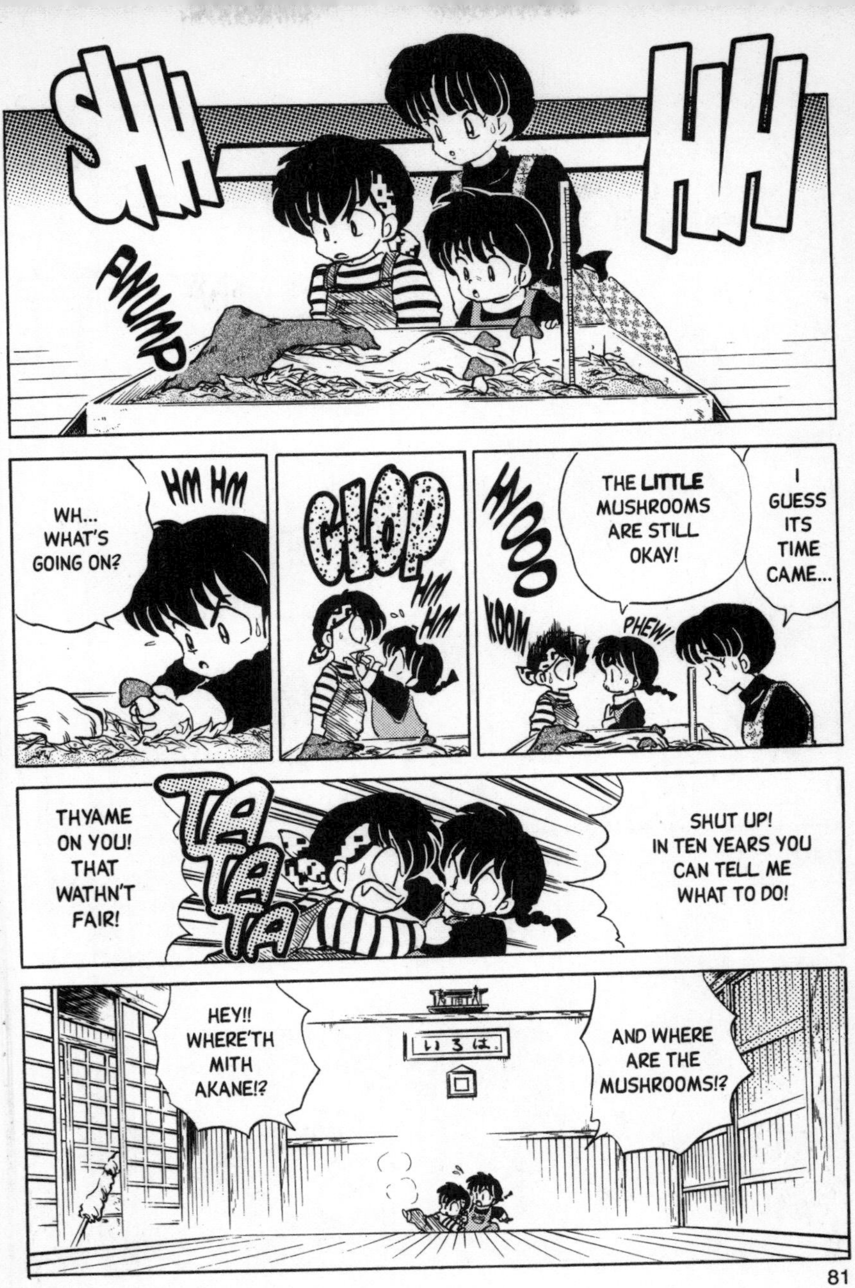
SHH
HH
AWUMP
HM HM
WH... WHAT'S GOING ON?
GLOP
HM HM
HWOOO
KOOM
THE LITTLE MUSHROOMS ARE STILL OKAY!
PHEW!
I GUESS ITS TIME CAME...
THYAME ON YOU! THAT WATHN'T FAIR!
TA TA TA
SHUT UP! IN TEN YEARS YOU CAN TELL ME WHAT TO DO!
HEY!! WHERE'TH MITH AKANE!?
いろは。
AND WHERE ARE THE MUSHROOMS!?

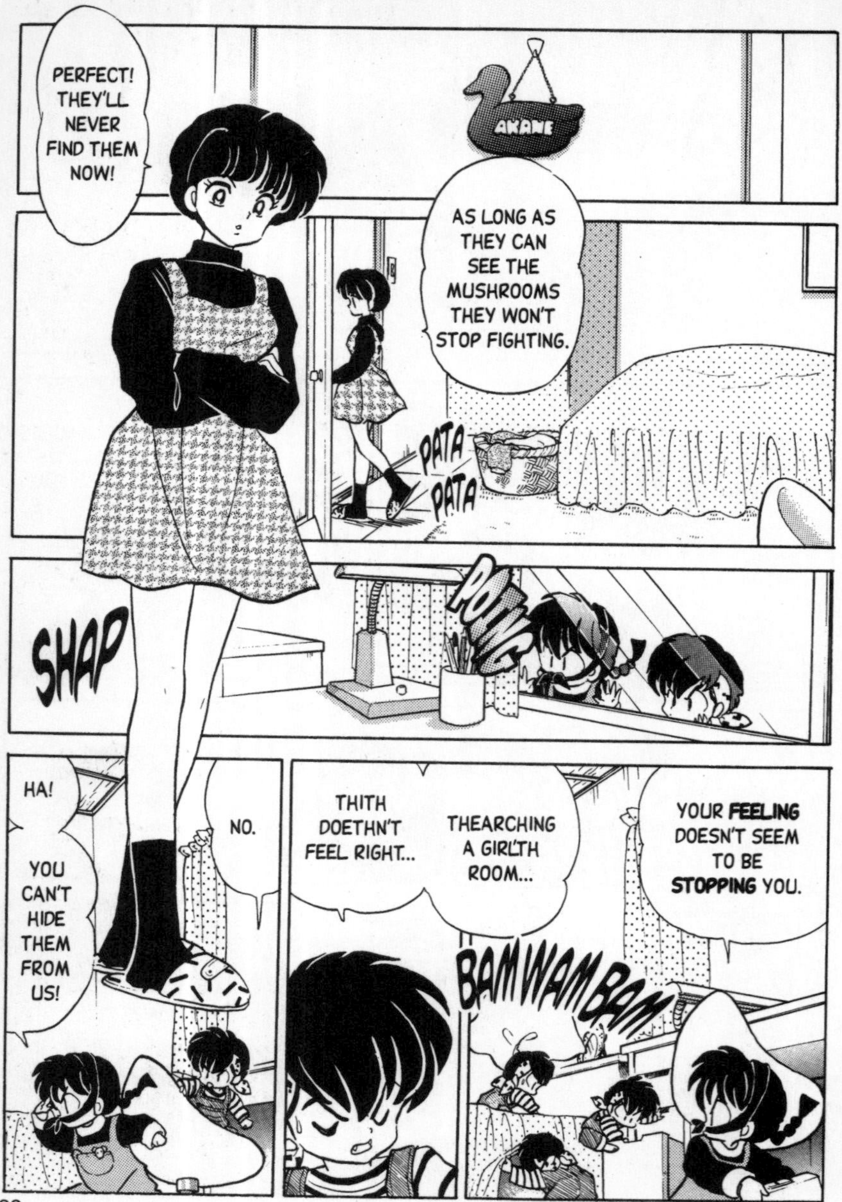

PERFECT! THEY'LL NEVER FIND THEM NOW!
AKANE
AS LONG AS THEY CAN SEE THE MUSHROOMS THEY WON'T STOP FIGHTING.
PATA PATA
SHAP
POING
HA!
YOU CAN'T HIDE THEM FROM US!
NO.
THITH DOETHN'T FEEL RIGHT...
THEARCHING A GIRL'TH ROOM...
YOUR FEELING DOESN'T SEEM TO BE STOPPING YOU.
BAM WAM BAM

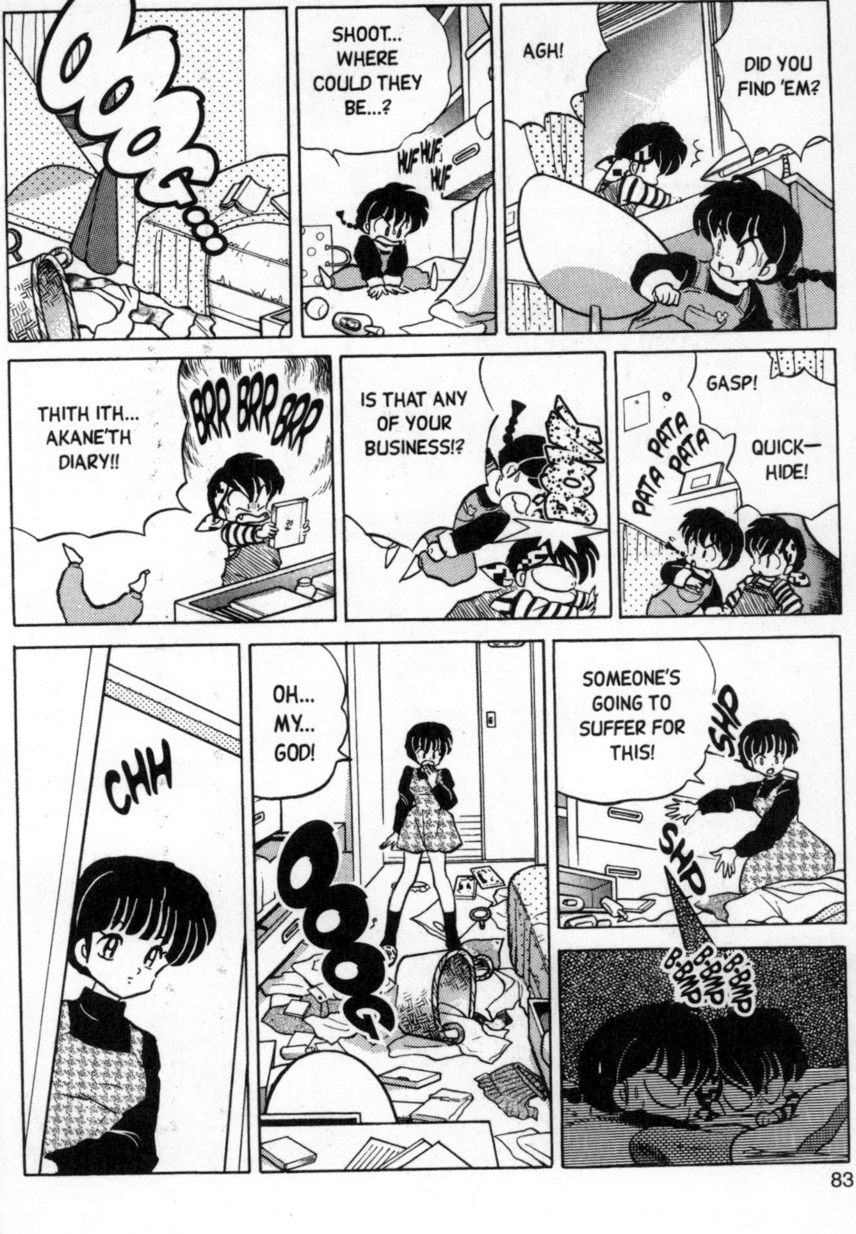
OOOOGOOO
SHOOT... WHERE COULD THEY BE...?
HUF HUF HUF
AGH!
DID YOU FIND 'EM?
THITH ITH... AKANE'TH DIARY!!
BRR BRR BRR
IS THAT ANY OF YOUR BUSINESS!?
BOOM
GASP!
PATA PATA PATA
QUICK— HIDE!
CHH
OH... MY... GOD!
OOOOG
SOMEONE'S GOING TO SUFFER FOR THIS!
SHP
SHP
B-BMP B-BMP B-BMP

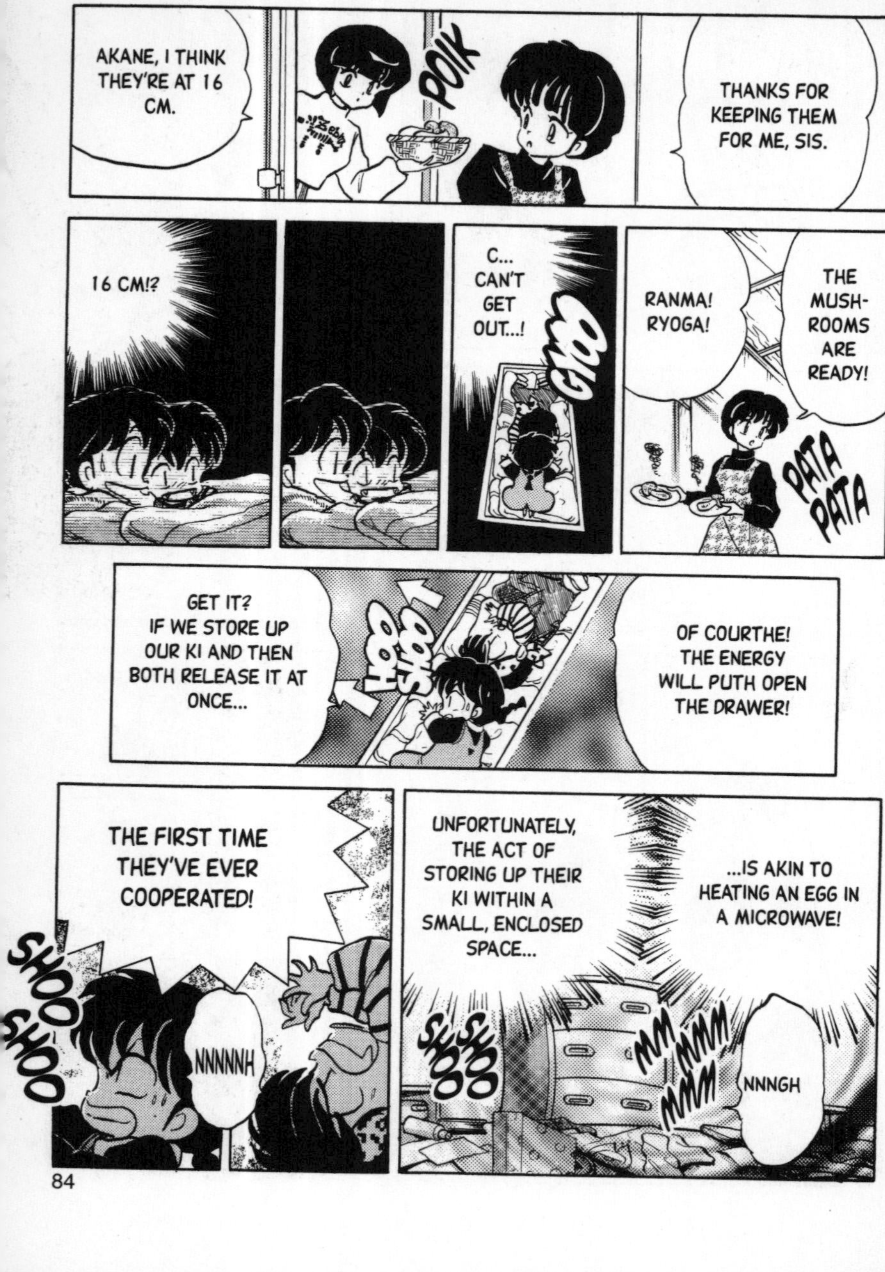
AKANE, I THINK THEY'RE AT 16 CM.
POIK
THANKS FOR KEEPING THEM FOR ME, SIS.
16 CM!?
C... CAN'T GET OUT...!
RANMA! RYOGA!
THE MUSH-ROOMS ARE READY!
PATA PATA
GET IT? IF WE STORE UP OUR KI AND THEN BOTH RELEASE IT AT ONCE...
OF COURTHE! THE ENERGY WILL PUTH OPEN THE DRAWER!
THE FIRST TIME THEY'VE EVER COOPERATED!
SHOO SHOO
NNNNNH
UNFORTUNATELY, THE ACT OF STORING UP THEIR KI WITHIN A SMALL, ENCLOSED SPACE...
...IS AKIN TO HEATING AN EGG IN A MICROWAVE!
SHOO SHOO
NNNGH

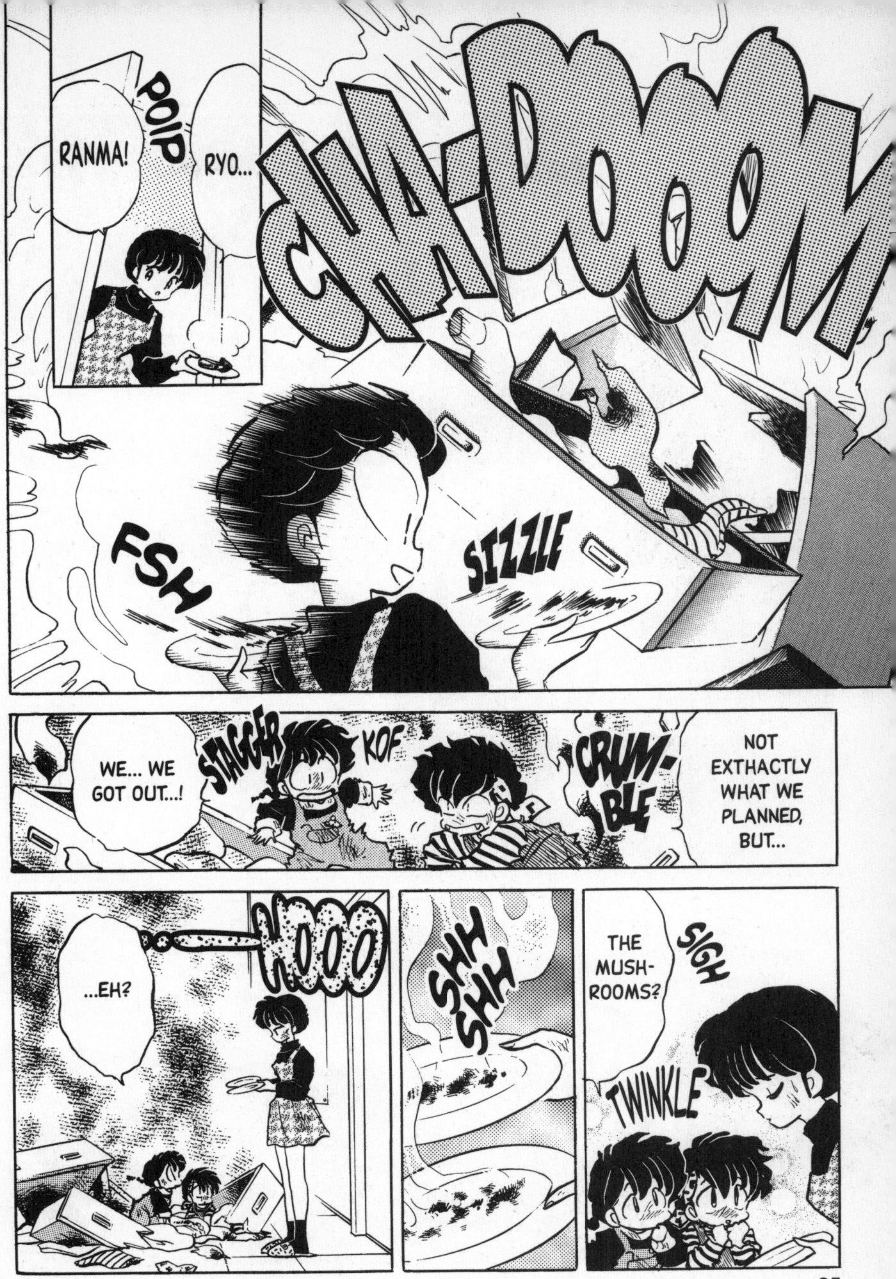
RANMA!
POIP
RYO...
CHA-DOOOM
FSH
SIZZLE
WE... WE GOT OUT...!
STAGGER
KOF
CRUM-BLE
NOT EXTHACTLY WHAT WE PLANNED, BUT...
...EH?
HOOO
SHH SHH
THE MUSH-ROOMS?
SIGH
TWINKLE

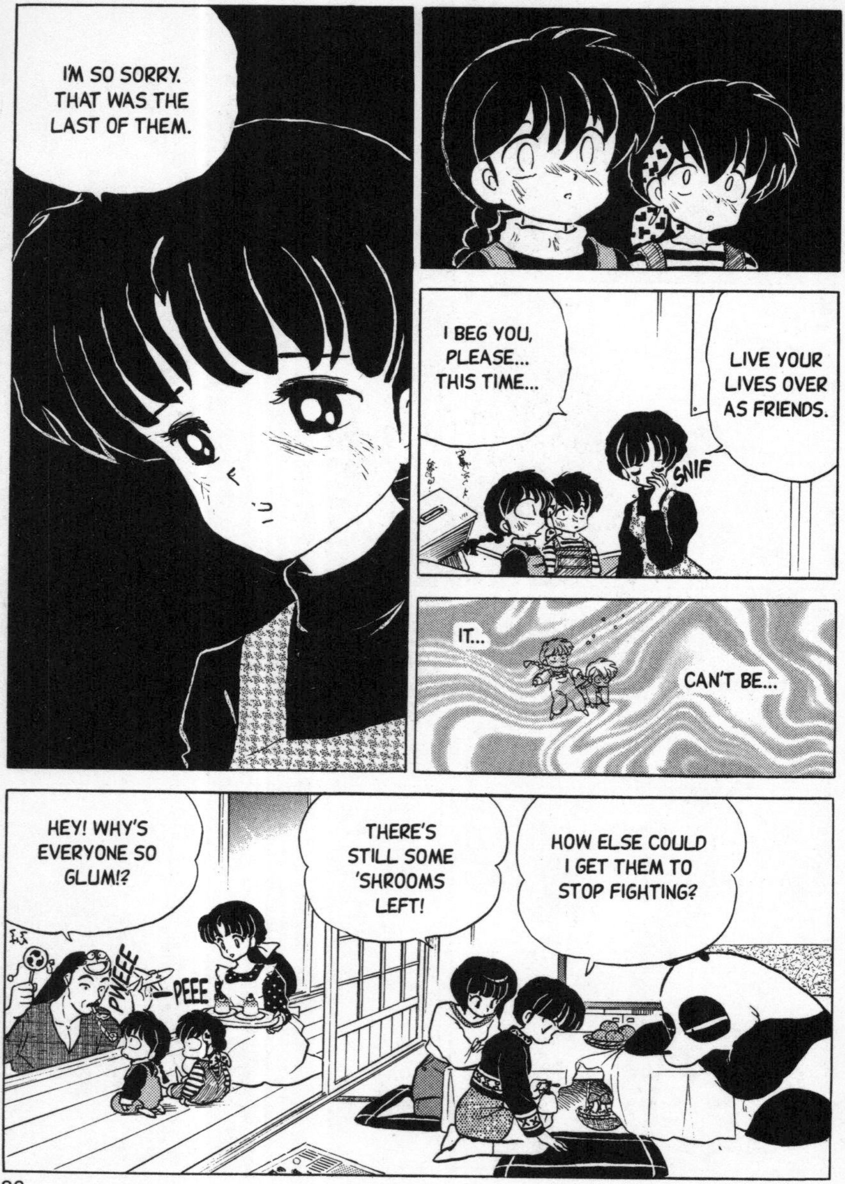
I'M SO SORRY. THAT WAS THE LAST OF THEM.
I BEG YOU, PLEASE... THIS TIME...
LIVE YOUR LIVES OVER AS FRIENDS.
SNIF
IT...
CAN'T BE...
HEY! WHY'S EVERYONE SO GLUM!?
PWEEE
—PEEE
THERE'S STILL SOME 'SHROOMS LEFT!
HOW ELSE COULD I GET THEM TO STOP FIGHTING?

PART 6
THE TWO SHAMPOOS

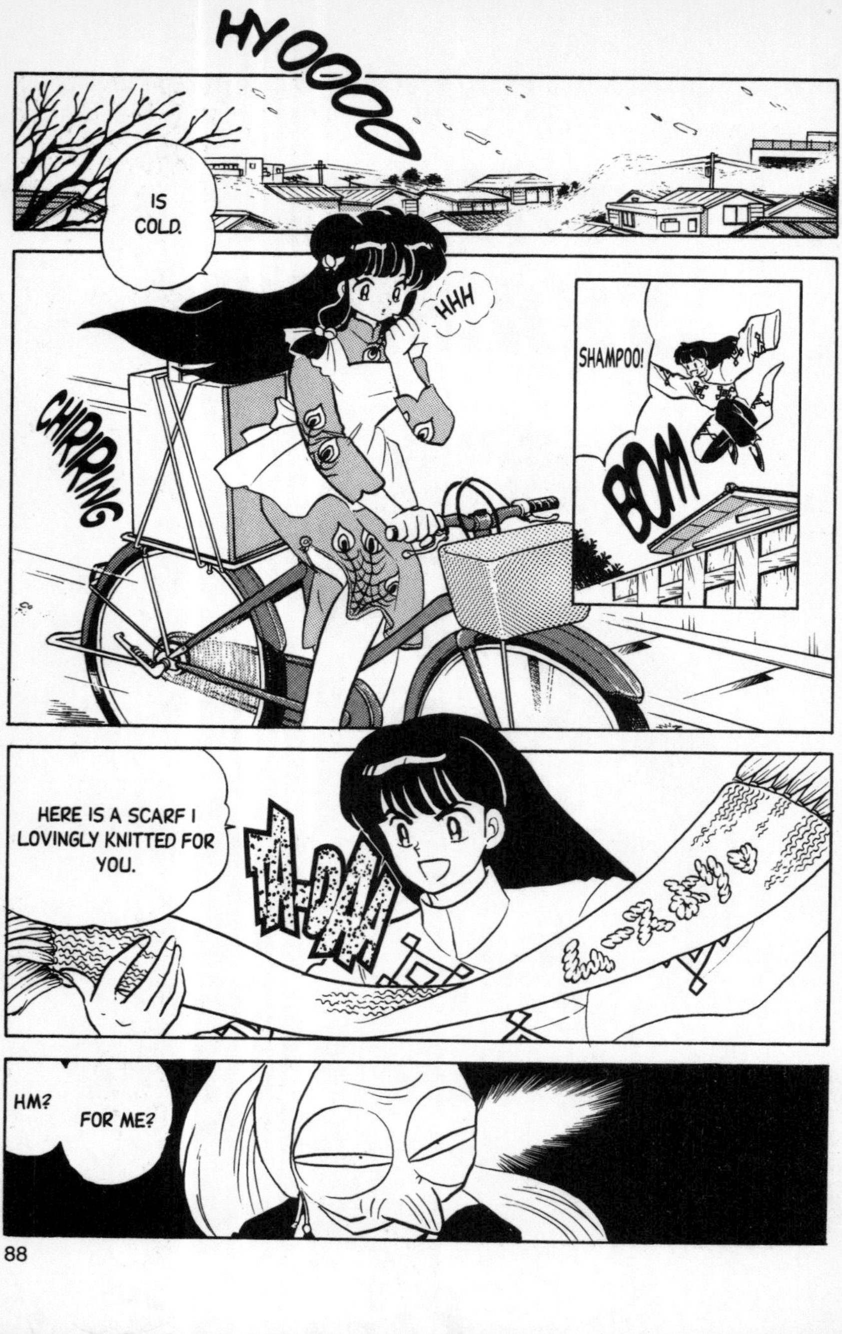
HYOOOO
IS COLD.
HHH
CHIRIRING
SHAMPOO!
BOM
HERE IS A SCARF I LOVINGLY KNITTED FOR YOU.
TA-DA
HM?
FOR ME?

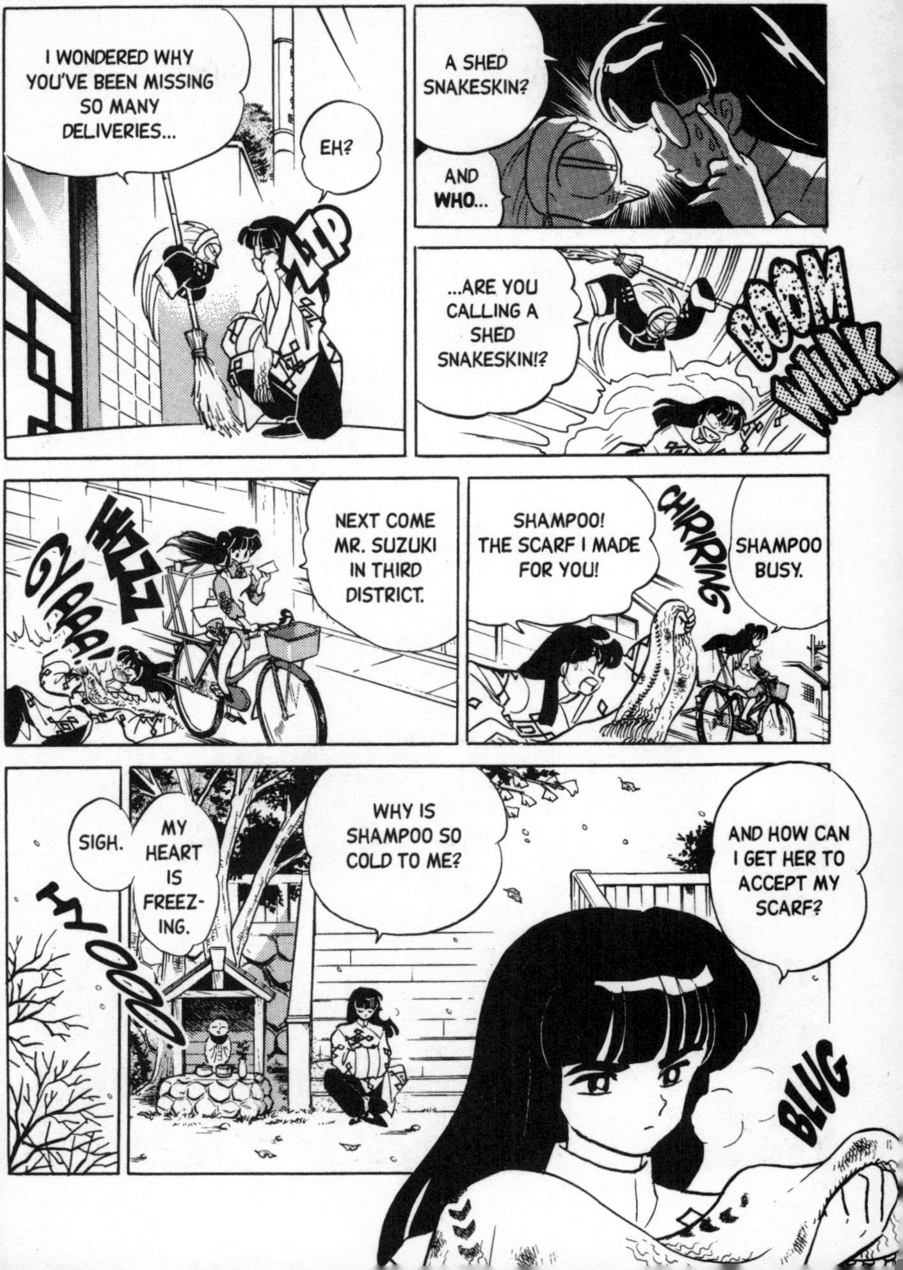
I WONDERED WHY YOU'VE BEEN MISSING SO MANY DELIVERIES...
EH?
ZIP
A SHED SNAKESKIN?
AND WHO...
...ARE YOU CALLING A SHED SNAKESKIN!?
BOOM
WHAK
GYAAA!
NEXT COME MR. SUZUKI IN THIRD DISTRICT.
SHAMPOO! THE SCARF I MADE FOR YOU!
CHIRIRING
SHAMPOO BUSY.
SIGH.
MY HEART IS FREEZ-ING.
HYOOO
WHY IS SHAMPOO SO COLD TO ME?
AND HOW CAN I GET HER TO ACCEPT MY SCARF?
BLUG

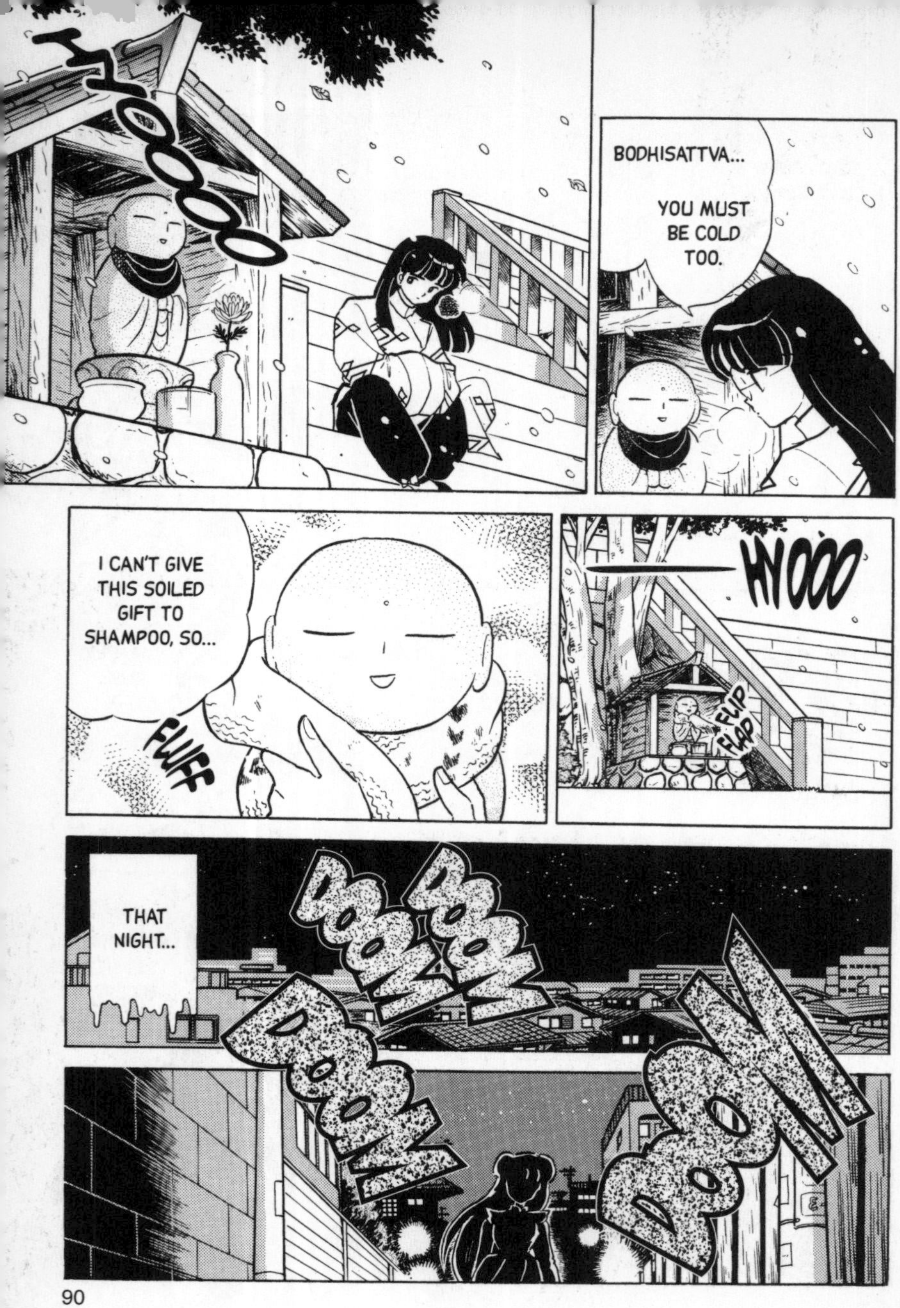
HYOOOOO
BODHISATTVA...
YOU MUST BE COLD TOO.
I CAN'T GIVE THIS SOILED GIFT TO SHAMPOO, SO...
FWIFF
HYOOO
FLIP FLAP
THAT NIGHT...
DOOON
DOOON
DOOON
BOOM

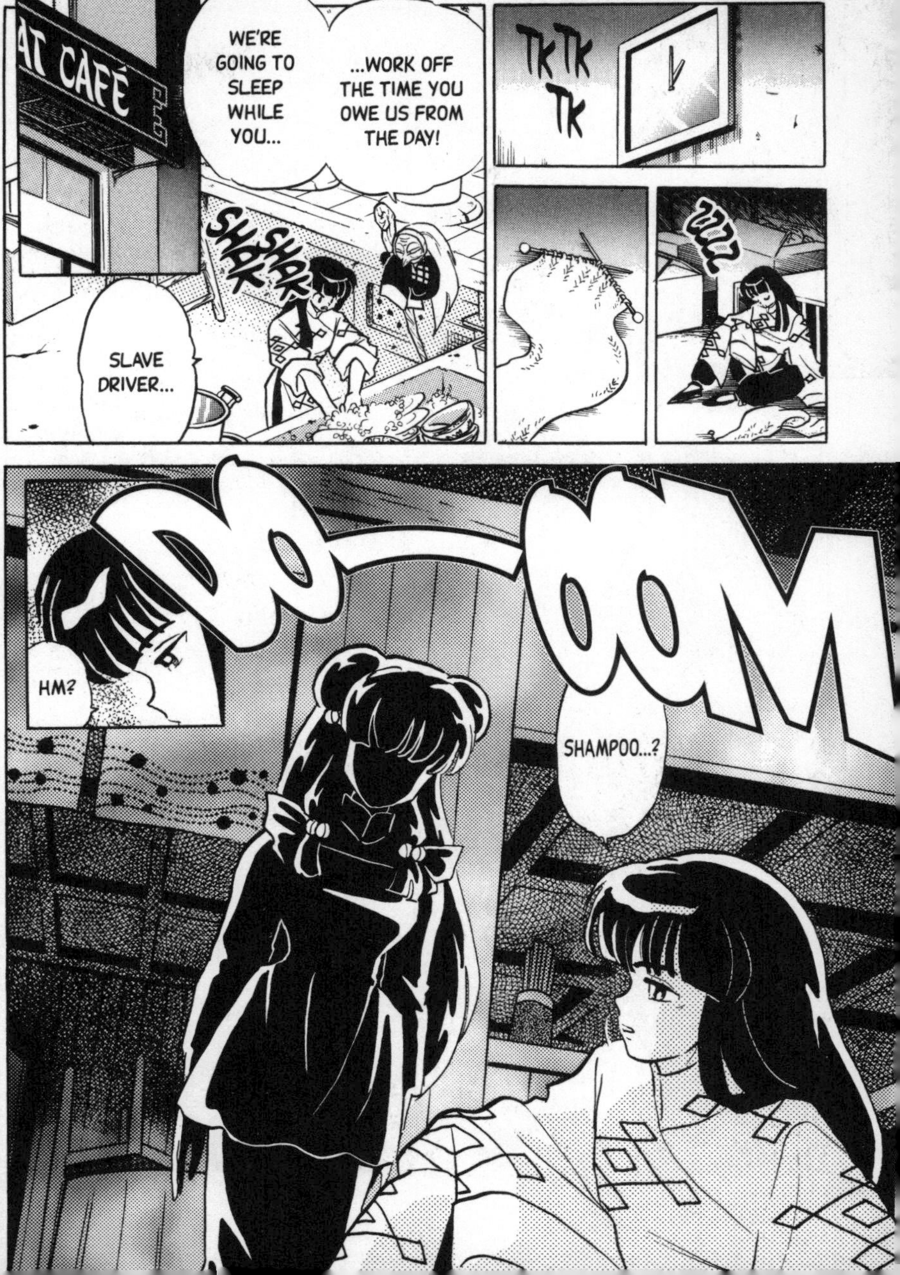
AT CAFÉ
WE'RE GOING TO SLEEP WHILE YOU...
...WORK OFF THE TIME YOU OWE US FROM THE DAY!
SHAK SHAK
SLAVE DRIVER...
TKTK TK
ZZZZ
DOOOM
HM?
SHAMPOO...?

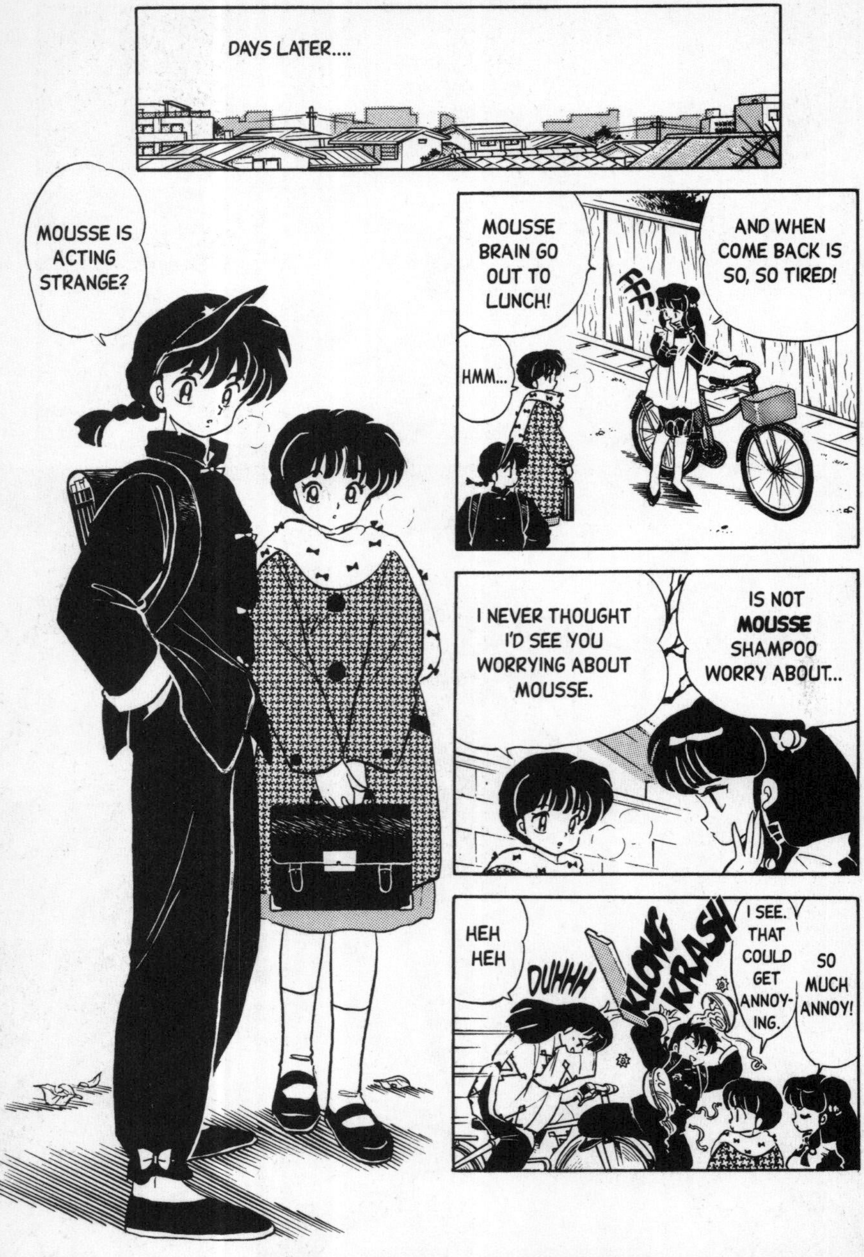
DAYS LATER....
MOUSSE IS ACTING STRANGE?
MOUSSE BRAIN GO OUT TO LUNCH!
AND WHEN COME BACK IS SO, SO TIRED!
FFF
HMM...
I NEVER THOUGHT I'D SEE YOU WORRYING ABOUT MOUSSE.
IS NOT **MOUSSE** SHAMPOO WORRY ABOUT...
HEH HEH
DUHHH
KLONG
KRASH
I SEE. THAT COULD GET ANNOY-ING.
SO MUCH ANNOY!

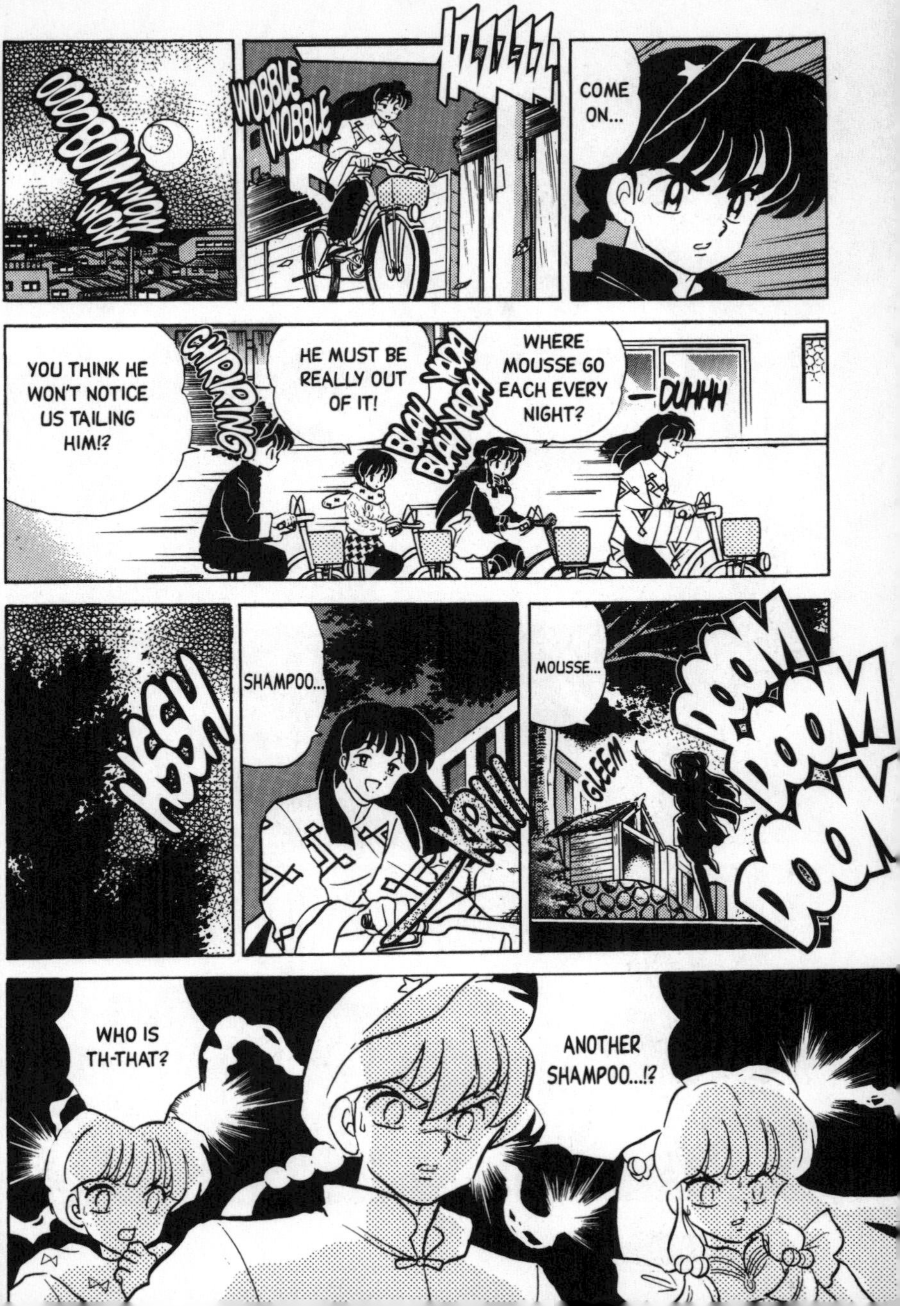
OOOOBOWWOWWOW
WOBBLE WOBBLE
COME ON...
YOU THINK HE WON'T NOTICE US TAILING HIM!?
CHIRRING
HE MUST BE REALLY OUT OF IT!
BLAH BLAH YADA YADA
WHERE MOUSSE GO EACH EVERY NIGHT?
—DUHHH
SHAMPOO...
MOUSSE...
GLEEM
DOOM DOOM DOOM
WHO IS TH-THAT?
ANOTHER SHAMPOO...!?

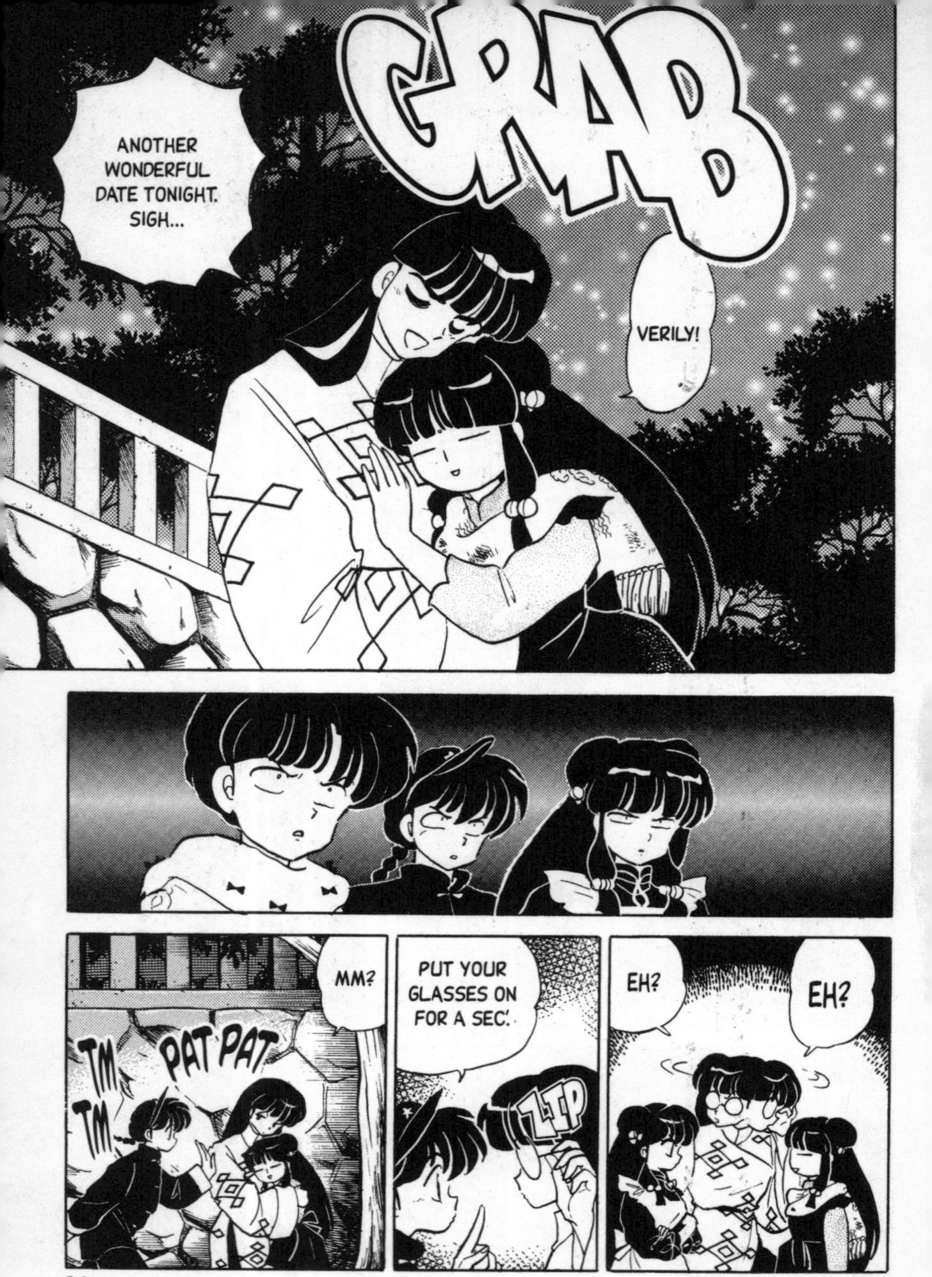
ANOTHER WONDERFUL DATE TONIGHT. SIGH...
GRAB
VERILY!
MM?
TM TM
PAT PAT
PUT YOUR GLASSES ON FOR A SEC.
ZIP
EH?
EH?

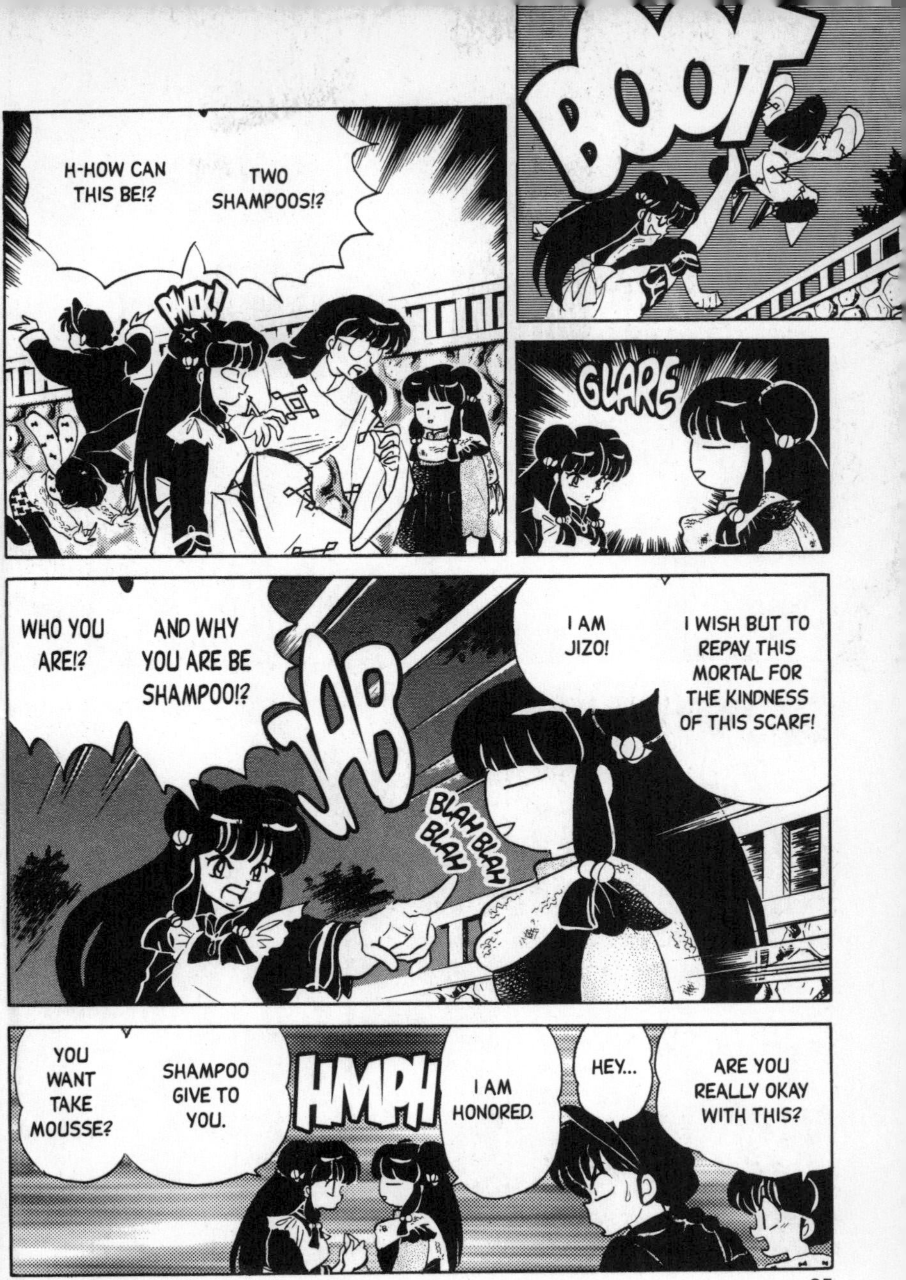
H-HOW CAN THIS BE!?
TWO SHAMPOOS!?
PWOK!
BOOT
GLARE
WHO YOU ARE!?
AND WHY YOU ARE BE SHAMPOO!?
JAB
BLAH BLAH BLAH
I AM JIZO!
I WISH BUT TO REPAY THIS MORTAL FOR THE KINDNESS OF THIS SCARF!
YOU WANT TAKE MOUSSE?
SHAMPOO GIVE TO YOU.
HMPH
I AM HONORED.
HEY...
ARE YOU REALLY OKAY WITH THIS?

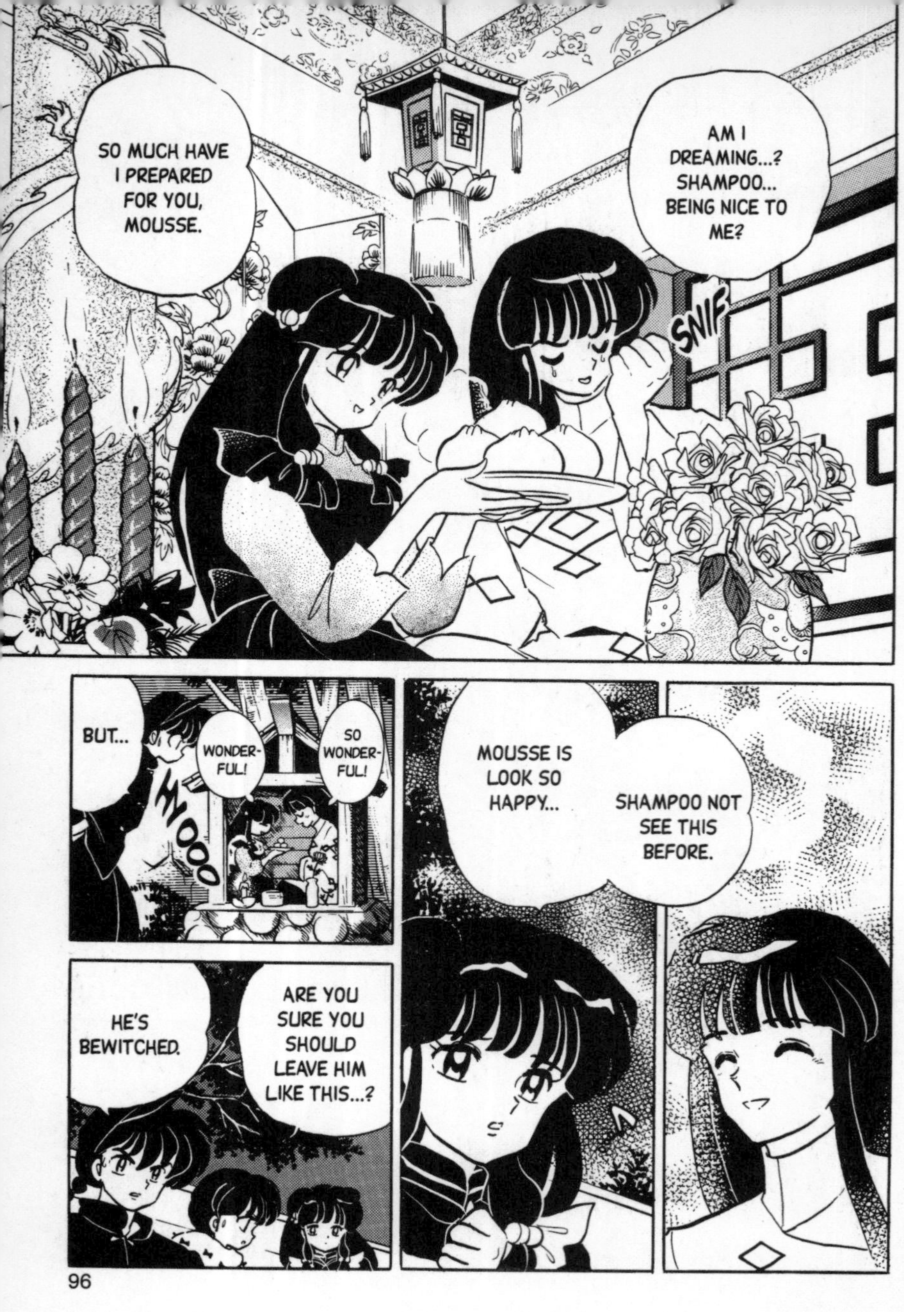
SO MUCH HAVE I PREPARED FOR YOU, MOUSSE.
AM I DREAMING...? SHAMPOO... BEING NICE TO ME?
SNIF
BUT...
WONDER-FUL!
SO WONDER-FUL!
HOOO
HE'S BEWITCHED.
ARE YOU SURE YOU SHOULD LEAVE HIM LIKE THIS...?
MOUSSE IS LOOK SO HAPPY...
SHAMPOO NOT SEE THIS BEFORE.

SHAMPOO CANNOT...

..DESTROY THIS DREAM FOR MOUSSE!

OH, SHAM-POO...

SO SHE'S GOTTEN SICK OF HIM, HUH?

DOOOM

KRAK

HO!

HHMM... A PROTECTIVE STATUE REPAYING A FAVOR...?

FLAP FLAP

THAT SOUNDS A BIT ODD TO ME.

YOU THINK SO TOO, HUH?

YOUR RAMEN. TH-THANK YOU FOR WAITING.

WOBBLE

WAAUGH!

MOUSSE IS SO EXHAUSTED...

IT'S AS IF HIS LIFE FORCE IS BEING SUCKED OUT OF HIM...

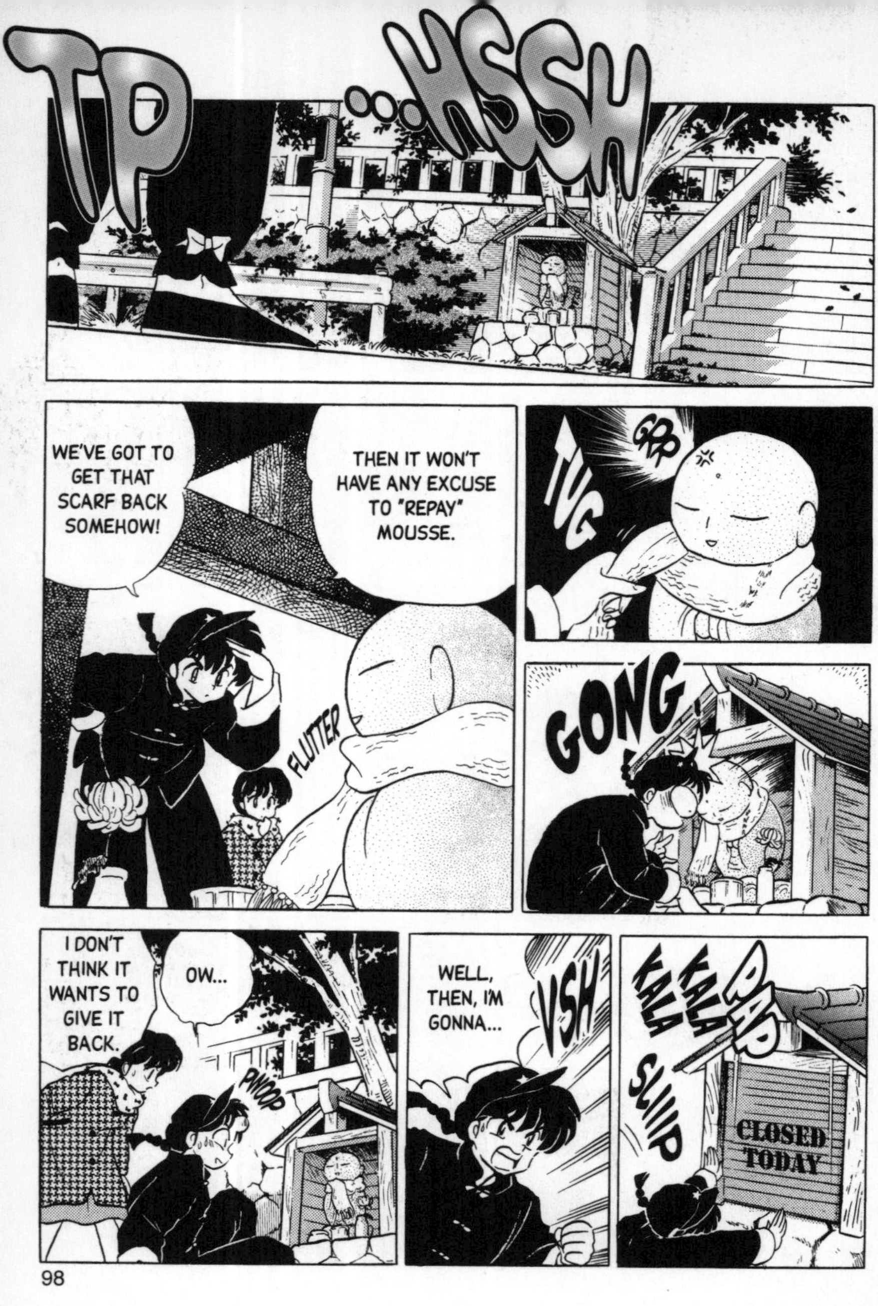

TP
...HSSH
WE'VE GOT TO GET THAT SCARF BACK SOMEHOW!
THEN IT WON'T HAVE ANY EXCUSE TO "REPAY" MOUSSE.
FLUTTER
GRR
TUG
GONG
I DON'T THINK IT WANTS TO GIVE IT BACK.
OW...
PWOOP
WELL, THEN, I'M GONNA...
VSH
PAP
KALA KALA
SLIIIP
CLOSED TODAY

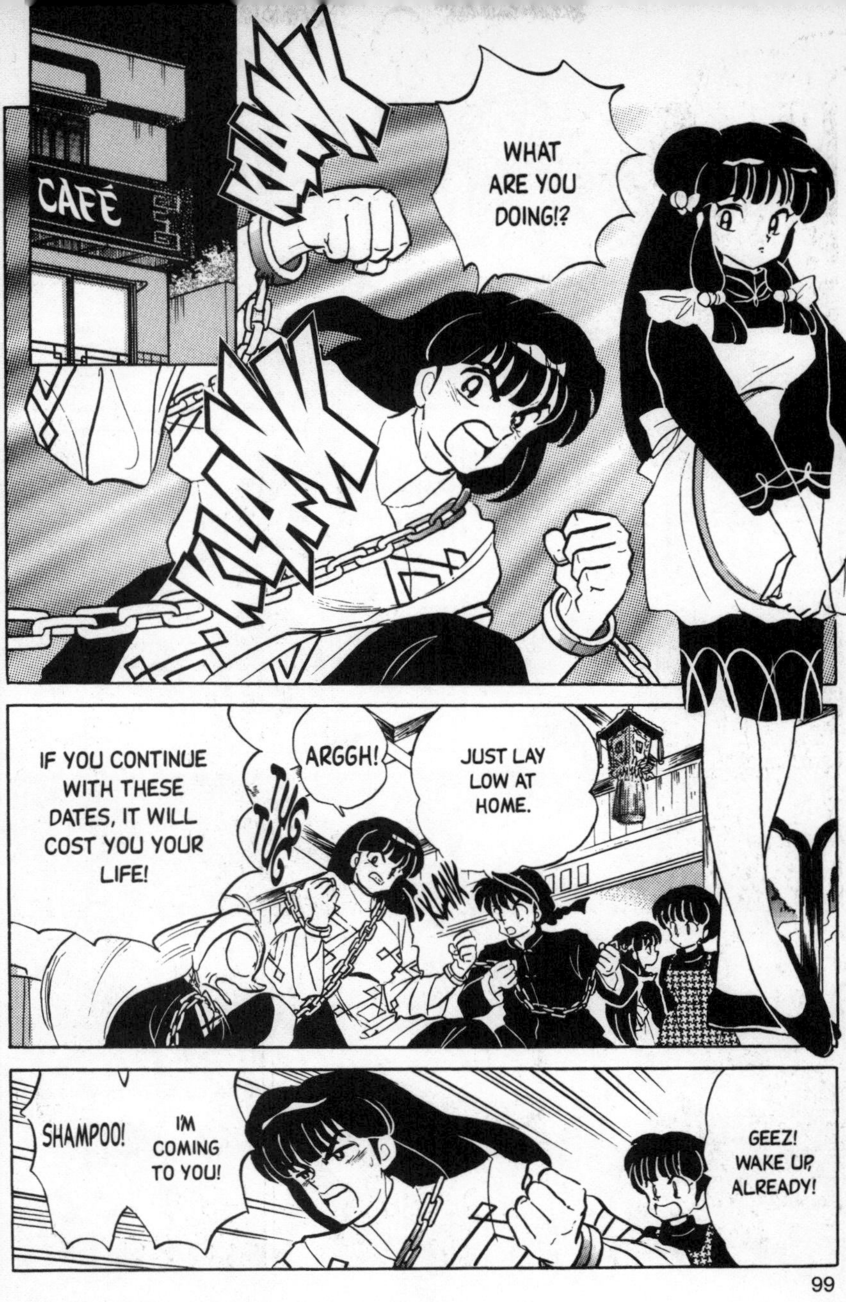
WHAT ARE YOU DOING!?
IF YOU CONTINUE WITH THESE DATES, IT WILL COST YOU YOUR LIFE!
ARGGH!
JUST LAY LOW AT HOME.
SHAMPOO!
I'M COMING TO YOU!
GEEZ! WAKE UP, ALREADY!

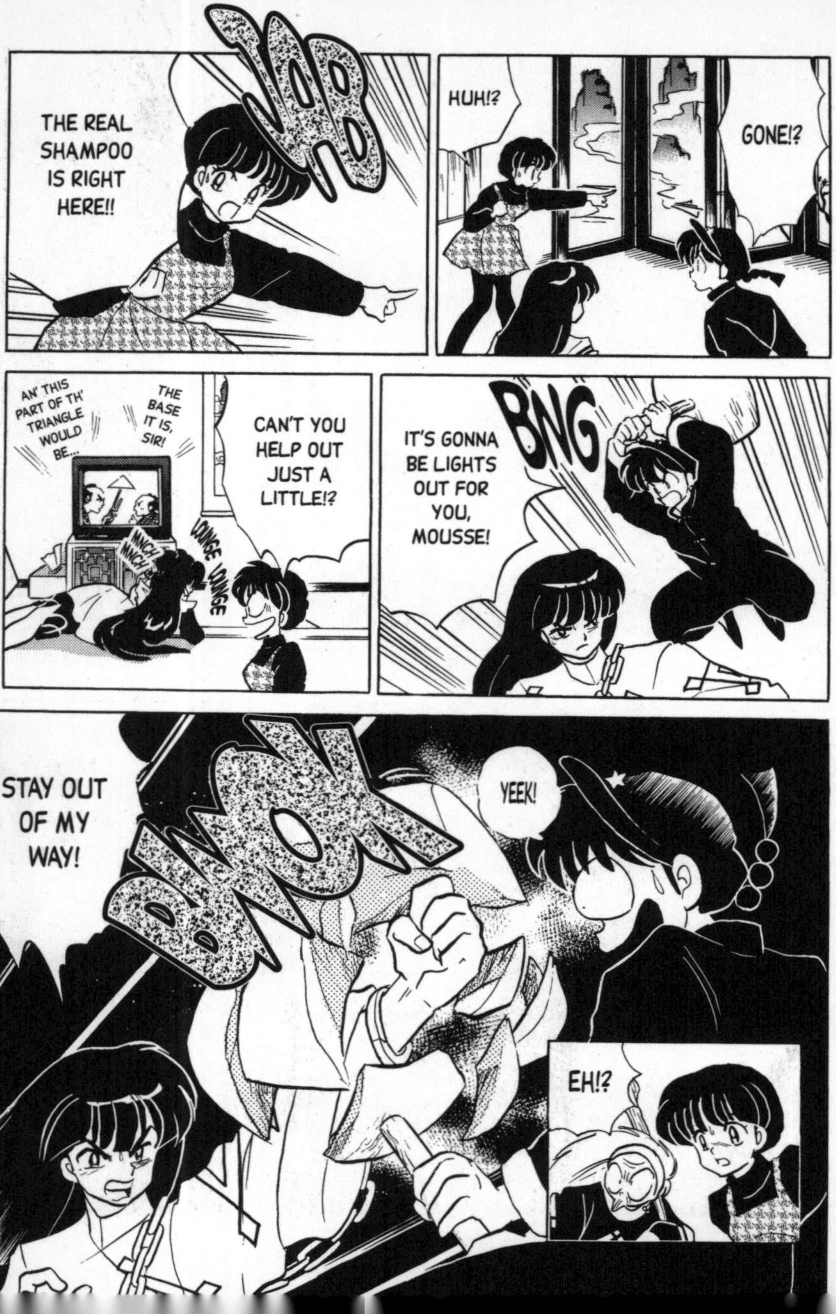
THE REAL SHAMPOO IS RIGHT HERE!!
HUH!?
GONE!?
AN' THIS PART OF TH' TRIANGLE WOULD BE...
THE BASE IT IS, SIR!
MNCH MNCH
LOUNGE LOUNGE
CAN'T YOU HELP OUT JUST A LITTLE!?
BNG
IT'S GONNA BE LIGHTS OUT FOR YOU, MOUSSE!
STAY OUT OF MY WAY!
YEEK!
EH!?

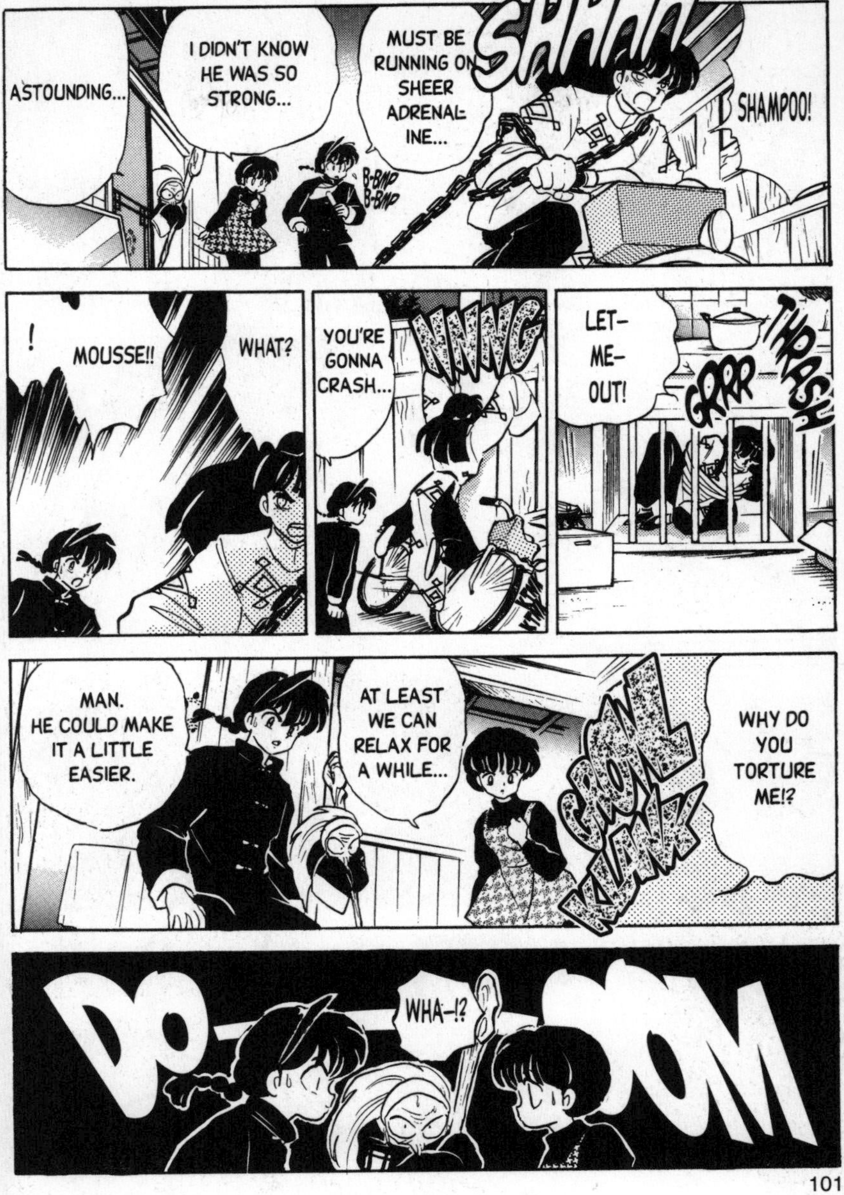
ASTOUNDING...
I DIDN'T KNOW HE WAS SO STRONG...
B-BMP B-BMP
MUST BE RUNNING ON SHEER ADRENAL-INE...
SHHH
SHAMPOO!
!
MOUSSE!!
WHAT?
YOU'RE GONNA CRASH...
NNNG
LET-ME-OUT!
GRRR
THRASH
MAN. HE COULD MAKE IT A LITTLE EASIER.
AT LEAST WE CAN RELAX FOR A WHILE...
CRONK
KLANK
WHY DO YOU TORTURE ME!?
DO-
WHA-!?
OOM

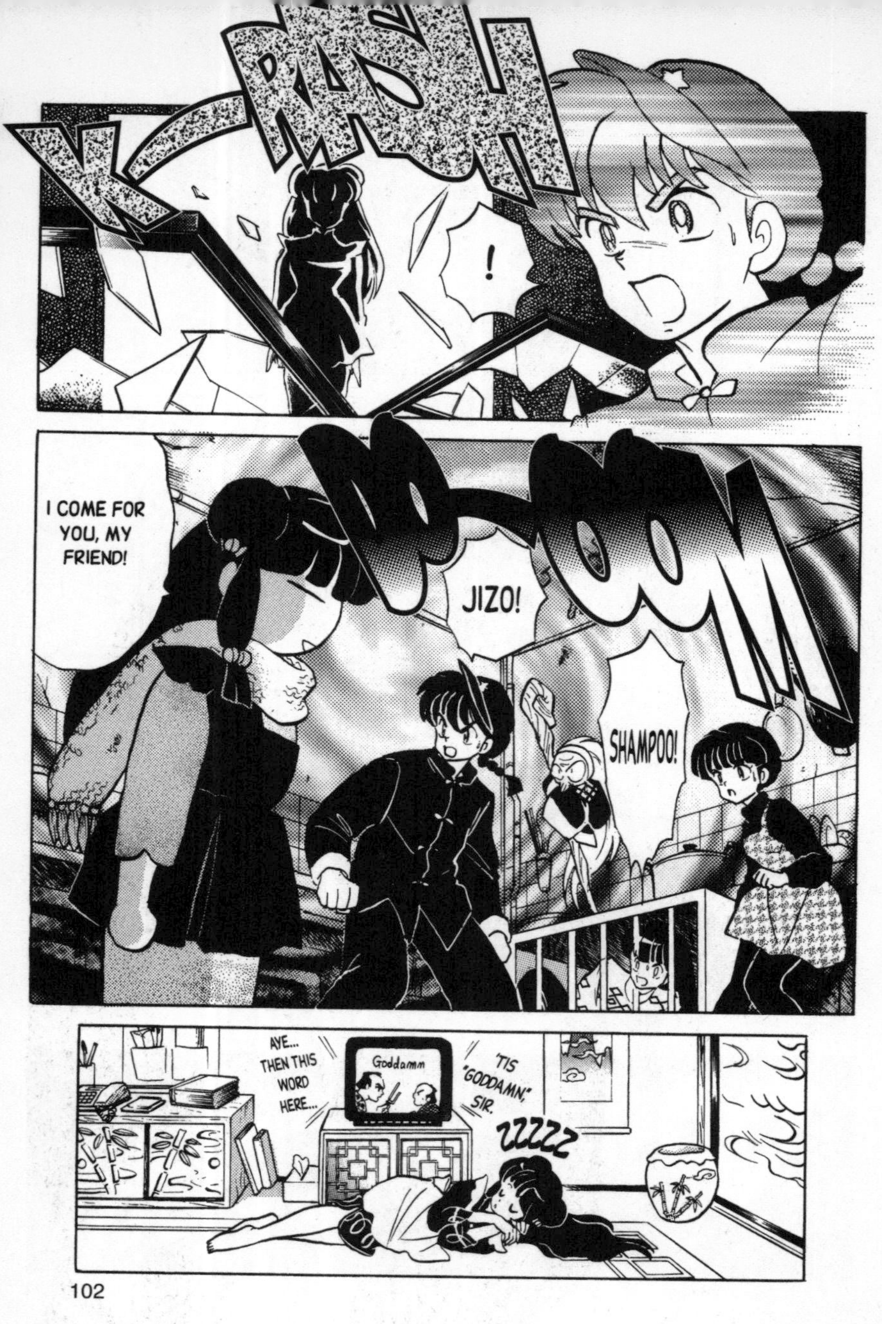
K-RASH
!
I COME FOR YOU, MY FRIEND!
JIZO!
SHAMPOO!
AYE... THEN THIS WORD HERE...
Goddamn
'TIS "GODDAMN," SIR.
ZZZZZ

PART 7

PAYBACK'S A SAINT

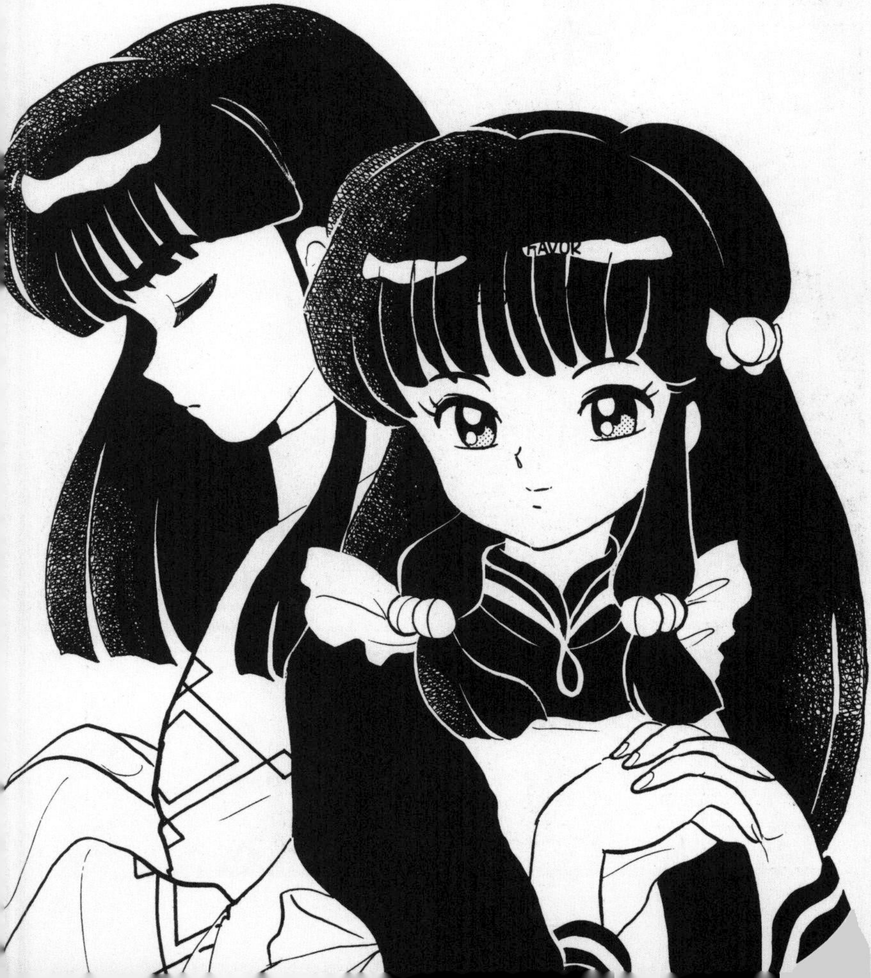

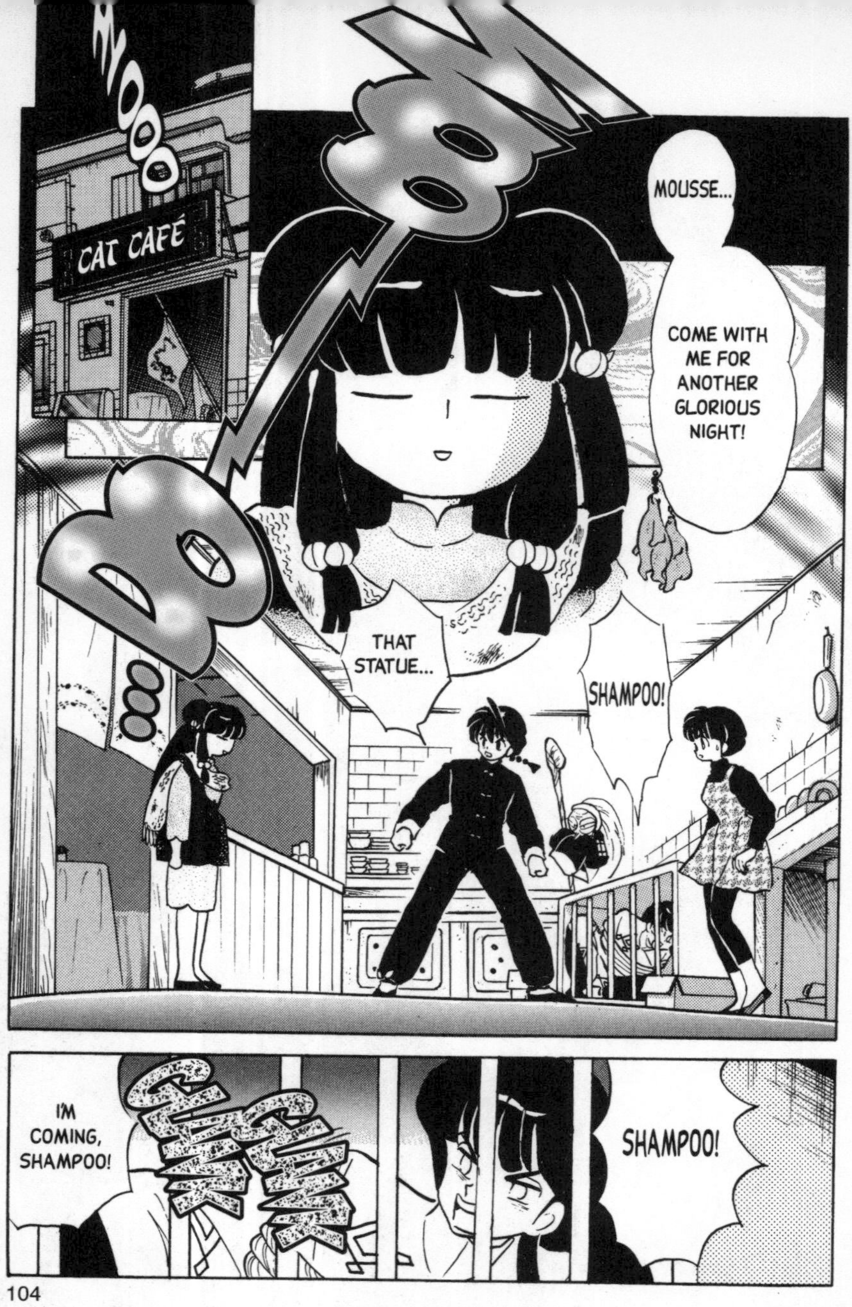
CAT CAFÉ
MOUSSE...
COME WITH ME FOR ANOTHER GLORIOUS NIGHT!
THAT STATUE...
SHAMPOO!
I'M COMING, SHAMPOO!
SHAMPOO!

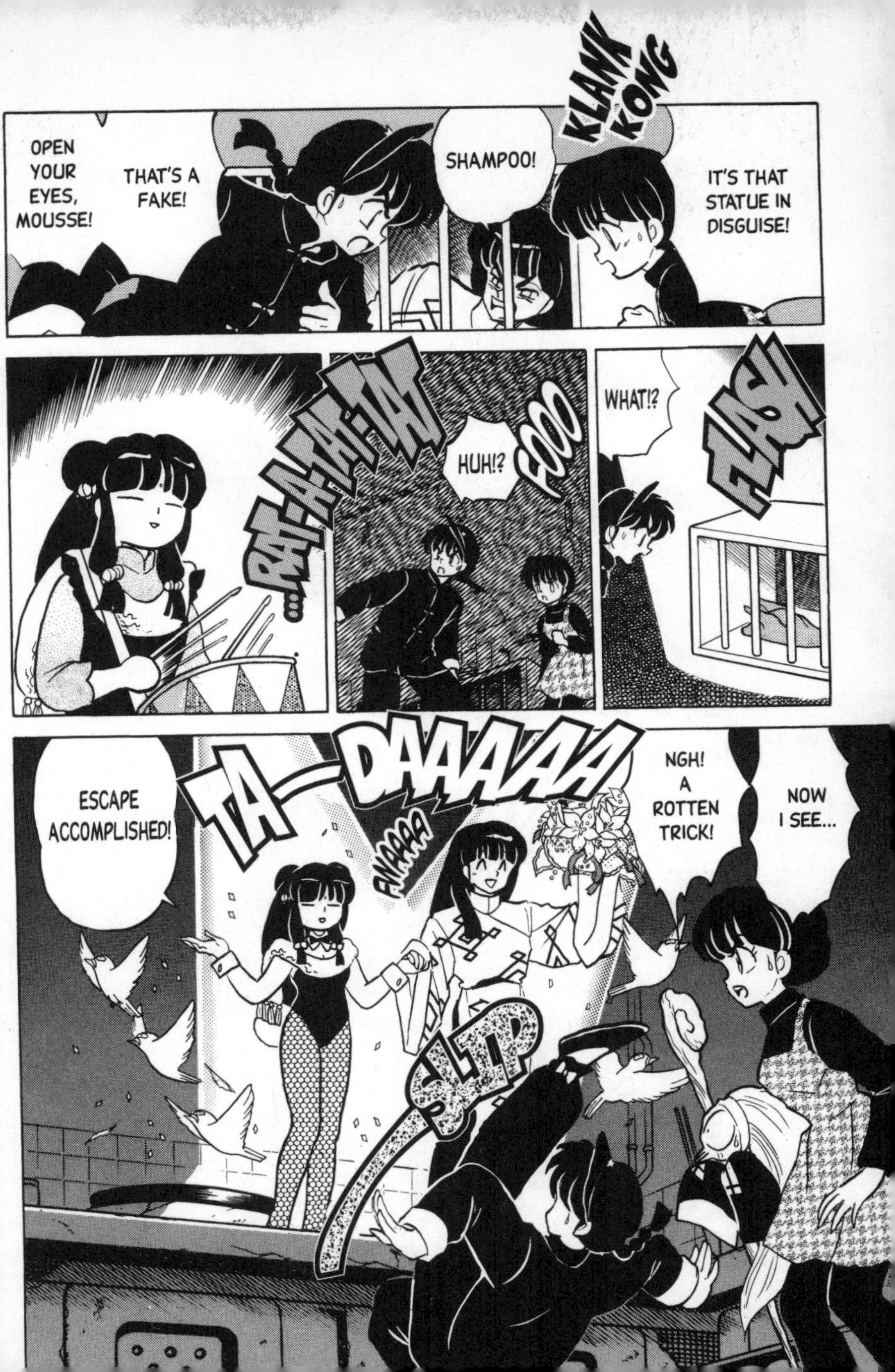
KLANK
KONG
OPEN YOUR EYES, MOUSSE!
THAT'S A FAKE!
SHAMPOO!
IT'S THAT STATUE IN DISGUISE!
...RAT-A-TAT-TAT
HUH!?
FOOOO
WHAT!?
FLASH
ESCAPE ACCOMPLISHED!
TA-DAAAAAA
AAAAAA
NGH! A ROTTEN TRICK!
NOW I SEE...
SLIP

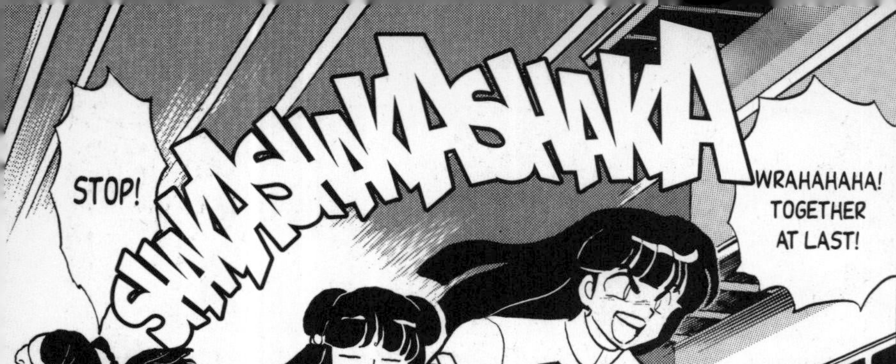
STOP!
SHAKASHAKASHAKA
WRAHAHAHA! TOGETHER AT LAST!

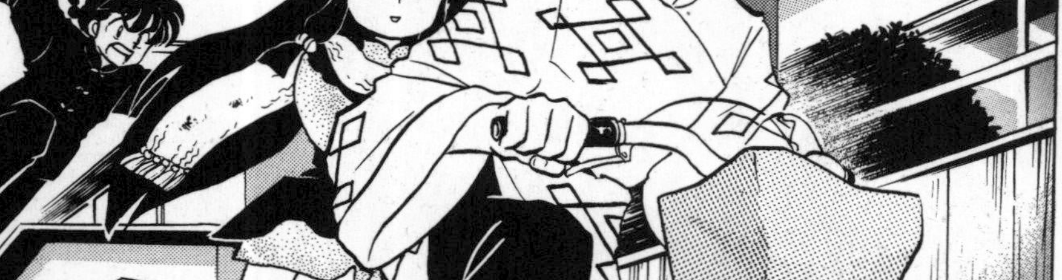
THE ONLY WAY TO BREAK THE SPELL BETWEEN MOUSSE AND THE STATUE IS TO...
TM TM TM
...GET THAT SCARF BACK!?

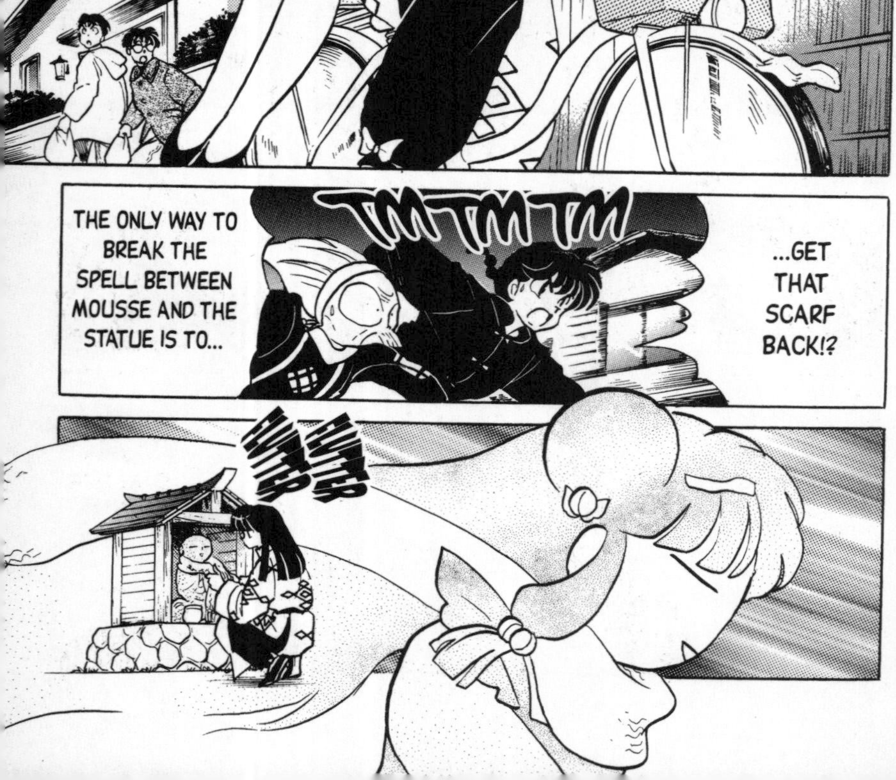
FLUTTER
FLUTTER

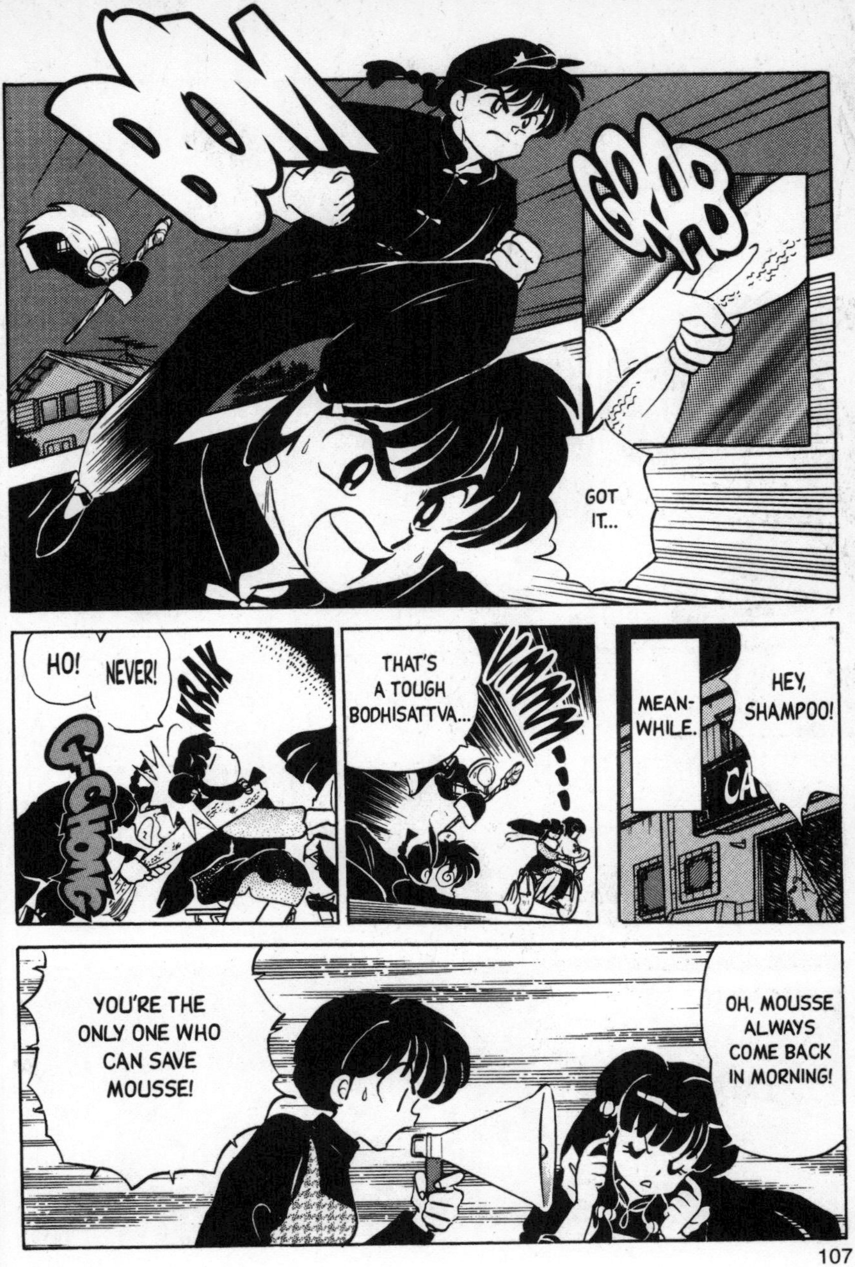
BOM
GRAB
GOT IT...
HO!
NEVER!
KRAK
G-CHONG
THAT'S A TOUGH BODHISATTVA...
MEAN-WHILE.
HEY, SHAMPOO!
YOU'RE THE ONLY ONE WHO CAN SAVE MOUSSE!
OH, MOUSSE ALWAYS COME BACK IN MORNING!

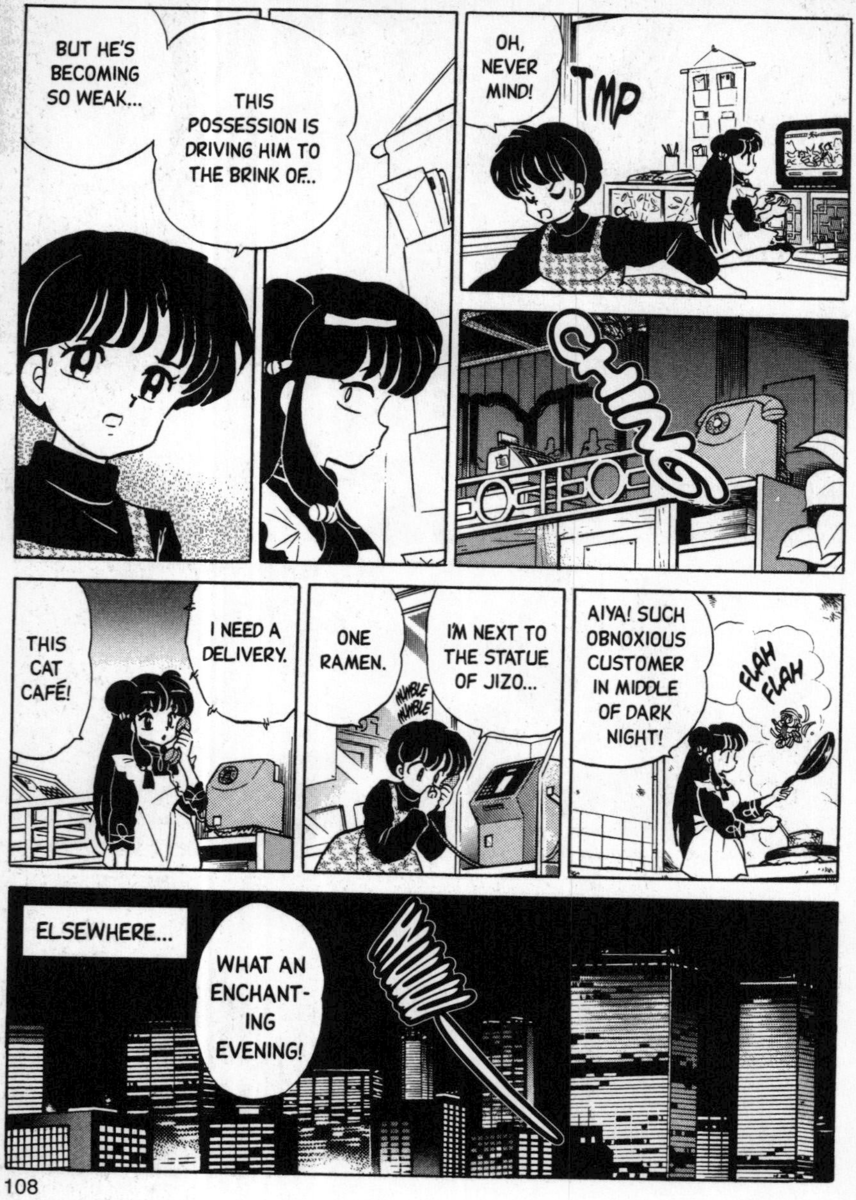
BUT HE'S BECOMING SO WEAK...
THIS POSSESSION IS DRIVING HIM TO THE BRINK OF..
OH, NEVER MIND!
TMP
CHING
THIS CAT CAFÉ!
I NEED A DELIVERY.
ONE RAMEN.
MUMBLE MUMBLE
I'M NEXT TO THE STATUE OF JIZO...
AIYA! SUCH OBNOXIOUS CUSTOMER IN MIDDLE OF DARK NIGHT!
FLAH FLAH
ELSEWHERE...
WHAT AN ENCHANT-ING EVENING!

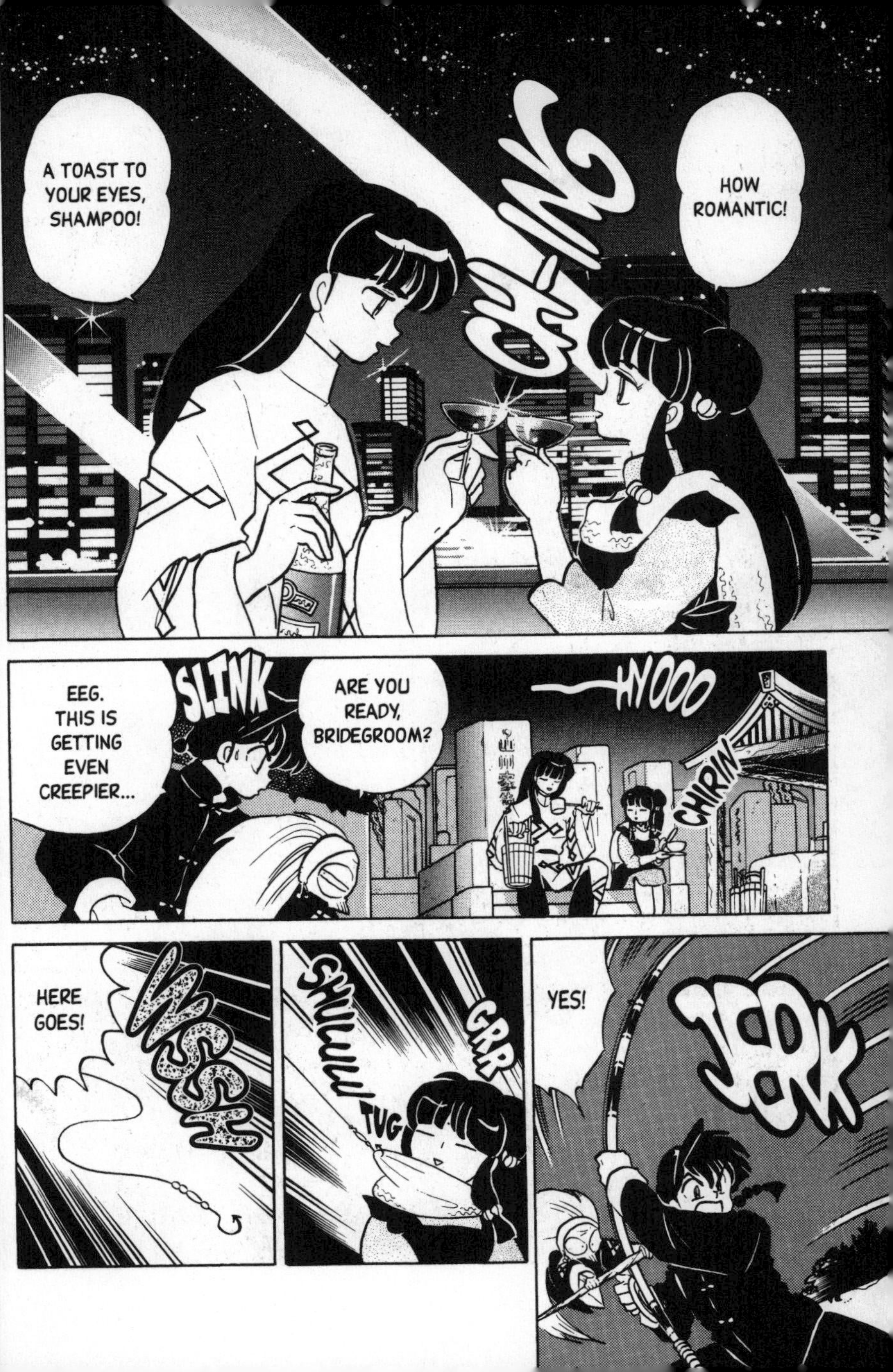
A TOAST TO YOUR EYES, SHAMPOO!
CHING
HOW ROMANTIC!
EEG. THIS IS GETTING EVEN CREEPIER...
SLINK
ARE YOU READY, BRIDEGROOM?
HYOOO
CHIRIN
HERE GOES!
WSSH
SHUUU
GRR
TUG
YES!
JERK

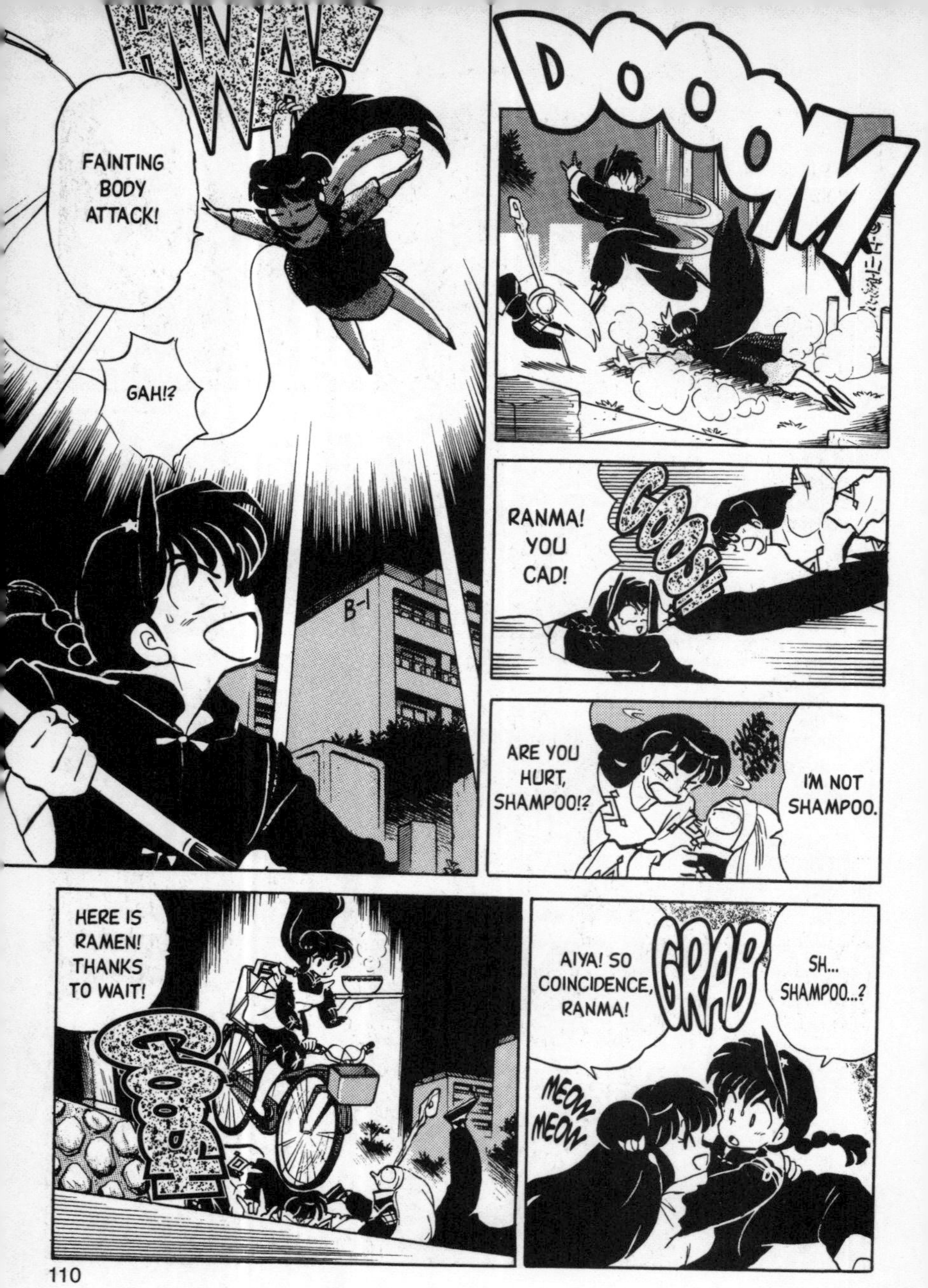
HWA!
FAINTING BODY ATTACK!
GAH!?
DOOOOM
RANMA! YOU CAD!
ARE YOU HURT, SHAMPOO!?
I'M NOT SHAMPOO.
HERE IS RAMEN! THANKS TO WAIT!
AIYA! SO COINCIDENCE, RANMA!
GRAB
SH... SHAMPOO...?
MEOW MEOW

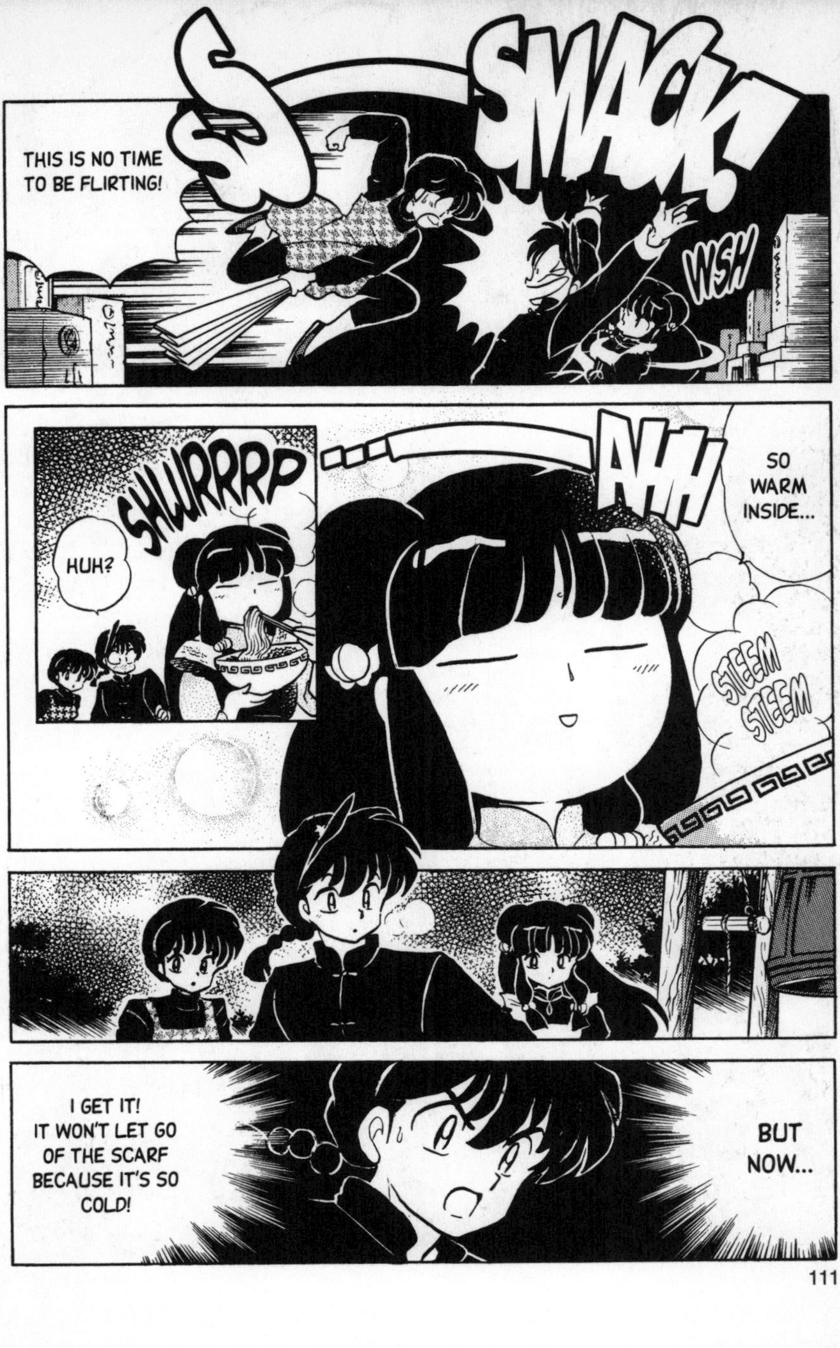

THIS IS NO TIME TO BE FLIRTING!
S—SMACK!
WSH
SHWURRRP
HUH?
...AHH
SO WARM INSIDE...
STEEM STEEM
I GET IT! IT WON'T LET GO OF THE SCARF BECAUSE IT'S SO COLD!
BUT NOW...

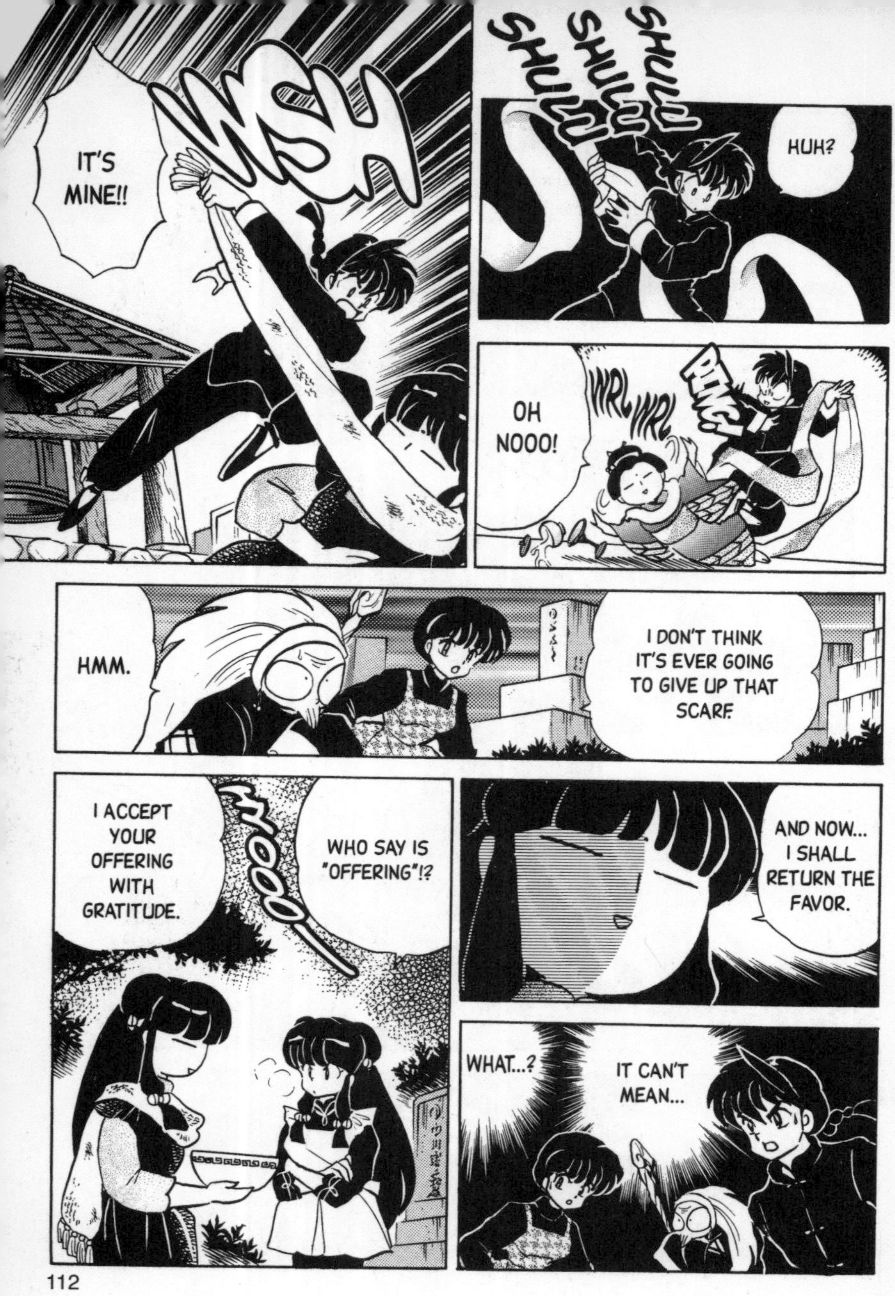

IT'S MINE!!
WSH
SHULU SHULU SHULU
HUH?
OH NOOO!
WRL WRL
HMM.
I DON'T THINK IT'S EVER GOING TO GIVE UP THAT SCARF.
I ACCEPT YOUR OFFERING WITH GRATITUDE.
WHO SAY IS "OFFERING"!?
AND NOW... I SHALL RETURN THE FAVOR.
WHAT...?
IT CAN'T MEAN...

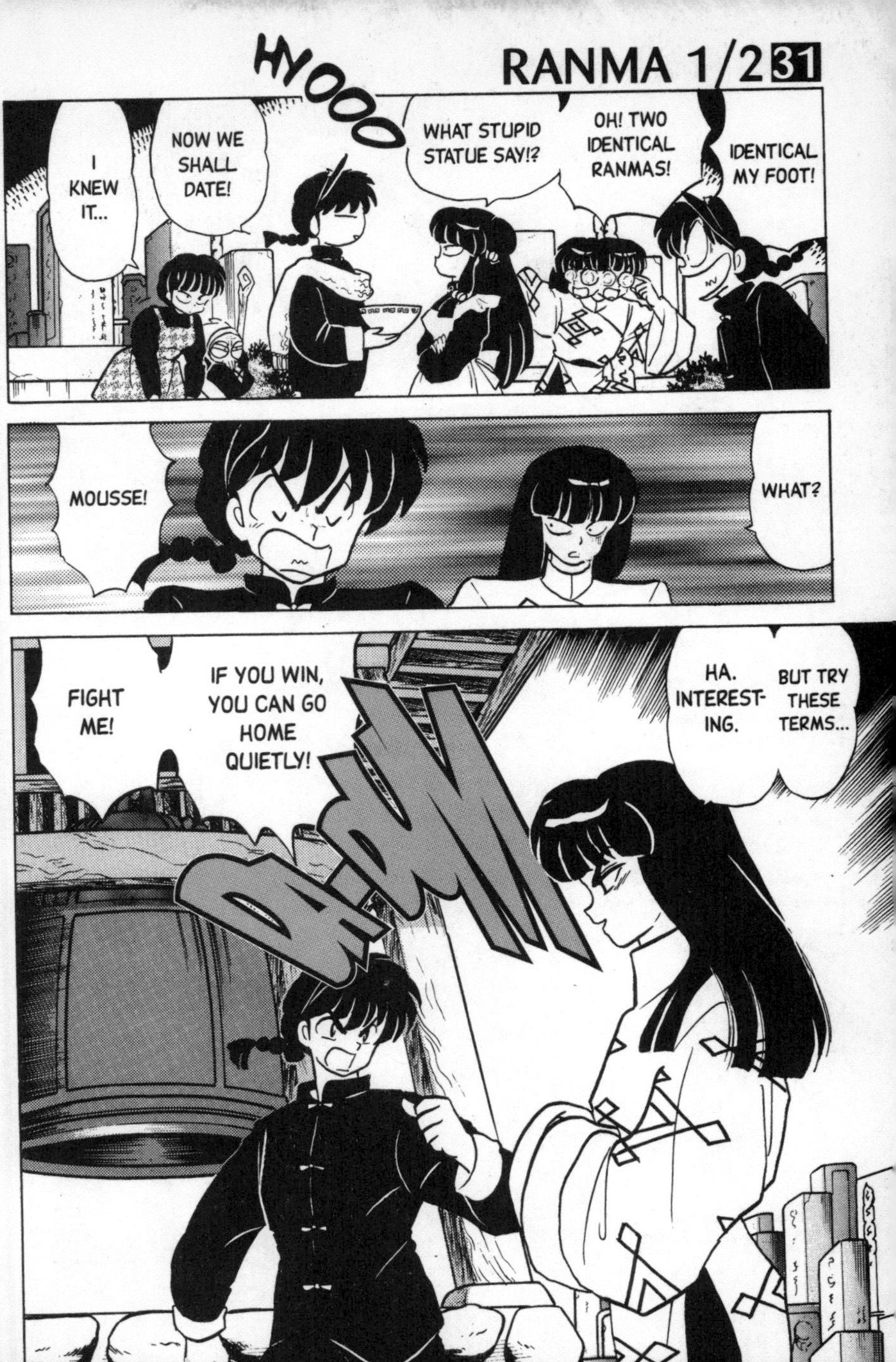
HYOOO
I KNEW IT...
NOW WE SHALL DATE!
WHAT STUPID STATUE SAY!?
OH! TWO IDENTICAL RANMAS!
IDENTICAL MY FOOT!
MOUSSE!
WHAT?
FIGHT ME!
IF YOU WIN, YOU CAN GO HOME QUIETLY!
BAM
HA. INTEREST-ING.
BUT TRY THESE TERMS...

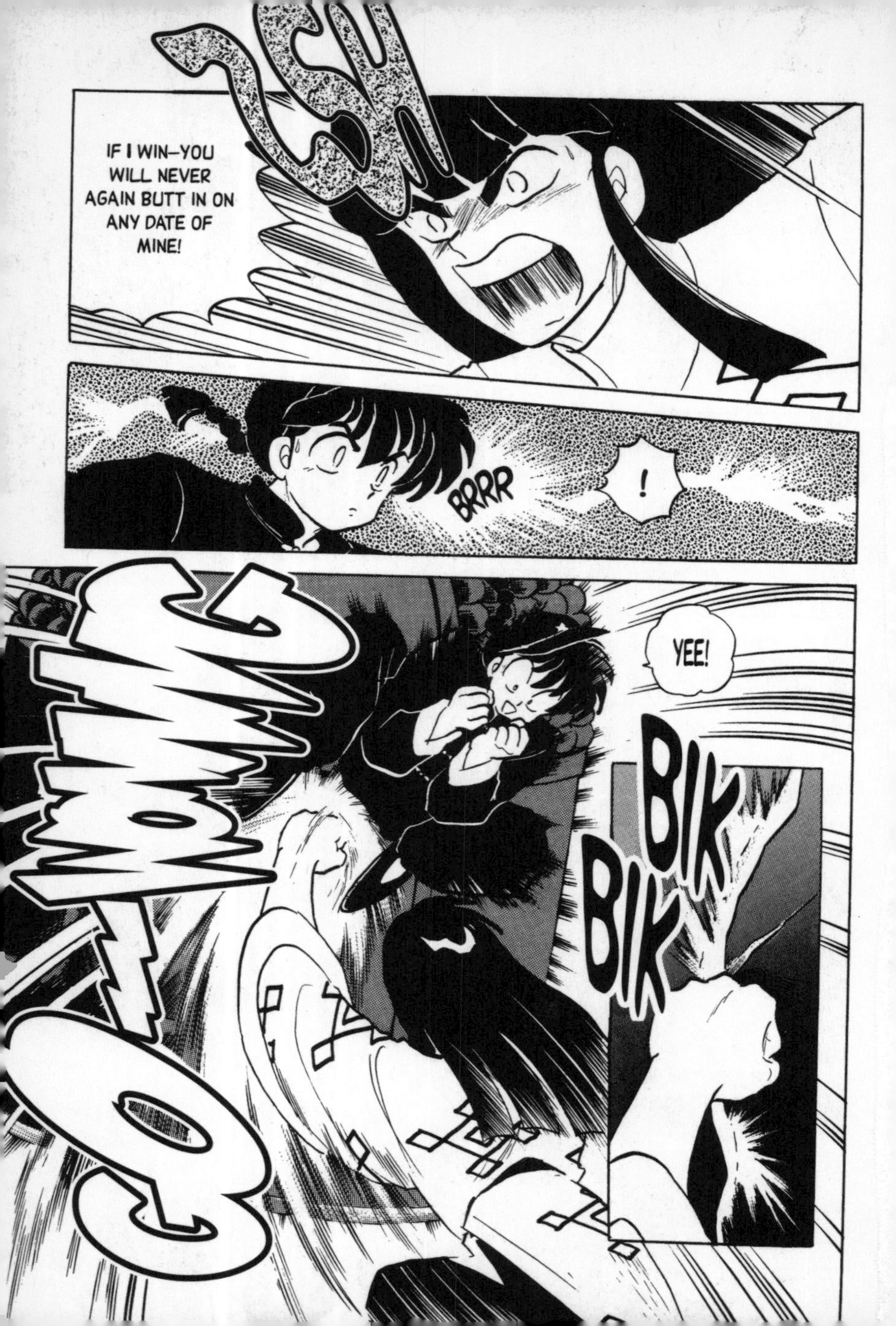
IF I WIN—YOU WILL NEVER AGAIN BUTT IN ON ANY DATE OF MINE!
BRRR
!
YEE!
BIK
BIK

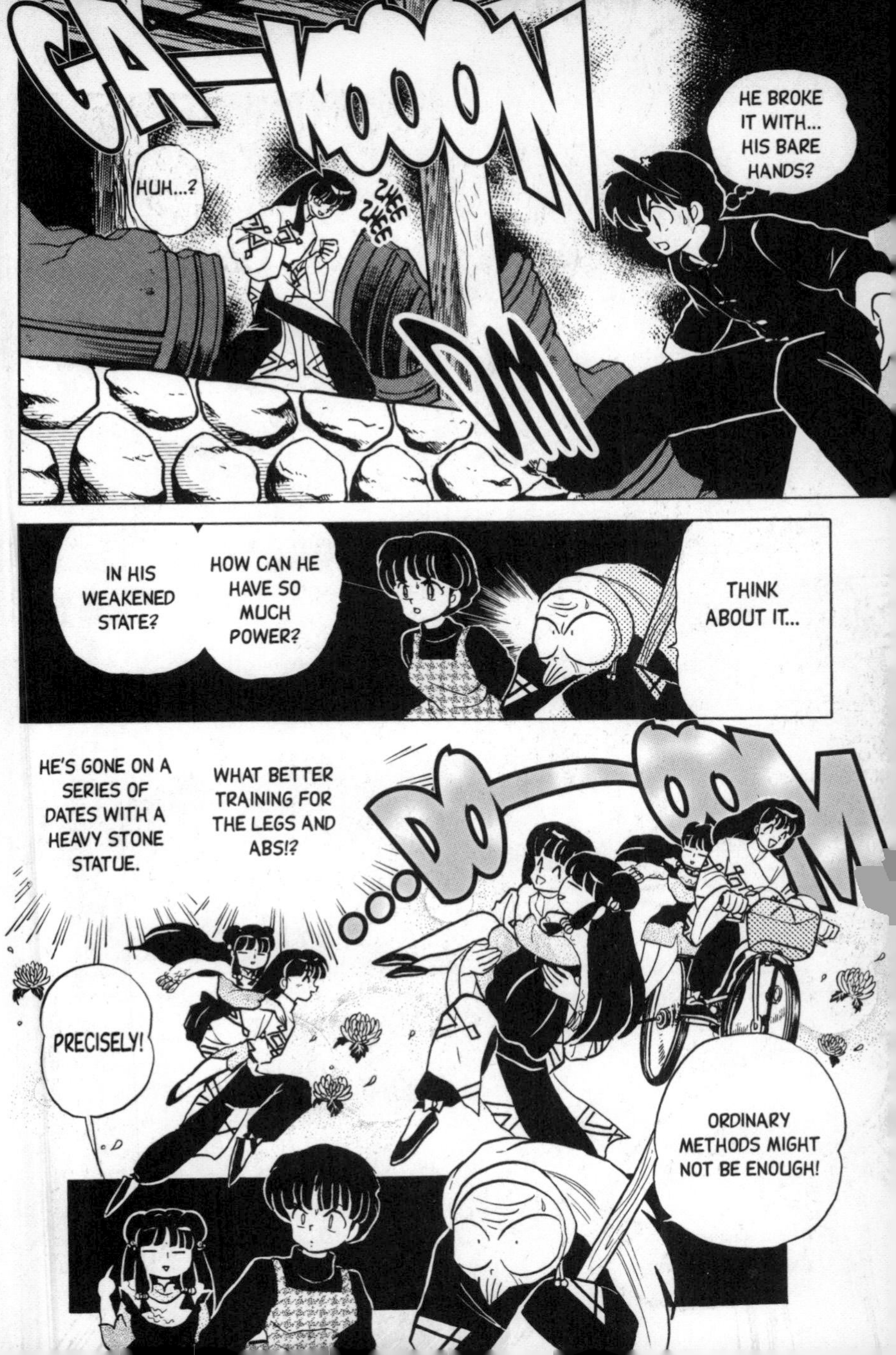
GA-KOOOON
HUH...?
DM
HE BROKE IT WITH... HIS BARE HANDS?
IN HIS WEAKENED STATE?
HOW CAN HE HAVE SO MUCH POWER?
THINK ABOUT IT...
HE'S GONE ON A SERIES OF DATES WITH A HEAVY STONE STATUE.
WHAT BETTER TRAINING FOR THE LEGS AND ABS!?
PRECISELY!
ORDINARY METHODS MIGHT NOT BE ENOUGH!

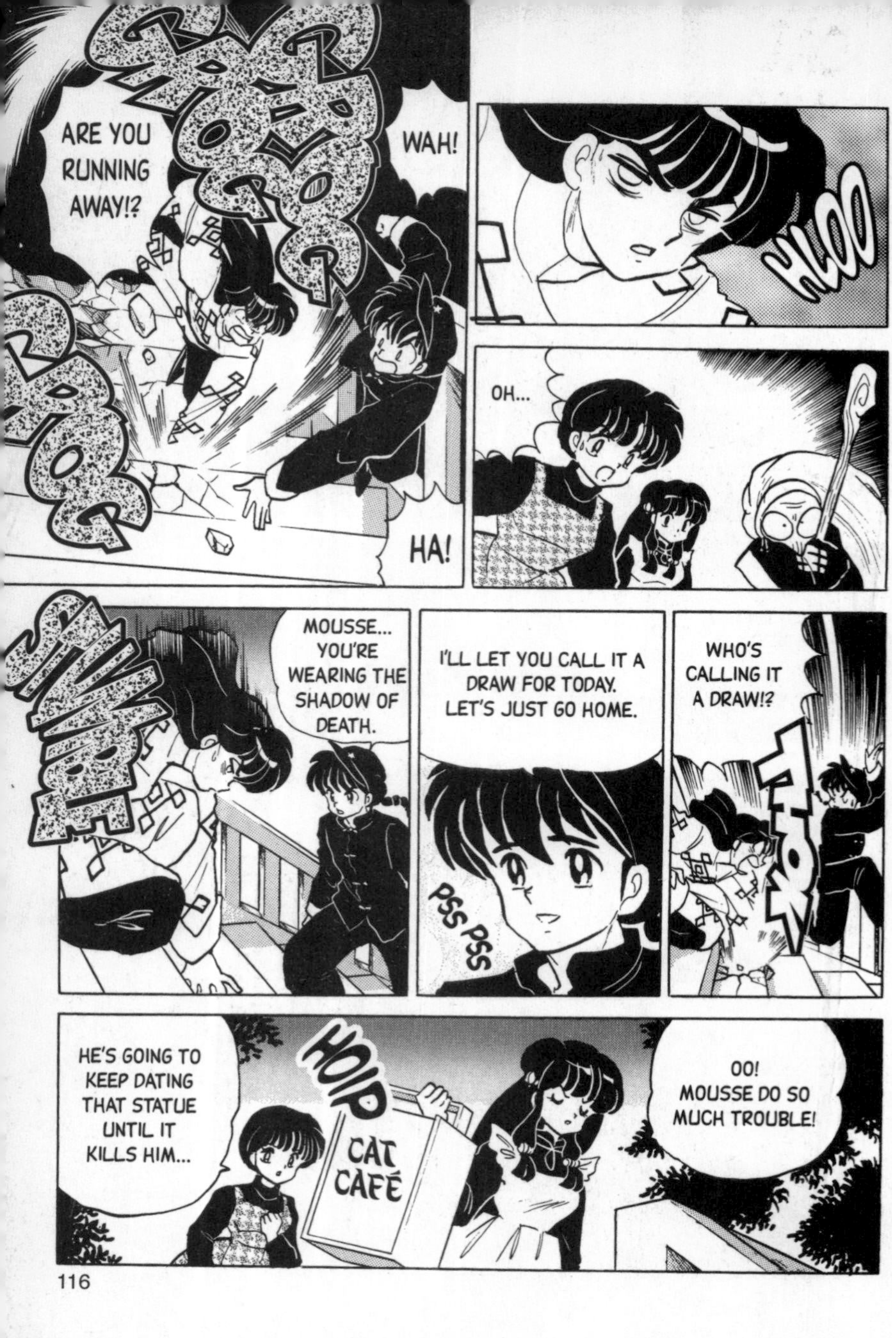
ARE YOU RUNNING AWAY!?
WAH!
HA!
OH...
MOUSSE... YOU'RE WEARING THE SHADOW OF DEATH.
I'LL LET YOU CALL IT A DRAW FOR TODAY. LET'S JUST GO HOME.
PSS PSS
WHO'S CALLING IT A DRAW!?
HE'S GOING TO KEEP DATING THAT STATUE UNTIL IT KILLS HIM...
HOIP
CAT CAFÉ
OO! MOUSSE DO SO MUCH TROUBLE!

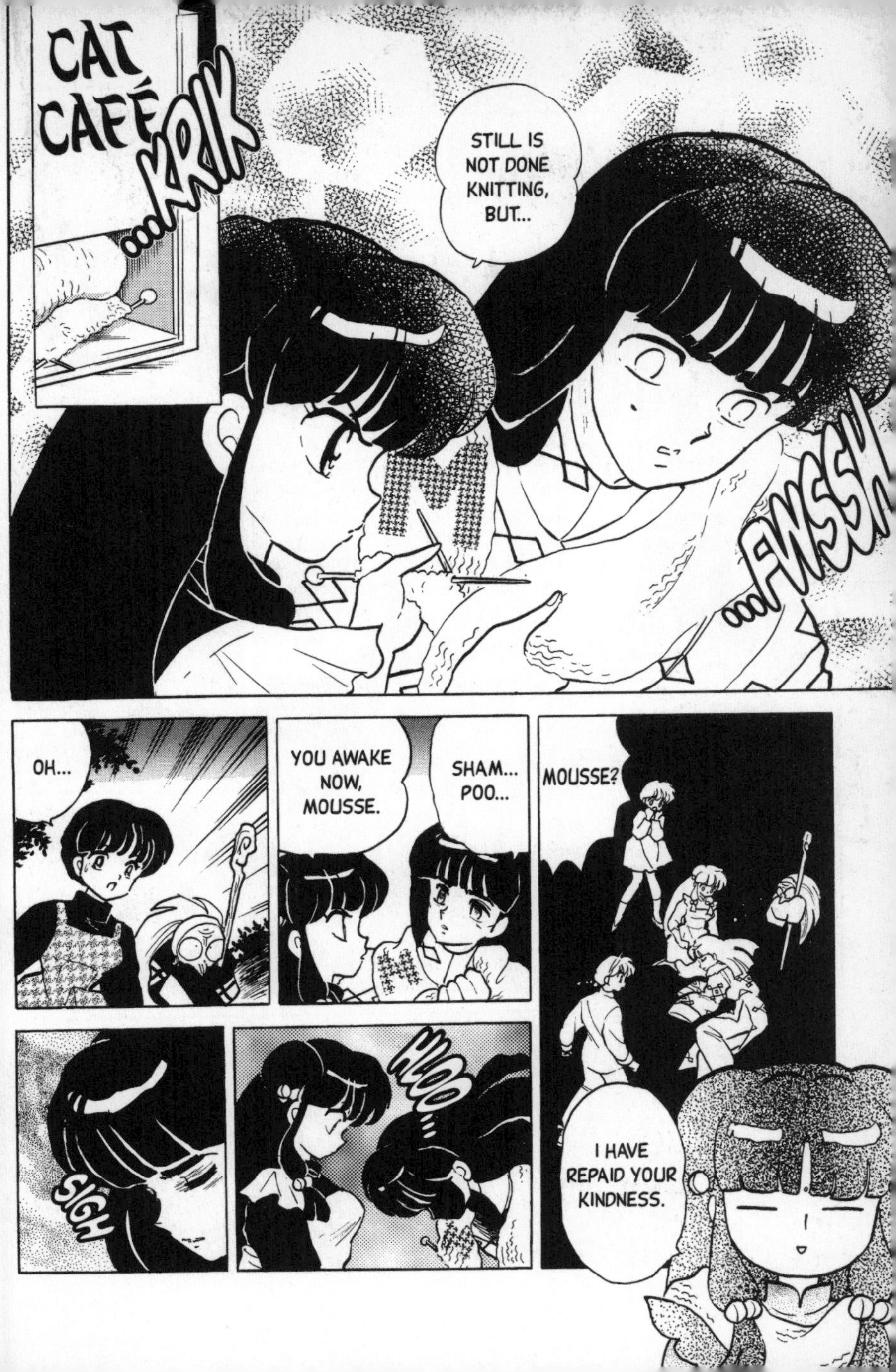
CAT CAFÉ
...KRIK
STILL IS NOT DONE KNITTING, BUT...
...FWSSH
OH...
YOU AWAKE NOW, MOUSSE.
SHAM... POO...
MOUSSE?
SIGH
HWOO...
I HAVE REPAID YOUR KINDNESS.

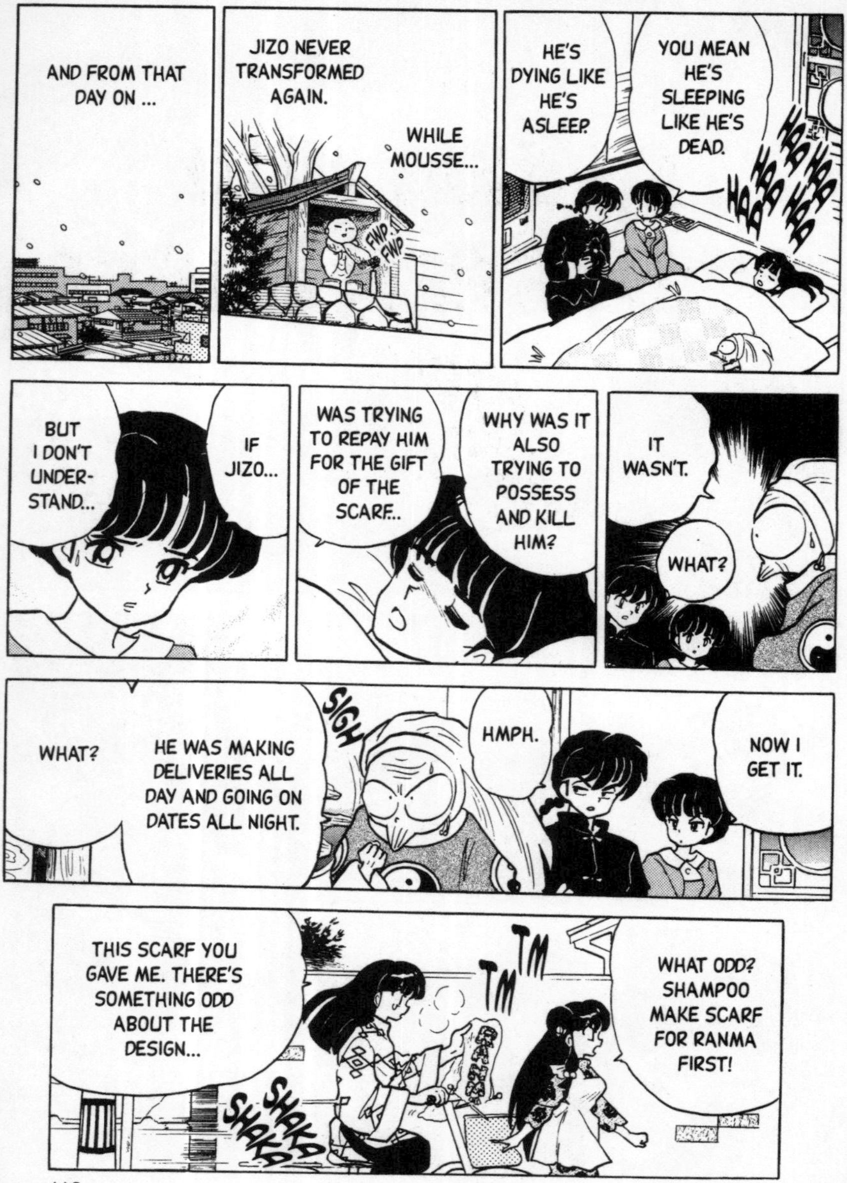
AND FROM THAT DAY ON ...
JIZO NEVER TRANSFORMED AGAIN.
WHILE MOUSSE...
FWP FWP
HE'S DYING LIKE HE'S ASLEEP?
YOU MEAN HE'S SLEEPING LIKE HE'S DEAD.
HAA HAA HAA HAA
BUT I DON'T UNDER-STAND...
IF JIZO...
WAS TRYING TO REPAY HIM FOR THE GIFT OF THE SCARF...
WHY WAS IT ALSO TRYING TO POSSESS AND KILL HIM?
IT WASN'T.
WHAT?
WHAT?
HE WAS MAKING DELIVERIES ALL DAY AND GOING ON DATES ALL NIGHT.
SIGH
HMPH.
NOW I GET IT.
THIS SCARF YOU GAVE ME. THERE'S SOMETHING ODD ABOUT THE DESIGN...
TM TM TM
SHAKA SHAKA
WHAT ODD? SHAMPOO MAKE SCARF FOR RANMA FIRST!

PART 8

DRAWN AND QUARTERED HORSE

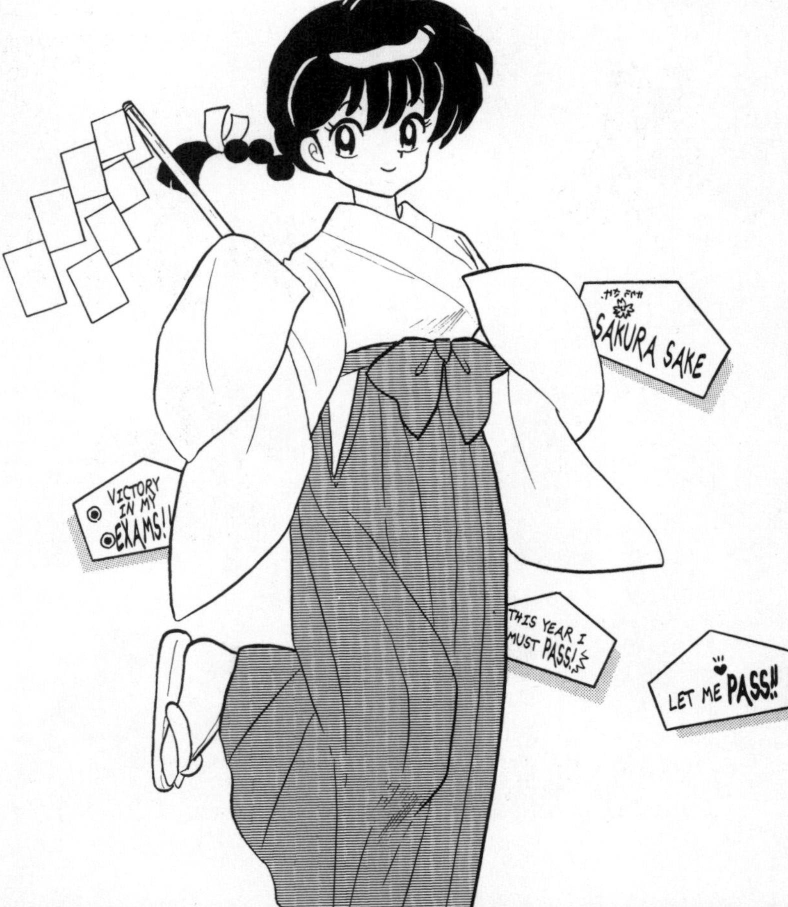
SAKURA SAKE
VICTORY IN MY EXAMS!!
THIS YEAR I MUST PASS!
LET ME PASS!!

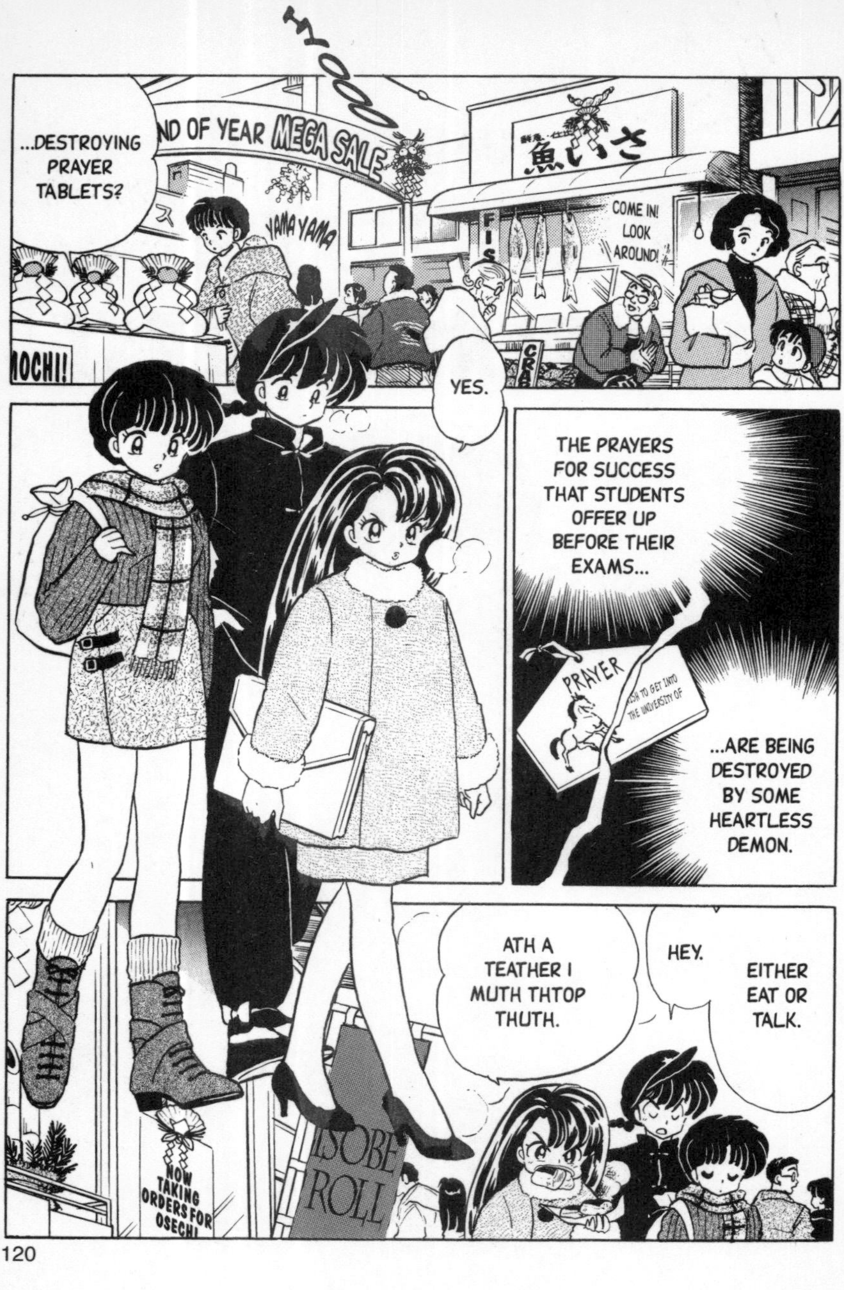
HYOOOO
...DESTROYING PRAYER TABLETS?
ND OF YEAR MEGA SALE
YAMA YAMA
COME IN! LOOK AROUND!
魚いさ
MOCHI!
YES.
THE PRAYERS FOR SUCCESS THAT STUDENTS OFFER UP BEFORE THEIR EXAMS...
PRAYER
THE UNIVERSITY OF
...ARE BEING DESTROYED BY SOME HEARTLESS DEMON.
NOW TAKING ORDERS FOR OSECHI
ISOBE ROLL
ATH A TEATHER I MUTH THTOP THUTH.
HEY.
EITHER EAT OR TALK.

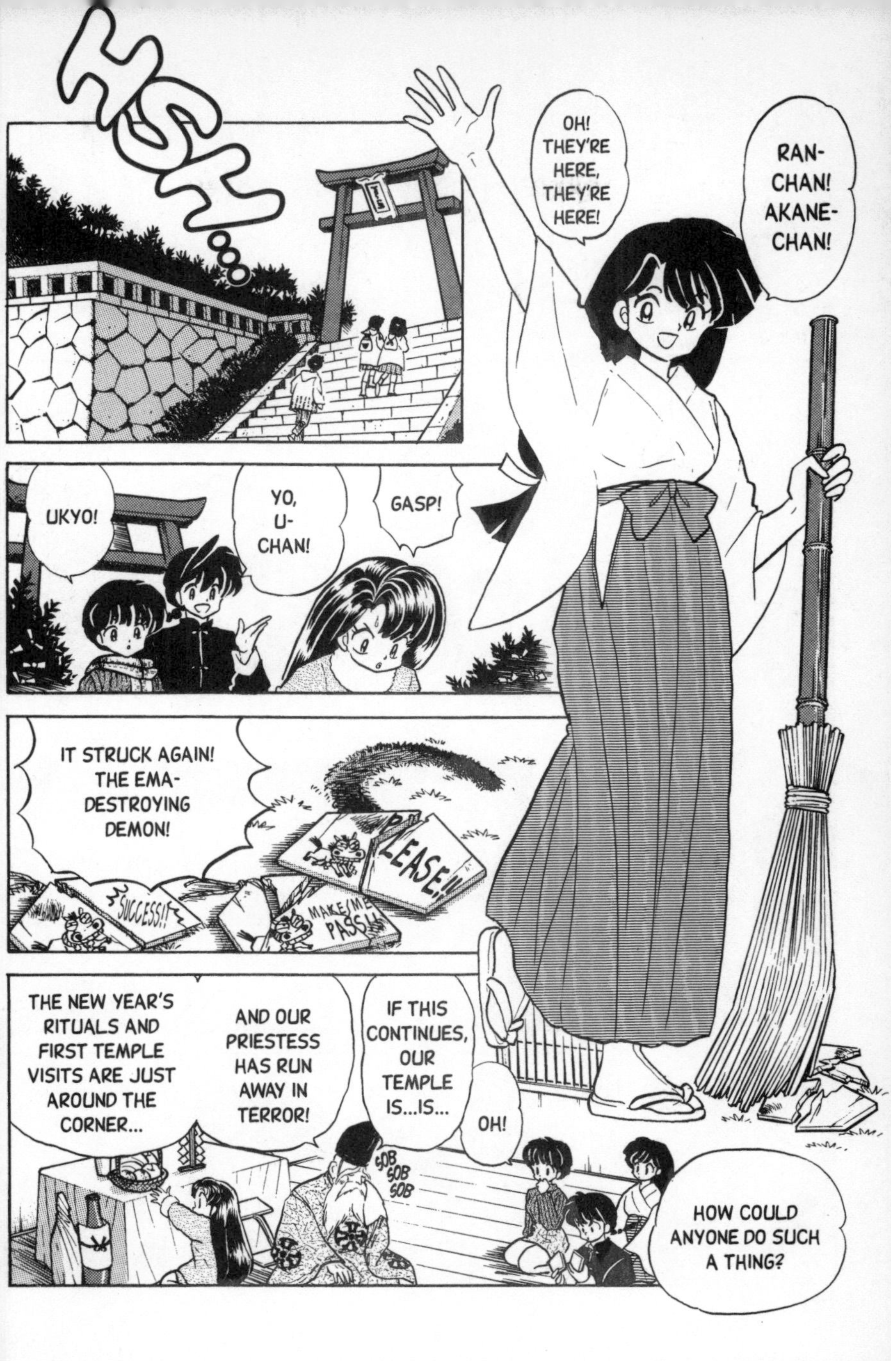
HSH...
UKYO!
YO, U-CHAN!
GASP!
IT STRUCK AGAIN! THE EMA-DESTROYING DEMON!
SUCCESS!!
MAKE ME PASS!!
PLEASE!!
OH! THEY'RE HERE, THEY'RE HERE!
RAN-CHAN! AKANE-CHAN!
THE NEW YEAR'S RITUALS AND FIRST TEMPLE VISITS ARE JUST AROUND THE CORNER...
AND OUR PRIESTESS HAS RUN AWAY IN TERROR!
IF THIS CONTINUES, OUR TEMPLE IS...IS...
OH!
SOB SOB SOB
HOW COULD ANYONE DO SUCH A THING?

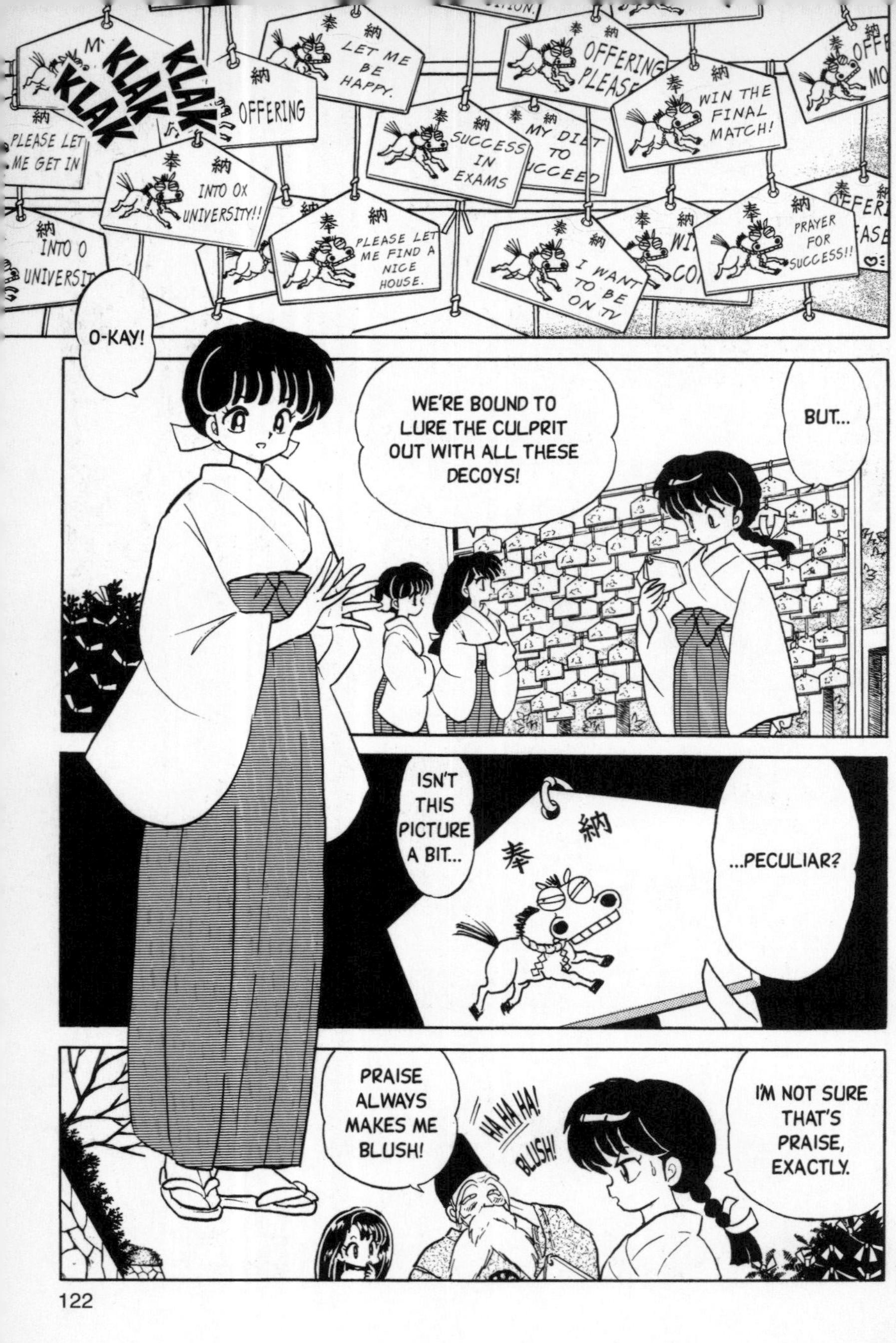

PLEASE LET ME GET IN
KLAK KLAK KLAK
OFFERING
INTO OX UNIVERSITY!!
INTO O UNIVERSIT
LET ME BE HAPPY.
PLEASE LET ME FIND A NICE HOUSE.
SUCCESS IN EXAMS
MY DIET TO SUCCEED
OFFERING PLEASE
I WANT TO BE ON TV
WIN THE FINAL MATCH!
PRAYER FOR SUCCESS!!
O-KAY!
WE'RE BOUND TO LURE THE CULPRIT OUT WITH ALL THESE DECOYS!
BUT...
ISN'T THIS PICTURE A BIT...
...PECULIAR?
PRAISE ALWAYS MAKES ME BLUSH!
HA HA HA!
BLUSH!
I'M NOT SURE THAT'S PRAISE, EXACTLY.

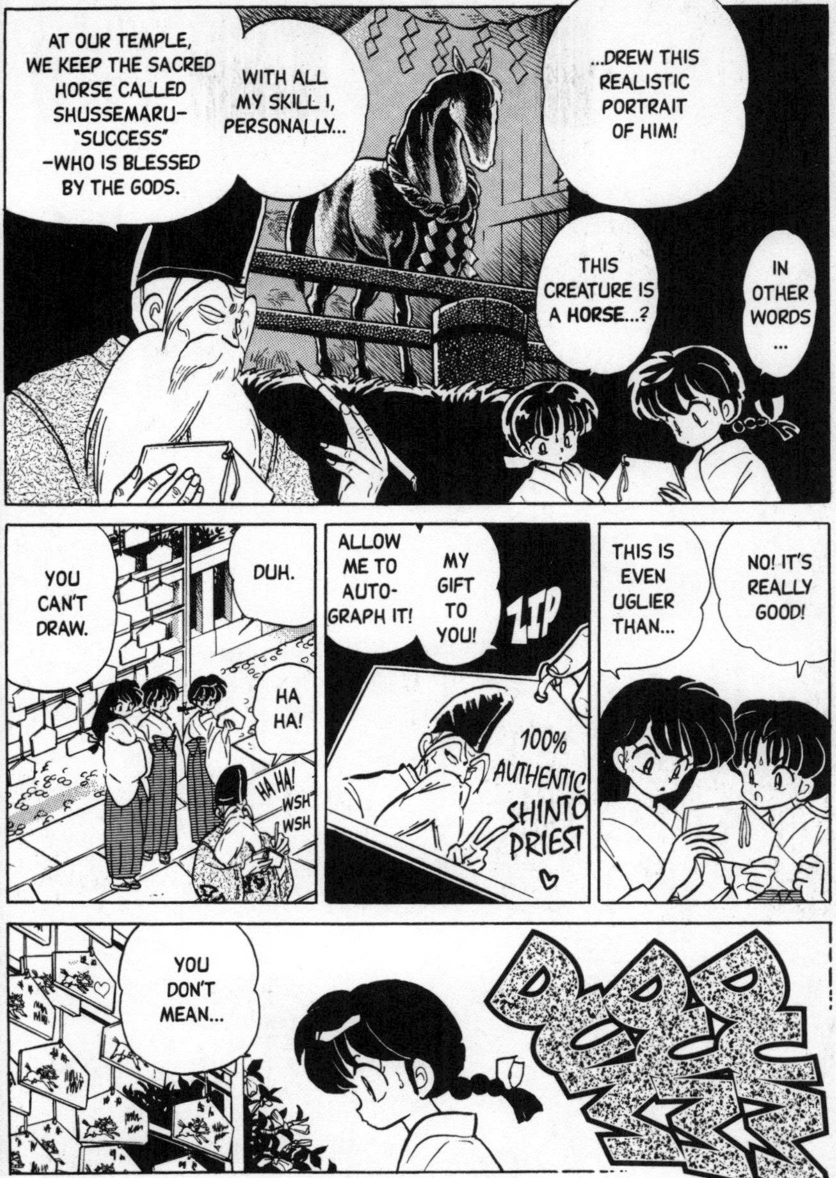
AT OUR TEMPLE, WE KEEP THE SACRED HORSE CALLED SHUSSEMARU– "SUCCESS" –WHO IS BLESSED BY THE GODS.
WITH ALL MY SKILL I, PERSONALLY...
...DREW THIS REALISTIC PORTRAIT OF HIM!
THIS CREATURE IS A HORSE...?
IN OTHER WORDS ...
YOU CAN'T DRAW.
DUH.
HA HA!
HA HA!
WSH WSH
ALLOW ME TO AUTO-GRAPH IT!
MY GIFT TO YOU!
ZIP
100% AUTHENTIC SHINTO PRIEST
THIS IS EVEN UGLIER THAN...
NO! IT'S REALLY GOOD!
YOU DON'T MEAN...
DODODODODO

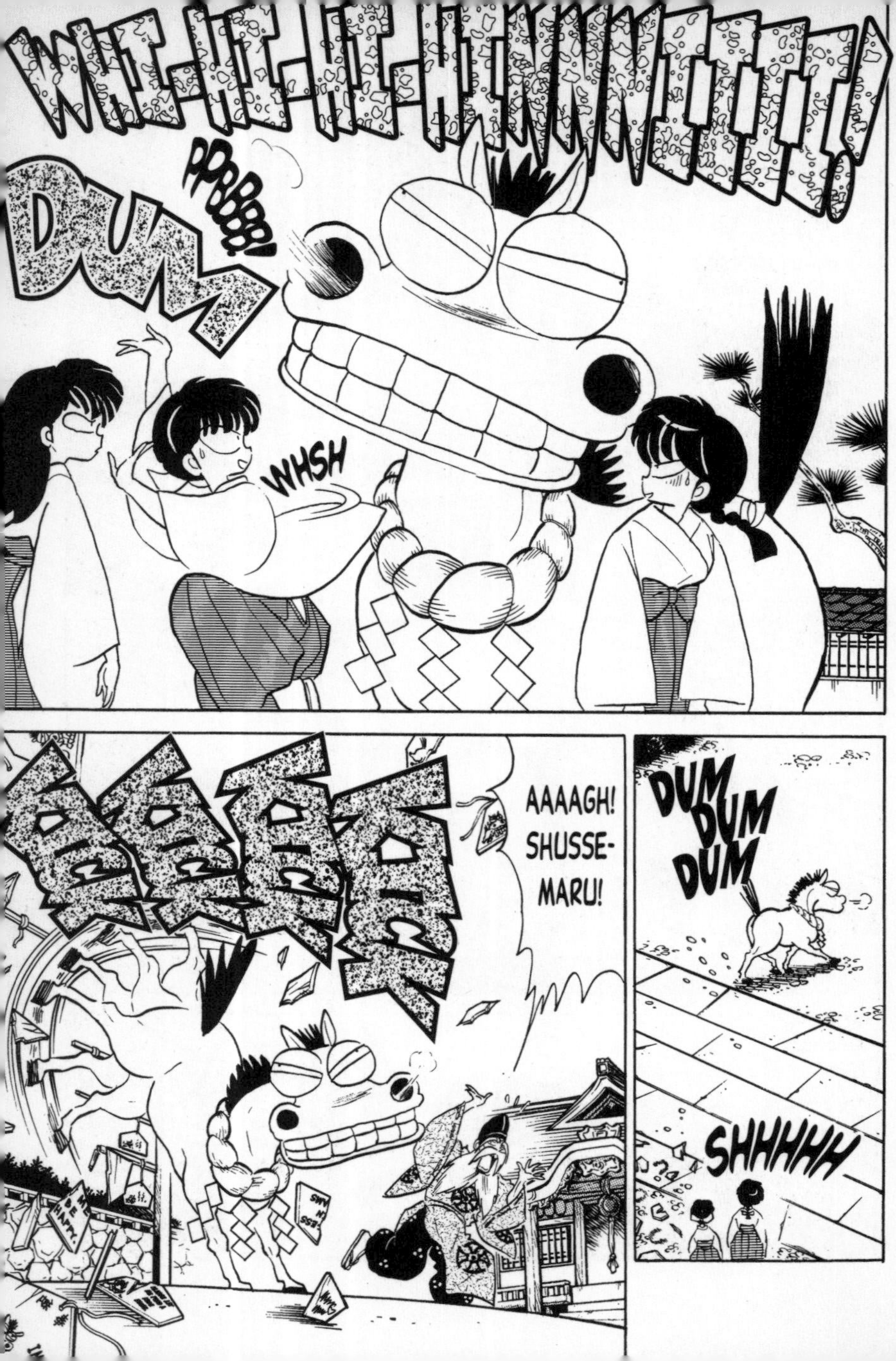

WHI-HI-HI-HINNNOOOT!
DUM
PPRRBBB!
WHSH
AAAAGH! SHUSSE-MARU!
DUM DUM DUM
SHHHHH

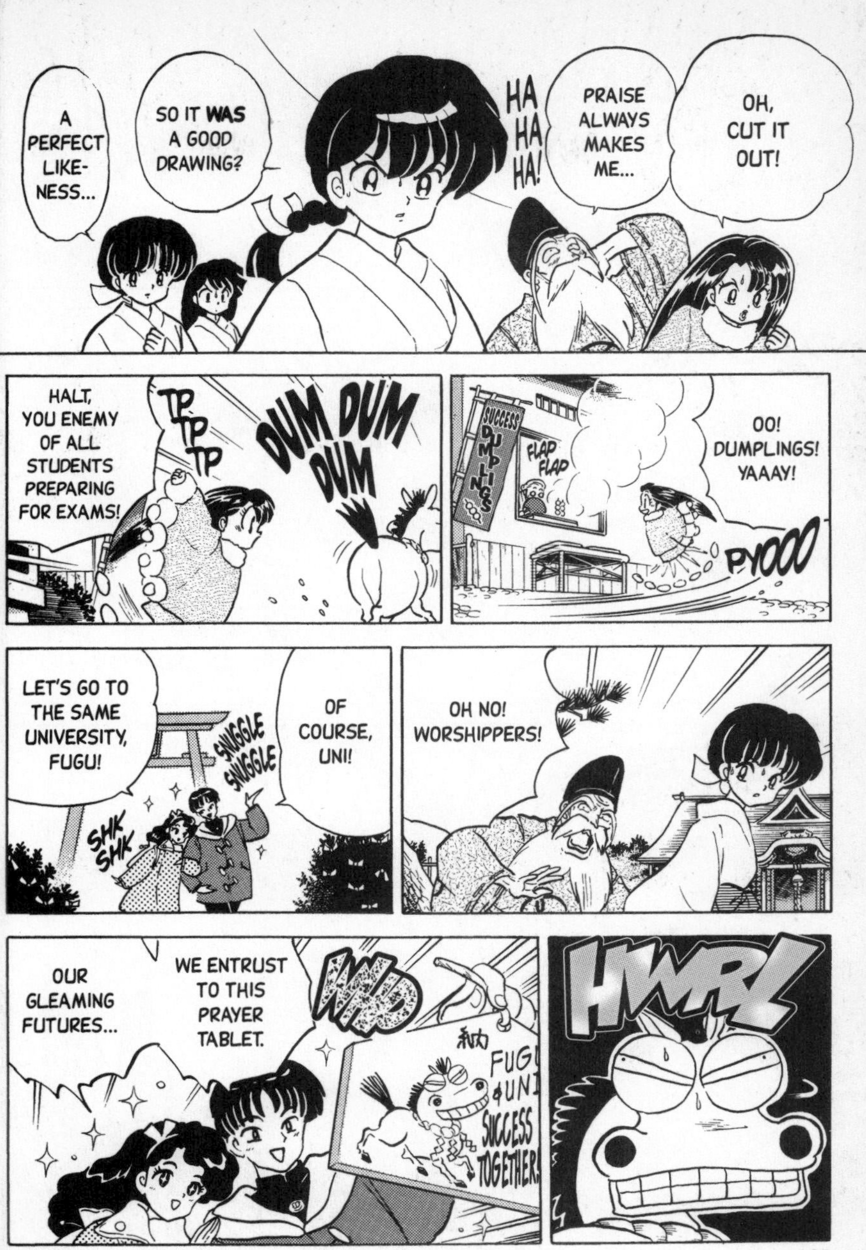
A PERFECT LIKE-NESS...
SO IT WAS A GOOD DRAWING?
HA HA HA!
PRAISE ALWAYS MAKES ME...
OH, CUT IT OUT!
HALT, YOU ENEMY OF ALL STUDENTS PREPARING FOR EXAMS!
TP TP TP
DUM DUM DUM
SUCCESS DUMPLINGS
FLAP FLAP
OO! DUMPLINGS! YAAAY!
PYOOO
LET'S GO TO THE SAME UNIVERSITY, FUGU!
SNUGGLE SNUGGLE
SHK SHK
OF COURSE, UNI!
OH NO! WORSHIPPERS!
OUR GLEAMING FUTURES...
WE ENTRUST TO THIS PRAYER TABLET.
WHD
FUGU & UNI SUCCESS TOGETHER!
HWRL

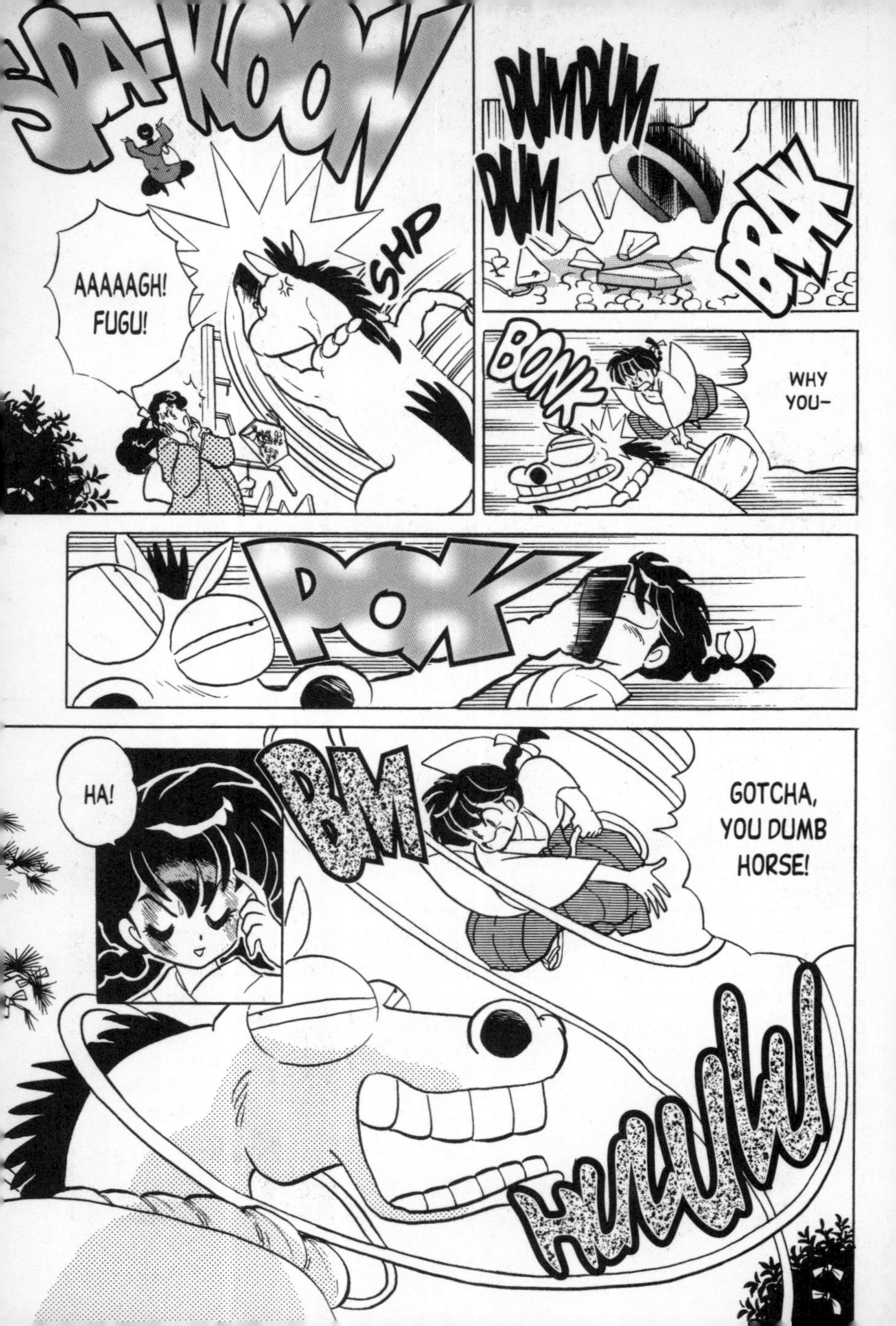
SPA-KOOON
AAAAAGH! FUGU!
SHP
DUMDUM DUM
BRAK
BONK
WHY YOU–
POK
HA!
BAM
GOTCHA, YOU DUMB HORSE!
HUUUW

WAHOO!

BUM-HHHHHIIII

DUM

SO SMOOTH.

WHIP WHIP

GULLUP GULLUP GULLUP

ONE PRAYER TABLET PLEASE.

ALWAYS SEIZE OPPORTUNITY...

BLAH BLAH

WELCOME, WELCOME, WELCOME!

HA! THEY MIGHT CALL YOU A SACRED HORSE, BUT YOU'RE STILL AN ANIMAL!

GULLUP GULLUP GULLUP

IF I DRIVE YOU FAR FROM THE PRAYER TABLETS—

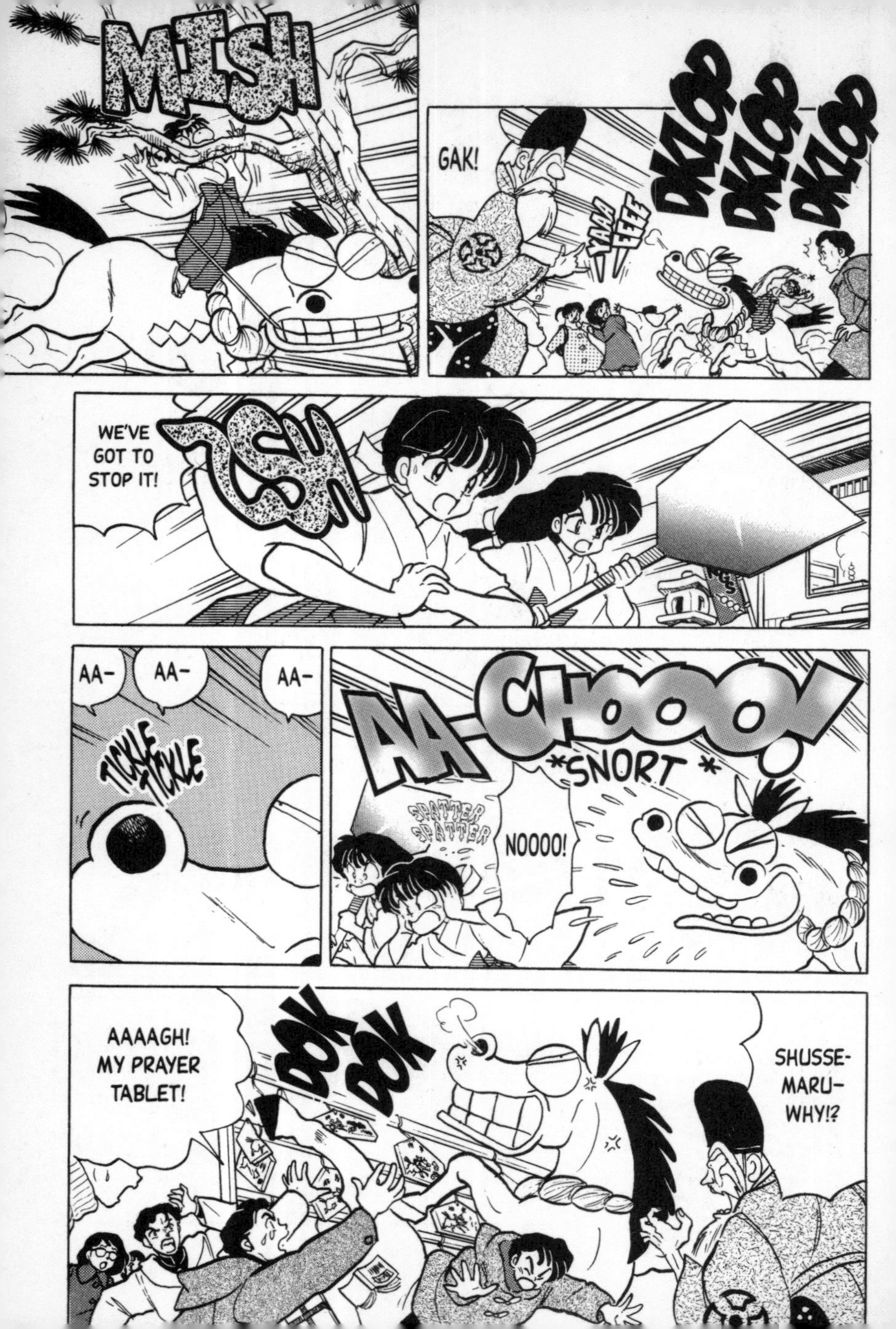
MISH
GAK!
YAAAEEEE
DKLOP DKLOP DKLOP
WE'VE GOT TO STOP IT!
TSSH
AA-
AA-
AA-
TICKLE TICKLE
AA-CHOOO!
SNORT
SPATTER SPATTER
NOOOO!
AAAAGH! MY PRAYER TABLET!
BOK BOK
SHUSSE-MARU-WHY!?

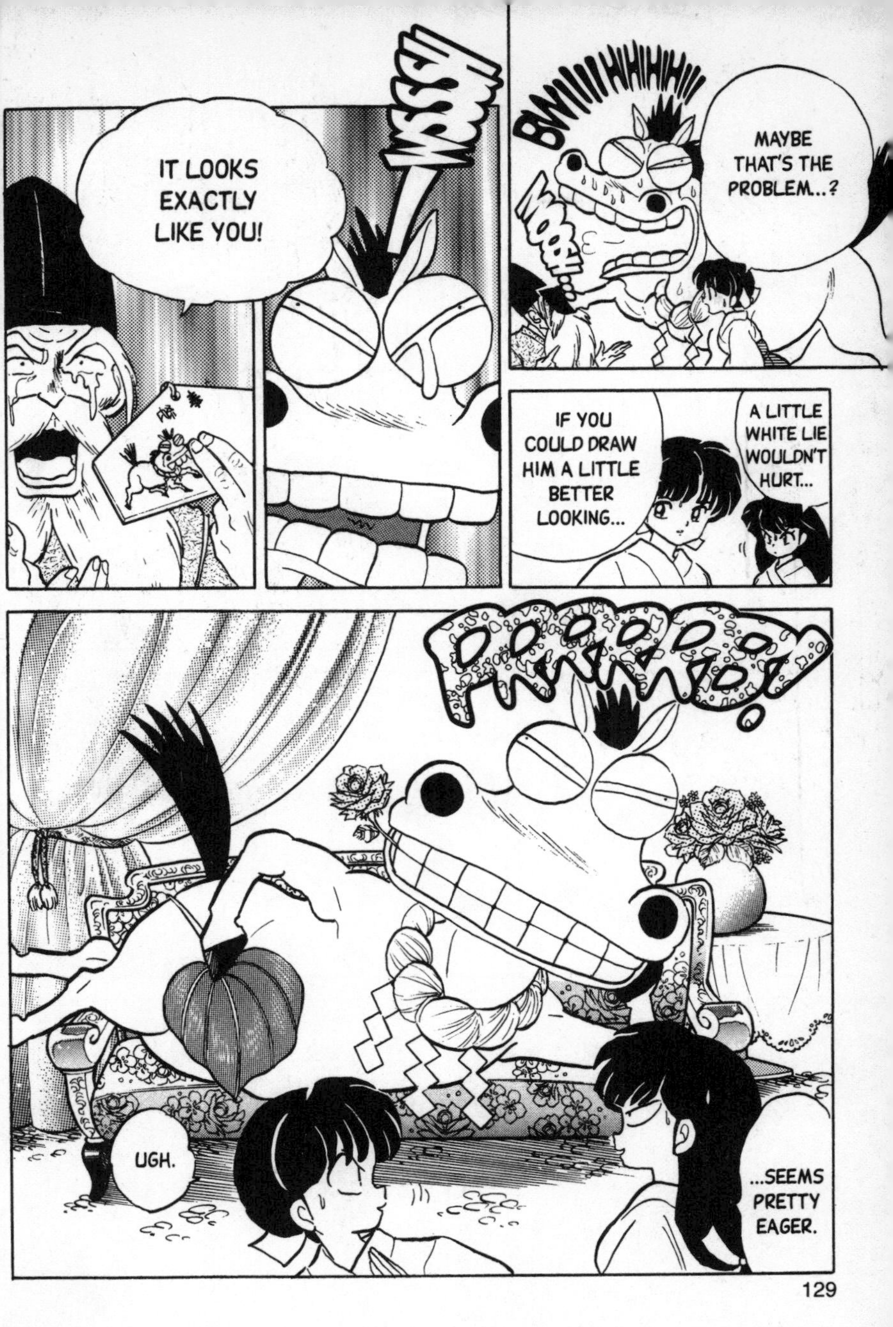
IT LOOKS EXACTLY LIKE YOU!
MAYBE THAT'S THE PROBLEM...?
IF YOU COULD DRAW HIM A LITTLE BETTER LOOKING...
A LITTLE WHITE LIE WOULDN'T HURT...
UGH.
...SEEMS PRETTY EAGER.

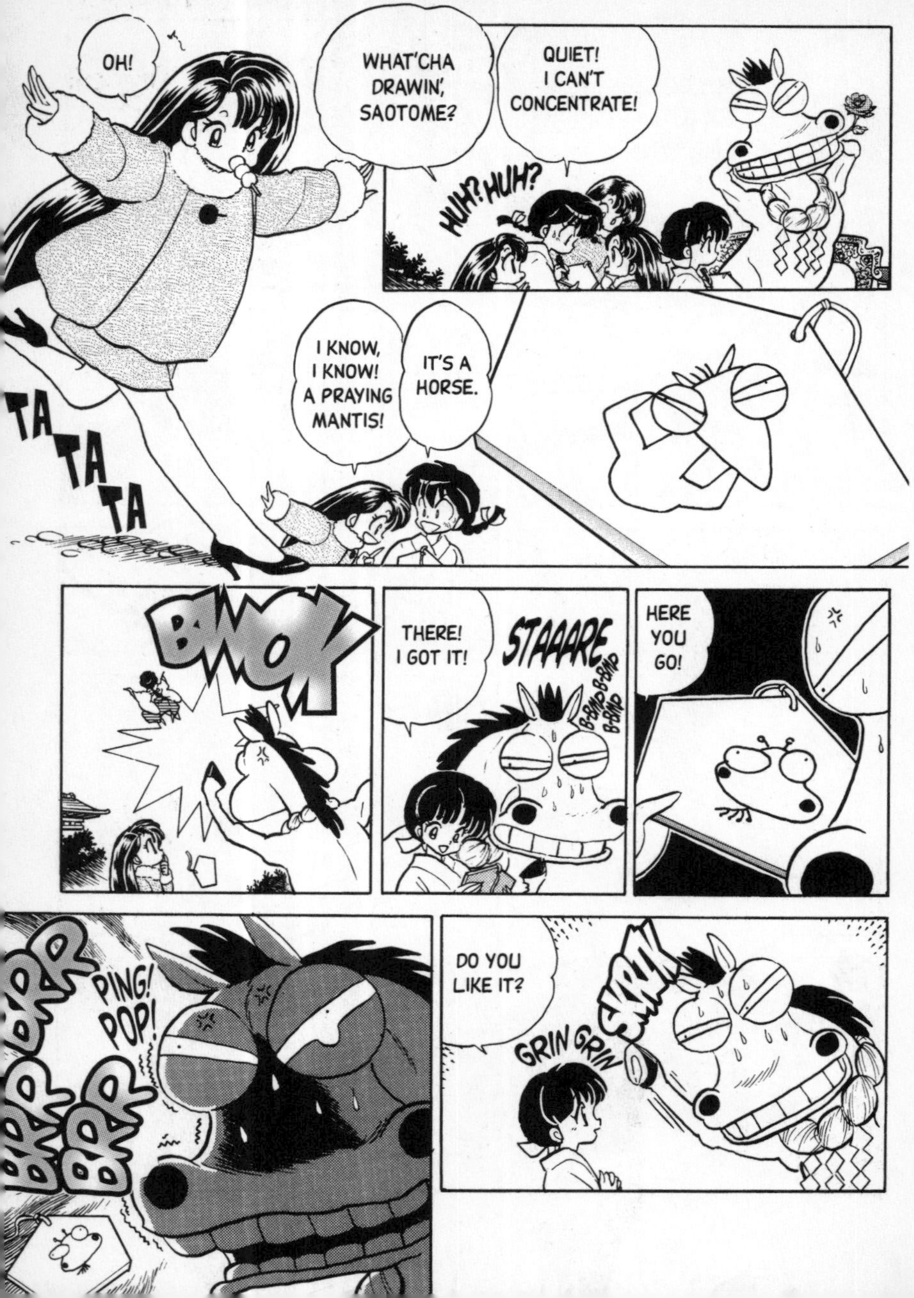
OH!
TA TA TA
WHAT'CHA DRAWIN', SAOTOME?
QUIET! I CAN'T CONCENTRATE!
HUH? HUH?
I KNOW, I KNOW! A PRAYING MANTIS!
IT'S A HORSE.
BWOK
THERE! I GOT IT!
STAAARE
B-BMP B-BMP B-BMP
HERE YOU GO!
BRRR BRRR
PING! POP!
DO YOU LIKE IT?
GRIN GRIN

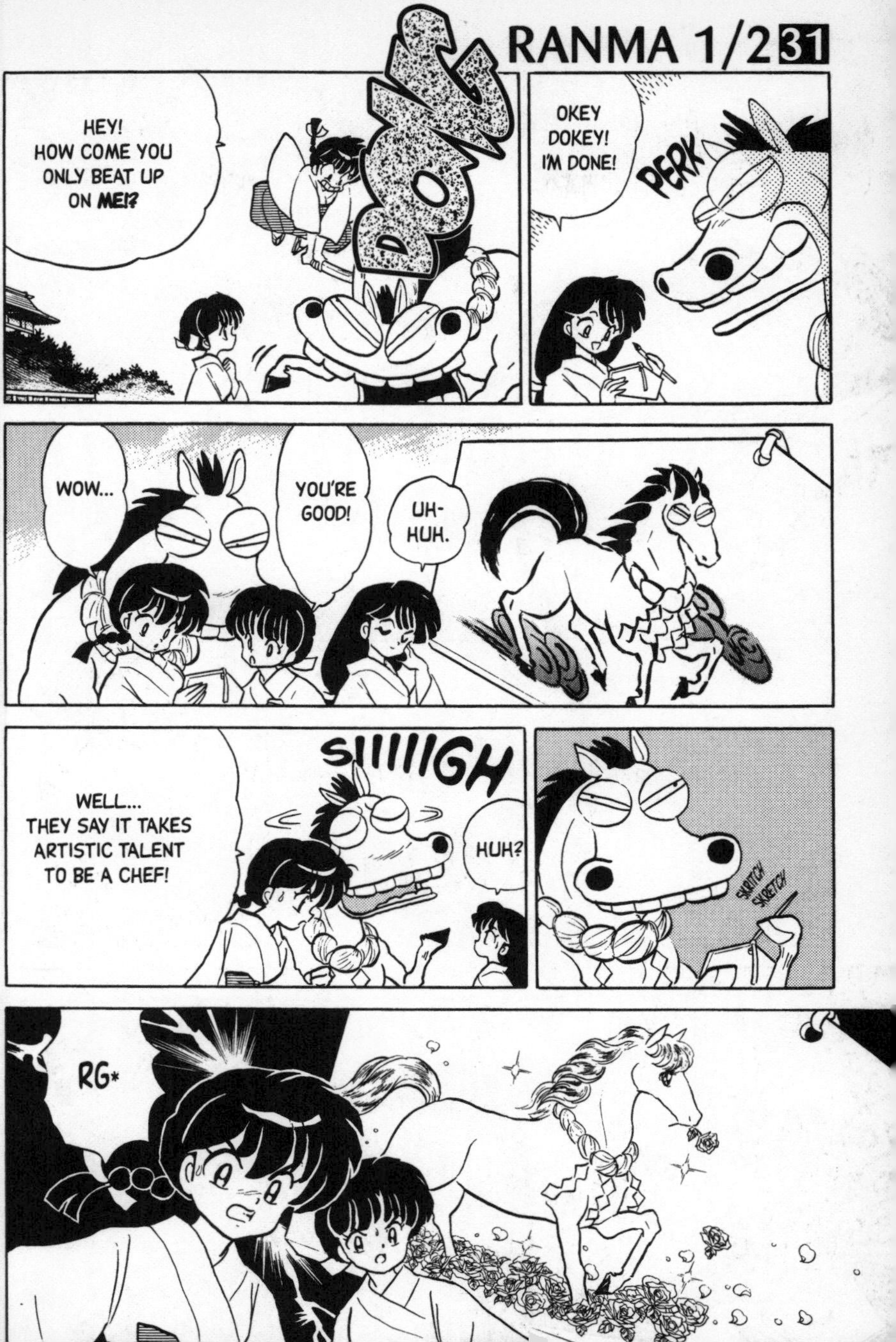
HEY!
HOW COME YOU ONLY BEAT UP ON ME!?
DOING
OKEY DOKEY! I'M DONE!
PERK
WOW...
YOU'RE GOOD!
UH-HUH.
WELL... THEY SAY IT TAKES ARTISTIC TALENT TO BE A CHEF!
SIIIIIGH
HUH?
SKRITCH
SKRITCH
RG*

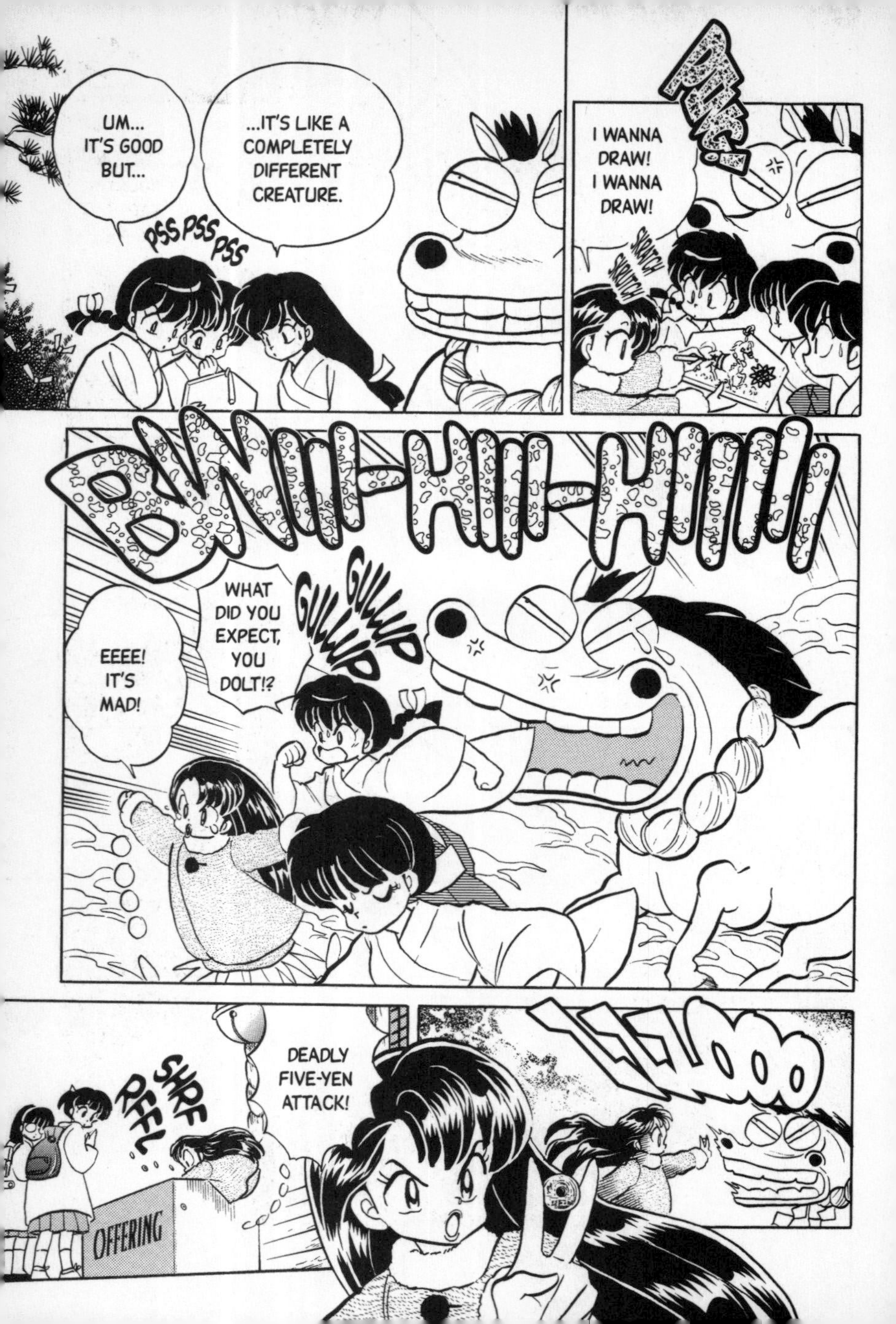
UM... IT'S GOOD BUT...
...IT'S LIKE A COMPLETELY DIFFERENT CREATURE.
PSS PSS PSS
PTING!
I WANNA DRAW! I WANNA DRAW!
SKRATCH SKRATCH
BWHII-HII-HIII!!
EEEE! IT'S MAD!
WHAT DID YOU EXPECT, YOU DOLT!?
GULLUP GULLUP
SHRF RFFL
OFFERING
DEADLY FIVE-YEN ATTACK!

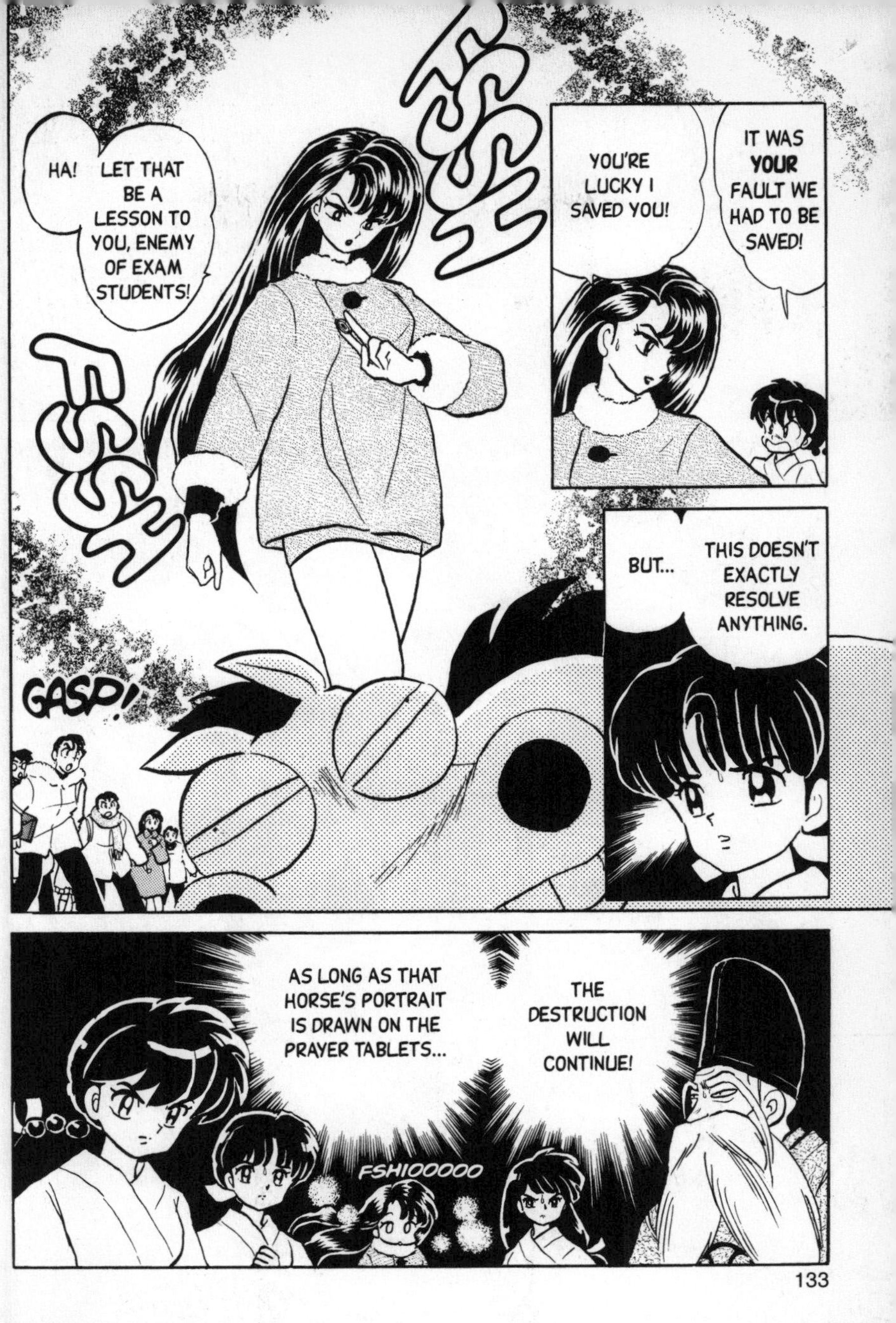
HA! LET THAT BE A LESSON TO YOU, ENEMY OF EXAM STUDENTS!
FSSH
FSSH
GASP!
YOU'RE LUCKY I SAVED YOU!
IT WAS **YOUR** FAULT WE HAD TO BE SAVED!
BUT...
THIS DOESN'T EXACTLY RESOLVE ANYTHING.
AS LONG AS THAT HORSE'S PORTRAIT IS DRAWN ON THE PRAYER TABLETS...
THE DESTRUCTION WILL CONTINUE!
FSHIOOOOO

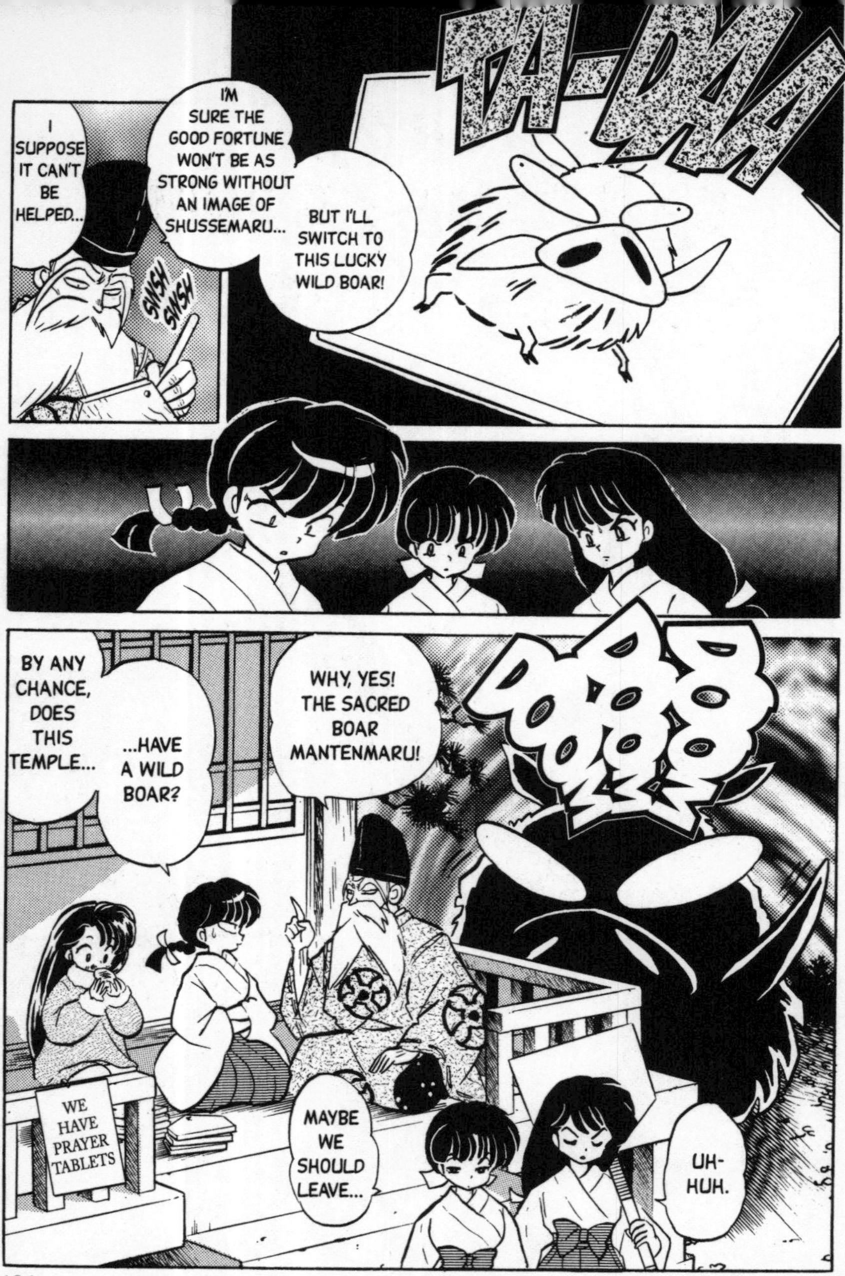
I SUPPOSE IT CAN'T BE HELPED...
SWSH SWSH
I'M SURE THE GOOD FORTUNE WON'T BE AS STRONG WITHOUT AN IMAGE OF SHUSSEMARU...
BUT I'LL SWITCH TO THIS LUCKY WILD BOAR!
TA-DAA
BY ANY CHANCE, DOES THIS TEMPLE...
...HAVE A WILD BOAR?
WHY, YES! THE SACRED BOAR MANTENMARU!
WE HAVE PRAYER TABLETS
MAYBE WE SHOULD LEAVE...
UH-HUH.

PART 9
SAOTOME FAMILY (ONSEN) VACATION

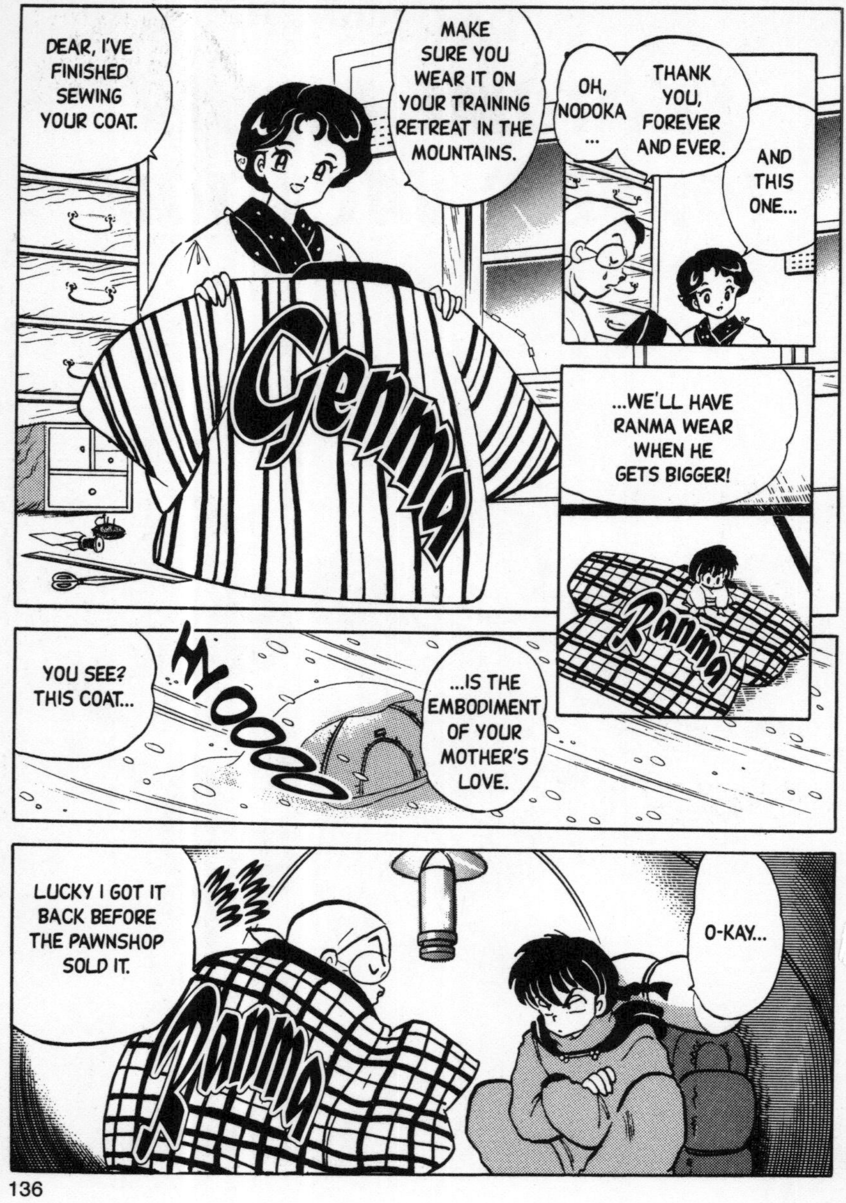
DEAR, I'VE FINISHED SEWING YOUR COAT.
MAKE SURE YOU WEAR IT ON YOUR TRAINING RETREAT IN THE MOUNTAINS.
Genma
OH, NODOKA ...
THANK YOU, FOREVER AND EVER.
AND THIS ONE...
...WE'LL HAVE RANMA WEAR WHEN HE GETS BIGGER!
Ranma
YOU SEE? THIS COAT...
HYOOOOO
...IS THE EMBODIMENT OF YOUR MOTHER'S LOVE.
LUCKY I GOT IT BACK BEFORE THE PAWNSHOP SOLD IT.
Ranma
O-KAY...

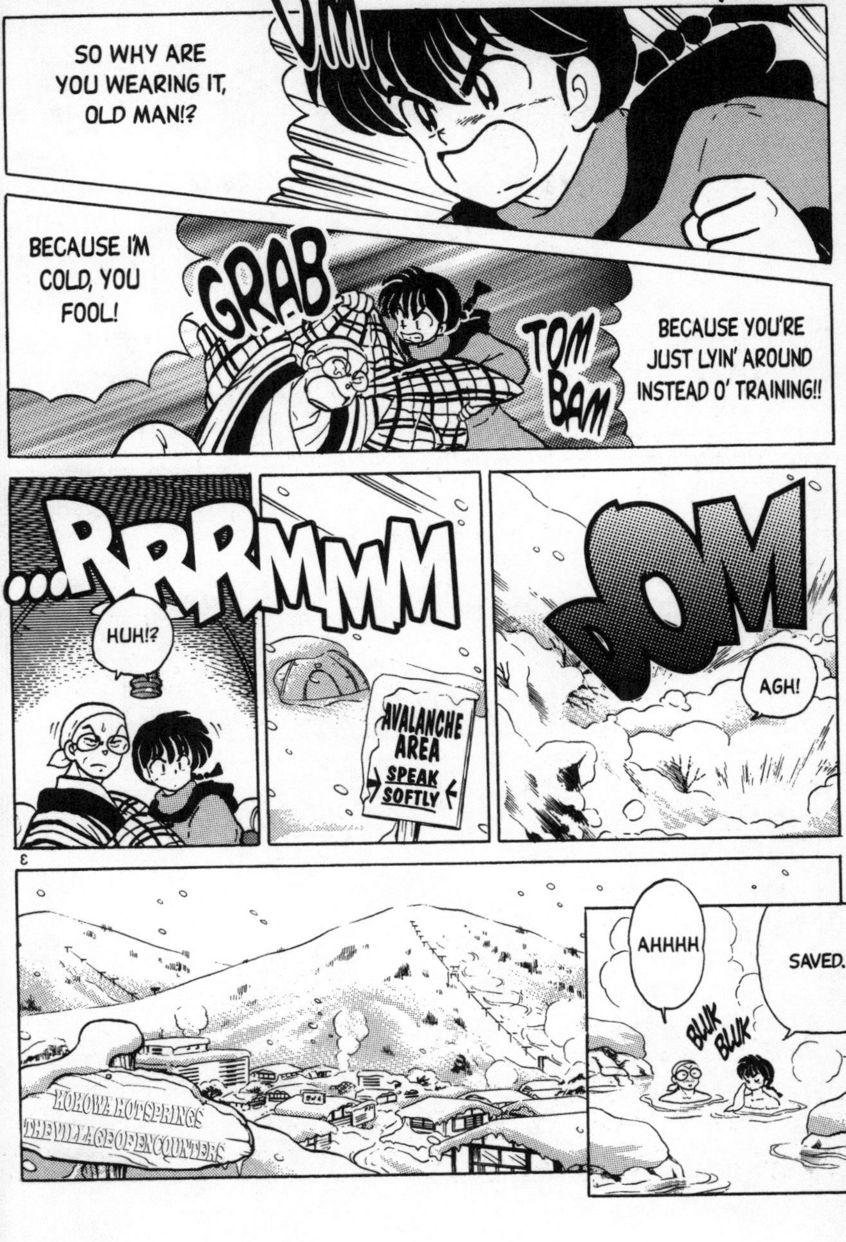
SO WHY ARE YOU WEARING IT, OLD MAN!?
DM
BECAUSE I'M COLD, YOU FOOL!
GRAB
TOM BAM
BECAUSE YOU'RE JUST LYIN' AROUND INSTEAD O' TRAINING!!
...RRRMMMM
HUH!?
AVALANCHE AREA
SPEAK SOFTLY
DOM
AGH!
KOKOWA HOTSPRINGS
THE VILLAGE OF ENCOUNTERS
AHHHH
BLUK BLUK
SAVED.

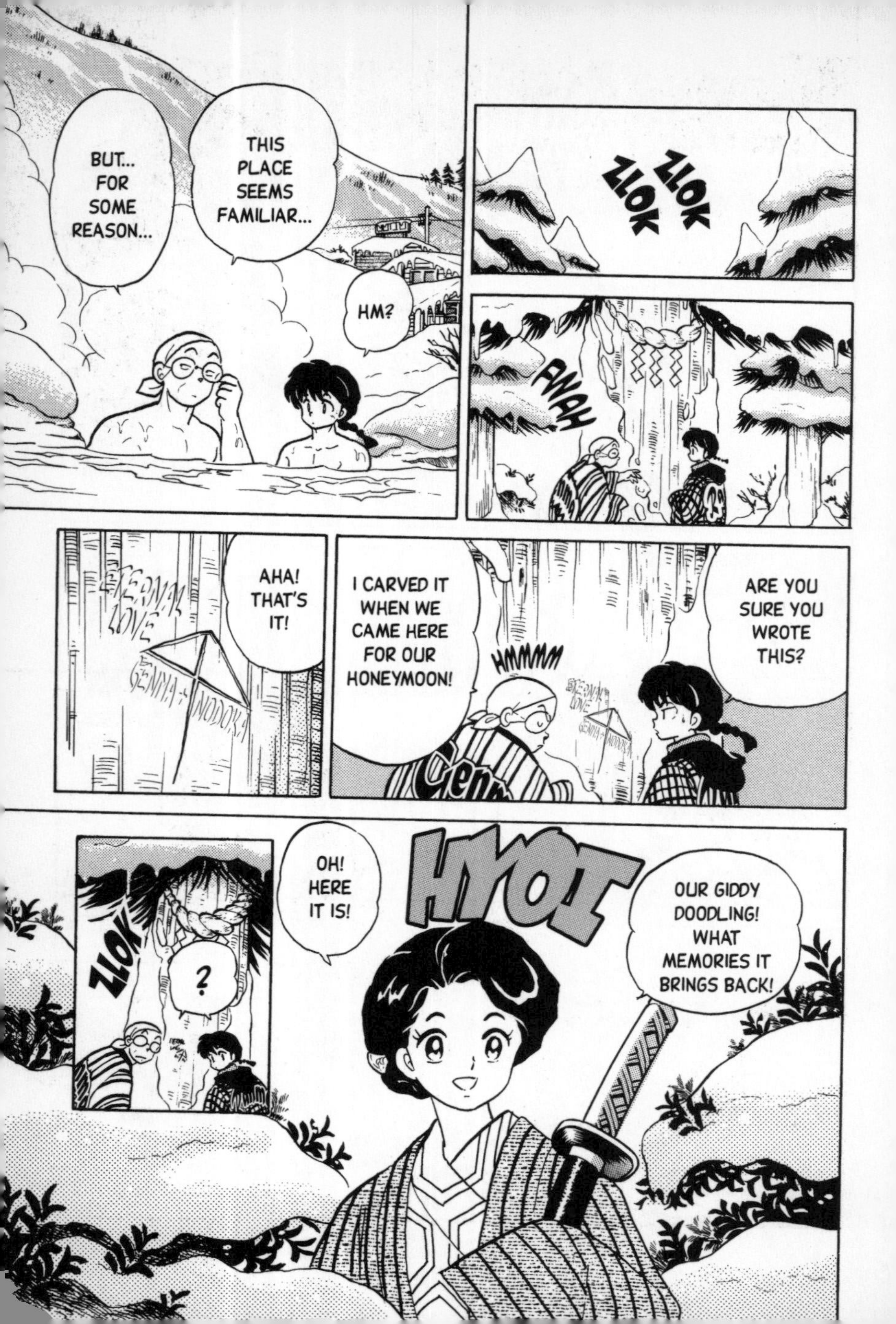
BUT... FOR SOME REASON...
THIS PLACE SEEMS FAMILIAR...
HM?
ZLOK ZLOK
AWAH
ETERNAL LOVE
GENMA + NODOKA
AHA! THAT'S IT!
I CARVED IT WHEN WE CAME HERE FOR OUR HONEYMOON!
HMMMM
ARE YOU SURE YOU WROTE THIS?
ZLOK
?
OH! HERE IT IS!
HYOI
OUR GIDDY DOODLING! WHAT MEMORIES IT BRINGS BACK!

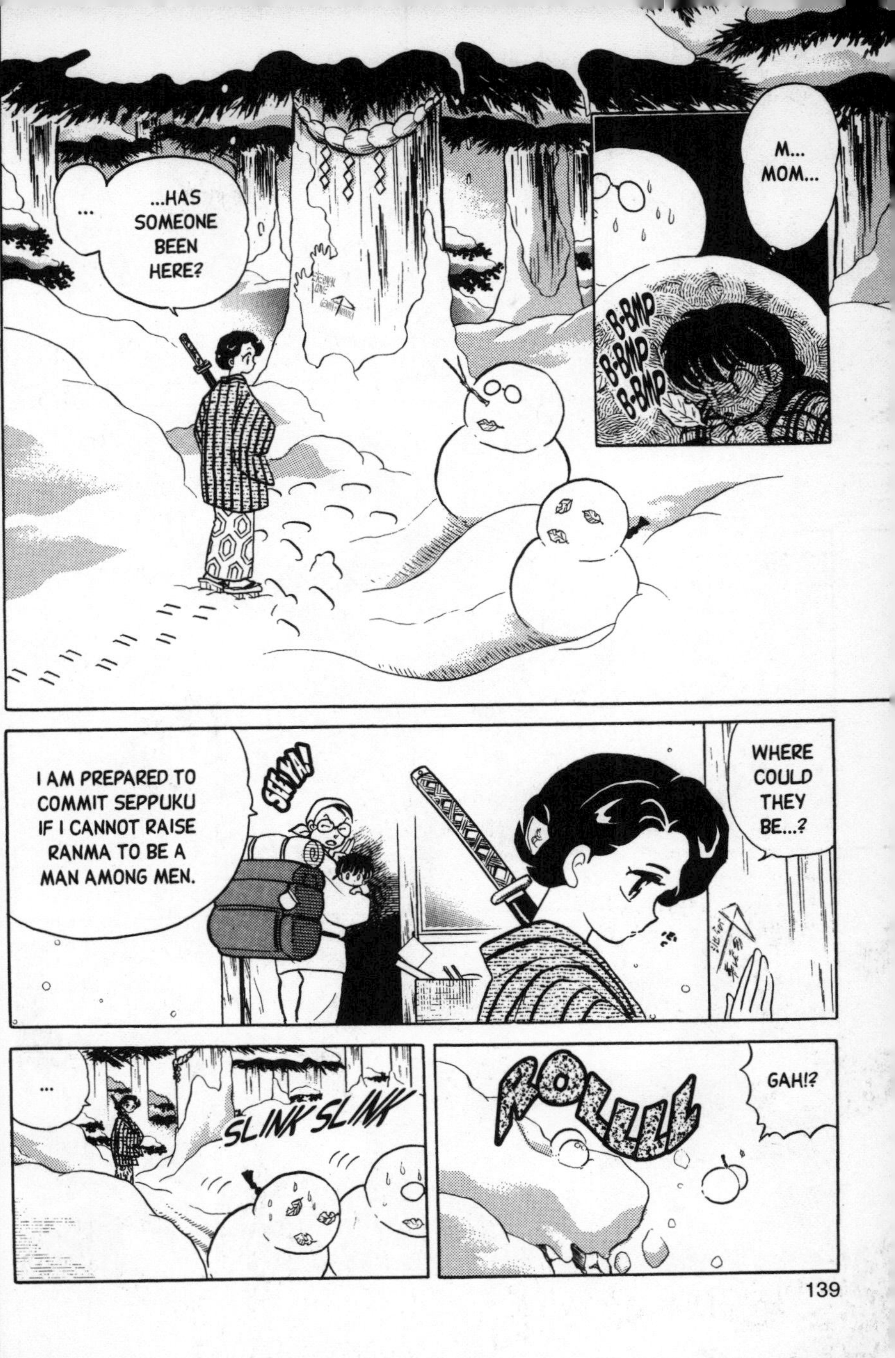
...
...HAS SOMEONE BEEN HERE?
M... MOM...
B-BMP B-BMP B-BMP
I AM PREPARED TO COMMIT SEPPUKU IF I CANNOT RAISE RANMA TO BE A MAN AMONG MEN.
WHERE COULD THEY BE...?
...
SLINK SLINK
ROLLLL
GAH!?

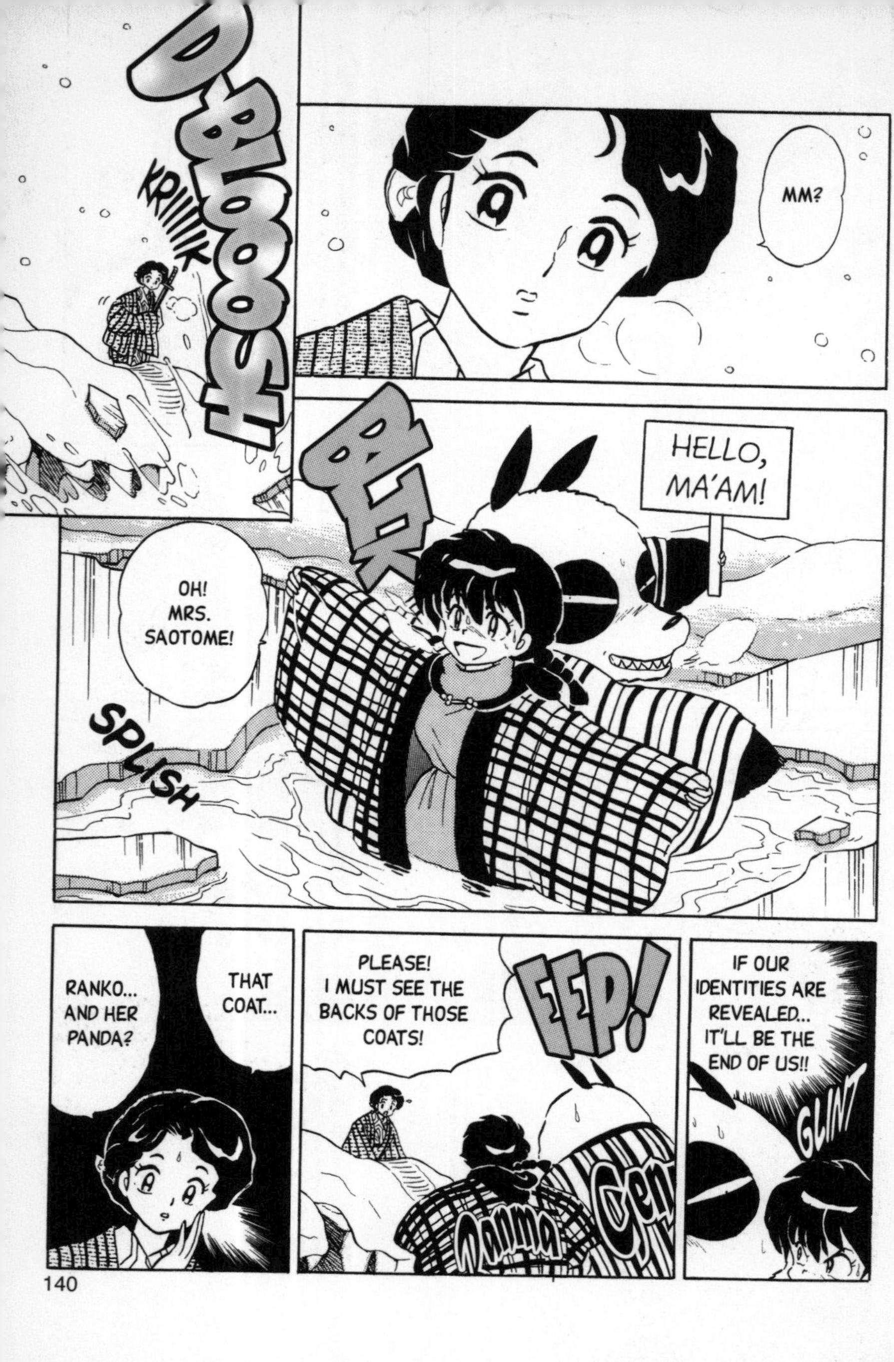
DBLOOOOSH
KRIIIIIK
MM?
BLIK
HELLO, MA'AM!
OH! MRS. SAOTOME!
SPLISH
RANKO... AND HER PANDA?
THAT COAT...
PLEASE! I MUST SEE THE BACKS OF THOSE COATS!
EEP!
IF OUR IDENTITIES ARE REVEALED... IT'LL BE THE END OF US!!
GLINT

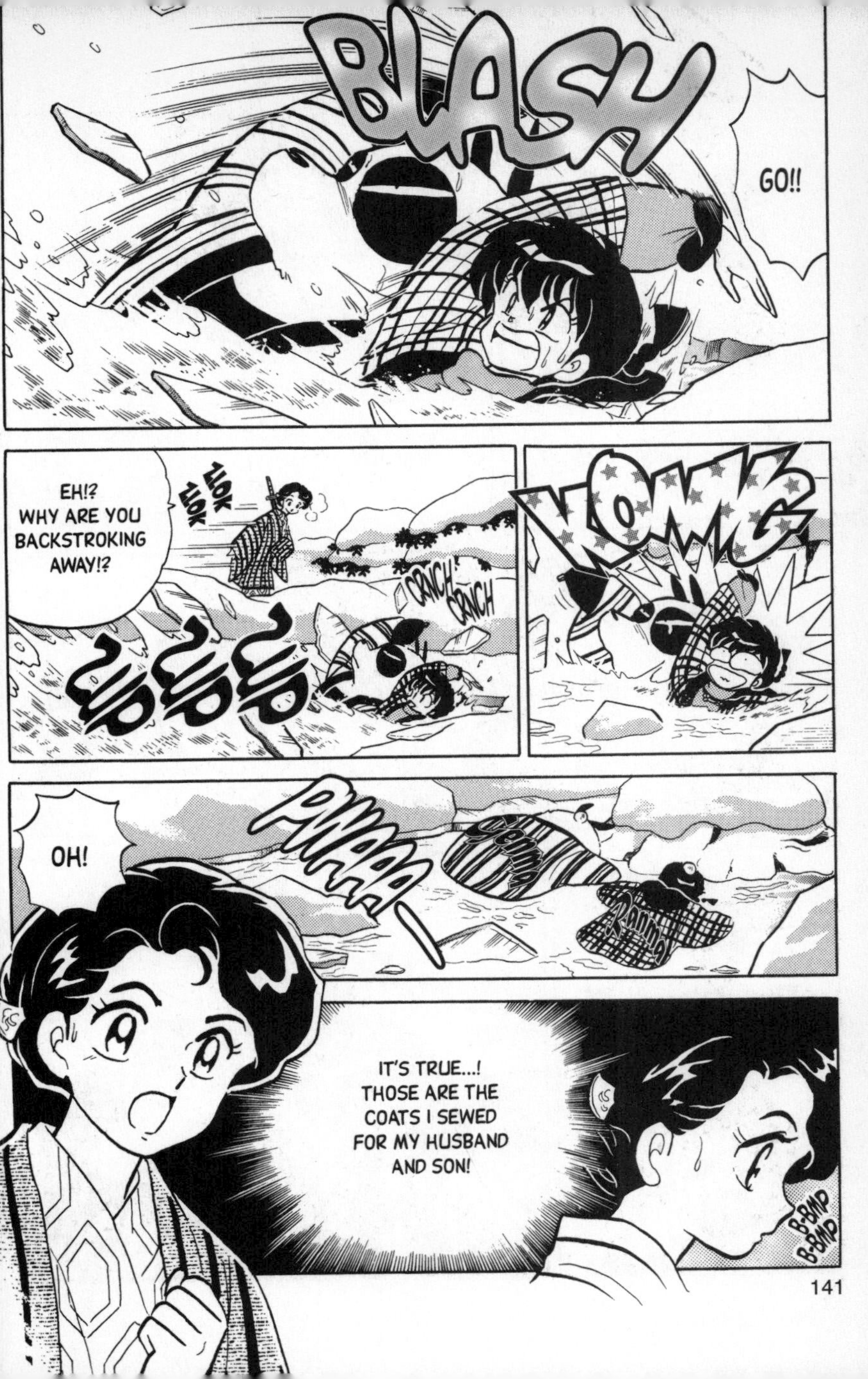
BLASH
GO!!
EH!? WHY ARE YOU BACKSTROKING AWAY!?
KLOK KLOK
ZUIP ZUIP ZUIP
CRNCH CRNCH
KOMG
OH!
PWAAA!
Genma
Ranma
IT'S TRUE...! THOSE ARE THE COATS I SEWED FOR MY HUSBAND AND SON!
B-BMP B-BMP

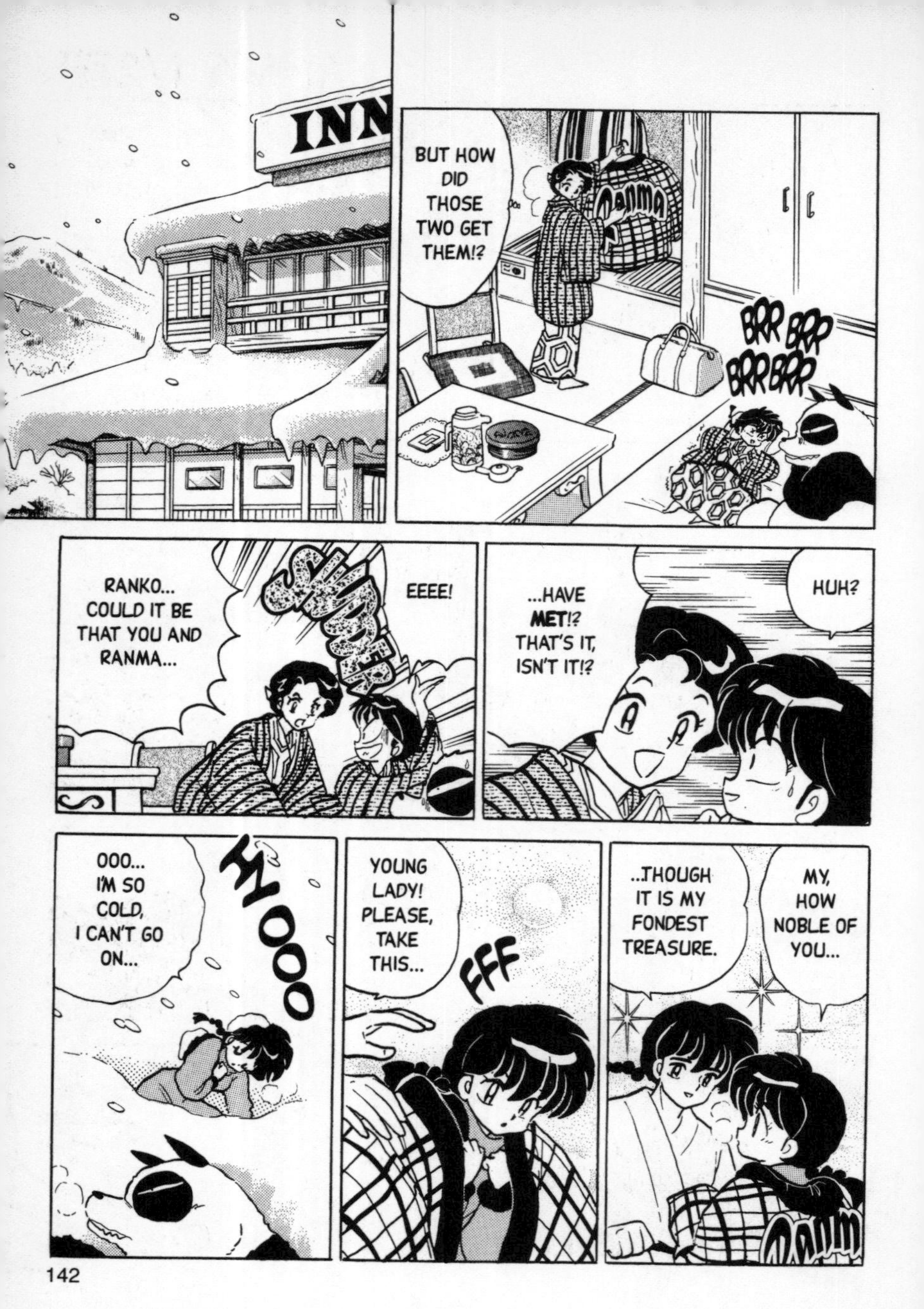
INN
BUT HOW DID THOSE TWO GET THEM!?
RANMA
BRR BRR BRR BRR
RANKO... COULD IT BE THAT YOU AND RANMA...
SHUDDER
EEEE!
...HAVE MET!? THAT'S IT, ISN'T IT!?
HUH?
OOO... I'M SO COLD, I CAN'T GO ON...
HOOOO
YOUNG LADY! PLEASE, TAKE THIS...
FFF
...THOUGH IT IS MY FONDEST TREASURE.
MY, HOW NOBLE OF YOU...

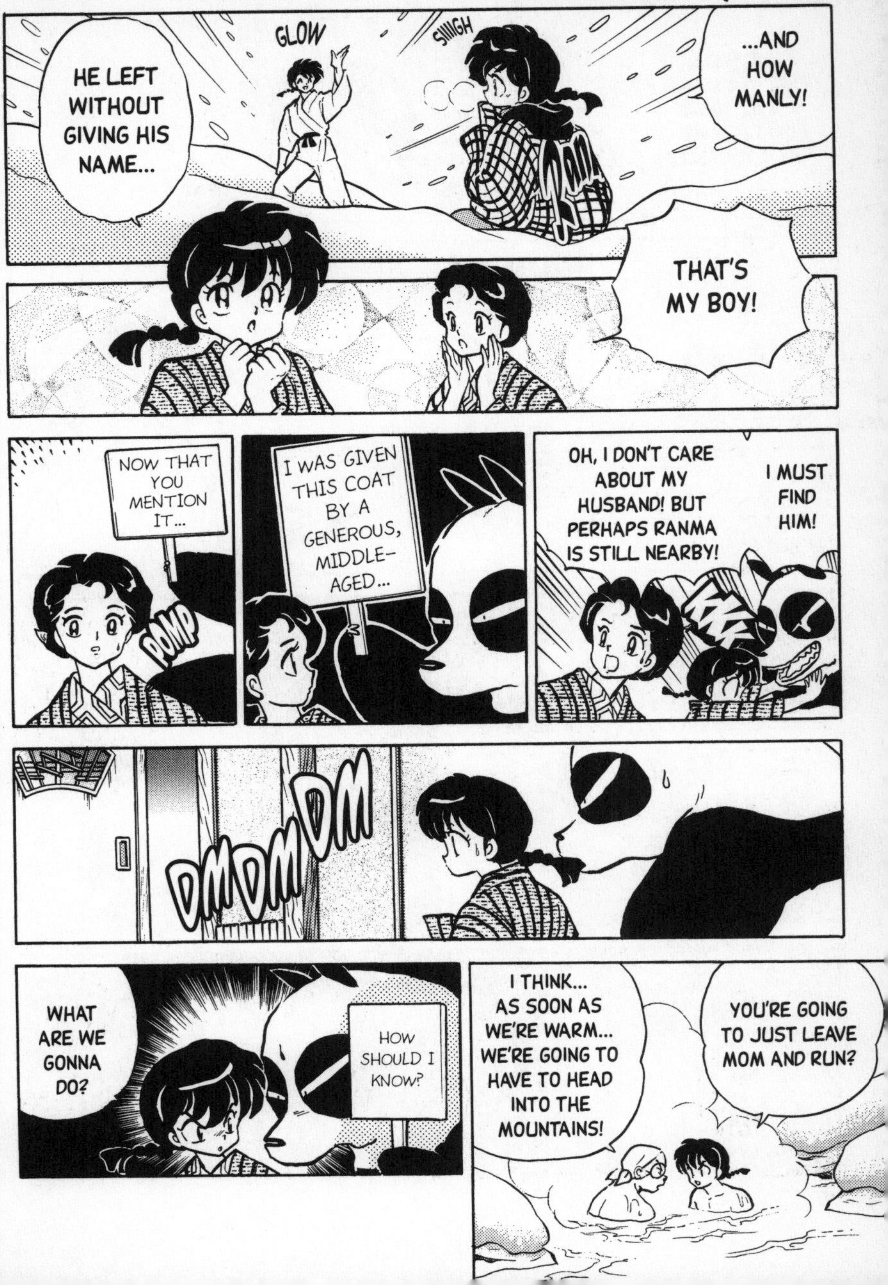
HE LEFT WITHOUT GIVING HIS NAME...
GLOW
SIIIGH
...AND HOW MANLY!
THAT'S MY BOY!
NOW THAT YOU MENTION IT...
POMP
I WAS GIVEN THIS COAT BY A GENEROUS, MIDDLE-AGED...
OH, I DON'T CARE ABOUT MY HUSBAND! BUT PERHAPS RANMA IS STILL NEARBY!
I MUST FIND HIM!
KKK
DMDMDMDM
WHAT ARE WE GONNA DO?
HOW SHOULD I KNOW?
I THINK... AS SOON AS WE'RE WARM... WE'RE GOING TO HAVE TO HEAD INTO THE MOUNTAINS!
YOU'RE GOING TO JUST LEAVE MOM AND RUN?

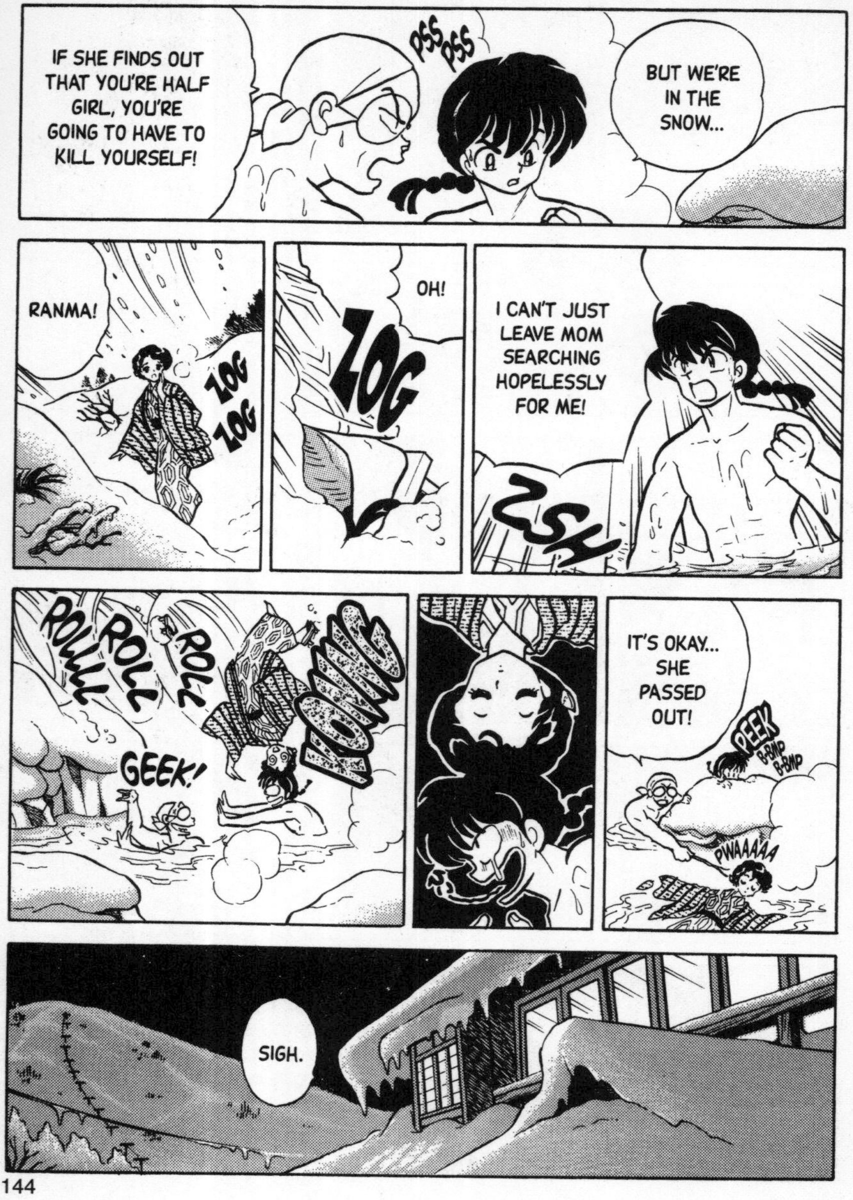
IF SHE FINDS OUT THAT YOU'RE HALF GIRL, YOU'RE GOING TO HAVE TO KILL YOURSELF!
PSS PSS
BUT WE'RE IN THE SNOW...
RANMA!
ZOG ZOG
OH!
ZOG
I CAN'T JUST LEAVE MOM SEARCHING HOPELESSLY FOR ME!
ZSH
ROWLL
ROLL
ROLL
GEEK!
IT'S OKAY... SHE PASSED OUT!
PEEK
B-BMP B-BMP
PWAAAAA
SIGH.

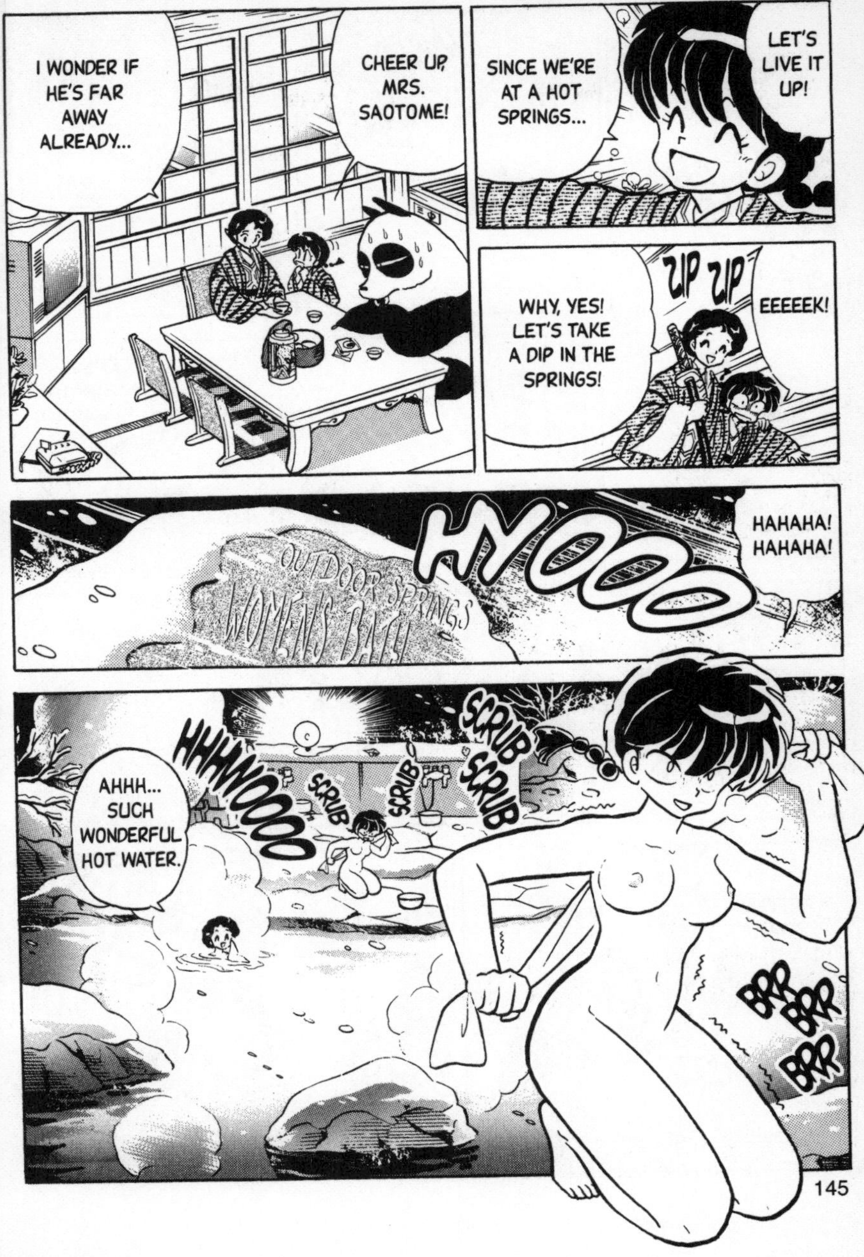
I WONDER IF HE'S FAR AWAY ALREADY...
CHEER UP, MRS. SAOTOME!
SINCE WE'RE AT A HOT SPRINGS...
LET'S LIVE IT UP!
WHY, YES! LET'S TAKE A DIP IN THE SPRINGS!
ZIP ZIP
EEEEEK!
OUTDOOR SPRINGS
WOMEN'S BATH
HYOOO
HAHAHA! HAHAHA!
HHHNOOOO
AHHH... SUCH WONDERFUL HOT WATER.
SCRUB
SCRUB
SCRUB SCRUB
SCRUB
BRR BRR BRR BRR

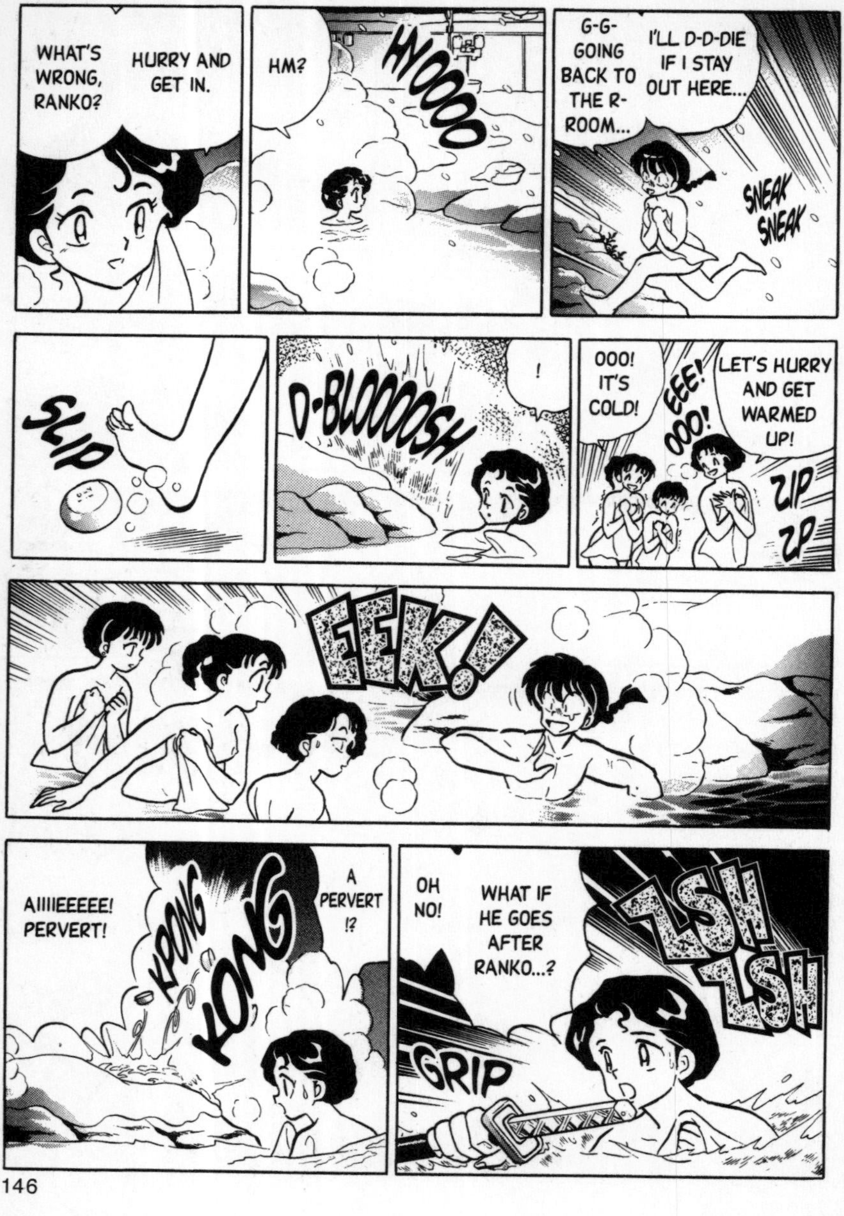

WHAT'S WRONG, RANKO?
HURRY AND GET IN.
HM?
HYOOOO
G-G-GOING BACK TO THE R-ROOM...
I'LL D-D-DIE IF I STAY OUT HERE...
SNEAK SNEAK
SLIP
D-BLOOOOSH
!
OOO! IT'S COLD!
EEE! OOO!
LET'S HURRY AND GET WARMED UP!
ZIP ZIP
EEK!
AIIIIEEEEE! PERVERT!
KPONG
KONG
A PERVERT !?
OH NO!
WHAT IF HE GOES AFTER RANKO...?
GRIP
TSH! TSH!

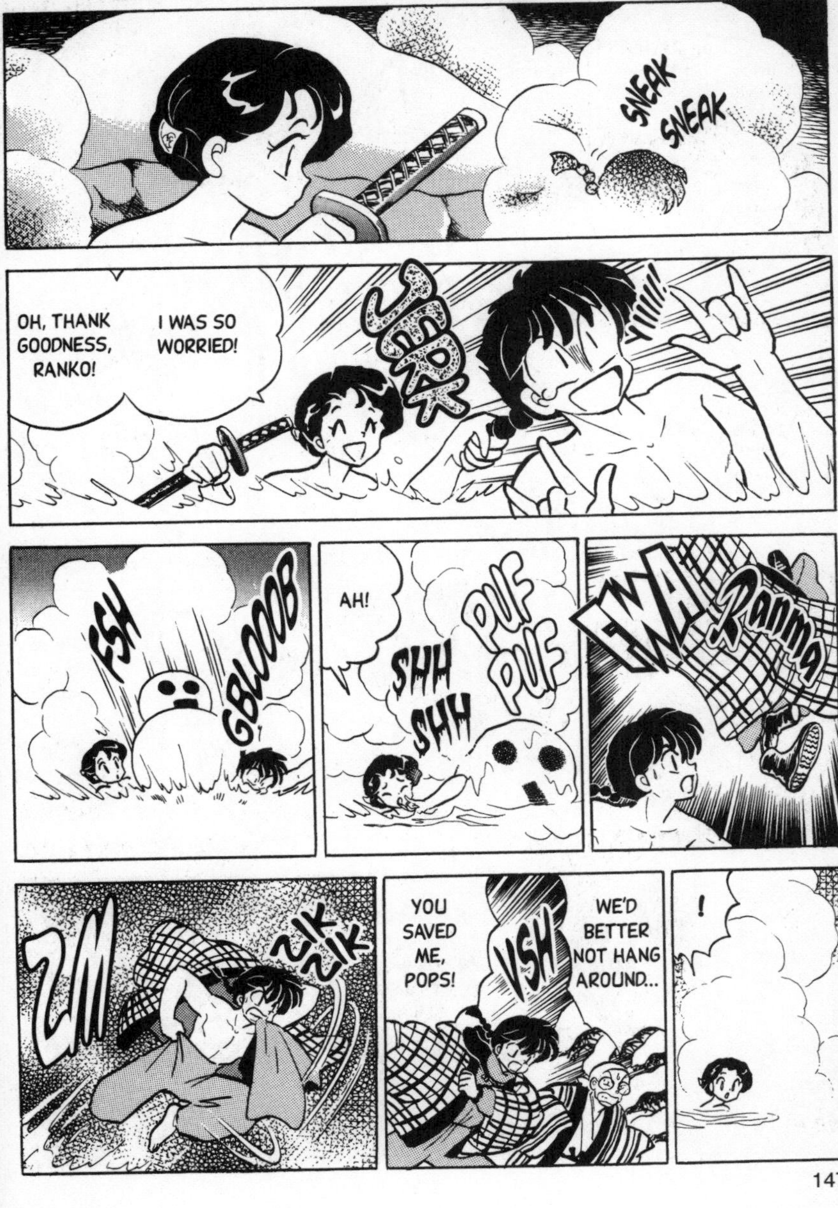
SNEAK
SNEAK
OH, THANK GOODNESS, RANKO!
I WAS SO WORRIED!
JERK
YIIIII!
FSH
GBLOOOB
AH!
SHH SHH
PUF PUF
FWA!
Ranma
ZM
ZIK ZIK
YOU SAVED ME, POPS!
VSH
WE'D BETTER NOT HANG AROUND...
!

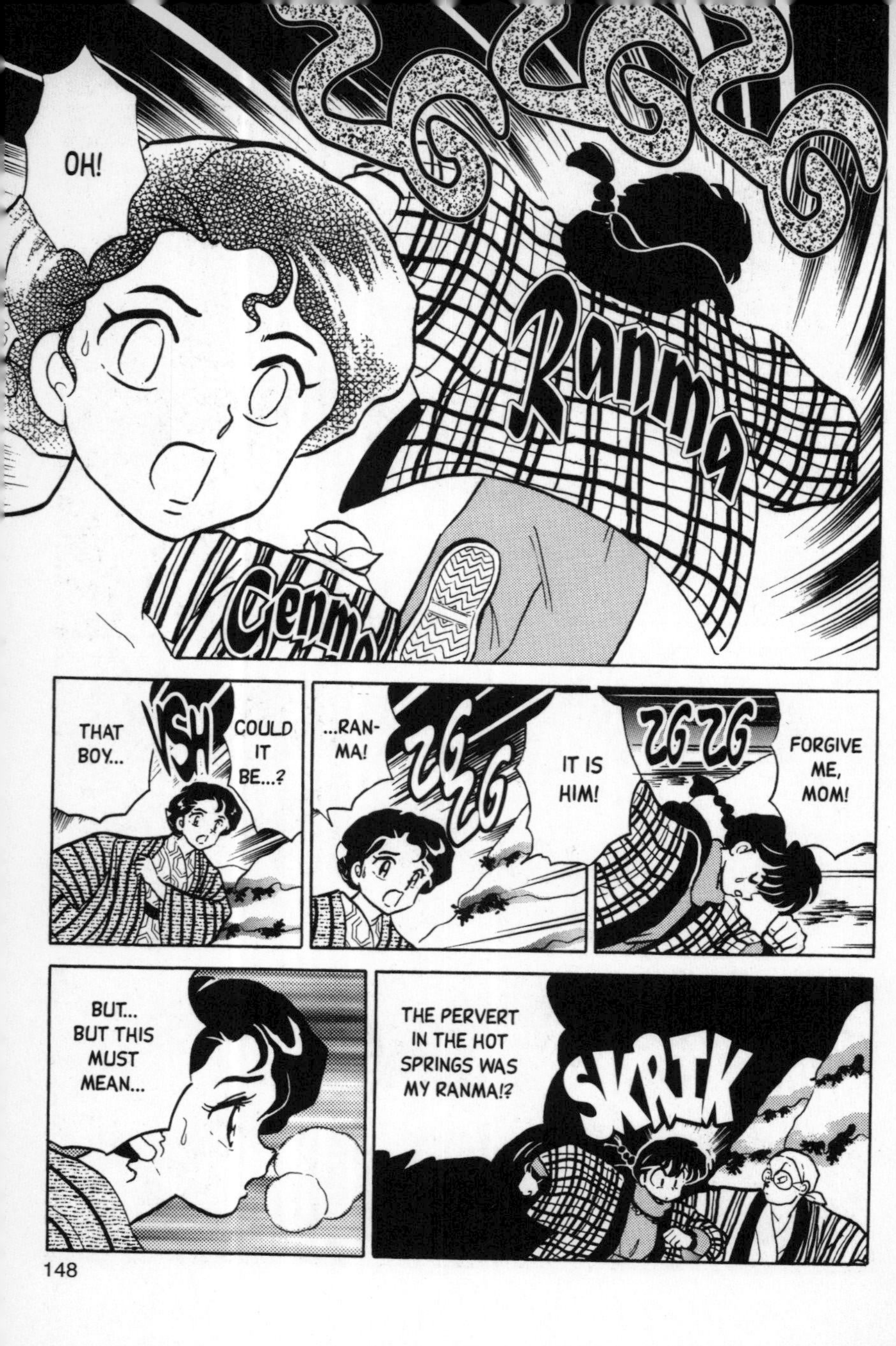
OH!
Ranma
THAT BOY...
VSH
COULD IT BE...?
...RAN-MA!
IT IS HIM!
FORGIVE ME, MOM!
BUT... BUT THIS MUST MEAN...
THE PERVERT IN THE HOT SPRINGS WAS MY RANMA!?
SKRIK

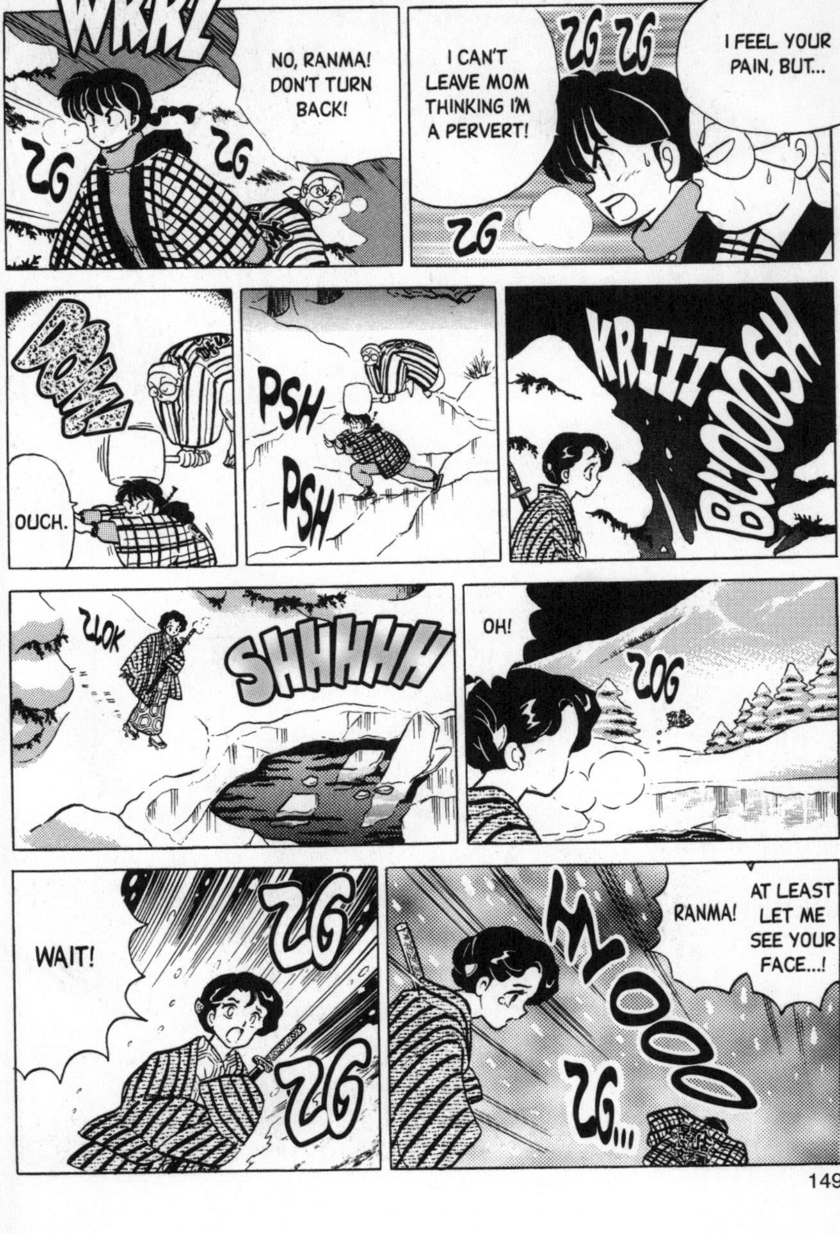
WRRL
NO, RANMA! DON'T TURN BACK!
ZG
ZG
ZG ZG
I CAN'T LEAVE MOM THINKING I'M A PERVERT!
I FEEL YOUR PAIN, BUT...
ZG
DOM!
OUCH.
PSH
PSH
KRIIIT
BWOOOSH
ZLOK
SHHHHH
OH!
ZOG
WAIT!
ZG
ZG
HYOOO
ZG...
RANMA!
AT LEAST LET ME SEE YOUR FACE...!

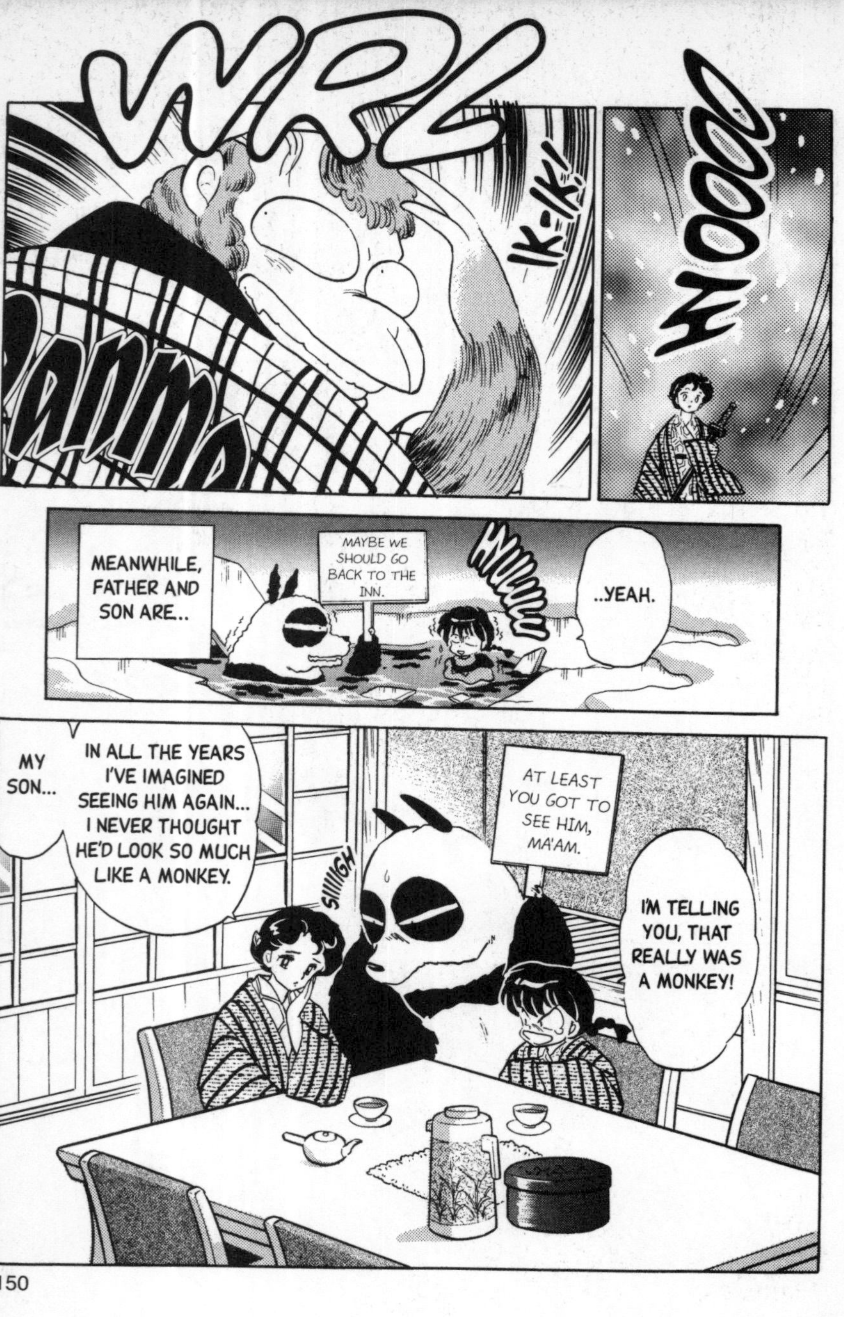
WRL
IK-IK!
WHOOOOO
MEANWHILE, FATHER AND SON ARE...
MAYBE WE SHOULD GO BACK TO THE INN.
..YEAH.
MY SON...
IN ALL THE YEARS I'VE IMAGINED SEEING HIM AGAIN... I NEVER THOUGHT HE'D LOOK SO MUCH LIKE A MONKEY.
SIIIIGH
AT LEAST YOU GOT TO SEE HIM, MA'AM.
I'M TELLING YOU, THAT REALLY WAS A MONKEY!

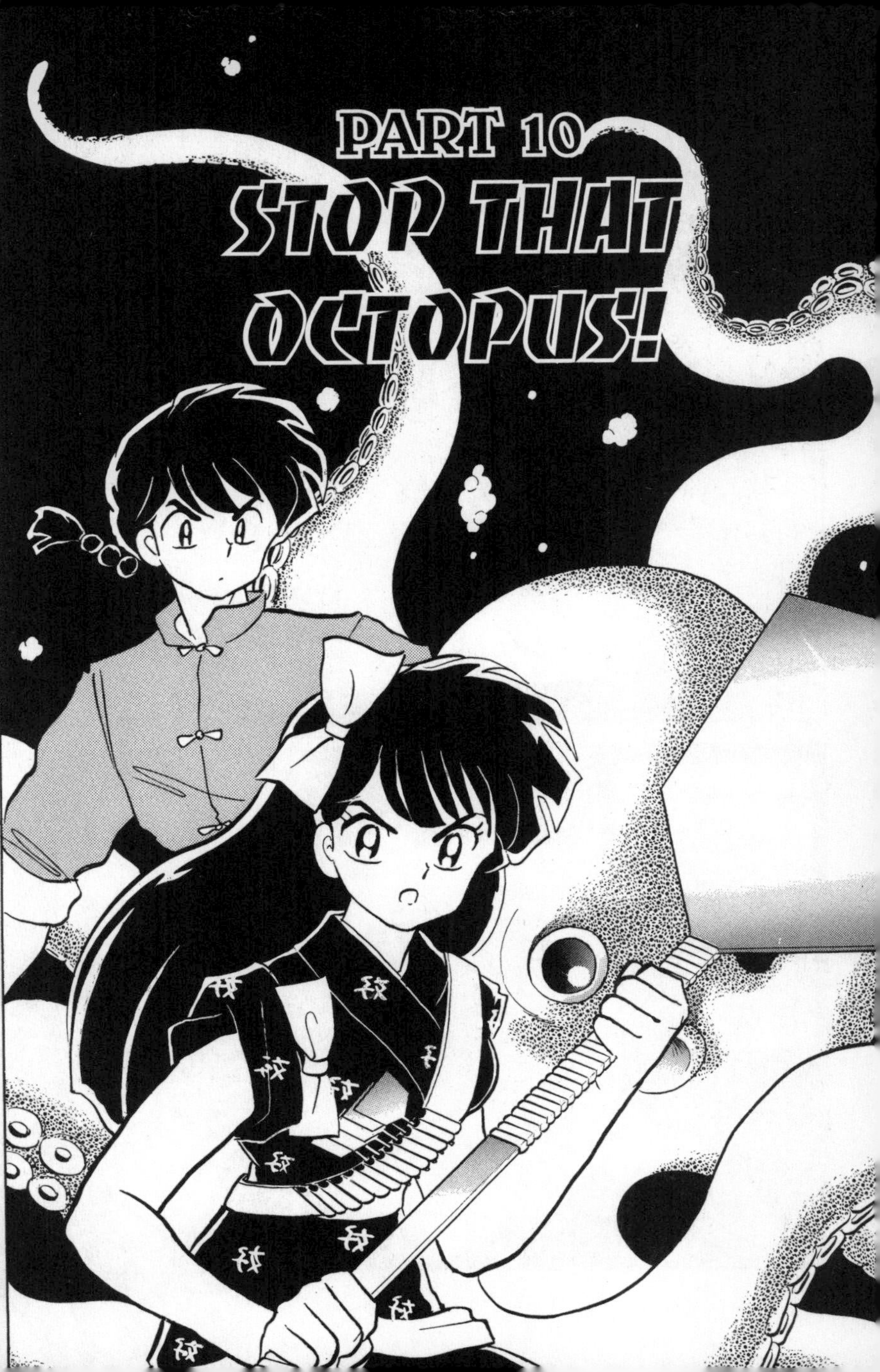
PART 10
STOP THAT OCTOPUS!

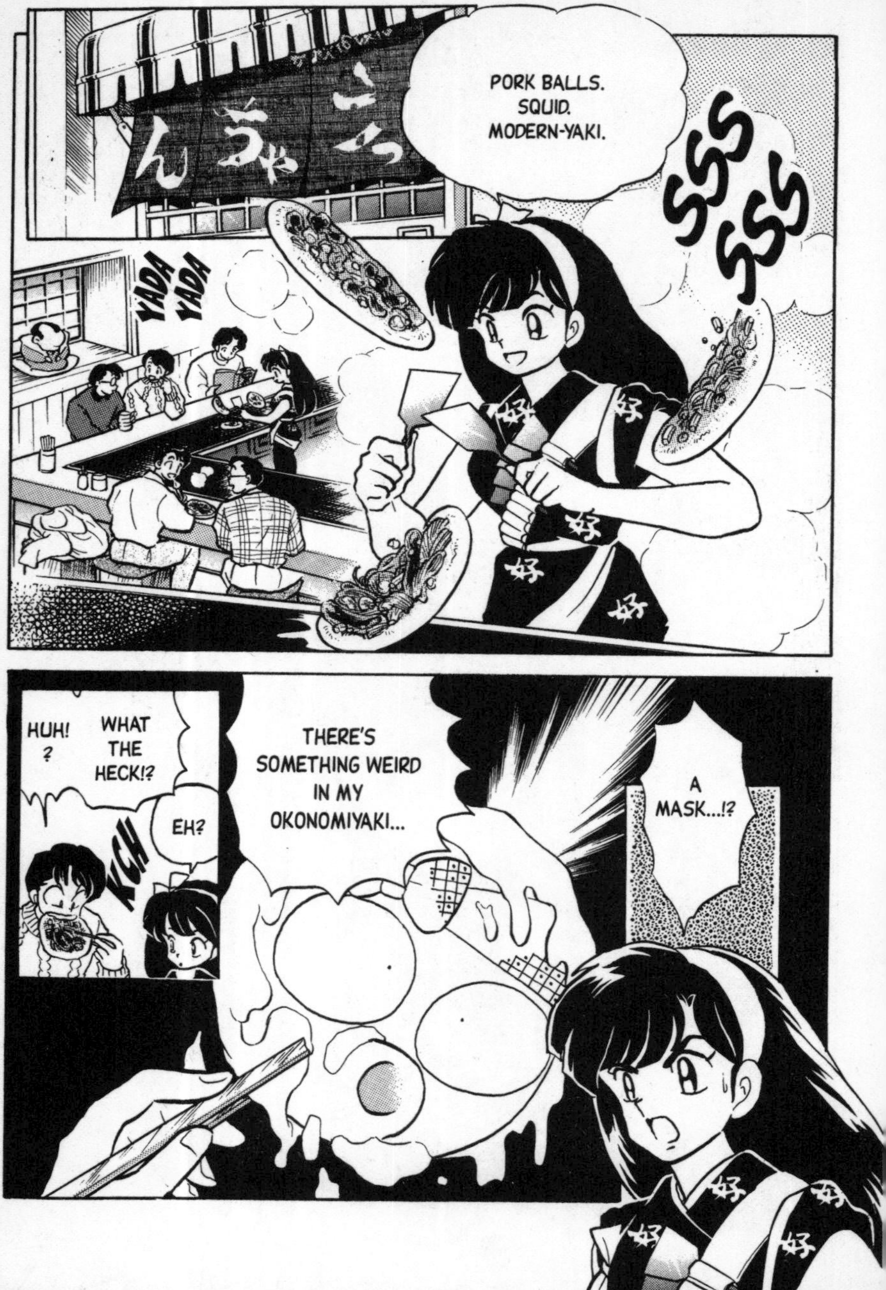
PORK BALLS. SQUID. MODERN-YAKI.
SSS SSS
YADA YADA
HUH! ?
WHAT THE HECK!?
KCH
EH?
THERE'S SOMETHING WEIRD IN MY OKONOMIYAKI...
A MASK...!?

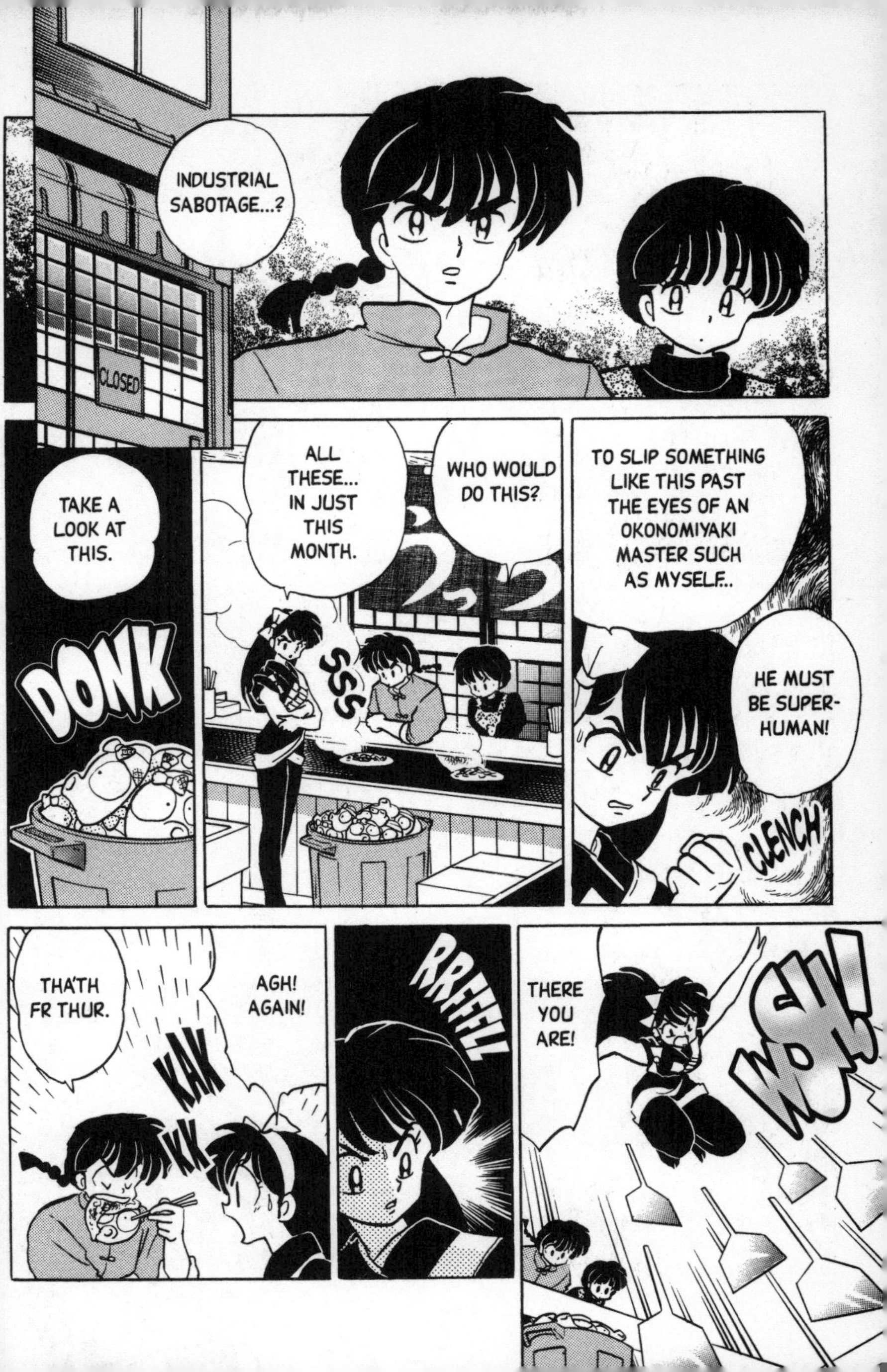
INDUSTRIAL SABOTAGE...?
CLOSED
TAKE A LOOK AT THIS.
DONK
ALL THESE... IN JUST THIS MONTH.
WHO WOULD DO THIS?
SSS
TO SLIP SOMETHING LIKE THIS PAST THE EYES OF AN OKONOMIYAKI MASTER SUCH AS MYSELF...
HE MUST BE SUPER-HUMAN!
CLENCH
THA'TH FR THUR.
AGH! AGAIN!
KAK
KK
RREFFLL
THERE YOU ARE!

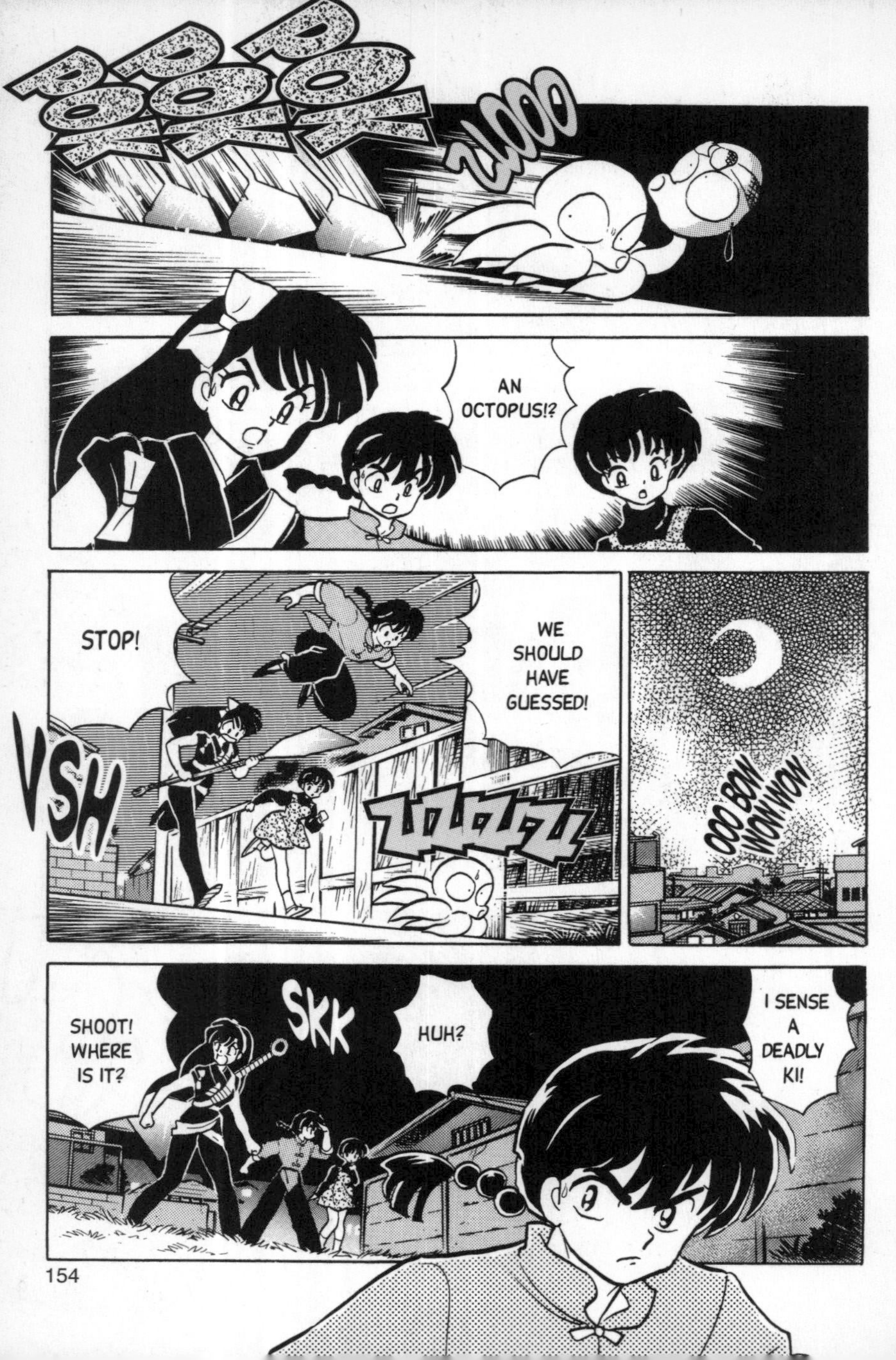
POK
POK
POK
ZOOO
AN OCTOPUS!?
STOP!
WE SHOULD HAVE GUESSED!
VSH
OOO BOW WOW WOW
SHOOT! WHERE IS IT?
SKK
HUH?
I SENSE A DEADLY KI!

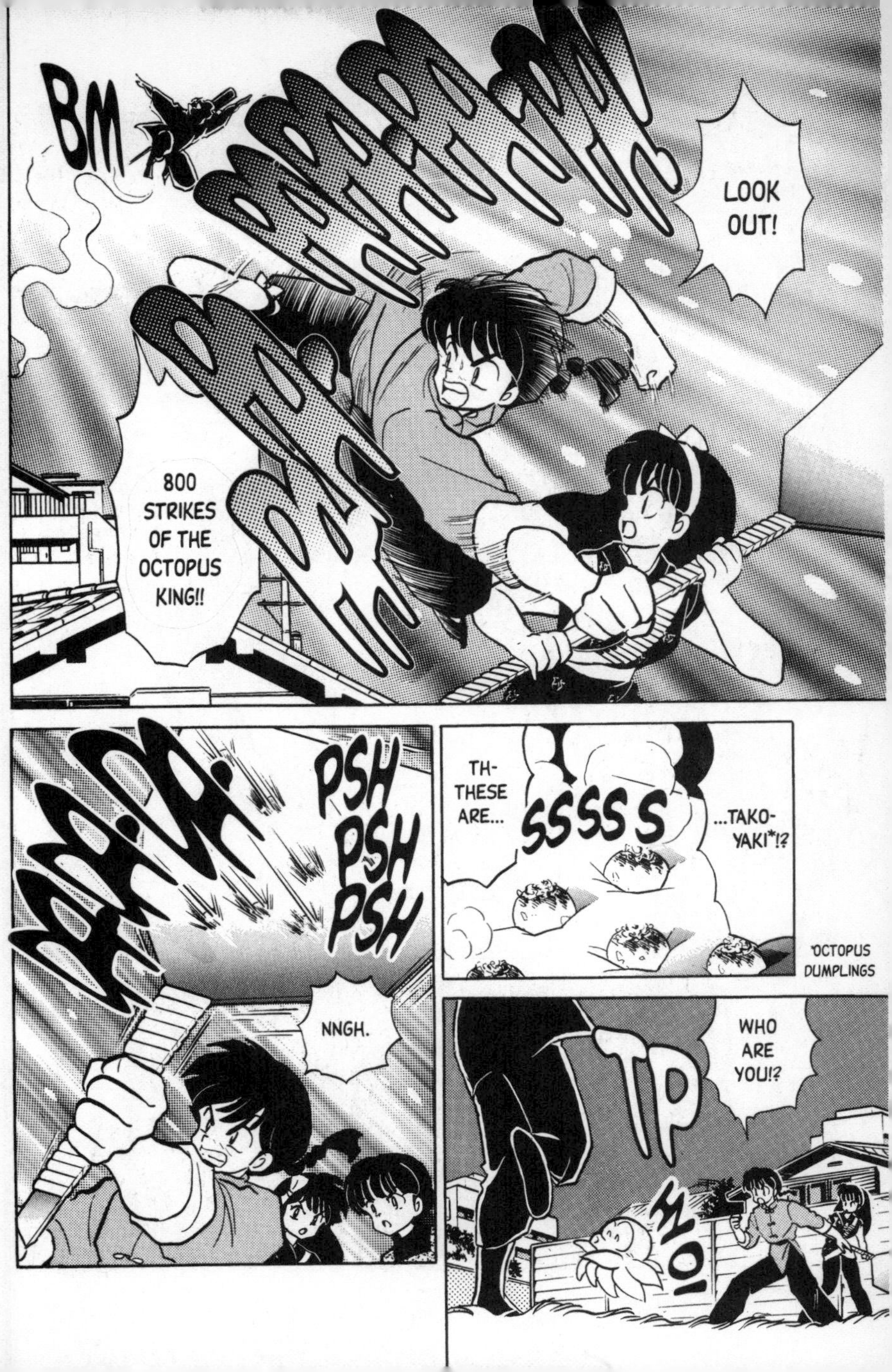
BM
LOOK OUT!
800 STRIKES OF THE OCTOPUS KING!!
PSH PSH PSH
NNGH.
TH- THESE ARE...
SSSS S
...TAKO-YAKI*!?
WHO ARE YOU!?
TP

*OCTOPUS DUMPLINGS

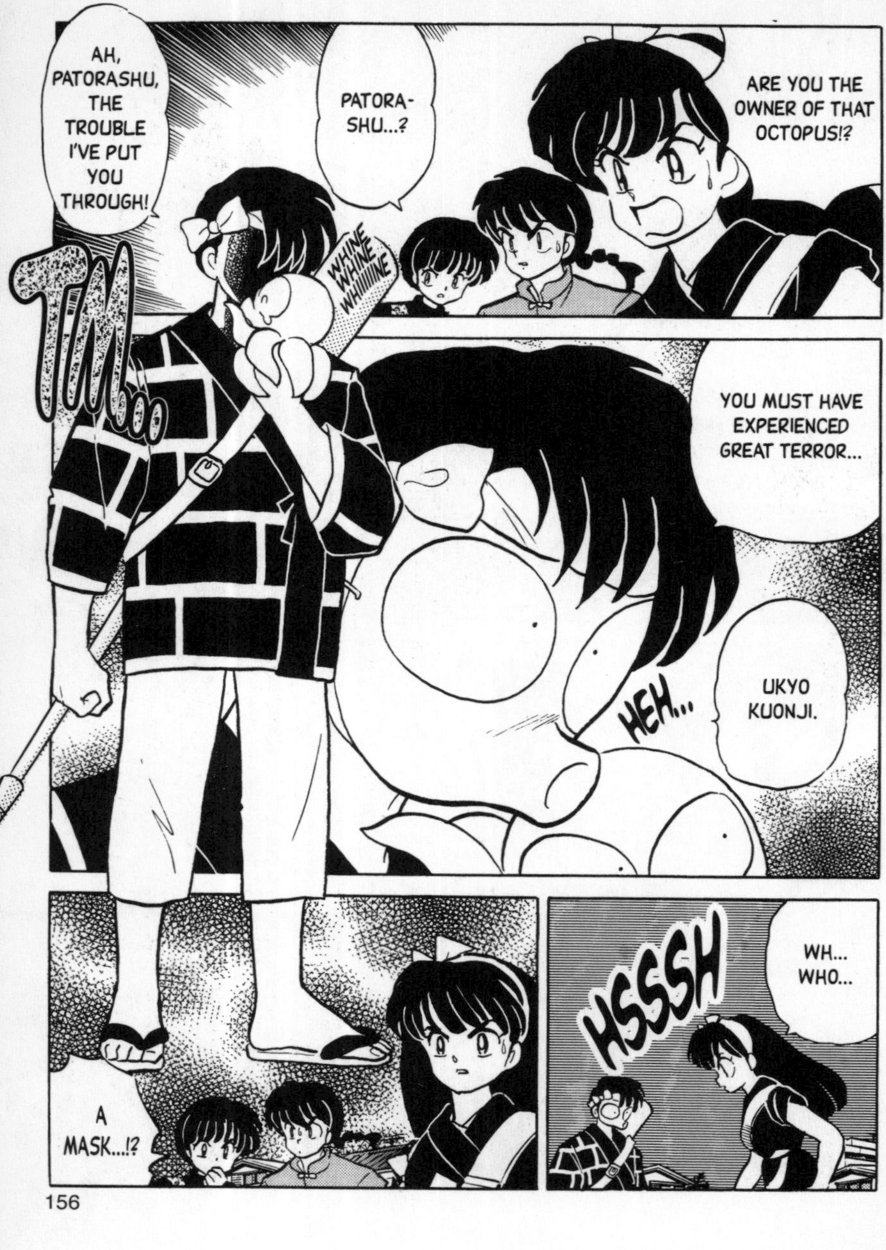
AH, PATORASHU, THE TROUBLE I'VE PUT YOU THROUGH!
PATORA-SHU...?
ARE YOU THE OWNER OF THAT OCTOPUS!?
TM...
WHINE WHINE WHIIIINE
YOU MUST HAVE EXPERIENCED GREAT TERROR...
HEH...
UKYO KUONJI.
A MASK...!?
HSSSH
WH... WHO...

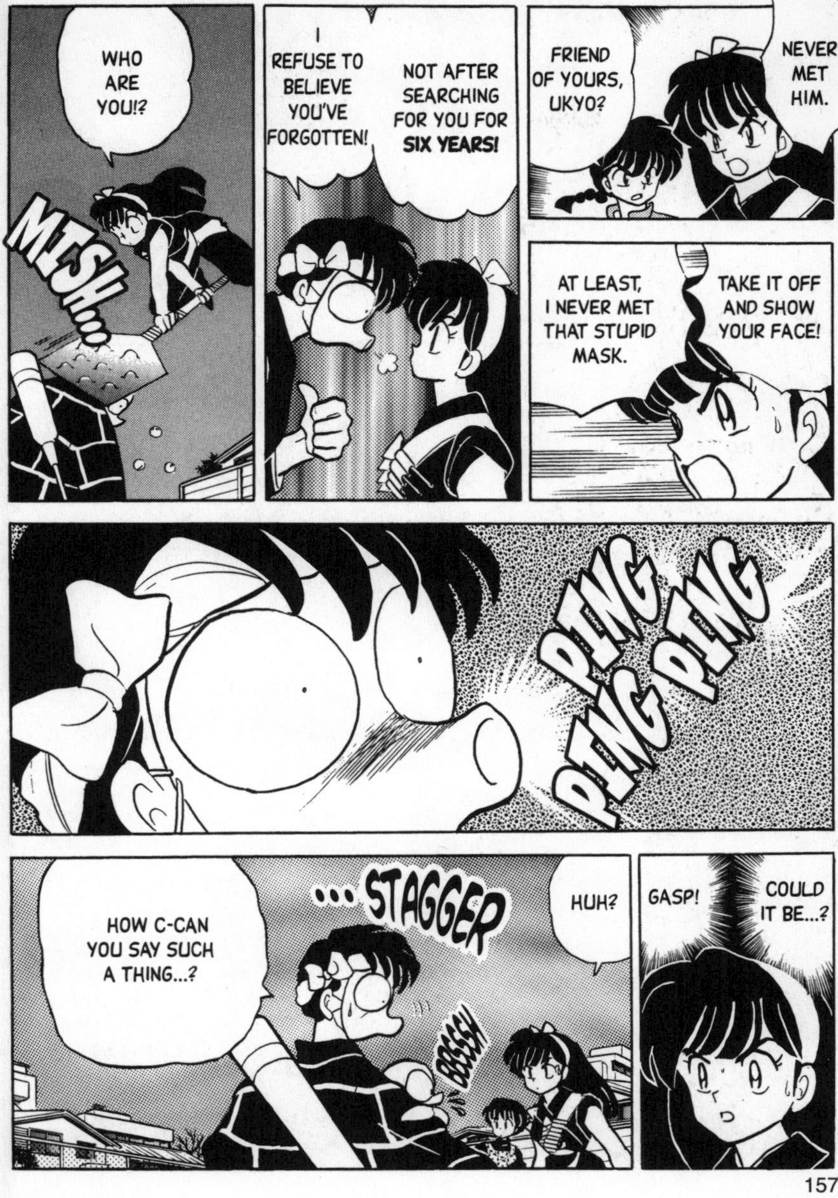

WHO ARE YOU!?
MTSH...
I REFUSE TO BELIEVE YOU'VE FORGOTTEN!
NOT AFTER SEARCHING FOR YOU FOR SIX YEARS!
FRIEND OF YOURS, UKYO?
NEVER MET HIM.
AT LEAST, I NEVER MET THAT STUPID MASK.
TAKE IT OFF AND SHOW YOUR FACE!
PING PING PING PING
HOW C-CAN YOU SAY SUCH A THING...?
...STAGGER
BSSSH
HUH?
GASP!
COULD IT BE...?

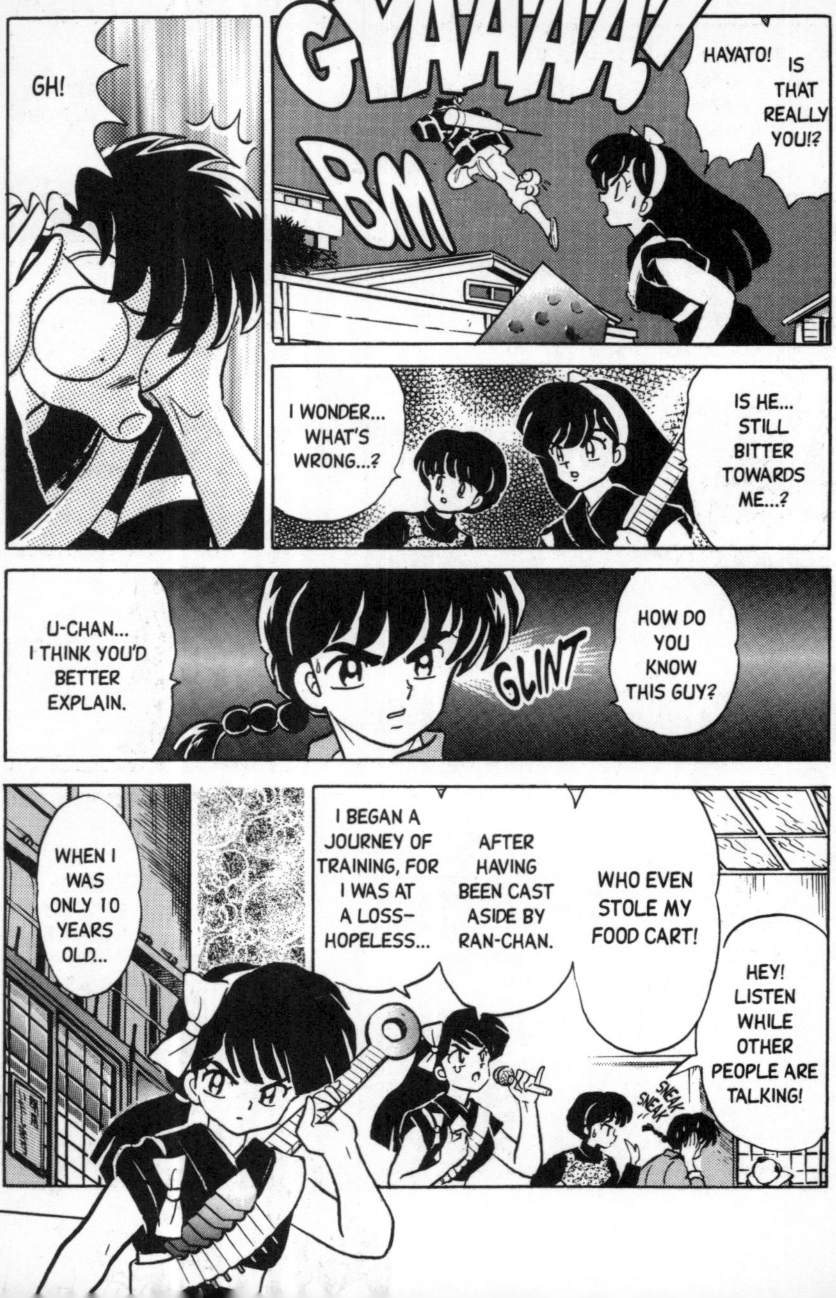
GH!
GYAAAA!
HAYATO! IS THAT REALLY YOU!?
BM
I WONDER... WHAT'S WRONG...?
IS HE... STILL BITTER TOWARDS ME...?
U-CHAN... I THINK YOU'D BETTER EXPLAIN.
GLINT
HOW DO YOU KNOW THIS GUY?
WHEN I WAS ONLY 10 YEARS OLD...
I BEGAN A JOURNEY OF TRAINING, FOR I WAS AT A LOSS— HOPELESS...
AFTER HAVING BEEN CAST ASIDE BY RAN-CHAN.
WHO EVEN STOLE MY FOOD CART!
HEY! LISTEN WHILE OTHER PEOPLE ARE TALKING!
SNEAK SNEAK

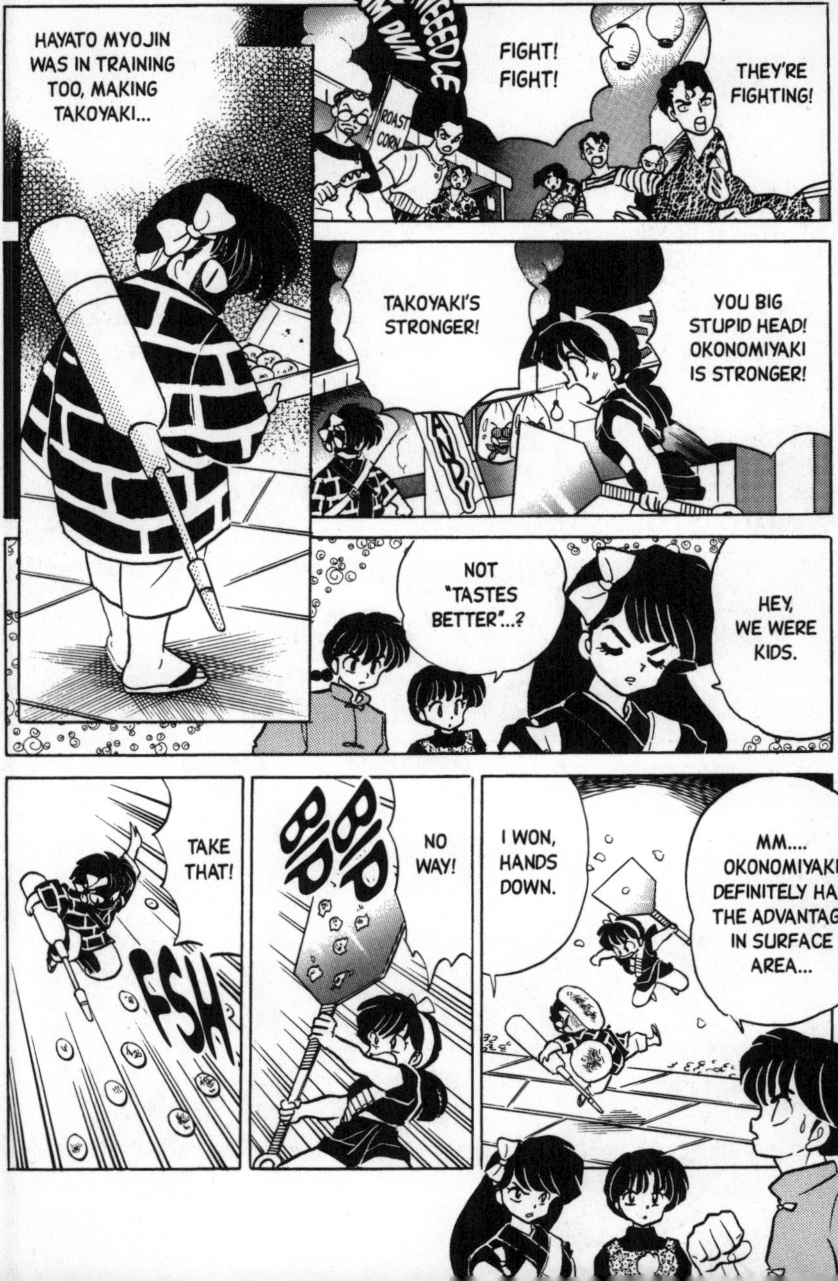
HAYATO MYOJIN WAS IN TRAINING TOO, MAKING TAKOYAKI...
PWEEEDLE
DUM DUM
ROAST CORN
FIGHT! FIGHT!
THEY'RE FIGHTING!
TAKOYAKI'S STRONGER!
YOU BIG STUPID HEAD! OKONOMIYAKI IS STRONGER!
ANDY
NOT "TASTES BETTER"...?
HEY, WE WERE KIDS.
TAKE THAT!
FSH
NO WAY!
BIP BIP
I WON, HANDS DOWN.
MM.... OKONOMIYAKI DEFINITELY HAS THE ADVANTAGE IN SURFACE AREA...

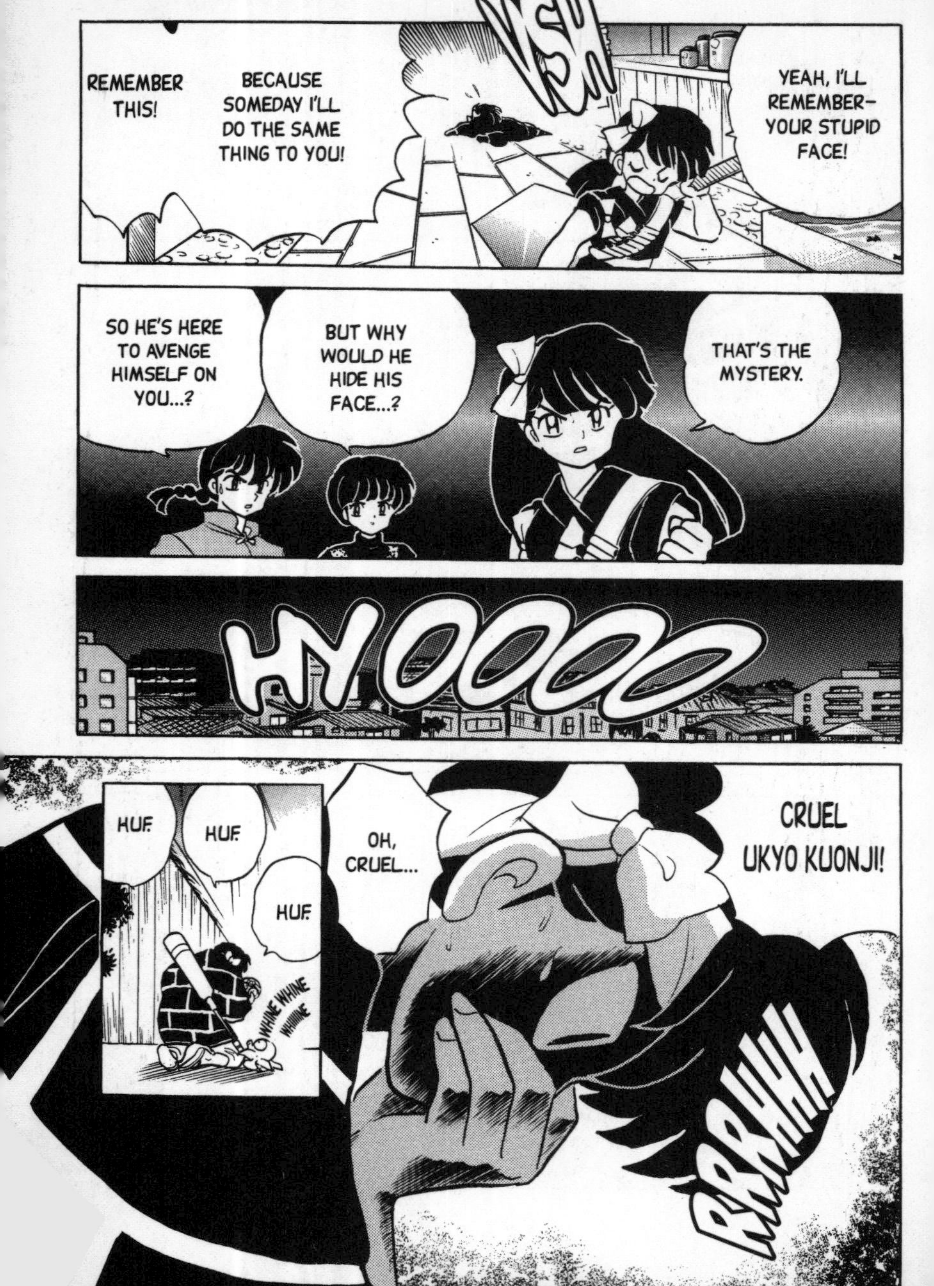
REMEMBER THIS!
BECAUSE SOMEDAY I'LL DO THE SAME THING TO YOU!
VSH
YEAH, I'LL REMEMBER— YOUR STUPID FACE!
SO HE'S HERE TO AVENGE HIMSELF ON YOU...?
BUT WHY WOULD HE HIDE HIS FACE...?
THAT'S THE MYSTERY.
HYOOOO
HUF.
HUF.
HUF.
WHINE WHINE WHINE
OH, CRUEL...
CRUEL UKYO KUONJI!
BRRWAH

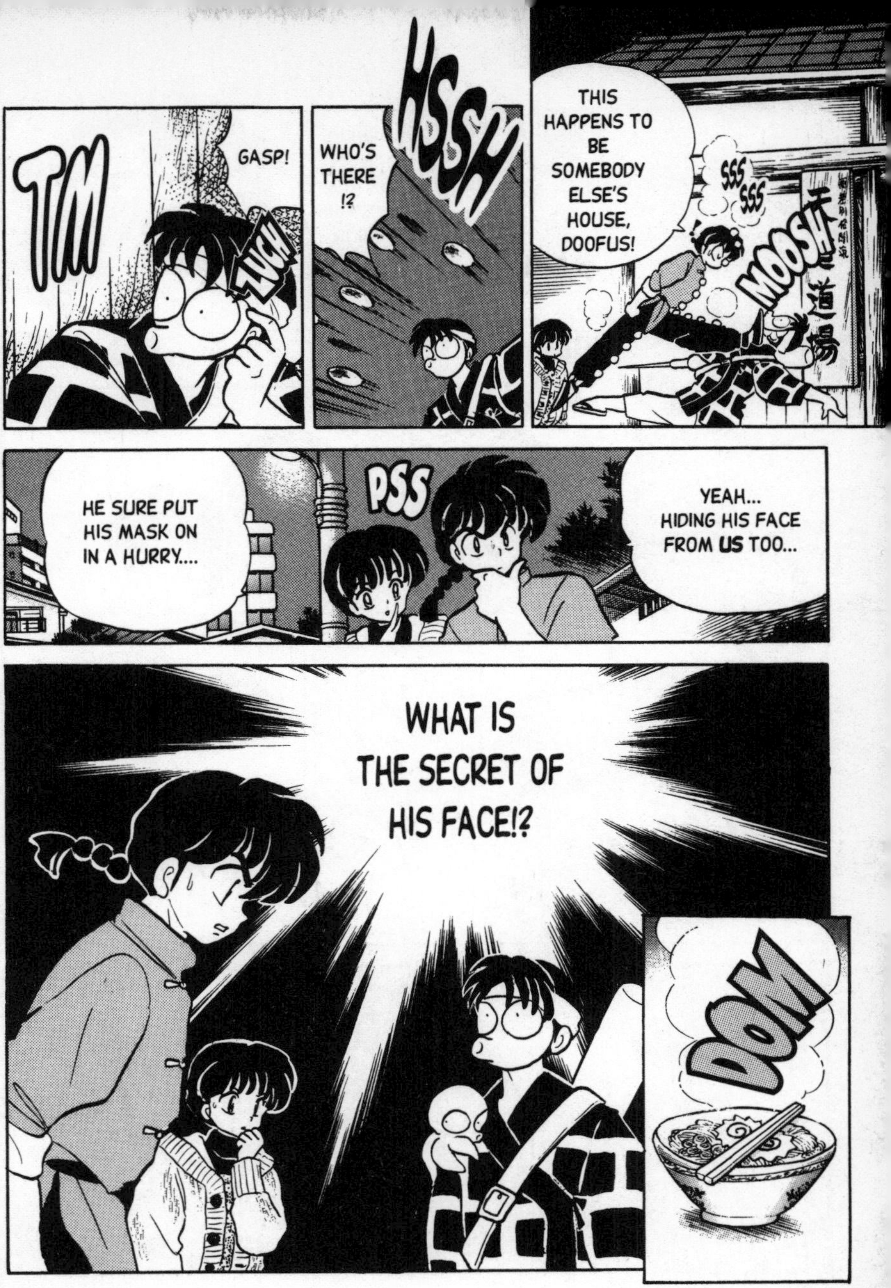
TM
GASP!
LUCH
WHO'S THERE !?
HSSH
THIS HAPPENS TO BE SOMEBODY ELSE'S HOUSE, DOOFUS!
SSS
SSS
MOOSH
HE SURE PUT HIS MASK ON IN A HURRY....
PSS
YEAH... HIDING HIS FACE FROM **US** TOO...
WHAT IS THE SECRET OF HIS FACE!?
DOM

HERE. EAT.

WE'RE BIG BELIEVERS IN HOSPITALITY.

YOU'RE TOO KIND.

SIIIGH

WELL, THEN... WITH YOUR PERMISSION...

SS

OKAY...

HE'S TAKING OFF THE MASK!!

SLRRRP

PONG

YOUR GENEROSITY IS BEYOND...

DON'T WORRY ABOUT IT.

NOW, TO WASH MY FACE.

SHH

YES!

SLPPPPPT

GUB GUB GUB

WHY DON'T YOU STAY FOR THE NIGHT?

I DO APPRECIATE ALL YOUR TROUBLE...

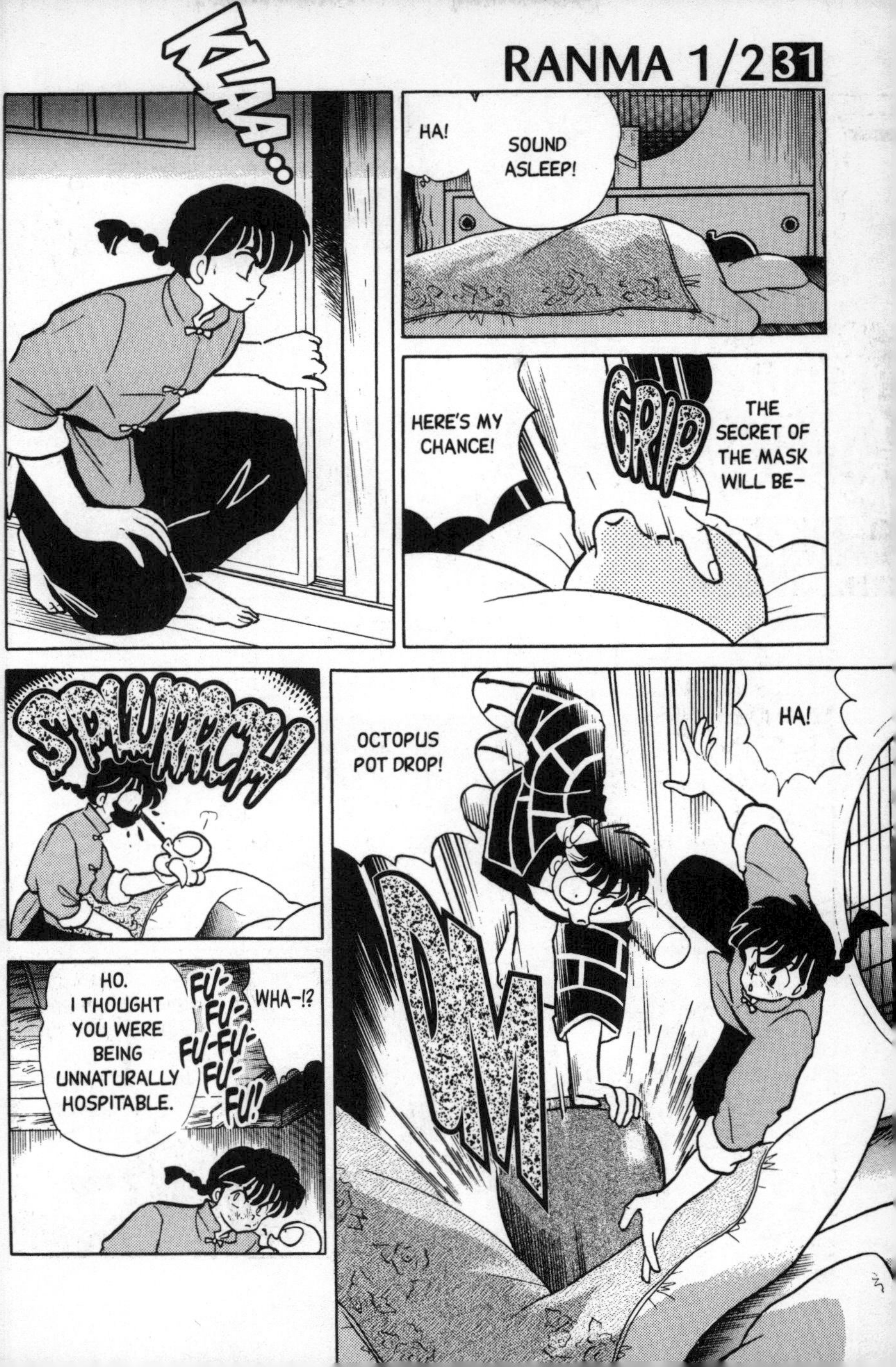
KLAA...
HA!
SOUND ASLEEP!
HERE'S MY CHANCE!
GRIP
THE SECRET OF THE MASK WILL BE-
HO. I THOUGHT YOU WERE BEING UNNATURALLY HOSPITABLE.
FU-FU-FU-FU-FU-FU!
WHA-!?
OCTOPUS POT DROP!
HA!
DM

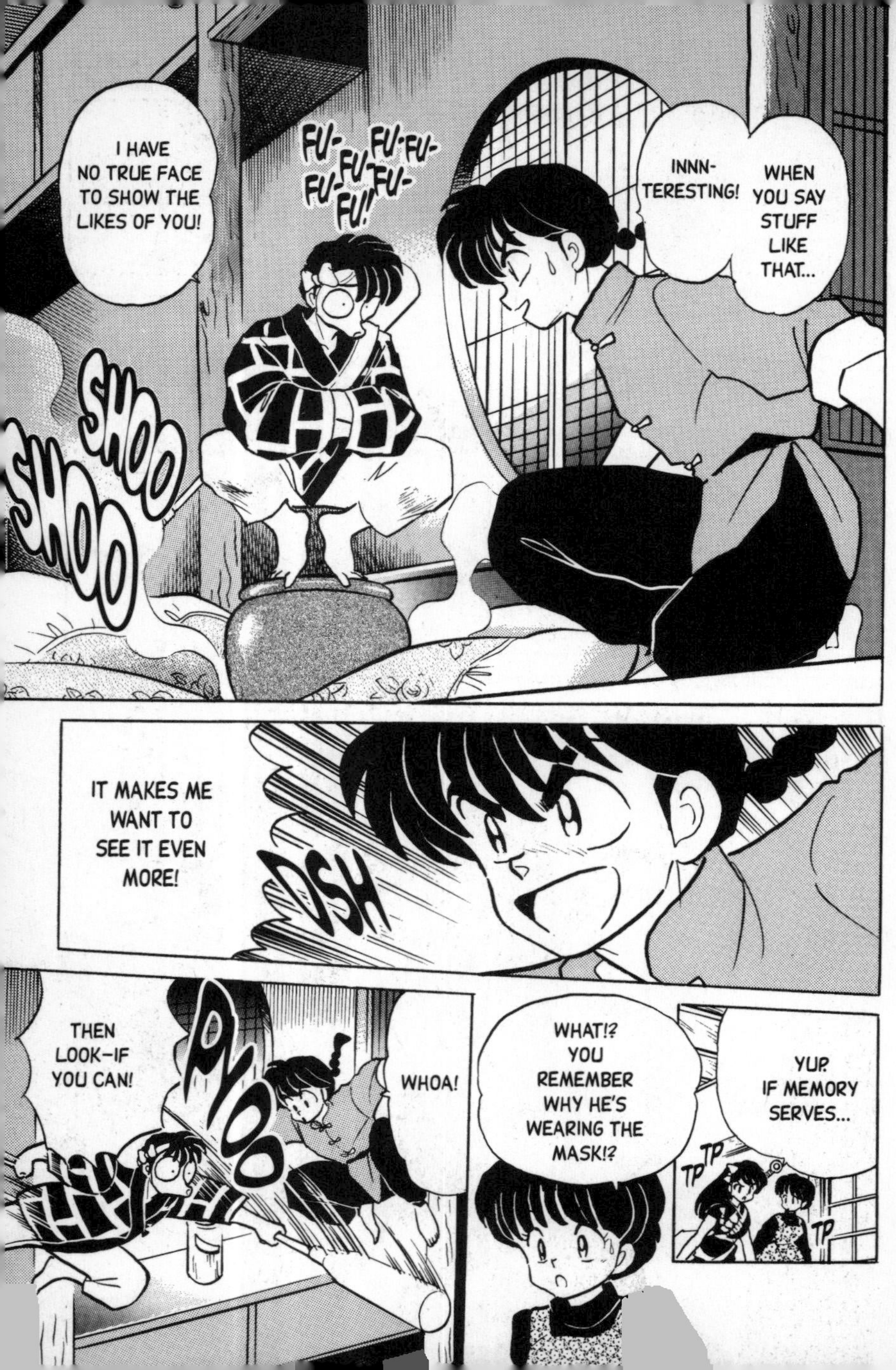
I HAVE NO TRUE FACE TO SHOW THE LIKES OF YOU!
FU-FU-FU-FU-FU-FU-FU!
SHOO SHOO
INNN-TERESTING!
WHEN YOU SAY STUFF LIKE THAT...
IT MAKES ME WANT TO SEE IT EVEN MORE!
DSH
THEN LOOK—IF YOU CAN!
PYOO
WHOA!
WHAT!? YOU REMEMBER WHY HE'S WEARING THE MASK!?
YUP. IF MEMORY SERVES...
TP TP
TP

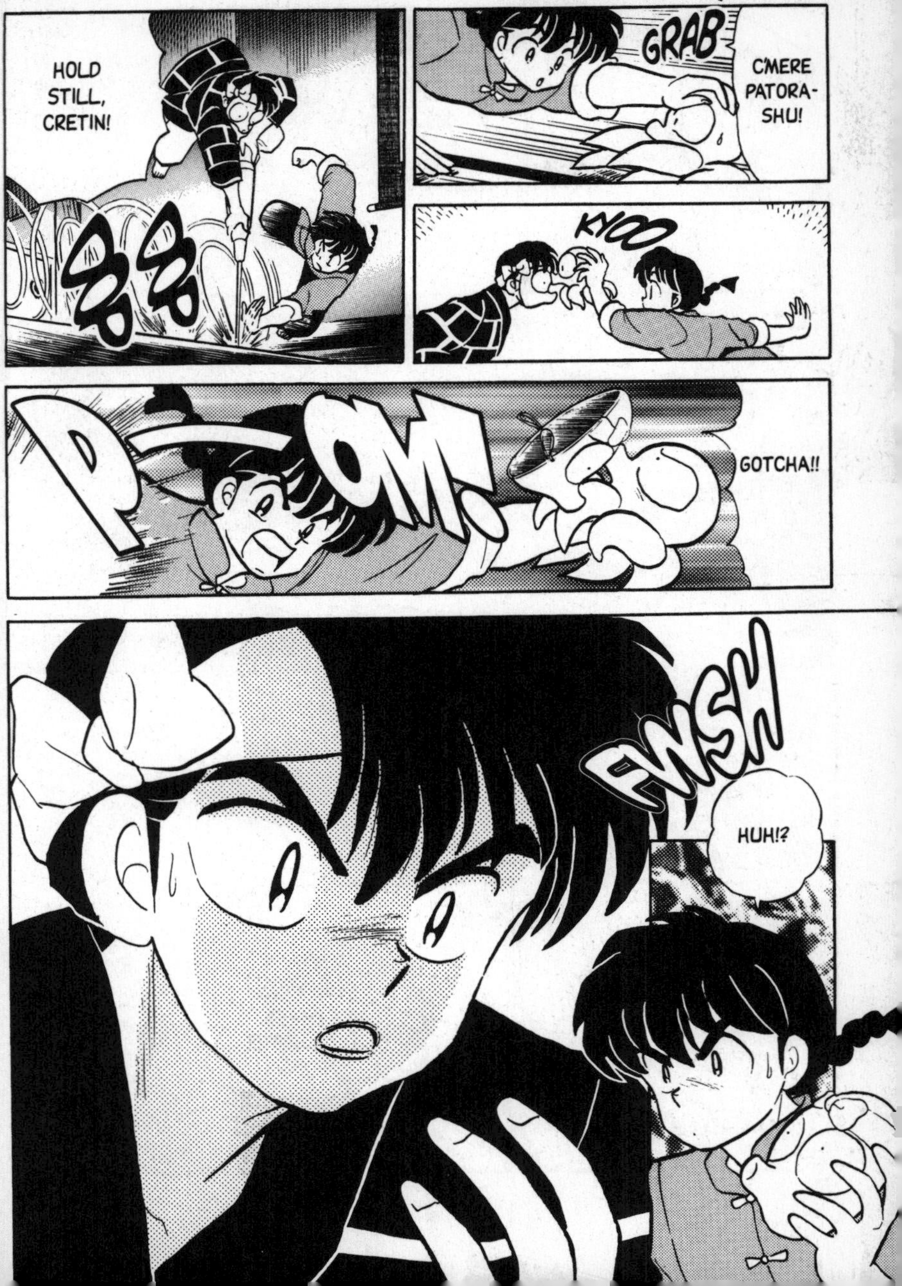
HOLD STILL, CRETIN!
DOP DOP
GRAB
C'MERE PATORA-SHU!
KYOO
POM!
GOTCHA!!
FWSH
HUH!?

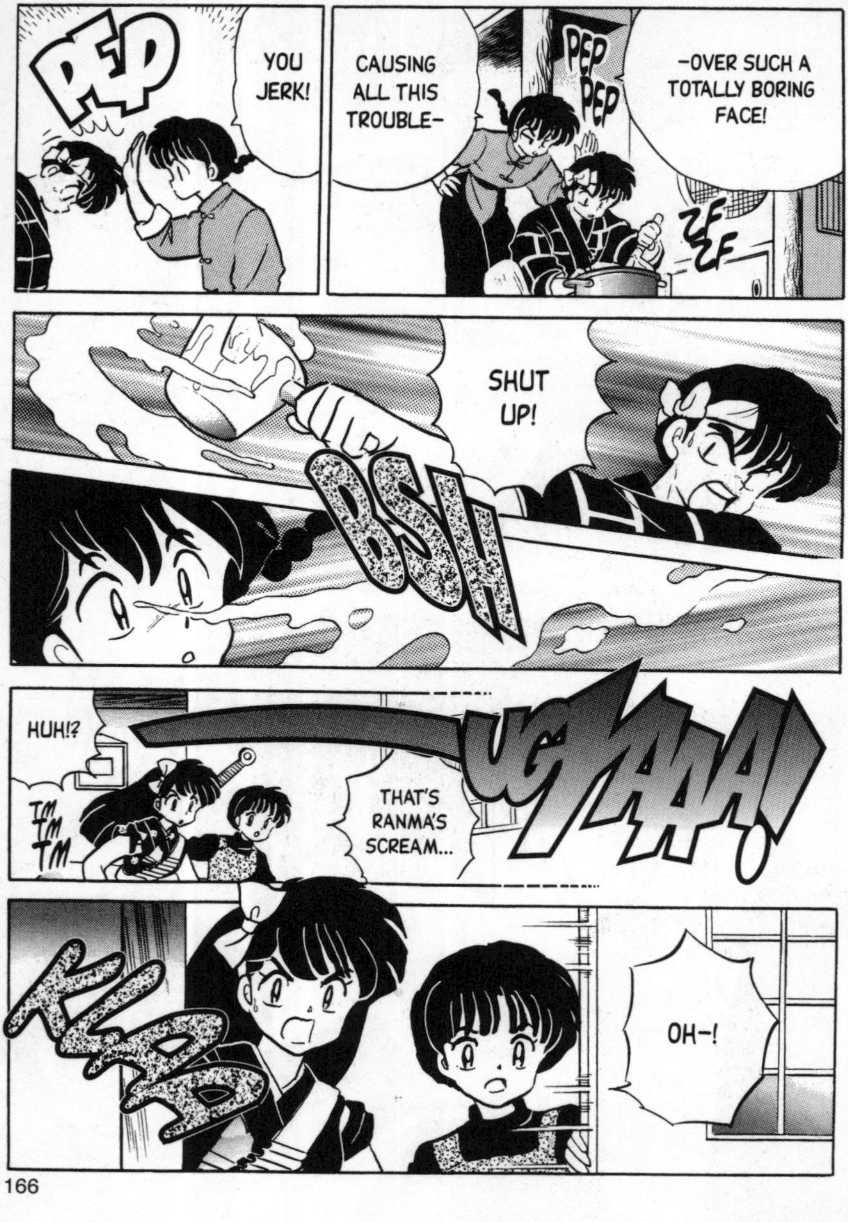
PEP
YOU JERK!
CAUSING ALL THIS TROUBLE–
PEP PEP
–OVER SUCH A TOTALLY BORING FACE!
SHUT UP!
BSH
HUH!?
TM TM TM
THAT'S RANMA'S SCREAM...
UGYAAA!
OH–!

PART 11
MASKED DEATH MATCH!

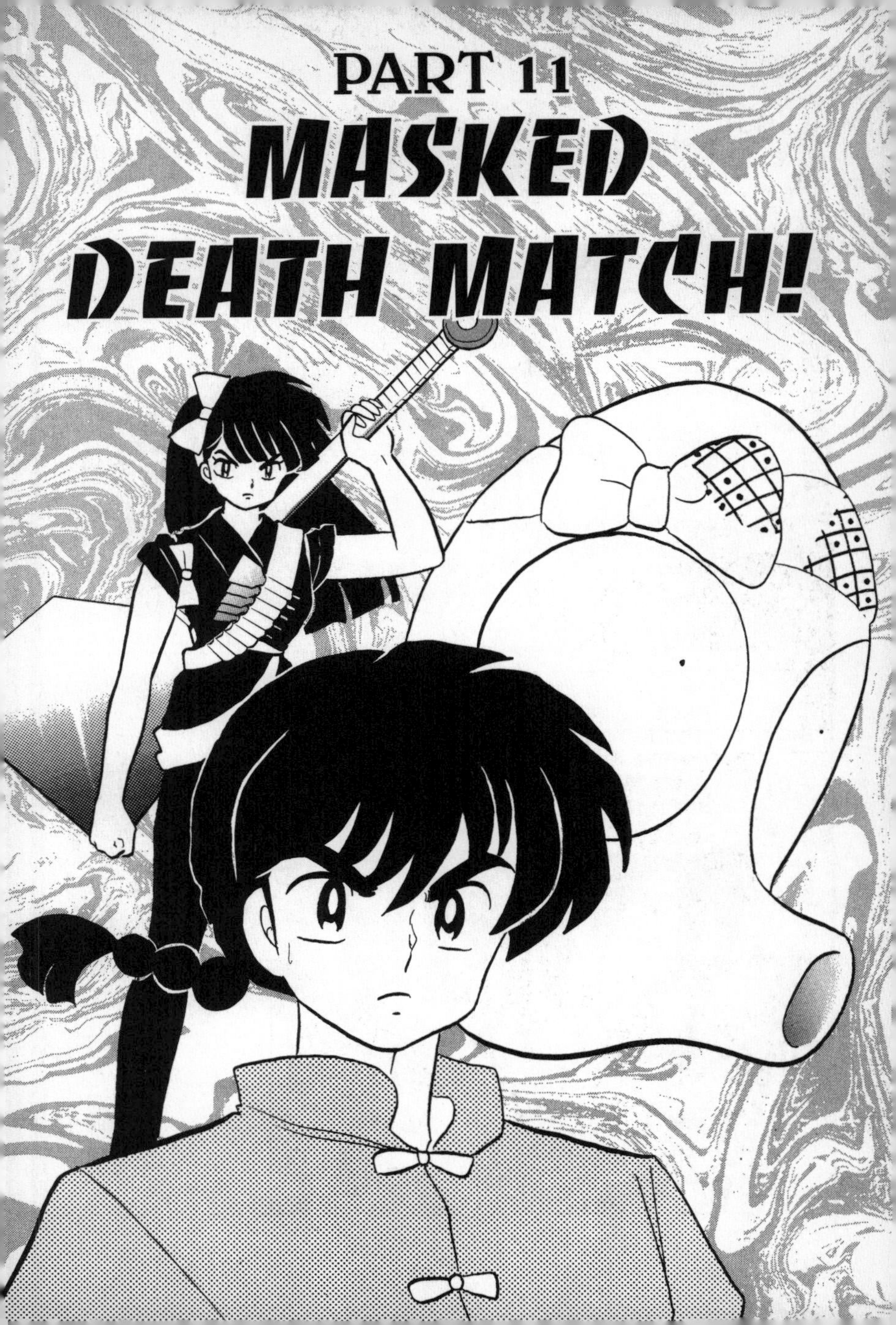

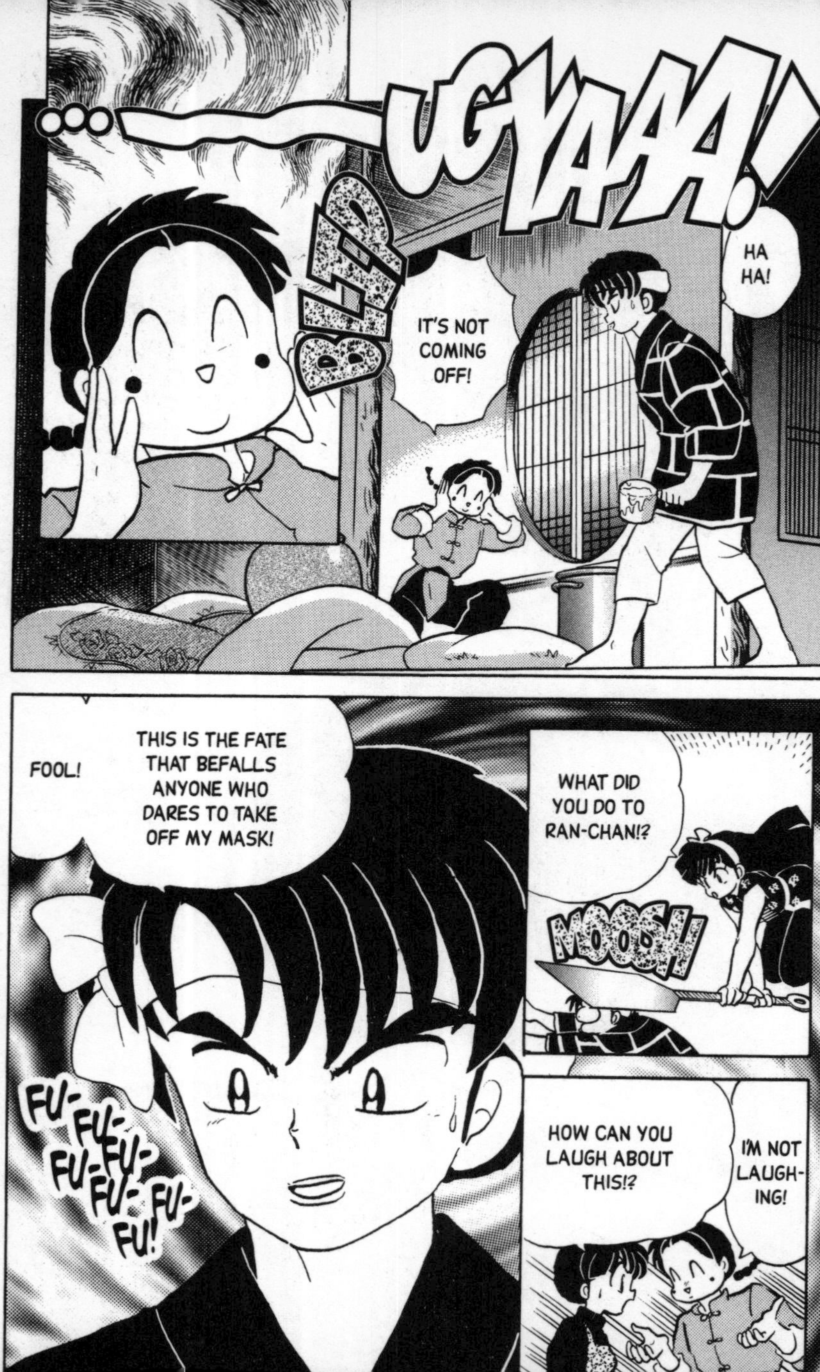
...—UGYAAA!
BLIP
IT'S NOT COMING OFF!
HA HA!
FOOL!
THIS IS THE FATE THAT BEFALLS ANYONE WHO DARES TO TAKE OFF MY MASK!
FU-FU-FU-FU-FU-FU-FU-FU!
WHAT DID YOU DO TO RAN-CHAN!?
MOOSH
HOW CAN YOU LAUGH ABOUT THIS!?
I'M NOT LAUGHING!

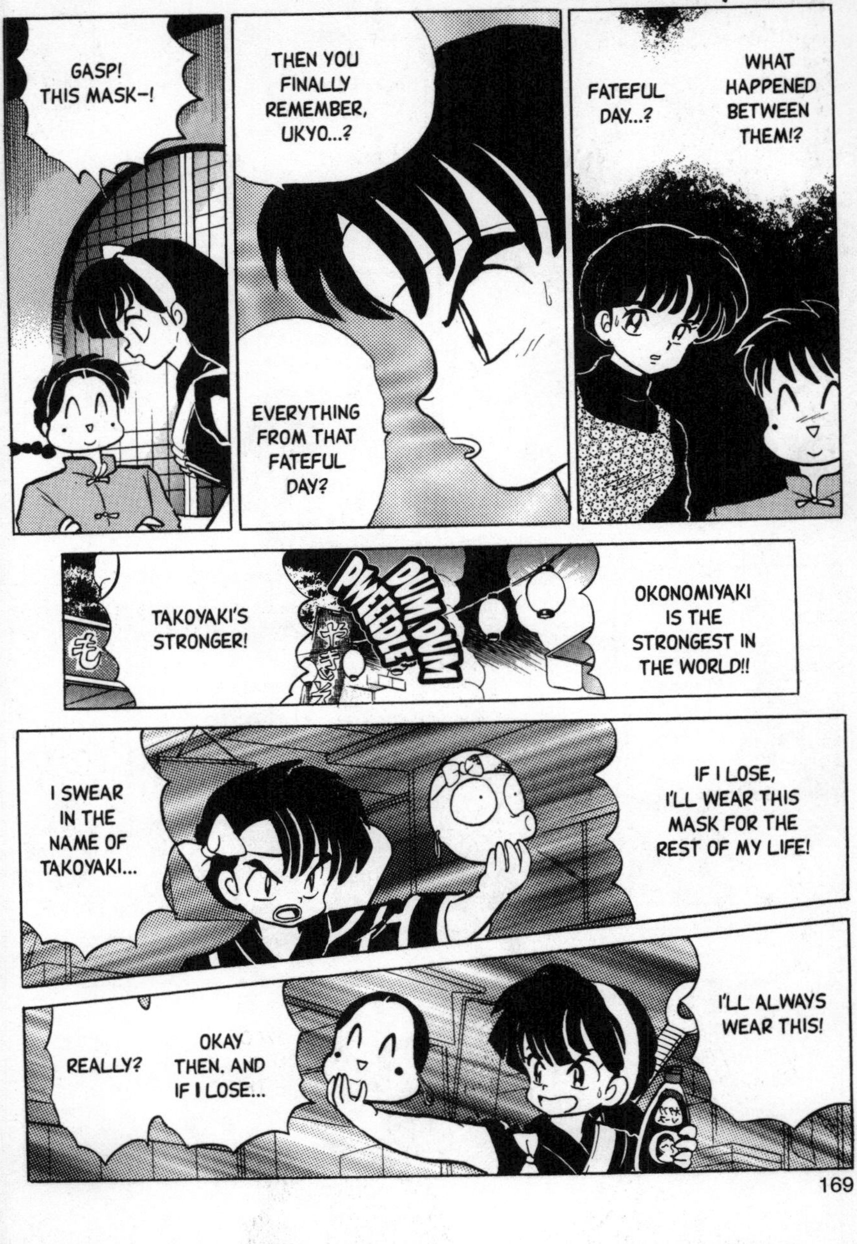
GASP! THIS MASK—!
THEN YOU FINALLY REMEMBER, UKYO...?
EVERYTHING FROM THAT FATEFUL DAY?
FATEFUL DAY...?
WHAT HAPPENED BETWEEN THEM!?
TAKOYAKI'S STRONGER!
DUM DUM PWEEEDLE
OKONOMIYAKI IS THE STRONGEST IN THE WORLD!!
I SWEAR IN THE NAME OF TAKOYAKI...
IF I LOSE, I'LL WEAR THIS MASK FOR THE REST OF MY LIFE!
REALLY?
OKAY THEN. AND IF I LOSE...
I'LL ALWAYS WEAR THIS!

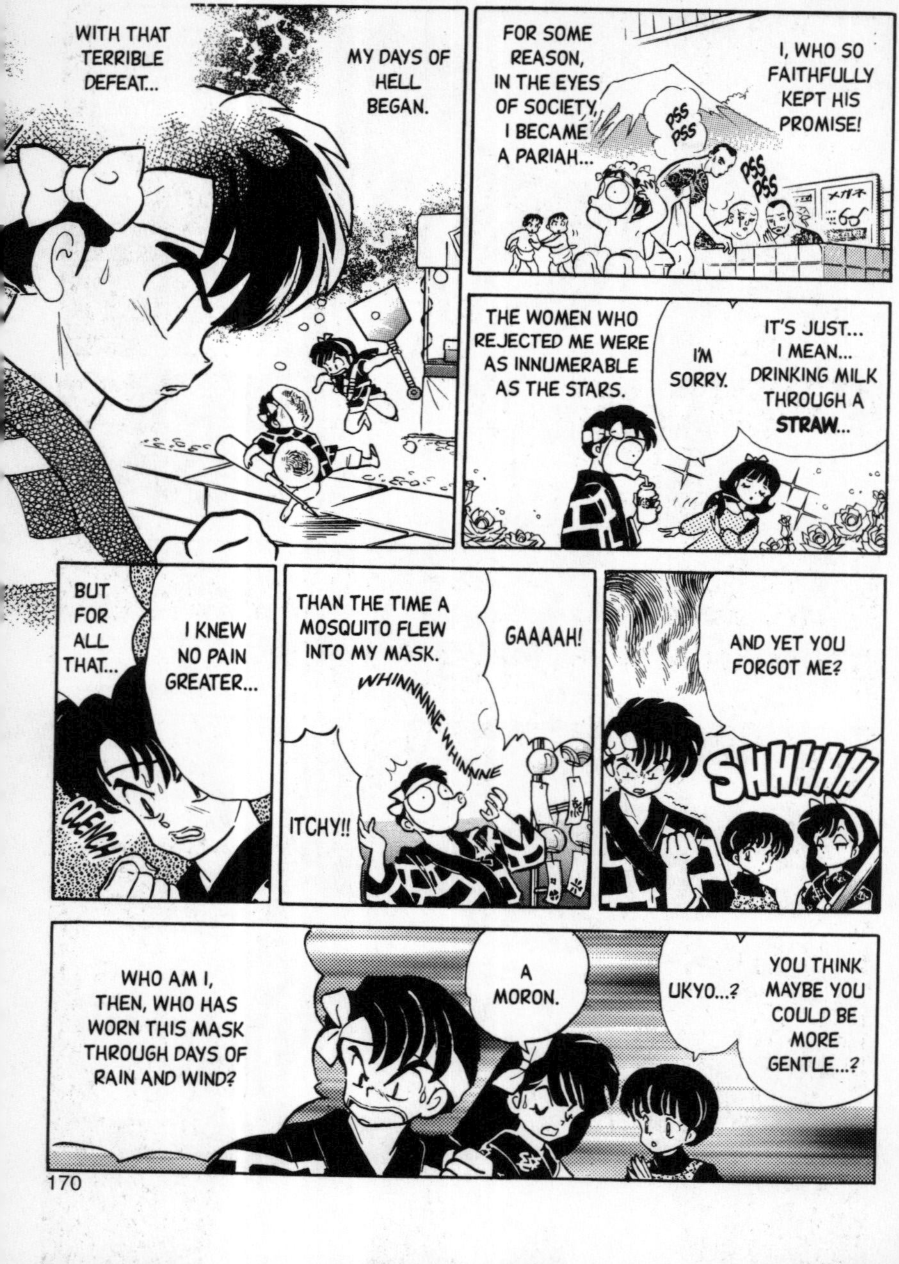
WITH THAT TERRIBLE DEFEAT...
MY DAYS OF HELL BEGAN.
FOR SOME REASON, IN THE EYES OF SOCIETY, I BECAME A PARIAH...
PSS PSS
PSS PSS
I, WHO SO FAITHFULLY KEPT HIS PROMISE!
THE WOMEN WHO REJECTED ME WERE AS INNUMERABLE AS THE STARS.
I'M SORRY.
IT'S JUST... I MEAN... DRINKING MILK THROUGH A STRAW...
BUT FOR ALL THAT...
I KNEW NO PAIN GREATER...
CLENCH
THAN THE TIME A MOSQUITO FLEW INTO MY MASK.
GAAAAH!
WHINNNNNE WHINNNNE
ITCHY!!
AND YET YOU FORGOT ME?
SHHHHH
WHO AM I, THEN, WHO HAS WORN THIS MASK THROUGH DAYS OF RAIN AND WIND?
A MORON.
UKYO...?
YOU THINK MAYBE YOU COULD BE MORE GENTLE...?

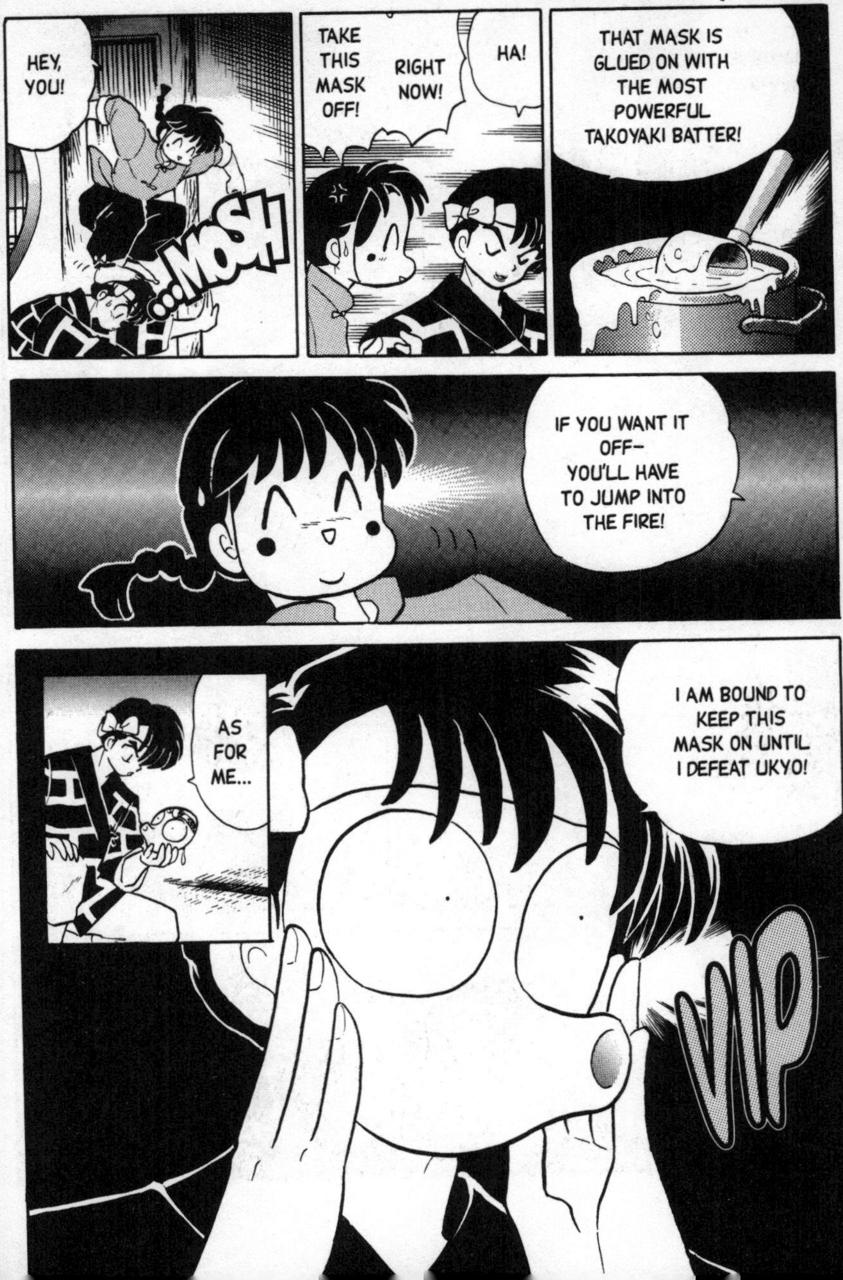
HEY, YOU!
...MOSH
TAKE THIS MASK OFF!
RIGHT NOW!
HA!
THAT MASK IS GLUED ON WITH THE MOST POWERFUL TAKOYAKI BATTER!
IF YOU WANT IT OFF— YOU'LL HAVE TO JUMP INTO THE FIRE!
AS FOR ME...
I AM BOUND TO KEEP THIS MASK ON UNTIL I DEFEAT UKYO!
VIP

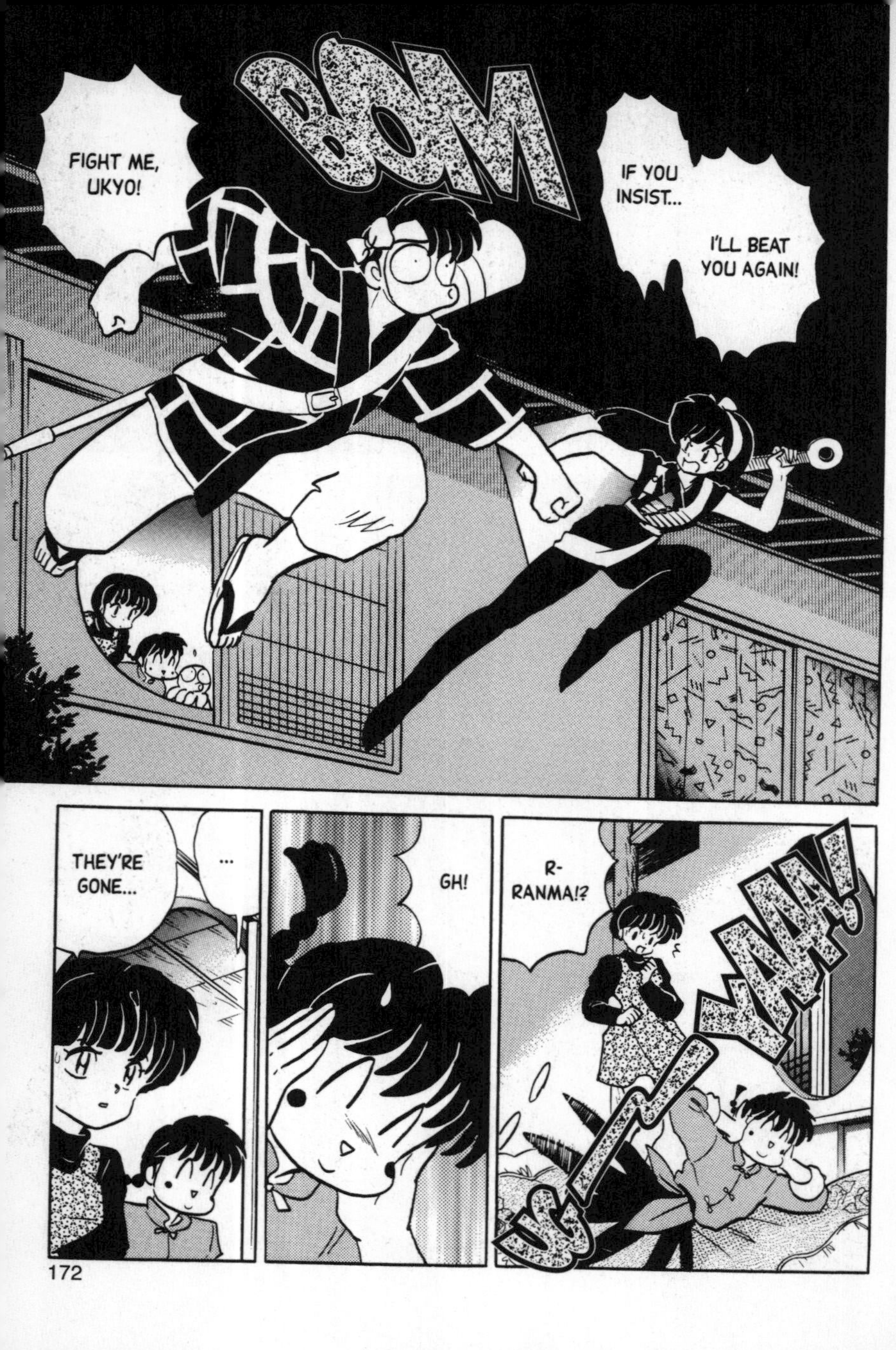
FIGHT ME, UKYO!
BOOM
IF YOU INSIST...
I'LL BEAT YOU AGAIN!
THEY'RE GONE...
...
GH!
R- RANMA!?

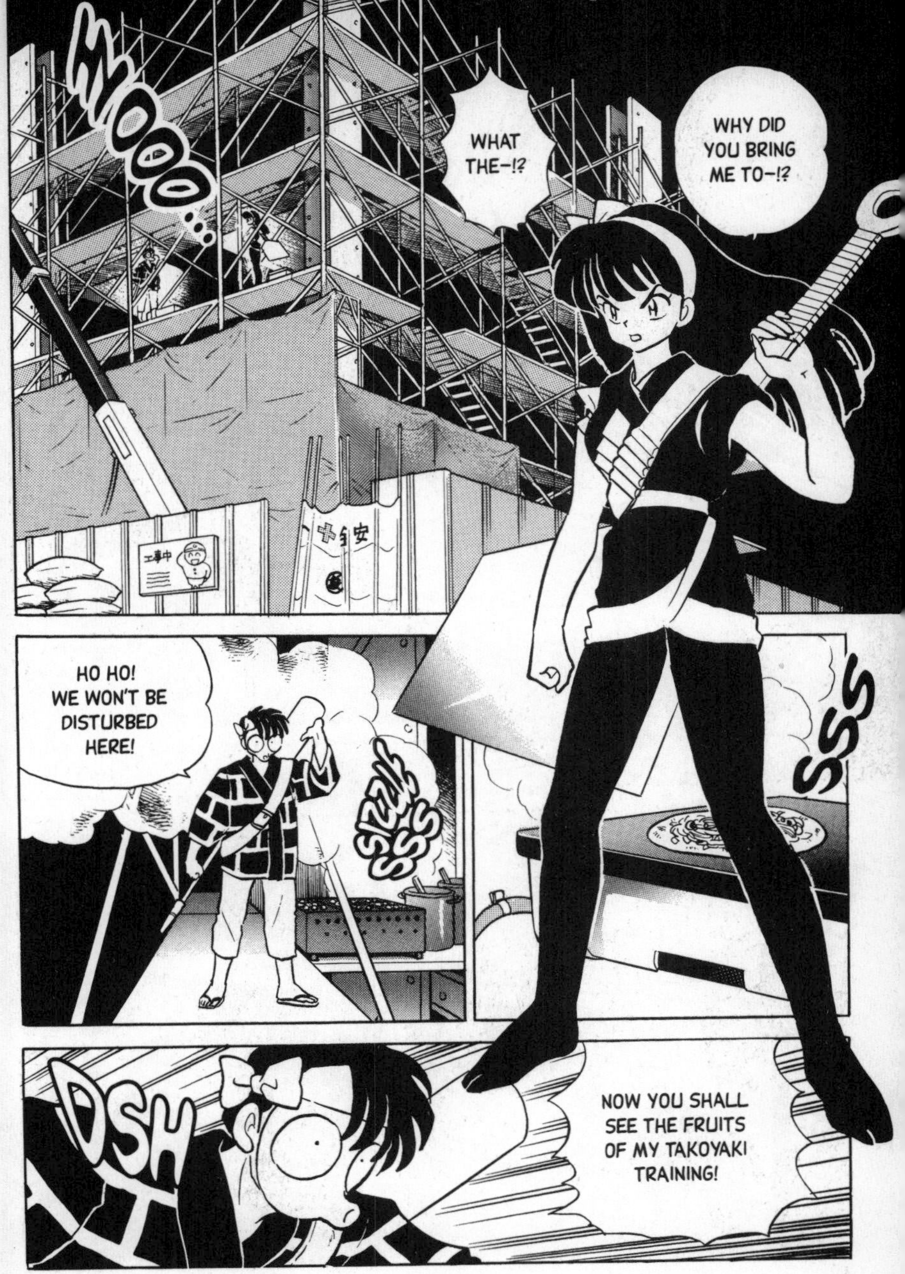
WHOOOO...
WHAT THE–!?
WHY DID YOU BRING ME TO–!?
HO HO! WE WON'T BE DISTURBED HERE!
SIZZLE
SSS
DSH
NOW YOU SHALL SEE THE FRUITS OF MY TAKOYAKI TRAINING!

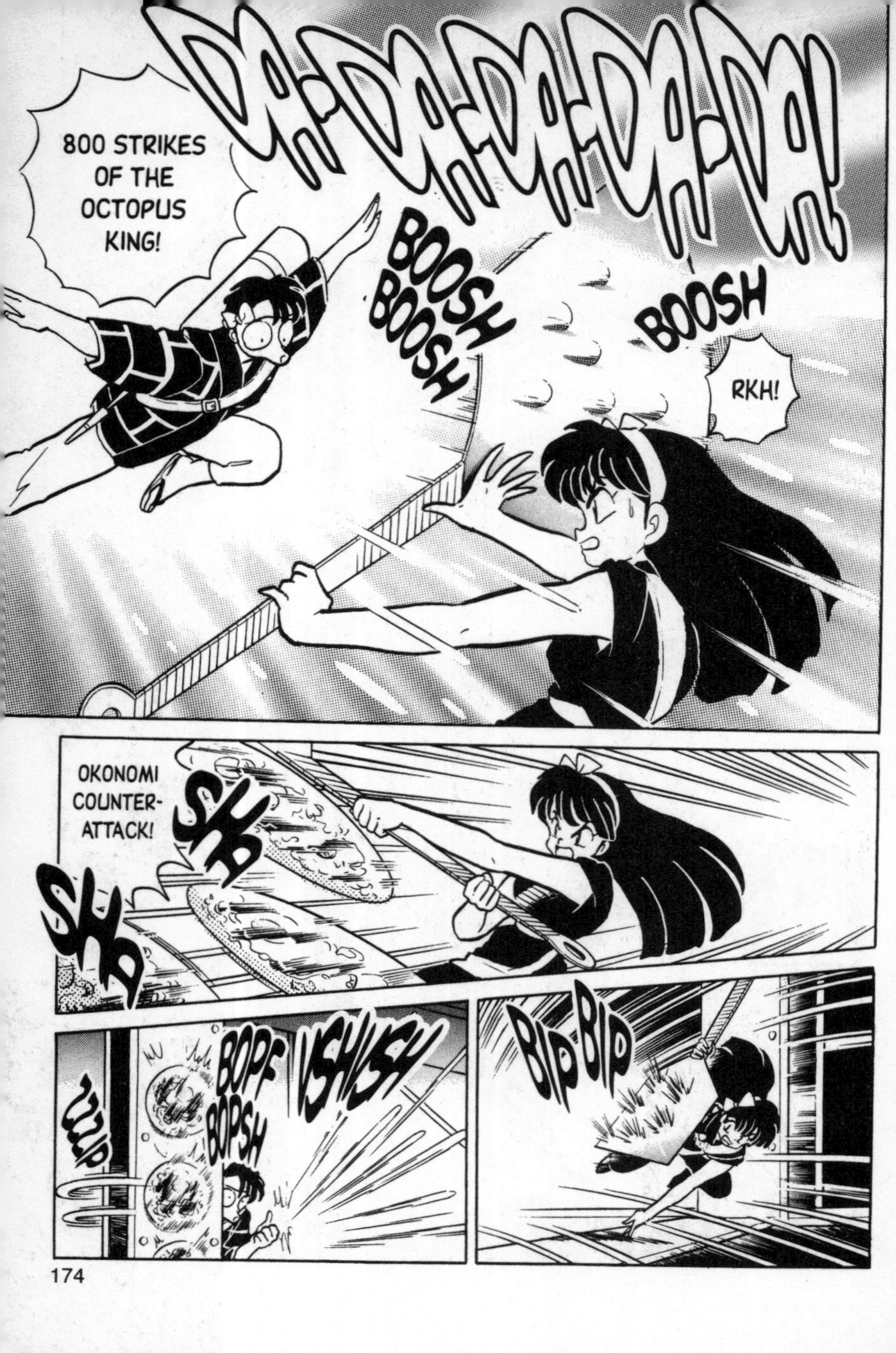
800 STRIKES OF THE OCTOPUS KING!
BOOSH BOOSH BOOSH
BOOSH
RKH!
OKONOMI COUNTER-ATTACK!
SHA
SHA
BOPF BOPSH
VSHVSH
BIP BIP

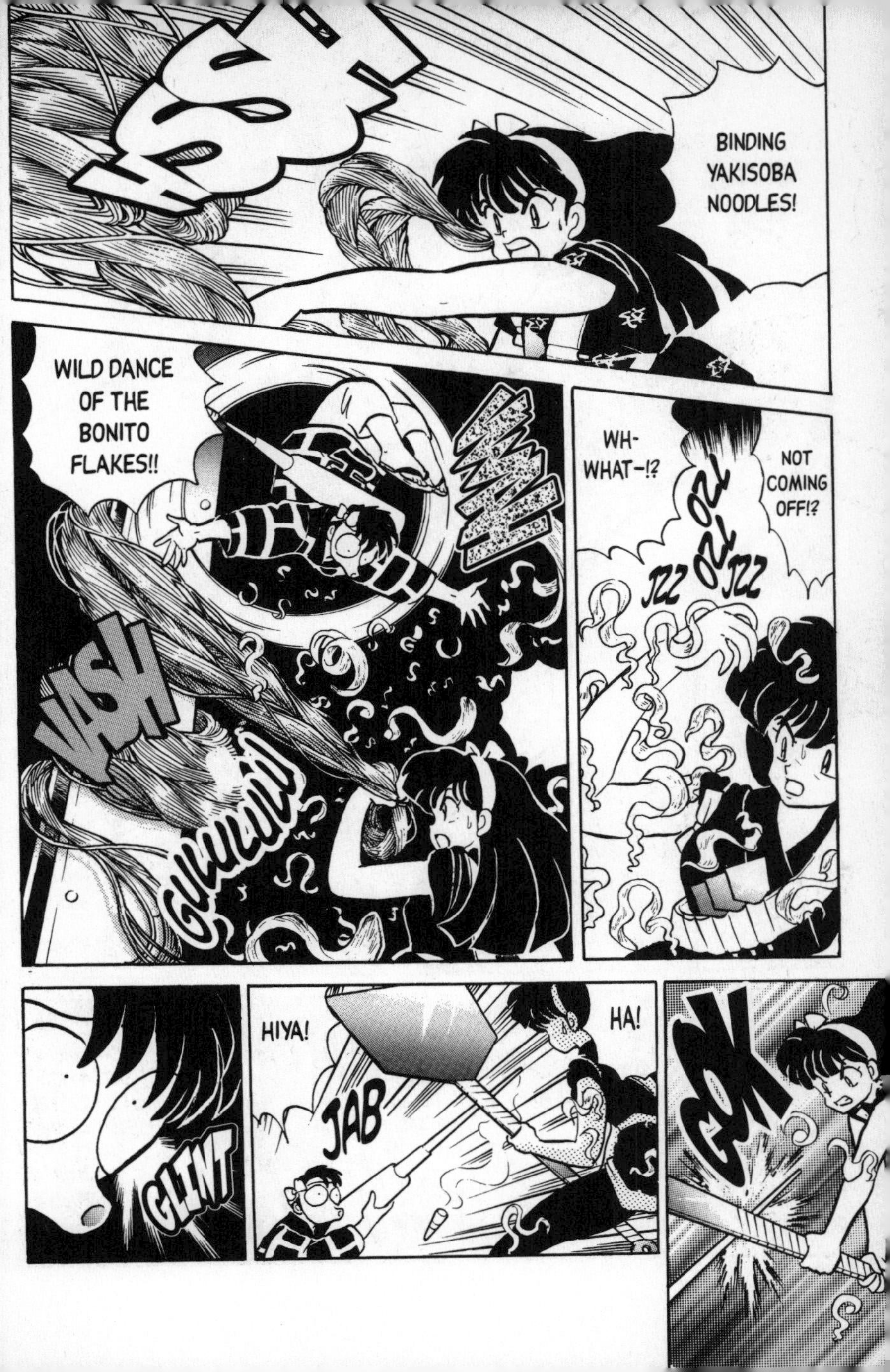
BINDING YAKISOBA NOODLES!
WILD DANCE OF THE BONITO FLAKES!!
VASH
WH- WHAT-!?
NOT COMING OFF!?
JZZ
JZZ
GLINT
HIYA!
JAB
HA!
GOK

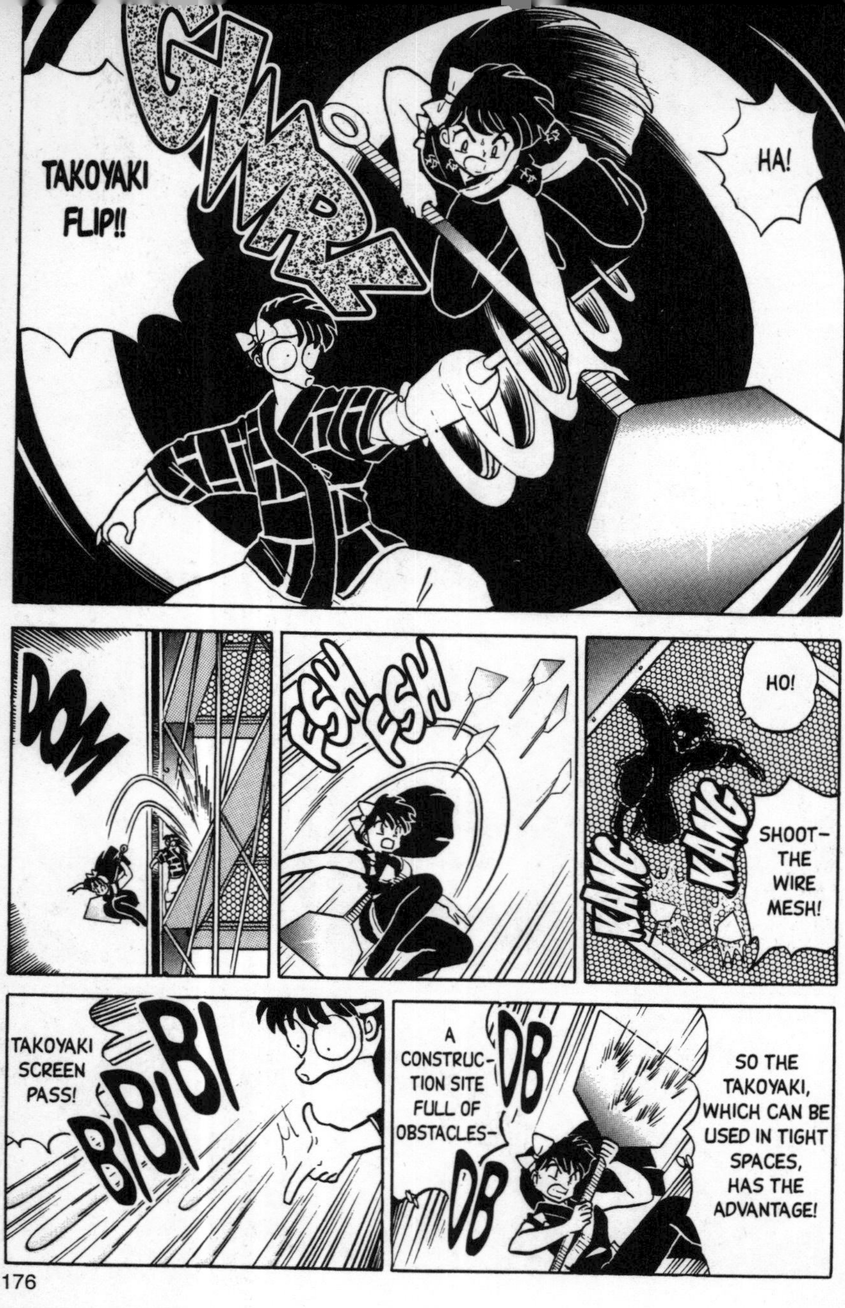
TAKOYAKI FLIP!!
HA!
DOM
FSH FSH
HO!
KANG KANG
SHOOT—THE WIRE MESH!
TAKOYAKI SCREEN PASS!
BIBIBI BIBIBI
A CONSTRUCTION SITE FULL OF OBSTACLES—
DB DB
SO THE TAKOYAKI, WHICH CAN BE USED IN TIGHT SPACES, HAS THE ADVANTAGE!

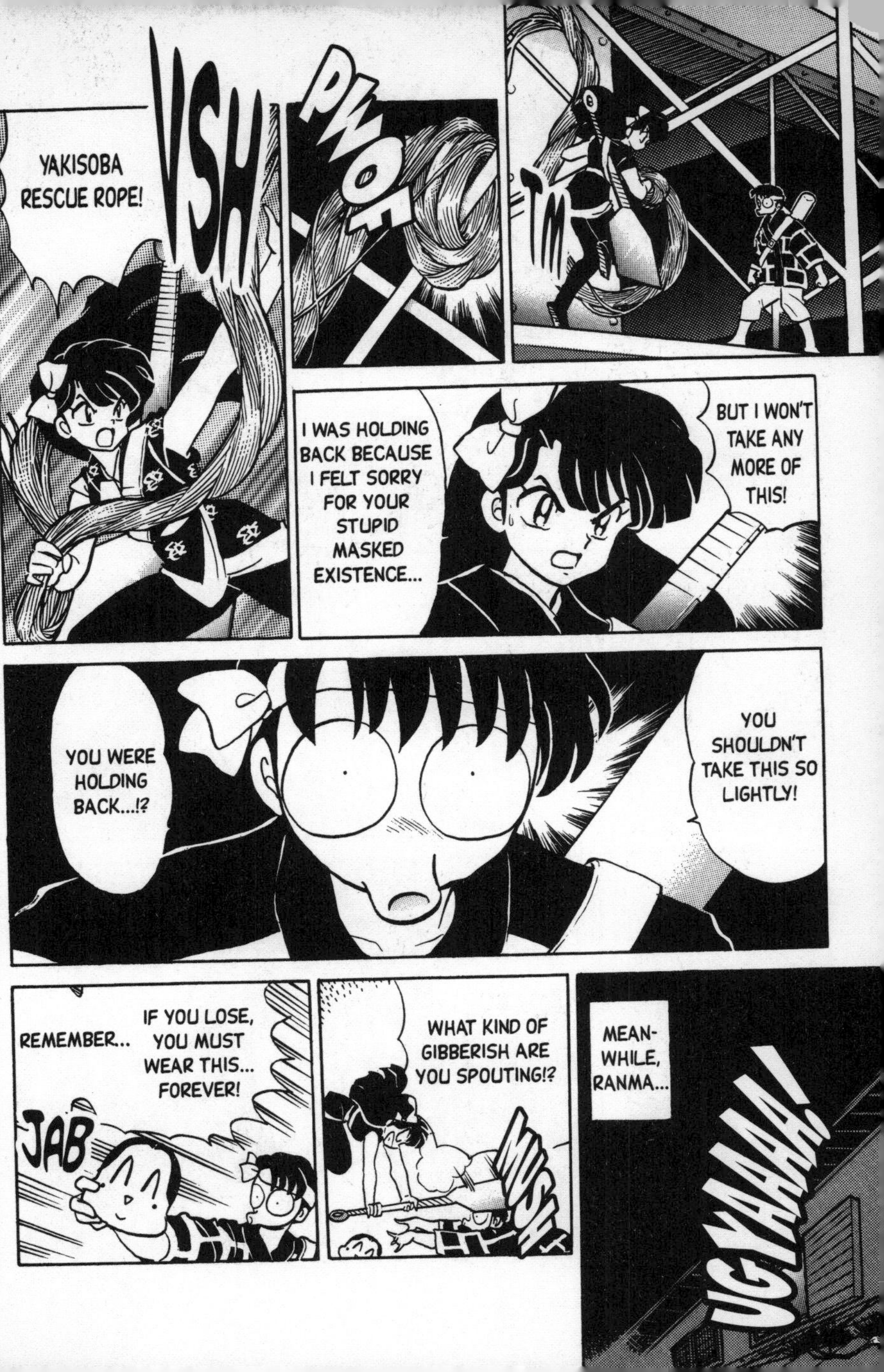
YAKISOBA RESCUE ROPE!
VSHH
PWOF
TM
I WAS HOLDING BACK BECAUSE I FELT SORRY FOR YOUR STUPID MASKED EXISTENCE...
BUT I WON'T TAKE ANY MORE OF THIS!
YOU WERE HOLDING BACK...!?
YOU SHOULDN'T TAKE THIS SO LIGHTLY!
REMEMBER...
IF YOU LOSE, YOU MUST WEAR THIS... FOREVER!
JAB
WHAT KIND OF GIBBERISH ARE YOU SPOUTING!?
WUSH
MEAN-WHILE, RANMA...
UGYAAA!

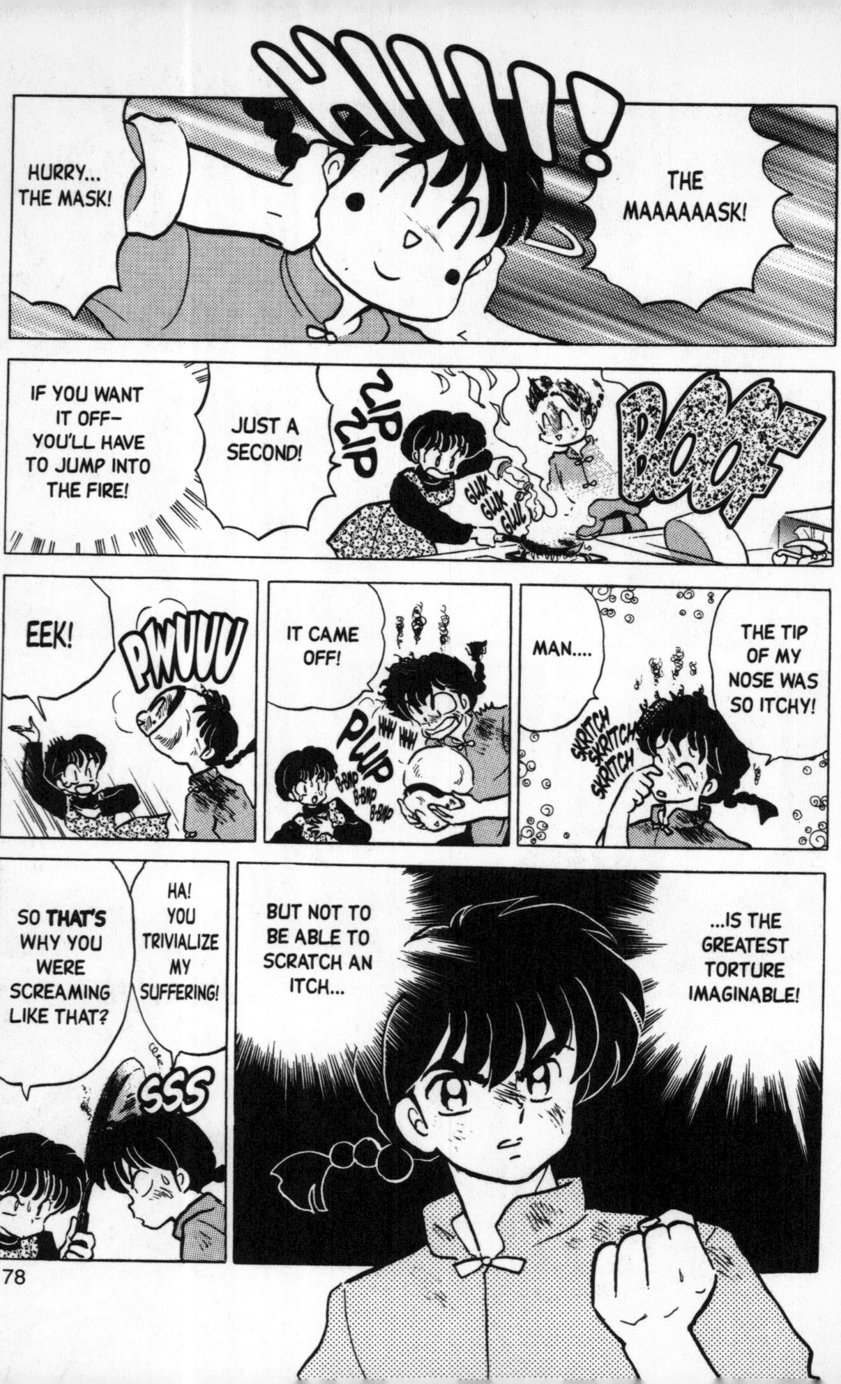
WAAAH!
HURRY... THE MASK!
THE MAAAAAASK!
IF YOU WANT IT OFF— YOU'LL HAVE TO JUMP INTO THE FIRE!
JUST A SECOND!
ZIP ZIP
GLUK GLUK GLUK
BOOF
EEK!
PWUUU
IT CAME OFF!
PWIP
B-BMP B-BMP B-BMP
MAN....
THE TIP OF MY NOSE WAS SO ITCHY!
SKRITCH SKRITCH SKRITCH
SO **THAT'S** WHY YOU WERE SCREAMING LIKE THAT?
HA! YOU TRIVIALIZE MY SUFFERING!
SSS
BUT NOT TO BE ABLE TO SCRATCH AN ITCH...
...IS THE GREATEST TORTURE IMAGINABLE!

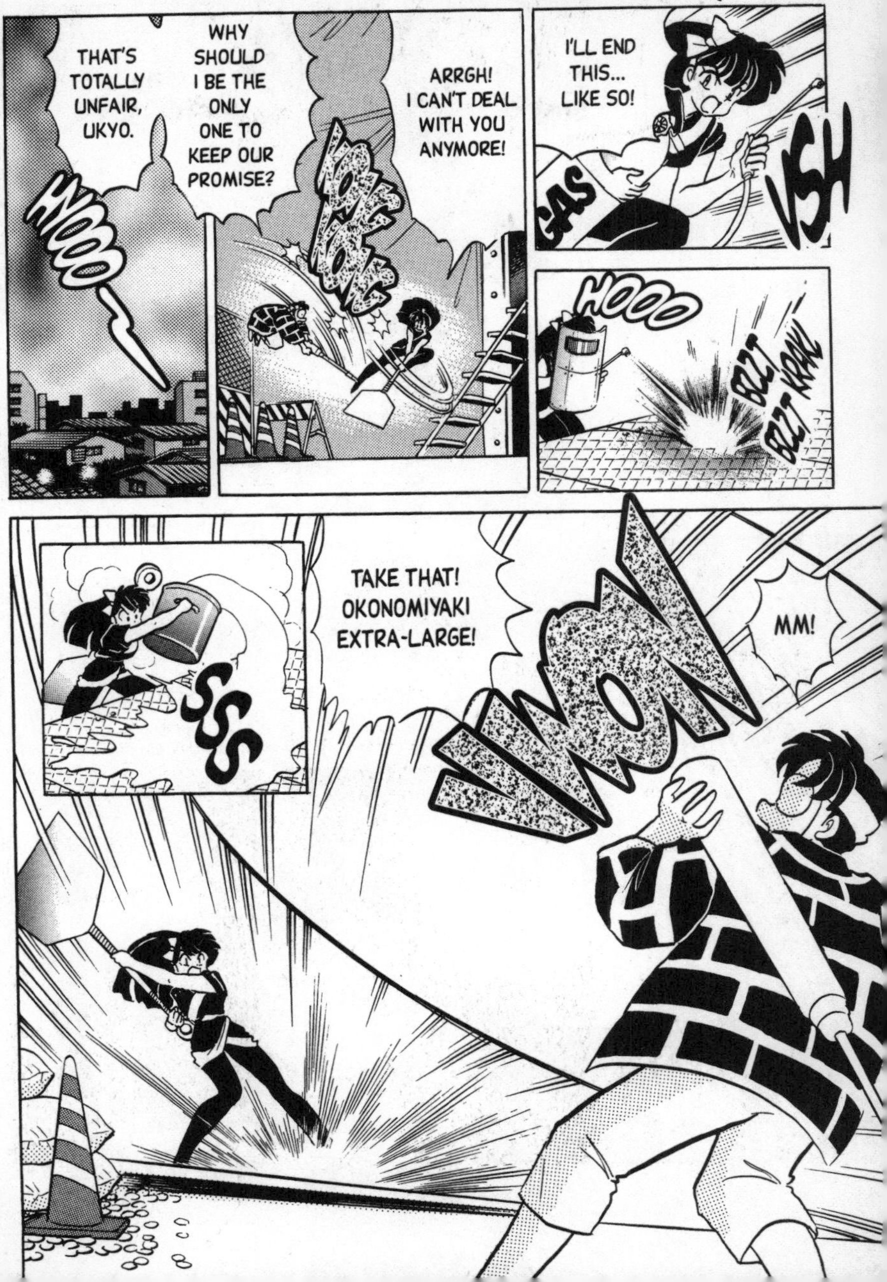
THAT'S TOTALLY UNFAIR, UKYO.
HWOOO
WHY SHOULD I BE THE ONLY ONE TO KEEP OUR PROMISE?
ARRGH! I CAN'T DEAL WITH YOU ANYMORE!
I'LL END THIS... LIKE SO!
GAS
VSH
HOOO
BZZT BZZT KRAK
SSS
TAKE THAT! OKONOMIYAKI EXTRA-LARGE!
WOW
MM!

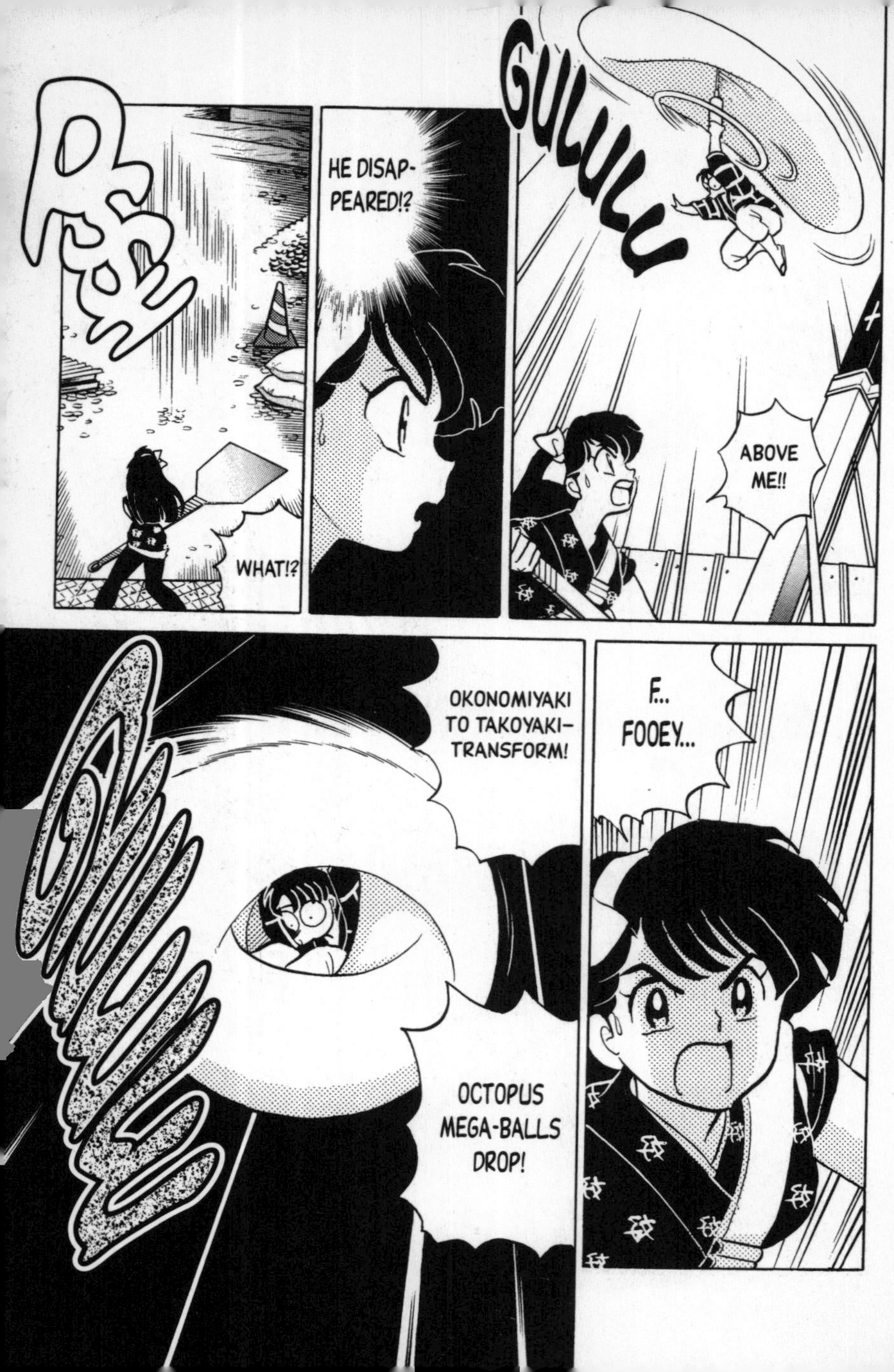
WHAT!?
HE DISAP-PEARED!?
GULULU
ABOVE ME!!
OKONOMIYAKI TO TAKOYAKI-TRANSFORM!
OCTOPUS MEGA-BALLS DROP!
F... FOOEY...

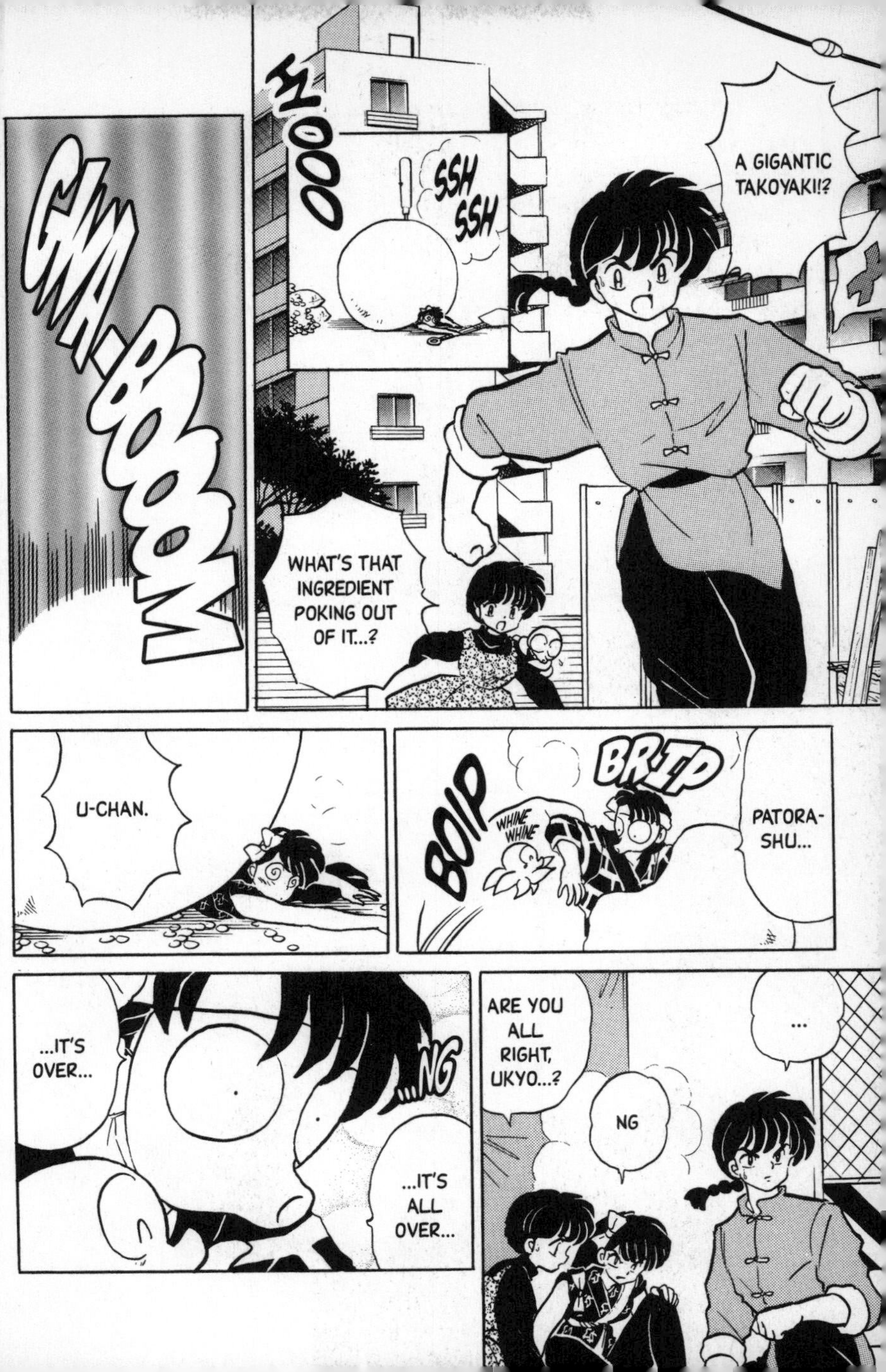
GHA-BOOOM
HOOOO
SSH SSH
A GIGANTIC TAKOYAKI!?
WHAT'S THAT INGREDIENT POKING OUT OF IT...?
U-CHAN.
BOIP
WHINE WHINE
BRIP
PATORA-SHU...
...IT'S OVER...
...NG
...IT'S ALL OVER...
ARE YOU ALL RIGHT, UKYO...?
NG
...

I HATE TO DO IT, BUT... I ACKNOWLEDGE DEFEAT.

STILL....

I'M NOT PUTTING ON THAT MASK!

SIGH...

IT'S ALL RIGHT NOW.

AT LEAST I...

...AM FINALLY FREE OF THIS MASKED LIFE!!

SORRY, PAL...

EH?

PAT

GAH!?

IT'S NOT COMING OFF!!

YOU PAINTED ON TAKOYAKI BATTER!?

I COULDN'T LET HIM DO A THING LIKE THAT TO ME WITHOUT RETALIATING, COULD I?

ARRGH! THE TIP OF MY NOSE ITCHES!

SHAKA SHAK

IT'LL COME OFF IF YOU JUMP INTO FLAMES,

WANT ME TO GRILL YOU?

About Rumiko Takahashi

Born in 1957 in Niigata, Japan, Rumiko Takahashi attended women's college in Tokyo, where she began studying comics with Kazuo Koike, author of CRYING FREEMAN. She later became an assistant to horror-manga artist Kazuo Umezu (OROCHI). In 1978, she won a prize in Shogakukan's annual "New Comic Artist Contest," and in that same year her boy-meets-alien comedy series URUSEI YATSURA began appearing in the weekly manga magazine SHÔNEN SUNDAY. This phenomenally successful series ran for nine years and sold over 22 million copies. Takahashi's later RANMA 1/2 series enjoyed even greater popularity.

Takahashi is considered by many to be one of the world's most popular manga artists. With the publication of Volume 34 of her RANMA 1/2 series in Japan, Takahashi's total sales passed one hundred million copies of her compiled works.

Takahashi's serial titles include URUSEI YATSURA, RANMA 1/2, ONE-POUND GOSPEL, MAISON IKKOKU and INUYASHA. Additionally, Takahashi has drawn many short stories which have been published in America under the title "Rumic Theater," and several installments of a saga known as her "Mermaid" series. Most of Takahashi's major stories have also been animated and are widely available in translation worldwide. INUYASHA is her most recent serial story, first published in SHÔNEN SUNDAY in 1996.

EDITOR'S RECOMMENDATIONS

If you enjoyed this volume of Ranma 1/2, then here is some more manga you might be interested in:

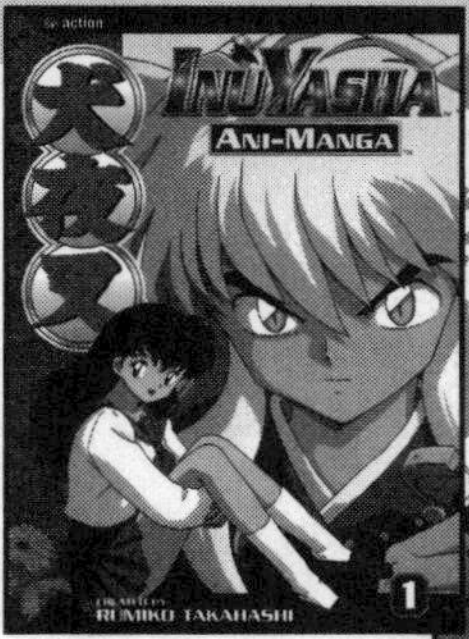
action
InuYasha
Ani-Manga
Rumiko Takahashi
1

InuYasha Ani-Manga

The story you've come to love using actual frames of film in full color from the TV and video series *Inuyasha!*

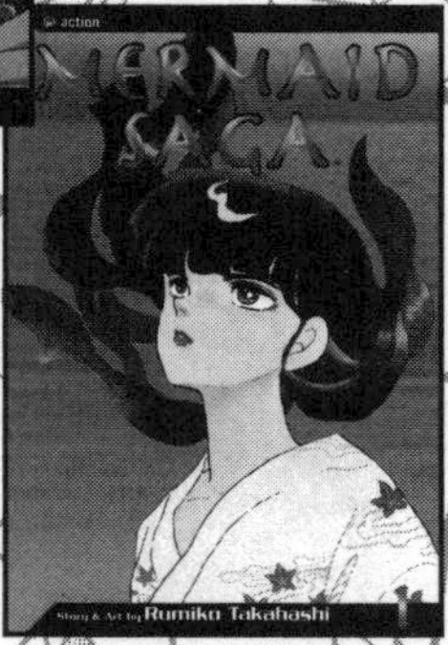
action
Mermaid Saga
Story & Art by Rumiko Takahashi

Mermaid Saga

This is the series Rumiko Takahashi created as her "hobby." Unpressured by editors and deadlines, she lets her creativity flow in this romantic-horror epic. Eating the flesh of a mermaid grants eternal life. But living forever can be a blessing or a curse. Immortal lovers Yuta and Mana are relatively lucky...others who partake of the mermaid's flesh are transformed into savage lost souls!

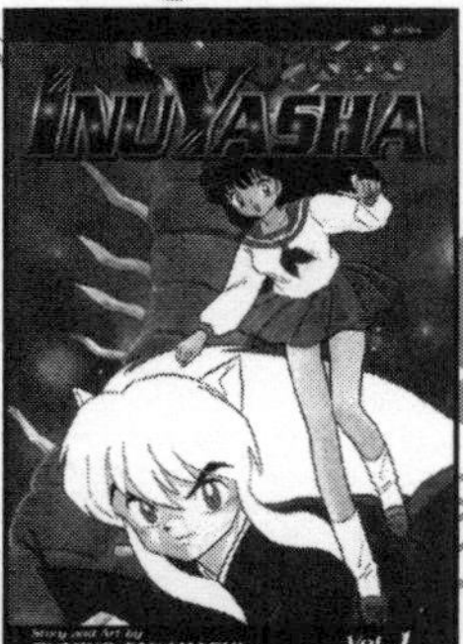
InuYasha
Story and Art by
Rumiko Takahashi
Vol. 1

Inuyasha

When high school student Kagome is transported back in time to Japan's feudal era, she accidentally releases the feral half-demon dog-boy Inu-Yasha from his imprisonment for stealing the "Jewel of Four Souls." But after a battle with fearsome demons, the jewel has been shattered and its countless shards scattered all over Japan. Now, bound together by a spell, Inu-Yasha and Kagome must join forces to reclaim the jewel and its terrifying powers from demons and mortals alike that would use it as a tool of unspeakable evil!

Half Human, Half

When Kagome discovers a well that transports her to feudal era Japan, she unwittingly frees a half-demon, Inuyasha, and shatters the sacred Jewel of Four Souls. Now they must work together to restore the jewel before it falls into the wrong hands...

INUYASHA

The manga that inspired a phenomenon!

Only $9.95!

FULL COLOR adaptation of the TV series!

Only $11.95!

LOVE MANGA? LET US KNOW!

☐ Please do NOT send me information about VIZ products, news and events, special offers, or other information.

☐ Please do NOT send me information from VIZ' trusted business partners.

Name: _____

Address: _____

City: _____ **State:** _____ **Zip:** _____

E-mail: _____

☐ **Male** ☐ **Female**   **Date of Birth** (mm/dd/yyyy): ___ / ___ / _____ (Under 13? Parental consent required)

What race/ethnicity do you consider yourself? (check all that apply)

☐ White/Caucasian   ☐ Black/African American   ☐ Hispanic/Latino

☐ Asian/Pacific Islander   ☐ Native American/Alaskan Native ☐ Other: _____

What VIZ shojo title(s) did you purchase? (indicate title(s) purchased)

_____

What other VIZ shojo titles do you own? _____

_____

Reason for purchase: (check all that apply)

☐ Special offer   ☐ Favorite title / author / artist / genre

☐ Gift   ☐ Recommendation   ☐ Collection

☐ Read excerpt in VIZ manga sampler   ☐ Other _____

Where did you make your purchase? (please check one)

☐ Comic store   ☐ Bookstore   ☐ Grocery Store

☐ Convention   ☐ Newsstand   ☐ Video Game Store

☐ Online (site:_____) ☐ Other _____

How many manga titles have you purchased in the last year? How many were VIZ titles?
(please check one from each column)

MANGA

- ☐ None
- ☐ 1 – 4
- ☐ 5 – 10
- ☐ 11+

VIZ

- ☐ None
- ☐ 1 – 4
- ☐ 5 – 10
- ☐ 11+

How much influence do special promotions and gifts-with-purchase have on the titles you buy?
(please circle, with 5 being great influence and 1 being none)

1   2   3   4   5

Do you purchase every volume of your favorite series?

☐ Yes! Gotta have 'em as my own   ☐ No. Please explain: _____

What kind of manga storylines do you most enjoy? (check all that apply)

- ☐ Action / Adventure
- ☐ Comedy
- ☐ Fighting
- ☐ Artistic / Alternative
- ☐ Science Fiction
- ☐ Romance (shojo)
- ☐ Sports
- ☐ Other _____
- ☐ Horror
- ☐ Fantasy (shojo)
- ☐ Historical

If you watch the anime or play a video or TCG game from a series, how likely are you to buy the manga? (please circle, with 5 being very likely and 1 being unlikely)

1   2   3   4   5

If unlikely, please explain: _____

Who are your favorite authors / artists? _____

_____

What titles would like you translated and sold in English? _____

_____

THANK YOU! Please send the completed form to:

NJW Research
42 Catharine Street
Poughkeepsie, NY 12601

Your privacy is very important to us. All information provided will be used for internal purposes only and will not be sold or otherwise divulged.